LITERARY REPRESENTATIONS OF THE PALESTINE/ISRAEL CONFLICT AFTER THE SECOND INTIFADA

Edited by
Ned Curthoys and Isabelle Hesse

EDINBURGH
University Press

Edinburgh University Press is one of the leading university presses in the UK. We publish academic books and journals in our selected subject areas across the humanities and social sciences, combining cutting-edge scholarship with high editorial and production values to produce academic works of lasting importance. For more information visit our website: edinburghuniversitypress.com

© editorial matter and organisation Ned Curthoys and Isabelle Hesse, 2022, 2024
© the chapters their several authors, 2022, 2024

Edinburgh University Press Ltd
The Tun – Holyrood Road
12 (2f) Jackson's Entry
Edinburgh EH8 8PJ

First published in hardback by Edinburgh University Press 2022

Typeset in 11/15 Adobe Garamond by
IDSUK (DataConnection) Ltd, and

A CIP record for this book is available from the British Library

ISBN 978 1 4744 9973 6 (hardback)
ISBN 978 1 4744 9974 3 (paperback)
ISBN 978 1 4744 9975 0 (webready PDF)
ISBN 978 1 4744 9976 7 (epub)

The rights of Ned Curthoys and Isabelle Hesse to be identified as editors, and the contributors to be identified as the authors, of this work have been asserted in accordance with the Copyright, Designs and Patent Act 1988, and the Copyright and Related Rights Regulations 2003 (SI No. 2498).

Chapter 4, 'The Palestinian Rebel: Liberty and Statehood in Literature', was funded by the Australian Research Council.

CONTENTS

List of Figures v
Acknowledgements vi
Notes on Contributors vii

Introduction 1
    Ned Curthoys and Isabelle Hesse

Part 1 The Aesthetics of Occupation

1 The Severed Limb: Relational Life Writing Against Techno-
  biopolitical Violence in Atef Abu Saif's *The Drone Eats with Me* 13
    Rita Sakr

2 Daily Encounters: Diary Writing and the Politics of the
  Mundane in Occupied Palestine 33
    Hiyem Cheurfa

3 American Palestinian Women as Public Intellectuals:
  New Narratives of Resistance 51
    Sahar al-Shoubaki

4 The Palestinian Rebel: Liberty and Statehood in Literature 69
    Jumana Bayeh

5 The Israeli/Palestinian Conflict in *To the End of the Land*:
  Some Thoughts on David Grossman's Hebrew in Translation 88
    Niva Kaspi

Part 2 Repurposing Form: Reimagining the Conflict outside of Palestine/Israel

6 'Public Confession' in Palestinian Literary Self-narratives after the Second Intifada — 107
Aarushi Punia

7 Detectives in Bethlehem: Crime Fiction in the Occupied Territories — 128
Anastasia Valassopoulos

8 Reframing Occupation after the Second Intifada: Drawing from Experience in Francophone Graphic Novels — 145
Lowry Martin

9 Coming of Age in Graphic Novels Representing the Palestine/Israel Conflict — 165
Ned Curthoys

10 The Palestine/Israel Conflict in the Young Adult Anglophone *Bildungsroman* — 184
Isabelle Hesse

11 Feeding Words with Sugar: Resurrecting Palestine in Children's Picture Books from Egypt — 200
Magda Mansour Hasabelnaby and Radwa R. Mahmoud

Afterword — 217
Anna Bernard

Works Cited — 222
Index — 245

FIGURES

4.1	Iconic image of Faris Odeh throwing a stone at an Israeli tank	70
4.2	Saber al-Ashqar, photographed by Mahmud Hams on 11 May 2018	70
4.3	A'ed Abu Amro, photographed by Mustafa Hassouna on 22 October 2018	70
4.4	Eugène Delacroix, *Liberty Leading the People*	71
9.1	'Harvey's consternation at Israeli settlement building'	172
9.2	'More like a maze than a process'	172
9.3	'Prejudging the situation'	176
9.4	'Our children'	181

ACKNOWLEDGEMENTS

Ned Curthoys would like to acknowledge the financial support of the School of Humanities at the University of Western Australia. Isabelle Hesse would like to acknowledge the financial support of the School of Literature, Art and Media and the Faculty of Arts and Social Sciences at the University of Sydney, Australia.

Particular thanks are due to Dr Blythe Worthy who played an essential role in compiling the full manuscript and in proofreading the references.

Following Edinburgh University Press house style, Arabic and Hebrew names and terms have not been transliterated in the main text. You can find the transliterated forms of these words in the index.

NOTES ON CONTRIBUTORS

Sahar al-Shoubaki is an instructor and doctoral candidate in the English Literature and Criticism programme at Indiana University of Pennsylvania. Her research interests include postcolonial and multi-ethnic literature, Arab American women's writings, resistance literature, feminism, and identity politics. She has written and presented several papers on these topics at various national and international conferences in the US and Canada. She is currently conducting research for her PhD dissertation on American Palestinian women writers and their feminist interventions and resistance as public intellectuals who are speaking truth to power in the age of war, imperialism and neoliberalism.

Jumana Bayeh is Senior Lecturer at Macquarie University, Australia. She is the author of *The Literature of the Lebanese Diaspora: Representations of Place and Transnational Identity* (2015) and several articles on Arab diaspora fiction. She co-edited *Democracy, Diaspora, Territory* (2020), and a special issue on 'Arabs in Australia' in *Mashriq & Mahjar: Journal of Middle East and North African Migration Studies*. She is working on two Australia Research Council-funded projects, one examining the representation of the nation state in Arab diaspora literature, and another, with Professors Helen Groth (UNSW) and Julian Murphet (Adelaide), looking at the global resurgence of riots.

Anna Bernard is Reader in Comparative Literature and English at King's College London. She is the author of *Rhetorics of Belonging: Nation, Narration, and Israel/Palestine* (2013) and co-editor of *Debating Orientalism* (2013) and *What Postcolonial Theory Doesn't Say* (2015). She has written a number of essays on the international representation of Palestine/Israel and on past and present solidarities with Palestine. She is currently working on two books: *Decolonizing Literature* and *International Solidarity and Culture: Nicaragua, South Africa, Palestine, 1975–1990*.

Hiyem Cheurfa has a PhD in English from Lancaster University and is an Associate Fellow of the UK's Higher Education Academy. She specialises in auto/biographical studies and postcolonial literature, with a focus on women's writings from the Middle East and North Africa. She has published her research in leading peer-reviewed international academic journals, including *Comedy Studies* (10:2, 2019), *A/B: Auto/Biography Studies* (35:2, 2020), and *Biography* (44:3, 2021). Her first monograph *Contemporary Arab Women's Life Writing and the Politics of Resistance* is forthcoming with Edinburgh University Press.

Ned Curthoys is Senior Lecturer in English and Literary Studies at the University of Western Australia. His research interests include literary and cinematic representations of the Holocaust, the thought of Hannah Arendt, neo-humanist public intellectuals, and the *Bildungsroman* and narrative theory. His monograph *The Legacy of Liberal Judaism: Ernst Cassirer and Hannah Arendt's Hidden Conversation* was published in 2013. He is currently working on a monograph on the *Bildungsroman* as it shapes the narrative strategies of recent historical fiction about the Second World War.

Magda Hasabelnaby is Professor of English Literature at Ain Shams University, Faculty of Women, and an adjunct professor at the American University in Cairo, where she teaches contemporary US literature, comparative literature and translation. She has published on Arab and Muslim women writers, and postcolonial readings of contemporary poetry and fiction. She has also translated American poetry and Ray Bradbury's novel *Fahrenheit 451* into Arabic. She has been a visiting scholar at the universities of Virginia; Miami, Florida; Oregon, Northeastern Illinois; and the University of Illinois at Urbana Champaign.

Isabelle Hesse is Senior Lecturer in the English Department at the University of Sydney, Australia. Her research is situated at the nexus of Jewish, Middle Eastern and postcolonial studies and she is the author of *The Politics of Jewishness in Contemporary World Literature: The Holocaust, Zionism and Colonialism* (2016). She has published on topics such as the twenty-first-century short story from Gaza, and British and German engagement with Israel and Palestine. She is currently completing a book entitled *Reimagining Israel and Palestine in Contemporary British and German Culture*.

Niva Kaspi holds a PhD from the University of Western Australia and her research focuses on the (un)translatability of Hebrew literature. Her study of David Grossman's novel *To the End of the Land* endorses visible translations with an emphasis on preserving and foregrounding features of the original language and culture. Niva's published translations from Hebrew to English include poetry and short prose for both adults and children, and she specialises in the translation of rhyme and humour. Niva lives in Perth, Western Australia where she lectures in Media and Culture and holds an Academic Coordinator position with Edith Cowan College.

Rawda R. Mahmoud is an associate professor of English literature at Faculty of Women for Arts, Science and Education, Ain Shams University, Egypt, where she teaches modern poetry and American literature. She is currently Head of the Scientific Publishing Unit, Ain Shams University. She received her PhD from Ain Shams University (2012). She has participated in international conferences in Poland, Canada and the US. Her publications include articles on trauma and war literature, prison poetry and American Sufi poetry. Her research interests are postcolonial literature, human rights, testimonial literature and American literature.

Lowry Martin is an associate professor of French at the University of Texas–El Paso and Chair of the Department of Languages and Linguistics. His primary fields of study are French literature during France's Third Republic, Francophone cinema, and the intersections of law, literature and sexuality. He has also written on Francophone and Israeli cinema. His book *Sapphic Mosaics: Fantasy, Desire, and the Cultural Production of Paris-Lesbos 1880–1939* is currently under review and he is working on a second monograph entitled *Imagining the Promised Land: Transnational Imaginaries and French Cultural Production*. He is a 2022 fellow at the Israel Institute at Brandeis University.

Aarushi Punia is a doctoral fellow in English Literature and a University Grants Commission senior research fellow at the Department of Humanities and Social Sciences, Indian Institute of Technology Delhi. She is formulating a comparative framework on narrative strategies of resistance against ethno-national states developed in Palestinian and Dalit literature. She has presented her research at several international conferences and has published articles related to gender, caste and Palestine in *The Print, News Laundry, Round Table India, Mondoweiss, New Politics, The Quint, News Laundry* and *Philosophy World Democracy.*

Rita Sakr is Lecturer/Assistant Professor in Postcolonial and Global Literatures at Maynooth University, Ireland. Among various other publications, she is the author of *Monumental Space in the Post-Imperial Novel: An Interdisciplinary Study* and of *'Anticipating' the 2011 Arab Uprisings: Revolutionary Literatures and Political Geographies*; co-editor of *The Ethics of Representation in Literature, Art and Journalism: Transnational Responses to the Siege of Beirut*; and co-director/co-producer of the RCUK-funded documentary on Beirut, *White Flags*. Her recent and forthcoming publications, including a new monograph project, focus on experimental aesthetics of forced displacement and 'necropolitics', especially in contemporary Arab literature.

Anastasia Valassopoulos is Senior Lecturer in World Literatures at the University of Manchester. Her research is on the postcolonial literature and culture of the Middle East. She is also very interested in the wider cultural production and reception of Arab film and music. Recent publications include work on the role of cinema in the Palestinian resistance movement, anti-colonial feminism in North Africa, as well as film, revolution and music in the Egyptian context (with Dalia Mostafa). Her co-written book *Postcolonial Locations* (with Robert Spencer) was published in 2020. She is currently working on a book-length project entitled 'Palestine in the Popular Imagination'.

INTRODUCTION: LITERARY REPRESENTATIONS AFTER THE SECOND INTIFADA

Ned Curthoys and Isabelle Hesse

In his 1999 multi-modal work, *After the Last Sky: Palestinian Lives*, Edward Said argued that '[p]articularly in fiction, the struggle to achieve form expresses the writer's efforts to construct a coherent scene, a narrative that might overcome the almost metaphysical impossibility of representing the present' (Said and Mohr 38). Said emphasises the capacity of literary form, which is often neglected at the expense of historical and political analysis, to represent an increasingly complicated present. Considerations of form permeate *After the Last Sky*, which combines narrative text with haunting photographs taken by Jean Mohr of Palestinians engaged in their everyday lives in familiar yet culturally significant settings. *Literary Representations of the Palestine/Israel Conflict After the Second Intifada* reprises Said's notion of form and the struggle to understand and represent an often mystified present, from a post-Second-Intifada perspective (2000–5 and its aftermath). Our cover image, Palestinian artist Hazem Harb's *Al Baseera #1*, exemplifies these ideas. While presenting an abstract image that needs deciphering and demystifying, Harb's work was inspired by the Arabic word 'Bazaar', which can be interpreted both as seeing and seeing through something (Google Arts and Culture). Hence, this image not only emphasises the importance of looking at and seeing the world from different perspectives but acknowledges how representation plays with and challenges our perceptions, which is also at the heart of our edited collection.

We take the onset of the Second Palestinian Intifada (2000–5) as a starting point for our examination of literary representations, as it marked a significant and material experiential change for both Palestinians and Israelis.

For Palestinians, this era constituted an important moment of (sometimes armed) resistance against Israel as an occupying power, the subjection to more intensive military control and surveillance through the proliferation of checkpoints, somatic vulnerability exacerbated by the use of drones, and the endurance of destructive military bombardment in Gaza after the Israeli withdrawal. For Palestinians, the Second Intifada also produced intense debate over strategies of resistance (violent nationalist struggle versus civil rights and BDS – Boycott, Divestment, Sanction – campaigns). For Israeli Jews, the new millennium marked a pronounced surge in Palestinian attacks, especially on civilians, which led to an increased sense of vulnerability and a desire for security during and after the Second Intifada. It was also a period of reflection on the trauma undergone by conscripts into the Israeli Defense Forces as documented for example by the testimonies collected by the organisation *Breaking the Silence*, and the corollary rise of the refusenik movement and other overlapping historical and postcolonial modes of inquiry grouped under the rubric of post-Zionism. Another key aspect of the Second Intifada is that during this period of time, the Israeli government started building the wall or 'separation barrier' between Israel and the West Bank, which has drastically impacted the ways in which Palestinians experience life under occupation but also influenced the ways in which Israelis engage with a seemingly more abstracted and mediatised conflict; the separation wall and the ever transforming 'architecture of enmity' has become one of the central elements that literary works invested in ameliorating this internecine situation now engage with.[1]

Our collection pays close attention to the innovative experiments in form that not only Palestinian and Israeli authors, but also writers and artists from across the globe, have used to depict Israel and Palestine to regional and international audiences in response to the Second Intifada and its aftermath. They have done so, our contributors suggest, in the hope of producing new, descriptively thicker, and cognitively disruptive imaginative cartographies of the conflict. The forms that interest this collection are both relatively new and increasingly influential media of literary expression, such as graphic novels as well as the repurposing of existing genres for various testimonial, ethical and political ends. These genres include the *Bildungsroman* or coming-of-age narrative; life writing in diaries and memoirs; the historical novel and its proclivity to generational saga and social panorama; the detective novel with its capacity for social exploration and psychogeography; and illustrated children's literature with its enchanting and redemptive appeal to child and adult readers. *Literary Representations of the Palestine/Israel Conflict after the Second Intifada* is mindful of the dynamic evolution of genres, once considered Western in origin, that now seek to 'undertake specific kinds of political and cultural work' as Anna Bernard argues, at a moment in which the region's history is contested yet intertwined, and in which different 'visions of its political future' need to be made to invested audiences in order to combat the fatalistic acceptance of a profoundly unjust and unsustainable situation (*Rhetorics* 5).

The forms and genres discussed in this volume articulate a range of tones and affects but there is a consistent emphasis, in the wake of the realisation that the *nakba* and *naksa* are less historical events than near permanent structures of everyday life, on the observant, quotidian and unheroic perspectives available to comedy, irony and satire. These perennial genres have been repurposed as expressions of *sumud*, a Palestinian term for a less spectacular dimension of resistance, that of steadfastness, a desire to stay put in one's home and on one's land and thereby counter the threat of physical and cultural erasure. As the Palestinian writer Raja Shehadeh has argued, such an attitude resists the submissive and humiliated posture demanded by the invasive and disruptive Israeli occupation, but also chafes against a normative Palestinian nationalist imaginary focused on the patriarchal interdiction of autonomous self-fashioning, and the sacrificial values of martyrdom (*Third Way* 39). Critical of Palestinian factionalism and the breakdown of community, much of the writing discussed in this collection protests in a sometimes 'unheroic' spirit against Israeli and Palestinian leaderships that have contributed to and legitimised political dysfunction and civic decay.

Yet our collection is also adapted to the needs of the present, the massive and inert reality of the colonial occupation of Palestinian lands and its profound but not always clearly understood impact on Palestinian and Israeli life worlds. We ask how recent key political and historical events, including the siege of Gaza (since 2006), Operation Cast Lead (2008–9), the Arab Spring (2010–11) and Operation Protective Edge (2014), the attempted mass Gaza crossings (2018), and the apparent death of any genuine peace process under Presidents Obama and Trump have impacted on the aesthetic choices made by writers of the conflict. Two decades into the twenty-first century our contributors are sensitive to the modelling of innovative conceptions of Palestinian subjectivity in the wake of the writings and activism of intellectuals such as Edward Said and poets such as Mahmoud Darwish, who have created a space for public intervention and performance that negotiates and resists accusations of terrorism, but also the conjunction of nationalism, patriarchy and martyrdom prevalent in some Palestinian nationalist narratives. At the same time, we see Israeli writers, such as David Grossman, grappling with the Second Intifada and its legacies which include an attenuation of the Israeli Left's drive for peace, questioning the divisions between self and other by exposing and interrogating the imagined and physical borders and divisions between Israelis and Palestinians. Our contributors also reflect on changing rhetorics of engagement in this highly charged literary cultural field with the rise of internet cultures and social media, as well as the increasing prominence of Israeli, Palestinian and diasporic writing that addresses transnational audiences.

Our collection, focused on changing formal and narrative schemes that influence and organise perceptions of Palestine/Israel, is interested in literary representations that must reckon with the reframing of encounters between Israel and Palestine less as a struggle of competing nationalisms and more through the prism of Israeli settler-colonialism and its repressive effects on the Palestinian population. It is curious about the consequences of this reframing, which has generated a (highly contested) 'anti-normalization discourse' focused on the rationale and legitimacy of Israel's actions that has combined with a commodification of Palestine into a 'tragic-hero fetish object' (Stein and Swedenburg 13–14), a symbol of impediments to human emancipation, as manifested in humanitarian discourses about Gaza in crisis under blockade and other solidarity movements. It joins a growing scholarship that has emerged since the end of the Second Intifada, which focuses on literary engagements with Palestine/Israel from a comparative perspective in which, for example, Palestinian and Israeli literary expression is read in intersectional ways as a modality of partition literature, as an extension of postcolonial attempts to rethink the nation, or as species of world literature. Similar to the work carried out by Lital Levy (2014), Gil Hochberg (2007), Anna Bernard (2013) and Kfir Cohen Lustig (2019), we are moving beyond a preoccupation with defining Palestinian and Israeli aspirations in terms of a dyadic national struggle, and instead examine the place of Israel and Palestine in larger networks of cultural representation in which various literary forms thrive as global commodities, and we share an emphasis on how popular cultural forms can reconfigure our sense of history, politics and ethics differently, building on the methodology developed by Rebecca L. Stein and Ted Swedenburg in their ground-breaking edited volume *Palestine, Israel, and the Politics of Popular Culture* (2005).

Literary Representations of the Palestine/Israel Conflict after the Second Intifada demonstrates that innovations and experiments with literary form can generate alternative visions that are radical in their departure from jaded representations of the situation in Palestine/Israel as hopelessly intractable and obscure, or motivated by religious ideology and ancient hatreds. As such, this collection contributes to unpacking the complexities of the conflict for a wider audience and draws attention to the role that literature and aesthetic representation plays in framing the conflict and its power dynamics in Palestine/Israel and beyond. Our collection is divided into two sections. The first section, entitled 'The Aesthetics of Occupation', focuses on how recent literature engages with the occupation of the Palestinian Territories since the Second Palestinian Intifada. Themes explored by this literature include embodied relationality and the politics of translation as well as the emergence of figures such as the satirical observer, rebel and public intellectual who generate innovative perspectives but uphold older prerogatives of witnessing, reportage and expressions of quotidian resistance that resist interpellation by nationalist imaginaries. Authors in this section ask how literature articulates the experience of occupation from both Israeli and Palestinian perspectives and how different literary works engage with the resultant traumatic disruption for a range of affected subjectivities.

In the first chapter, Rita Sakr explores Atef Abu Saif's *The Drone Eats with Me* (2016) as a Gazan mixed-genre illustrated prose–poetic war-chronicle in diary form, mediating the aesthetic and ethico-political implications of the severed limb in terms of the challenge of embodied relationality to the dismembering impact of techno-biopolitical violence not only on the bodies of Palestinians and their lived spaces of refuge but also on representational possibility, responsibility and communicability. Sakr demonstrates that Abu Saif presents the severed limb as the image that both complicates narrativity with respect to the Israeli Operation Protective Edge (8 July–26 August 2014) and enables radical narrative alternatives that are attuned to the (il)logic of wholesale destruction and the traumatic space-times that it produces.

Hiyem Cheurfa then turns to the public-facing Palestinian diary as a cultural form that redefines both the stereotypical reputation of the genre and geopolitical frameworks of the (literary) representation of the Palestinian–Israeli conflict in Chapter 2. Deploying postcolonial and autobiographical theories, she investigates the relationship between diary writing and the politics of the mundane in the post-Second-Intifada Palestinian–Israeli relationship in Suad Amiry's *Sharon and My Mother-in-Law: Ramallah Diaries* (2006), Sayed Kashua's *Native: Dispatches from a Palestinian-Israeli Life* (2016) and Atef Abu Saif's *The Drone Eats with Me: Diaries from a City Under Fire* (2015). The diary form of life writing, Cheurfa argues, reinvigorates the imbrication of personal and national narration and testifies to contemporary local Palestinian experience by privileging the representation of the quotidian dimensions of occupation.

Drawing on Edward Said's idea that the role of the intellectual is to speak truth to power, in Chapter 3, Sahar al-Shoubaki takes a postcolonial feminist approach to argue that diasporic American Palestinian women writers, such as Susan Abulhawa and Ibtisam Barakat, have claimed the role of the intellectual in order to universalise and bring attention to the issues at stake when it comes to the cause of Palestine, using their narratives as a creative form of resistance, not only against colonial power (the Israeli occupation), but also against patriarchy and all kinds of oppression, be they political, cultural, economic or gender based.

Jumana Bayeh's chapter focuses on the representation of the figure of the Palestinian rebel in three novels published since the Second Intifada, *The Parisian* (2019) by Isabella Hammad, *A Rebel in Gaza* (2018) by Asma al-Ghoul and *Mornings in Jenin* by Susan Abulhawa. The events of the Second Intifada indicated to Palestinians that statehood had not only been made more difficult to achieve since the 1993 Oslo Accords, but also that liberation from Israeli occupation must precede state-building. An ethics of liberation, Bayeh suggests, represents an apparent reversal of priorities and a critique of the assumption that statehood and liberation are coeval. Bayeh argues that in these novels, rebel characters are deployed to emphasise that liberation is both central to and a necessary precursor of the achievement of state-based independence.

In the fifth chapter, Niva Kaspi examines how David Grossman's *To the To the End of the Land* (2008) interrogates – and performs – the relationship between language and reality by creating a private and embodied idiolect that is at odds with the militaristic and binary rhetoric of the nation. This generative aspect of Grossman's writing offers some translational complexities that Kaspi's chapter sets out to make visible with its close attention to idioms, neologisms and coded significance in the Hebrew original. First, the chapter focuses on the geopolitical landscape in which real and imagined boundaries invoke problems of possession, occupation and trespass. Then, it turns to the proliferation of accents, language varieties and cultural emblems that encode meaning into the relationship between Arabs and Jews and between military and civilian life. Finally, the chapter illustrates how Grossman manipulates the mechanics of the Hebrew language in order to escape the confines of clichés, stereotypes and slogans that afflict depictions of the conflict.

The second section, entitled 'Repurposing Form: Reimagining the Conflict outside of Palestine/Israel', considers new ways of engaging with and reimagining Palestine and Israel in the twenty-first century in the Jewish and Palestinian diaspora as well as in literature from outside the region. It examines how supple literary genres such as the *Bildungsroman*, the detective genre, the graphic novel and the children's picture book are repurposed to reimagine the conflict for a variety of readerships. This section responds to a continuing problematic of representation that may indeed define the task of the non-resident writer in the twenty-first century, namely how writers in a variety of established and emerging literary forms can make the conflict in

Palestine/Israel accessible to a wider audience given the intense scrutiny of representations of the history, politics and morality of the conflict. It also asks to what extent literary works experiment with and recalibrate form and genre in order to draw attention to politics and power dynamics that shape encounters between Israelis and Palestinians but also between Palestine/Israel and the wider world.

In Chapter 6, Aarushi Punia considers the renewal of the narrative form of public confession which can be found in its most developed form in autobiographical and fictional self-narratives after the Second Intifada. This chapter demonstrates that the rhetorically adroit strategy of public confession in Sayed Kashua's *Dancing Arabs* (2002), Suad Amiry's *Sharon and My Mother-in-Law: Ramallah Diaries* (2004) and Samir El-Youssef's 'The Day the Beast Got Thirsty' (2004) articulates a selfhood that resists erasure under the Israeli occupation as well as assimilation into a homogenising nationalist and patriarchal narrative.

Anastasia Valassopoulos focuses on the crime novelist Matt Rees in Chapter 7. Rees is best known for his detective novels centred around the Palestinian investigator Omar Yussef. Yussef's investigations expose domestic power structures local to Palestinian communities and allow a form of socio-cultural complexity to emerge around political and social contexts. The novels pay attention to daily frustrations with the Israeli state but also bring to light the internal dynamics of the various ethnic and religious groups that work and live in and around the Occupied Territories. This chapter highlights the contribution of the detective novel genre to contemporary recognition of the role of popular literature in rendering the Palestine/Israel context accessible in a differentiated manner to audiences worldwide.

Examining two Francophone graphic novels, Maximilien Le Roy's *Faire le Mur* (a play on words that can alternately mean *Build the Wall, Go Over the Wall* or *Sneak Out*) (2010) and Anaële and Délphine Hermans's *Les Amandes vertes: Lettres de Palestine* (*Green Almonds: Letters from Palestine*) (2011), in Chapter 8 Lowry Martin explores how these works function in reframing and rethinking dominant representations of the Israeli–Palestinian conflict after the Second Intifada. His chapter analyses the twin pillars of graphic novels: their visual story-worlds as well as their discursive strategies, and contends that the use of the first-person in addition to the works' documentary and autofictional narrative styles are particularly effective in deconstructing ideas about terrorism. These visual/discursive accounts of Israeli–Palestinian life after the Second Intifada not only contribute to our understanding of decades-old tensions but they may also be one of the most effective and subversive forms of representation of 'life on the ground' after the Palestinian uprising that began in September 2000.

In Chapter 9, Ned Curthoys responds to recent genre analysis of the *Bildungsroman* which has focused on the mature narrator and their synthetic review of their memories as an important protagonist for a narrative of self-making once held to be focused on youth, and argues that failure, disillusionment and a degree of parody and satire have long been incorporated into the genre. He analyses two graphic novels: Harvey Pekar's *Not the Israel My Parents Promised Me* (2012), where Pekar's mature Jewish American avatar looks back on his life, in which he grew disenchanted with his parents' ardent support for Israel; and Sarah Glidden's *How to Understand Israel in 60 Days or Less* (2010), which deploys a young and liminally situated protagonist who learns to let go of preconceptions that she has been schooled in by Leftist orthodoxy. Curthoys argues that developments in our understanding of the genre of the *Bildungsroman* have ramifications for the graphic novel which focalises the increasingly ethical awareness of a protagonist or comic avatar as a conduit for destabilising modes of geopolitical analysis.

Isabelle Hesse examines how the *Bildungsroman* functions as a didactic tool in young adult fiction that uses a Palestinian, a thinly veiled Israeli Jewish, and a North American protagonist respectively, in Chapter 10. She argues that Elizabeth Laird's *A Little Piece of Ground* (2003), William Sutcliffe's *The Wall* (2013) and Deborah Ellis's *The Cat at the Wall* (2014) achieve what Joseph R. Slaughter has called the 'literary social work' of the *Bildungsroman* (7) through an engagement with the conflict in Palestine/Israel, which contributes to shaping the narrators' understanding of their identity and its relation to their community. The literary social work examined by Hesse manifests itself in the use of conventions of the *Bildungsroman* to allow audiences to be educated alongside the characters and to untangle and understand some of the perceived complexities of the conflict in the Middle East.

Magda Hasabelnaby and Radwa R. Mahmoud's chapter considers how children's picture books in Egypt offer alternatives to mainstream historical, political and cultural discourses about Palestine. It highlights how the Egyptian illustrator Sahar Abdallah, born in 1980, reinvents and canonises the work of the late Mahmoud Darwish (1964–2008), a poet who has been regarded widely as a Palestinian icon, and a spokesperson for the rights of Palestinians. By closely analysing three picture books by Abdallah, the authors show how these new drawings focus on both the suffering and the resilience of Palestinians and offer an alternative to mainstream discourses about Palestine in Egypt and beyond.

In her afterword, Anna Bernard provides a retrospective on the volume in the context of a geopolitical reality that has become even bleaker for the Palestinians in recent years. She suggests that the future of representing Palestine/Israel as a globally significant conflict will combine aesthetic innovation and flexibility of address to multiple audiences, with a form of steadfast commitment to edification and clarification, reprising an international 'civic tradition' of realist literature that 'exhorts its readers to recognize a bad reality and take a stand against it' (Bernard, this volume). While the salient political questions of this conflict await resolution, the personal, political and ethical rejuvenation such a literature gestures towards, is a task for all of us.

Taken together, these two sections of our edited volume demonstrate that writing can generate alternative visions that are radical in their departure from jaded representations of the conflict in Palestine/Israel but also draw on the vitality, dexterity, humour, self-awareness and global reach of genre literature and popular cultural forms. As such, this collection contributes to unpacking the complexities of the conflict for a wider audience and draws attention to the role that literature and aesthetic representation play in framing the conflict and seeking to transform the power dynamics in Palestine/Israel and beyond.

Note

1. We acknowledge the problems inherent in using the term 'conflict' as it suggests that Israel and Palestine are equally empowered and it does not directly reference the occupation of the Palestinian people and their land (see, for example, Collins 19). We – together with our contributors – critically interrogate the use of this term after the Second Intifada, including the ways in which it is circulated in and beyond Israel and the Occupied Palestinian Territories, and our collection is mindful of the power differentials that govern any encounter between Palestinians and Israelis that this term might conceal.

PART 1

THE AESTHETICS OF OCCUPATION

1

THE SEVERED LIMB: RELATIONAL LIFE WRITING AGAINST TECHNO-BIOPOLITICAL VIOLENCE IN ATEF ABU SAIF'S *THE DRONE EATS WITH ME*

Rita Sakr

> You, standing at our thresholds, come in,
> sip some Arab coffee with us!
> You may feel you're as human as we are.
>
> (Darwish, *State of Siege* 21)

In *The Palestinian Novel: From 1948 to the Present*, Bashir Abu-Manneh aptly charts a 'materialist framework for interpreting the Palestinian novel through two major trajectories: historical processes (including social and political developments) and literary form (including distinct aesthetic characteristics and features)' (4). More specifically, he insightfully emphasises the 'structurally disordered conditions of struggle, mass mobilization, and terrains of cultural production' in Palestine (4). While Abu-Manneh's study is concerned with the novel, this essay explores this 'uneven condition' of struggle and cultural production in relation to life writing and testimonial literature. The focus will be on the Gazan mixed-genre illustrated prose–poetic war-chronicle in diary form, exemplified by Atef Abu Saif's *The Drone Eats with Me: Diaries from a City Under Fire*, which both mediates the formal and ethico-political implications of the severed limb in Gaza in terms of the challenge of embodied relationality to the dismembering impact of techno-biopolitical violence and reconfigures the implications of the Derridean concept of 'hospitality' as 'a self-contradictory concept' (Derrida, 'Hostipitality' 5) in the context of the Israeli Operation Protective Edge (8 July–26 August 2014). From this perspective, Derrida's etymological and philosophical study of 'hospitality' as 'a word which carries its own contradiction incorporated into it, a Latin word which allows itself to be parasitized by its opposite, "hostility," the undesirable guest [hôte] which it harbors as the self-contradiction in its own body' ('Hostipitality' 3) can be the starting point for an investigation of the paradoxical state of co-extensive and disjointed embodiment as it is re-imagined in *The Drone Eats with Me*. In this work, Abu Saif delineates an aesthetics of the re-membered and reconstituted severed limb that brings together the structure of the diary with the resources of the prose–poetic war memoir, the philosophical treatise, the socio-political study, and the testimony.

Conditions of siege and war in both Ramallah and Gaza have initiated an increase in the production of the diary form. However, the uneven political geography of the Palestinian–Israeli conflict have inflected the two contexts with differing formal and socio-political parameters, particularities and potentials for the diary. Kimberly Katz's translation and edition of *A Young Palestinian's Diary, 1941–45: the Life of Sami 'Amr* indicates that the literary history of the Palestinian diary predates the establishment of Israel and the Israeli–Palestinian conflict. In the last two decades, the Ramallah context has produced several important diaristic prose engagements; Suad Amiry's *Sharon and My Mother-in-Law: Ramallah Diaries* (2005) and Raja Shehadeh's *Occupation Diaries* (2012) are perhaps the most notable. In each of these instances, the personal and the political intersect continuously even if differently, and the common structure of feeling is an imaginative approach to resilience outside ideologically driven nationalist spheres. This personal–political crossroads in literary Ramallah is anchored in Mahmoud Darwish's *State of Siege*, published in 2002. Confronting Israeli attacks on besieged Ramallah during the Second Intifada, Darwish produced the book-length poem in which he evokes a double sense of material and representational siege, bombardment and imposed silence that, according to Patrick Williams in his thought-provoking essay 'Gaps, Silences and Absences', the Palestinian poet resists through the sheer energy of resilient survival as it is articulated by the vibrant poetic imagination (99). Darwish's poem, from which this chapter's epigraph is excerpted, like the diaristic compositions, offers aesthetic reconfigurations of both disconnectedness and relationality through ironic, paradoxical hospitality amidst states of siege. These are poetics and politics that shift registers in twenty-first-century Palestinian life writing – rather than just strictly diaristic compositions – from Ramallah and Gaza, for example in Mourid Barghouti's *I Saw Ramallah* (2003), Ghada Karmi's *In Search of Fatima* (2009) and *Return* (2015), as well as Izzeldin Abuelaish's *I Shall Not Hate: A Gaza Doctor's Journey on the Road to Peace and Human Dignity* (2012) and the volume edited by

Norma Hashim, *The Prisoners' Diaries: Palestinian Voices from the Israeli Gulag* (2013) – given their distinct textures and trajectories.

Countering Violent Fragmentation and Bare Death with Embodied Relationality and De-familiarised Metaphor

Amidst this plethora of forms, Abu Saif's work is, however, most comparable to one of the earliest examples of the mixed-genre text in the context of the last three decades of testimonial Palestinian literature. Edward Said and Jean Mohr's photo-essay *After the Last Sky* (1986) renders the tensions between the ethico-political dimensions of the visual-textual representation of othering strategies and the disruptive relational recognition of shared humanity.[1] Amidst the violence and persistence of images, Said reflects on Palestinian narrative possibilities: 'Our characteristic mode, then is not a narrative, in which scenes take place seriatim, but rather broken narratives, fragmentary compositions, and self-consciously staged testimonials, in which the narrative voice keeps stumbling over itself, its obligations, and its limitations' (*After the Last Sky* 38). Atef Abu Saif's *The Drone Eats with Me* re-imagines narrative possibility through the relationality of its fragmentary compositions, in consideration of its obligations, and in defiance of its limitations. The text starts with a key paragraph that immediately introduces the urgency of representational militancy in the battlefield of factual-historical account(ability) by inscribing the Gazan relationship to war with a familiarity that combines everyday synaesthetic experience and uncanny absent presence:

> When it comes, it brings with it a smell, a fragrance even. You learn to recognise it as a kid growing up in these narrow streets. You develop a knack for detecting it, tasting it in the air. You can almost see it. Like a witch's familiar, it lurks in the shadows, follows you at a distance wherever you go. If you retain this skill, you can tell that it's coming – hours, sometimes days, before it actually arrives. You don't mistake it. حرب. Harb. War. (*Drone* 1)

The integrity of the war narrative is both threatened and enabled by the (un)translatability of حرب. This reconstitution of words as severed limbs acknowledges representational conflict and disfiguring violence but gestures towards narrative alternatives to fragments of ruptured lives in private and public spaces: 'Occasionally turning on the TV doesn't help: the body parts; the severed hand lying at the side of the road; the stomach dangling from a limp corpse; the face covered in blood; the skull rent open' (Abu Saif, *Drone* 34). Abu Saif, himself more recently the victim of familiar/familial violence that left his fingers smashed as a punishment for his uncompromising political stance in Gaza, explores the severed limb as the image that both complicates the ethics and politics of representation with respect to Operation Protective Edge, and enables radical narrative possibilities that are attuned to the (il)logic of wholesale destruction produced by what Elke Schwarz calls 'a deeper regime of techno-biopolitical expertise – an assemblage of discourses and technologies that produce and manage life on the basis of a specifically medical understanding of politics, treating the body politic as a *corpus organicus* in need of a cure . . . pushing this practice beyond the zone of ethical contestation' (61).[2]

To make sense of what he describes as 'the ingredients of nightmares, only they're not nightmares' (*Drone* 34), Abu Saif releases his perspective on the severed limb from the framework of spectacularisation and banality in news reportage and resituates it in connection to the familiarity of his own body and his children's bodies:[3] 'Whenever you see body parts on the news or hear a radio presenter describe them, you think of those parts of your own body, the hands and legs and arms of your children and loved ones' (*Drone* 35). This is an imaginative leap that communicates the need for embodied relationality as a platform for survival, solidarity and resistance. This perspective also accrues radical gendered implications relating to the revolutionary relational significance of Gazan women's affective labour, as will be discussed in the third section of the chapter.

Abu Saif's focus on the everyday lives of his family and friends (as well as details about families who lost members in the Gaza war) recovers their biological and social relationships as they confront the war machine. Throughout Abu Saif's text, narrative sequences that record the vital trajectories of meaningful lives resist techno-biopolitical violence that creates severed limbs. The crucial reconstitution of dismembered lives in their sensuously vibrant domestic settings militates against the debilitating force of shame, a practice that chimes with Zachary Manfredi's thoughts on 'the very particular way in which the power of life is the power of resistance in the camp' (Weizman and Manfredi 177). Abu Saif's text confronts the shameless gaze of the international community with the severed limbs of Gaza in all their material and symbolic urgency as interrupted lives that deserve more than the humanitarian intervention of the ambulance.

In one of the most aesthetically significant moments of the diary, Abu Saif writes:

> body parts of different people mixed up together, lying with flesh they shouldn't be with – as all these images build up, flesh becomes like the wreckage of a house: walls and ceilings, beams and staircases, windows and bits of roofs, all in the wrong places, scattered, amputated, lying on top of one another. (*Drone* 35)

The diary engages with the dismembering and disfiguring impacts of Israel's Operation Protective Edge not only on the bodies of Palestinians and their lived spaces of refuge but also on representational possibility, responsibility and communicability. As Raja Shehadeh notes: 'In true Orwellian fashion, the Gaza assault and the reporting of events were replete with enough misleading terms to give a discourse analyst years of explication' (*Language of War* 13–14). The challenge to counter the surplus of discursive trivialisation is summed up in Abu Saif's reflection on the destruction of Beit Hanoun in the 5 August entry: 'There is little point writing about the brutality and vulgarity that has befallen Beit Hanoun. No phrase or metaphor, no rhetoric can be quite honest enough or do justice to it' (*Drone* 154). Abu Saif's diary explores both familiar representational territory and uncharted figurative terrains with respect to what Dina Matar and Helga Tawil-Souri call 'Gaza as metaphor' (2016) in their eponymous volume of essays. As the space of refuge is turned into rubble, only a radical testimonial rendering of the raw experience of destruction seems to do it justice since 'All the media reports and first-hand accounts fail to come close to the reality of it' (Abu Saif, *Drone* 153). Yet, instead of being a mere account of victimhood and despair amidst the violence, *The Drone Eats with Me* creates a narrative form and aesthetic technique that ethico-politically approximate the transformative urgency and mundane repetition with a difference of the material and symbolic severed limb in Gaza. The resilience of the figurative connective tissue in Abu Saif's narrative militates against the representational negligence and violence, the scarcity and excess, which exacerbated the destructive force of the Israeli attack on the Strip and created the socio-spatial chaos exemplified in Beit Hanoun 'this village-turned-town-turned-bombsite' (*Drone* 153). In this context, the hyphenation of Beit Hanoun refracts the condition of the Gaza Strip as a severed limb in the Israeli–Palestinian political geography, or in Yves Winter's terms, 'a non-sovereign quasi-state over which Israel maintains military control; a territory that is under recurring military assault; and yet a space that has been detached from the spatial and political imaginary of the Israeli state' (312).

This paradoxical spatiality of dismemberment and sovereign incorporation is intertwined with the precarity of refuge across Gaza. In the first diary entry, Abu Saif traces the spatial history of Jabalia's refugee camp where he grew up: 'once a field of tents, then a forest of shacks, now a jungle of highrise apartment blocks crammed tightly together – has been beset by wars for as long as we've all been alive' (*Drone* 2). He registers the conflict's intensive incorporation of human beings and the other-than-human environment into a more-than-human spatiality where blurred ontological boundaries both expose the non-surgical scope of the 2014 attack, which violated an array of human and environmental rights, and enact radical resistance to material and representational destruction:[4]

> not seeing a yard in front of us and when we come across a pile of orange trees, scattered at our feet like an assassin's victims, we know that we are lucky. They were mistaken for us. Death is so close that it doesn't see you anymore. It mistakes you for trees, and trees for you. You pray in thanks for this strange fog, this blindness. (*Drone* 20)

What first seems to Abu Saif as an inexplicable confusion of the human and other-than-human as targets of the attack can be explained in terms of what Joseph Pugliese fittingly describes as

> local self-organizing fractals of militarized violence that expose clear patterns of self-similarity even in what appears to be the chaos and fog of war . . . reproduced at progressively smaller scales: the bulldozing of an orchard, the shooting of a tree, a man, a sheep, a dog, and so on. (89)

Still, the necropolitical guest seems to perceive the host through a 'strange fog' of paradoxically intense hostility and dense intimacy – what Achille Mbembe would have called 'spectral figure and figural presence' (53). From this perspective, Abu Saif's engagement with the 2014 war on Gaza is deeply attuned to a situated understanding of 'necropolitics' that Mbembe theorised in his eponymous book in relation to various contexts including – if not especially – the 'contemporary occupation of Palestine' that he describes as 'the most accomplished form of necropower' (80), signifying that 'weapons are deployed in the interest of maximally destroying persons and creating *death-worlds*' (92), which would encompass in Pugliese's words the broader spectrum of 'ecologies of destruction' (91) produced by the Israel Defense Forces in Gaza.

For Mbembe, the '*state of siege* [emphasis in the original]' involves a distinctive mechanism whereby '[i]nvisible killing is added to outright executions' (82–3). In the same first entry discussed above, Abu Saif describes weaponry as endowed with anthropomorphic qualities as either intruder or killer, but more frequently as both: 'An Israeli F16 attacked the family home while the children and parents were preparing the *iftar*. The F16 wasn't willing to let a family be happy together, to get on with life despite the war. It decided to put an end to such things' (*Drone* 12). It is at this more-than-human crossroads that Abu Saif's narrative may encounter the soldier's account of the violence since, as Isla Forsyth argues in a cultural geographical context, 'personal and embodied biographies of those who experience warfare, . . . although still anthropomorphic in focus reveal that control and power do not exclusively reside within the human but are produced through more-than-human relations' (798). However, the relational horizons opened up by this more-than-human crossroads have to come to terms with the pitfalls of the anthropomorphised drone warfare narrative whereby 'drones are posited as moral agents that can "act" rationally, dispassionately, and – at least in principle – ethically' (Schwarz 65). Here the defamiliarising effect of Abu Saif's anthropomorphising metaphorical descriptions of drones and other weaponry is contrapuntally readjusted by the recurrent reference to the human drone operator, thus continually alerting the reader to the ethico-political fallacies of techno-biopolitical accountability:

> a young man was driving his toktok when a rocket struck him directly, leaving a crater in the ground and unimaginable remains . . . A young man who sold kids' food – sweets, chocolates, crisps – became, in the eyes of the drone operator, a valid target, a danger to Israel. (*Drone* 12)

In this recalibrated representational space, it is neither abstract death nor the anthropomorphised non-human F16 that identifies or decides on targeting civilians but specifically the fully cognisant human operators of a state war machine.

The book abounds in instances of figurative assault on the mundane absent presence of the necropolitical technologies that are enveloped in material, legal and moral-philosophical darkness while being visually discerning and still voraciously consuming lives:

> They could hardly have been thinking about that gunship out there in the darkness, watching them, or the anger it stored, as they cheered and shouted at the match. They could hardly have imagined its maw, the gaping mouth of its gun turret, salivating with hunger for their souls. (Abu Saif, *Drone* 19)

In this densely figurative representational space where dystopian metaphor unsettles the familiar tropes of war reportage, the gunship that is wrapped in darkness becomes a monstrous predator, furiously and ferociously seeking its victims. The banality of 'collateral damage' is thus displaced by the intentionality of anger and hunger that target not only bodies but also souls.[5]

In the following entry for Friday, 11 July, titled 'Floodlit City', Abu Saif describes darkness through a similar textual bombardment of metaphors of the devouring monster who inflicts bodily and psychological violence on the Gazan: 'Darkness is a ghoul that grinds and chews and gnaws at our calm.

Worry courses through our veins. Uncertainty bites into our rest' (*Drone* 23). Similarly, in the 19 July entry, Abu Saif presents the targeting of a family who are killed while sleeping with the same barrage of metaphors: 'The ghoul of death ran up and down the Strip last night, swallowing everything in its path' (*Drone* 62). Yet 'the ghoul of death' is not simply a figurative leitmotif connecting the diary entries, for it is specifically used for its contextualised import signifying that the hostile guest violates the principles of good hospitality. This key figurative instance in the text not only engages the Derridean concept of hospitality as 'a self-contradictory concept' (Derrida, 'Hostipitality' 5) by gesturing to the inalienable dynamics of hostility in the extra-territorial practice of Israeli sovereignty but also more radically re-orientates hospitality's 'reaffirmation of mastery and being oneself in one's home' ('Hostipitality' 14) towards the precariously resident Gazan who is targeted by the violence of the familiar stranger – complicating further Mbembe's argument that '[w]ithin societies that continue to multiply the measures of separation and discrimination, the relation of care toward the Other has been replaced by a relation without desire . . . Never have hospitality and hostility been so directly opposed' (65).

In the 16 July entry, what mediates in no uncertain terms the connection between the gunship that is enveloped in darkness and the severed limb in Gaza is a combination of starkly realist war testimony and what can be described as 'horrific surrealism', a term coined by Omid Tofighian in reference to Behrouz Boochani's techniques of representation in his reflections on the production of refugee bare life in *No Friend but the Mountains* (366). Through horrific surrealist representation, *The Drone Eats with Me* repositions on the imaginative plane of resistance what has been referred to after Agamben's 'bare life' (2000) as bare death. Approaching what he calls 'one of the most brutal crimes of the war' (*Drone* 47), Abu Saif describes the death of four boys from the Bakir family as they were targeted by a warship while they were playing football, as they always did, on the beach facing their home: 'A series of missiles from a warship miles out to sea tore their game to shreds. Their blood mixed with the sand and the sea water, while their bodies were retrieved amid screams and continued shelling' (*Drone* 47). Abu Saif's description not only emphasises the civilian deaths, easily identifiable by the warship that nevertheless indiscriminately tears young lives into fragments, but also articulates the 'horrific surrealist' transfiguration of the Gazan sea amidst techno-biopolitical violence through the image of 'blood mixed with the sand and the sea water'. The warship fails to sever the connections of Gazans to their sea; blood affirms the unassailable links of the severed limb to a more-than-human geography of resistance and reclamation of rights to dignified life, land and sea. Moreover, blood is one of the lifelines of the narrative, a figurative representation of flow that combats fragmentation and boundaries paradoxically produced by Israeli necropolitical sovereignty, of generational continuity that resists political-historical fissures as well as of shared precariousness and shared narrativity that unravel the indeterminacy of hospitality–hostility, against the framework of Derridean 'hostipitality' (Derrida, 'Hostipitality' 3). If, according to Derrida, the host offers the guest 'a kind of right of asylum by authorizing him to cross . . . a threshold that is determinable because it is self-identical and indivisible' ('Hostipitality' 5), then the bloodied Gazan sea is the indeterminable threshold where the language of authority and rights is radically unsettled by a re-orientated, uneven exchange of hospitality and hostility that recalls the epigraph from Darwish.

Reconstituting Socio-spatial Connectivity and Reconfiguring Hospitality–Hostility through Postcolonial Witnessing

What emerges in *The Drone Eats with Me* in terms of a delineation of the ethico-political horizons of the sea as a paradoxical Gazan lifeline against necropolitical violence and as a threshold that redefines host–guest relationships in this geopolitical context becomes even clearer in light of the 2019 documentary *Gaza* that engages with the same Bakir family of fishermen. *Gaza* narrates, in fragments that are threaded together through the figure of the family's elderly figure, the violently intimate relation between the family and the sea. The documentary shows us that the family fished freely before the imposition of the three-mile limit in 2007 by the Israeli army and the aggressive securitisation of this sea border by military gunships. The documentary also features the release of the Bakir son, himself a father, from an Israeli jail after a fishing trip cost him a two-year prison sentence in the aftermath of the 2014 war in which the four Bakir boys were killed. Near the end of the documentary, the Bakir grandfather mutely looks out to sea in prayer. By virtue of its embeddedness into a realist narrative of enforced deprivation from everyday life pleasures and livelihood opportunities and of transgenerational persistence in unfaltering resilience, the older Bakir's silence inflects personal traumatic mourning with the collective impulse of what Stef Craps calls 'postcolonial witnessing'. This resonant silence indignantly and urgently gestures towards the need for new ethico-political horizons of representing, on his/her own terms, the traumatised victim of continued violence in oppressive time-spaces (Craps 4) – a representational need that is powerfully embodied in Abu Saif's work. The sea features in both Abu Saif's short story 'A Journey in the Opposite Direction' and *The Drone Eats with Me* as a geopolitically and ecocritically significant site of bearing witness. Alongside the home/camp, it is the most significant representational space with respect to the political geography of siege, dispossession and destruction in Gaza as well as the environmentalist scope of territorial reclamation and affirmative politics of life.

The challenge of reclaiming rights over a territory that is continually assaulted is at the heart of Abu Saif's postcolonial witnessing. *The Drone Eats with Me* reconstructs a history of violence from the British Mandate to Operation Protective Edge against Gaza's socio-spatial integrity since

> Every time the war machines roll up to feast on the city once more, they do not scratch at its face or scrape at its skin, they devour whole parts of it . . . with every conflict, a different, distinctive feature of the city is removed. (*Drone* 177)

Techno-biopolitical violence does not only sever bodily limbs creating physical disability but also actively aims at disabling socio-spatial connectivity among Palestinians displaced from Gaza. This is why '[s]omeone who moved away from Gaza ten years ago and then returned would not recognize it, let alone someone from 100 years ago' (*Drone* 178). This calculated socio-spatial dislocation is the result of the triple dynamic of 'separation, strangulation, and vivisection' (Mbembe 38) at the heart of necropower.

Socio-spatial chaos inflects the aforementioned 11 July entry, where Abu Saif figuratively articulates Gaza *in extremis*: 'Darkness is a ghoul . . . Explosions chase each other through the night, like nightmares one after the other. The reporters are panting now. They sound scared as well as exhausted and can no longer tell exactly where the missiles are landing' (*Drone* 23–5). Yet he quickly disrupts the familiar metaphor, of the darkness as a ghoul, with which he started by repeating it with a difference: 'Darkness is a ghoul. I have an urge to start a fire, burn the whole apartment, just to bring back some light' (*Drone* 25). Abu Saif brings back some light amidst the apocalyptic scene in Beit Hanoun through the precision of his eyewitness experience and the vast political geographical scope of the testimonial representational space that he reconstructs out of the rubble: 'We look over the devastation and, in the middle of it, I spot Nafiz . . . From a three-story house with a garden, to a tent. Nafiz's story sums up the catastrophe that has befallen Gaza' (*Drone* 181). Responding to Mourid Barghouti's warning 'Who would dare to make it [Palestine] into an abstraction' (6), Abu Saif reconnects the severed limbs of the signifying ongoing Palestinian *nakba* through the specific socio-spatiality of the Gazan catastrophe '[f]rom a three-story house with a garden, to a tent' while narrating the Gazan home as a hospitably and violently severed limb, detached from the resonant poetics of everyday domesticity and attached to the banal politics of humanitarianism. Against the eroded narrative of the homeland that is recurrently reconstructed through abstract symbolification,

Abu Saif situates his national consciousness in a literary geography anchored in the revolutionary prose–poetic representational space opened up by Ghassan Kanafani and Darwish as he states that: 'When I read them I feel at home; I feel as if I am reading about myself' (*Drone* 176).[6]

Across a global Arab literary geography of forced displacement, Abu Saif's assault on abstractions through narrative density and figurative precision is the closest equivalent in a Palestinian refugee literary context (in this case non-fictional) to what Hassan Blasim's refers to in an interview with Margaret Litvin and Johanna Sellman as 'nightmare realist' articulations both of representational breakdown in the spaces of the conflict in Iraq and on the asylum-seeking route as well as of the urge to counter this with radical ruptures of 'the whole apartment' (Abu Saif, *Drone* 25), which is here the whole framework of familiar narrative structure, stylistic techniques and metaphors. This is an aesthetic vision conceptualised and implemented in Blasim's short stories and novel that explore other forms of techno-biopolitical violence and necropower as well as defamiliarising imaginings of more-than-human resistance amidst the banality of media accounts. In Abu Saif's account, when '[o]ne missile strikes Sheikh Radwan Cemetery. A reporter comments on the strange fate of the corpses interred there – many of whom were killed in previous bombings – finding themselves once more under attack' (*Drone* 26). This reflection on the nightmarish implications of techno-biopolitical weaponry that attacks what it has already killed, a phenomenon that war reportage is unable to fit into a sequence and assigns to the discursive space of 'strange fate', gestures towards a reconsideration of the narrativity of necropolitical violence amidst Gaza's states of bare death, later articulated as: 'The dead do not fight wars, by and large, they're too busy being dead, but on this occasion they were forced to participate in the suffering of the living' (Abu Saif, *Drone* 88).

But it is particularly Abu Saif's figurative engagement with Israel's drone warfare that reconnects one of the crucially severed limbs in the narrative of Palestine, more specifically of Gaza under Israeli attack, by emphasising the links between the fragile structure of accountability for Israel's unjust wars and the erosion of the prospect of relationality between the Israeli army and the Palestinian civilian population. In one of the most analytically incisive and imaginatively expansive passages of the book, one in which the title gains definitive political-historical and bio-philosophical significance with respect to the here specifically ironic self-contradiction of 'hostipitality' in Gaza's relationship to the encroaching drone, Abu Saif writes:

> This is how Gaza looks on the computer screen – a thousand images captured by a speeding drone and relayed back to a computer, perhaps a laptop on a desk. The images might include any detail. One of them could be of Hanna

> [Abu Saif's wife] and I sitting on the blue sofa in our flat, staring into a darkness. Another might be of our children sleeping in the corridor, spied through the bathroom window at just the right angle . . .
>
> The drone keeps us company all night long. Its whirring, whirring, whirring is incessant – as if it wants to remind us it's there, it's not going anywhere. It hangs just a little way above our heads . . .
>
> The food is ready. I wake the children and bring them in. We all sit around five dishes . . . Darkness eats with us. Fear and anxiety eat with us. The unknown eats with us. The F16 eats with us. The drone, and its operator somewhere out in Israel, eat with us. (*Drone* 31–2)

The thousand images on the computer screen are non-sequential and anti-narrative. Yet the familial space of the home and slow time of the *suhur* counter the disparate images of the speeding drone. Starting with the title, *The Drone Eats with Me* disrupts the parameters of centuries-long philosophical reflections on the relations of hospitality to hostility by re-imagining the metaphor of the host *in extremis*, forcing the necropolitical war machine into the realm of the personal encounter and hence of accountability, and tracing the contours of an intimately terrorising relationality with the oppressor and their devouring war machine or what Barbara Harlow brilliantly names 'the omnivorous drone' (70). Ultimately, what Abu Saif's re-imagining of hospitality–hostility in Gaza under attack and siege emphasises is the intertwined biopolitical dynamics of food shortages and insecurity to which the Strip had been subject for more than a decade.

In the company of his friend Abu Annas, Abu Saif suggests: 'We have to put ourselves in the shoes of the drone operator; we have to think like a drone operator; we have to respect his blind following of commands', before asking: 'Who will convince the drone operator that the people of Gaza are not characters in a video game?' (*Drone* 66). The paradoxical relationality with the drone operator, or what Harlow calls 'a disconcerting gesture towards an aborted empathic connectivity' (69), correspondingly encapsulates, at one and the same time, an exposure of unreasoning empathy as complicit, an unravelling of the (im)personality of the operator as irreversibly accountable for their role in Operation Protective Edge, and an unmasking of the disavowed colonial logic of drone warfare as sanitised techno-biopolitical violence – or what Isabelle Hesse aptly describes as 'dromocolonial violence' (94) and John Collins as 'dromocratic violence' (144). Through its positing of paradoxical relationality, Abu Saif's diary unravels technologies of violence that shield the perpetrator from personal and collective recrimination by denying the life it attacks, before speedily obliterating it as 'ungrievable life' (J. Butler, *Frames of War* 38) in a video-game frame of war.

The literary–philosophical engagement with the relation of hospitality to hostility in the context of encroaching techno-biopolitical violence is reinforced by the testimonial, rigorous recording of the material impacts of this violence on the Gazan home that emerges as a perpetually precarious space of refuge:

> The Israeli army has struck more residential complexes. People are dying in their homes, lying asleep in their beds. In the last ten days, some 630 homes have been destroyed and around 13,550 have been damaged. Thousands of people have been left without a roof above their heads. Many have lost everything, including their loved ones. (Abu Saif, *Drone* 47)

Abu Saif's diary entries recurrently address the compounded erosion of refugee rights and the vulnerability of humanitarian spaces of refuge in Gaza: 'the same voice [of the UNRWA coordinator] reiterates another UNRWA rule: refugees entering the school must not be seen to be carrying anything heavy with them. "Your belongings might be mistaken for weaponry or rocket fuel," the voice explains' (*Drone* 56). The paradoxical imbrication of hospitality with hostility crosses over from the battlefield to the sites of humanitarian refuge, affirming that in the Gazan context, there is no real provision of sanctuary as sanctioned by international law for the twice-displaced refugee. The UNRWA coordinator's surrender to the demands of an oppressive system that constantly aims at recreating bare life as non-political, life that is deprived of its belongings – its rights, drives Abu Saif's defamiliarising diagnostic statement regarding Gazans' trauma: 'sleep deprivation will drive you mad in the end: the flares in the sky, the symphony of explosions, the roar of mortars, the whir of drones, the voice of the UNRWA man . . . all this chaos will beat you, if you let it' (*Drone* 57).

What emerges here is twofold. On the one hand, there is a clear critique of the failures of established institutions of humanitarian assistance to fulfil their mandate in Gaza; this becomes more explicit in the 30 July entry where Abu Saif writes: 'With each refugee centre, they've made a new prison – UN-sanctioned prison-within-a-prison. And even there, they're bombed and shelled and murdered' (*Drone* 124). This is a condemnation that is attuned to what Eyal Weizman explains as the collusion of 'humanitarian technologies in relation to the siege over Gaza and legal technologies when it came to the distribution of violence in attacks from the air or on the ground' (Weizman and Manfredi 168). On the other hand, there is a rebellion here against psychological defeatism, passive victimhood and fragmented responses to trauma that deny the possibility of organised action – if you let them. According to Craps: 'Insofar as it negates the need for taking collective action towards systemic change, the hegemonic trauma discourse can be seen to serve as a political palliative to the socially disempowered' (28). Similarly, without a materialist foundation to the narration of the trauma attesting to its uneven human geography and in the absence of imaginative frameworks for establishing relational engagements with the impact of techno-biopolitical violence on civilians and 'homes', human and other-than-human, it becomes ethico-politically futile to generally and abstractly document war crimes in Gaza.

In his seminal essay 'Permission to Narrate', Said writes: 'Facts do not at all speak for themselves, but require a socially acceptable narrative to absorb, sustain and circulate them' (34). He argues that

> [t]he very indiscriminateness of terrorism, actual and described, its tautological and circular character, is anti-narrative ... Israeli commentators have remarked that the systematic use by Begin, Sharon, Eitan and Arens of the rubric 'terrorist' to describe Palestinians made it possible for them to use phrases like 'terrorist nests,' 'cancerous growth' and 'two-legged beasts' in order to bomb refugee camps. (36–7)

Such abusive metaphorical outpouring in military rhetoric is closely linked to what Schwarz describes as drones 'repeatedly being referred to as instruments that enable cancerous terrorist cells to be eliminated with surgical precision' (67), while this military use of medical terminology is materially realised in Gaza in terms of what Glenn Bowman calls 'encystation' (114). Here Said's germinal argument is crucially relevant to an understanding of Abu Saif's aesthetic response to terrorising, anti-narrative, simultaneously anthropomorphising (of the exclusionary and exceptionalist body politic and its technologies of oppression) and othering (of the target of violence) representational methods. Abu Saif's reconstitution of the geographies of Gazan everyday life, under siege and indiscriminate attack, does not merely reconstruct what Said calls the 'sequence, the logic of cause and effect as between oppressors and victims' ('Permission to Narrate' 36–7) but more emphatically, by anthropomorphising with ironic difference the Israeli tools of destruction, re-establishes human responsibility for the illogical and terror-inflicting anti-terrorist language through which Likud and the Israeli Defense Forces, for over half a century, attempted to render Palestinians as non-human targets of techno-biopolitical violence that actively dismembers human and more-than-human beings – a tautology that could protect, through sheer anti-narrative power, from the reality of the disavowed, continued erosion of the originary Israeli military ethic of 'purity of arms'. As Stephen Nathanson writes with respect to the fallacy of 'just war': 'When people engage in or accept unintended killings that show callous disregard for their victims, it makes a mockery of their condemnations of terrorism' (98).

Abu Saif addresses the intertwined ethico-political and aesthetic implications of anti-narrative terrorising violence as he writes:

> When a human being is made into a number, his or her story disappears. Every number is a tale; every martyr is a tale, a life lost. Or rather, part of that life is lost; the rest tells another tale. The tale after . . . The Kawareh family – from Khan Younis, whom the drone decided to prevent from enjoying a meal on the roof of their small building under the moonlight – they were not just 'SIX.' They were six infinitely rich, infinitely unknowable stories that came to a stop when a dumb missile fell from a drone and tore their bodies apart. Six novels that Mahfouz, Dickens or Márquez could not have written satisfactorily. (*Drone* 77)

Here, not only does he critique reportage that both trivialises and sensationalises drone warfare, but he also directly tackles the aesthetic (im)possibilities and ethico-political risks of representing its targets as numbered victims rather than interrupted lives made paradoxically visible through necropolitical technology that obliterates. The abstract number that 'the ghoul of death' reproduces needs to be defeated as the power of grievable life persists through its immeasurability. In this context, Weizman argues that: 'Another aspect in the aesthetics of resistance [with respect to Gaza] in this field of visibility and calculability is to make oneself ungovernable, incalculable, immeasurable, uncountable' (Weizman and Manfredi 171). Moreover, while Abu Saif's comment on Mahfouz, Dickens or Márquez may indicate that the novel, in both its realist and magical realist versions, may be unsuitable, despite its breadth and length, for the articulation of the complexities of lives lost in the Gaza war(s), it also suggests alternative aesthetics that could reconstitute the narrative fragments created by this war. As Claire Gallien notes, 'Gazan literature is not only suturing broken territories, thus contesting the neo-colonial cartography of the region, it also seeks to hyphenate the local with the global and to think global connections from local and secluded space' (64). Abu Saif's contribution is distinctive in this respect in that *The Drone Eats with Me* both radically reinvents genres and representational spaces at the glocal level and masterfully communicates this aesthetic vision as a transformative intervention at the crossroads of disciplines.

Defeating the Unrepresentability of Techno-biopolitical Violence through an Emergent, Mixed-genre Gazan Testimonial Aesthetic

Against necropolitical anti-narrativity, *The Drone Eats with Me* delineates an emergent aesthetic of Gazan life writing in figurative terms that straddle architectural, visual-artistic and bio-philosophical grounds. Describing the streets during the first truce on 17 July, Abu Saif writes: 'Great twists of iron protrude from the concrete; chunks of masonry dangle from exposed ceilings, defying gravity, rubble of all kinds covers the ground' (*Drone* 49). What the excerpt mediates may resemble counter-monumental modernist art, but the representational gesture is painstakingly testimonial. Abu Saif affirms that this is a traumatically fragmented space, but suggests that the only way to impactfully confront the destructive force of techno-biopolitical violence is to piece together the fragments, through gestures of everyday survival and creative solidarity, rather than surrender to the anti-narrative techniques that disavow the meaningful transformation of this trauma. While '[t]he movement of the crowds in the street suggests people are happy; they finally have a few hours of normality after ten days of death,' Abu Saif notes

> image after image of devastated buildings in strange black and white – like undeveloped negatives . . . The street looks like a sculptor's workshop, fragments everywhere, and yet the form of his subject is still deep in the stone, yet to reveal itself. (*Drone* 49)

The relationship between the former observation of resistance through everyday life practice and the later suspended counter-monumental memorialising vision that emerges from the fragments becomes clear when Abu Saif in the same entry mentions his mother Amina as the epitome of 'the Gazan spirit: resilience, indefatigability, resourcefulness' (*Drone* 51) and he concludes that: 'there are no statues to the ordinary women of Gaza . . . They should be commemorated in stone' (*Drone* 51–2).

While cultural geographical and historical studies address the general tendency to replace ordinary women with symbolic figures in the iconography of both imperial/colonial and nationalist monumental landscapes, this disavowal of women's personal agency is vividly exposed and overturned in such instances of radical literary and cultural engagement with liberation struggles. Here, the representation of the visionary power of ordinary women, who disrupt material and figurative spaces of violence, unravels the often-gendered foreclosures and fissures of commemorative acts while revealing the possibility that the form of the post-traumatic nation may still be 'deep in the stone, yet to reveal itself'. In a Palestinian context – and more specifically a Gazan context – what is yet to reveal itself and demands our critical attention responds to Ruba Salih's argument that: 'Apprehending war and violence through [women's] embodied memories, and subjective, emotional articulations should be crucial for imagining a different kind of future and existence' (757). This specifically gendered perspective expands the scope of Abu Saif's engagement with the transformative power of embodied relationality in the context of representation and narrativity.

The Drone Eats with Me abounds with examples of Abu Saif's imaginatively incisive attention to the form of the Palestinian narrative after the 2014 war on Gaza, whereby a representational space of resistance needs to be attuned to the integrative power of women's affective labour amidst the destruction. In the 27 July entry on the Shuja'iyya massacre, he notes: 'People's homes now merge and weave together all over Gaza, like threads in a woollen scarf, knitted together by an old woman' (Abu Saif, *Drone* 101). Amidst the 151 dead, he singles out:

> One of the corpses found was of a woman who had been carrying both her children, one in each arm, when the tank shell hit her home ... She held them tight to her chest and, despite the weight of the masonry, she never let go. What they found under all that concrete was like a still life, apparently, a photograph, a perfect composition. (*Drone* 102)[7]

This is the closest delineation of the contours of the counter-monumental embodied relationality to which Abu Saif's aesthetic of life writing gestures: a statue to the ordinary women of Gaza *in extremis*, marking an irrevocable inter-generational resilience amidst the banality of necropolitical violence. The perfect composition merges modes of representation, painterly and photographic, while it features what approximates Boochani's mode of 'horrific surrealism'.

In *The Drone Eats with Me*, an engaged 'horrific surrealism' inflects images like '[b]ombs swim across the sky like tiny, luminous fish' (Abu Saif, *Drone* 115) whereby the seemingly irrational imagery that reorders subject-object relations (the bombs in the sky and the fish in the sea) quickly emerges as an instance of sharp eyewitness testimony on the dismembering impact of techno-biopolitical violence: 'I see everything: scattered organs, severed limbs. I have to pick them up. I touch them. I see how a human can be sliced into pieces like a cow in a butcher's shop' (*Drone* 117). This technique reconfigures the synaesthetic dynamics and testimonial implications of what Hesse astutely identifies as '[t]he suffering body as a marker of shared humanity [that] is still widely used in the political and cultural self-representation of Palestinians, often by drawing on visceral realism' (192) and what Pugliese powerfully notes as 'more-than-human entities who are also victims of military violence' (1), while it extends the visual–textual implications of Said's *After the Last Sky*. The socio-political import of Abu Saif's representational aesthetic, which combines aspects of nightmare realism, techniques of horrific surrealism, and a reconfigured visceral realism, as well as an insistence on personally seeing and touching the evidence of annihilation, runs as a counterforce against what Schwarz calls the techno-biopolitical mechanism 'made possible entirely through new visualization techniques for the identification and targeting of pathologies that disturb the optimization of health' (62). Still, Abu Saif acknowledges that the documentary force of the visual is recurrently disrupted by the erasures inflicted by technologically advanced tools of destruction and misrepresentation: 'Many buildings have completely disappeared, as if a designer somewhere had simply Photoshopped them out of the picture – the designer being an F16 pilot, a drone operator, a soldier sitting in a warship or a tank' (*Drone* 129).

In the 30 July entry, the legally impactful weight of eyewitness testimony, with which Abu Saif engages extensively, augments the transformative breadth of reinvented figurative language as the writer touches a piece of metal:

> It belongs to the rocket that struck an UNRWA school this morning, just a few hours ago, killing dozens . . . It may have feasted on their souls and torn at their flesh, passing from body to body before fully quenching its thirst for their blood. I turn it over in my hands. Death still lingers in it, like a djinn hiding quietly somewhere in its heavy metal, like a sleeping volcano ready to erupt at any time. (*Drone* 121)

Abu Saif's unrelenting figurative militancy not only counterbalances the unceasing military campaign by positing the radical relationality of bodies paradoxically connected by the destructive rocket, but it also traces the genealogical roots and routes of an emergent aesthetic of Gazan war literature that articulates its uneven conditions of trauma as severed limbs within the broad corpus of Arab literature and that of international war literature. This parameter of interpretation responds to Craps's invitation:

> Rather than positing a necessary relation between aesthetic form and political or ethical effectiveness, . . . trauma theory should take account of the specific social and historical contexts in which trauma narratives are produced and received, and be open and attentive to the diverse strategies of representation and resistance that these contexts invite or necessitate. (43)

At the same time, it instantiates what Roger Luckhurst views as 'that apparently paradoxical thing, the trauma narrative . . . if trauma is a crisis in representation, then this generates narrative possibility just as much as impossibility, a compulsive outpouring of attempts to formulate narrative knowledge' (83). Williams's poignant analysis of the fraught relationship between Postcolonial Studies and Palestine makes this assessment of the paradoxical parameters of the trauma narrative co-extensive with the Palestinian context in its long duration. Williams writes: 'What emerges, in direct opposition to the trauma theory model . . . is the persistent effort of Palestinians to represent themselves – to make themselves present and audible – that requires postcolonial engagement' (101). This is an engagement that must be cognisant of the shifting forms and modalities of both techno-biopolitical violence as well as of bodily and narrative resistance to this violence, not just generally with respect to Palestine, but also with a more focused attention on Gaza.

Against the 'hum of drones' that seek to erode connective resilience as they (re)produce severed limbs, Abu Saif reminds us that the last bastion of resistance and integrity is hope:

> The only part of you the drones or the F16s or the tanks or the warships can't reach. So you hug it to yourself. You do not let it go. The moment you give it up you lose the most precious possession endowed by nature and humanity. Hope is your only weapon. (*Drone* 143)

Hope enables the struggle for justice, a struggle that relies on imaginative resourcefulness, since, as Seamus Heaney wrote in *The Cure at Troy* with great vision in relation to the conflict in Northern Ireland: 'once in a lifetime/ The longed-for tidal wave/ Of justice can rise up,/ And hope and history rhyme' (77). From this perspective, *The Drone Eats with Me* re-envisions what emerges as the paradoxically optimistic horizons of Derridean hospitality: 'To think hospitality from the future – this future that does not present itself or will only present itself when it is not awaited as a present or presentable – is to think hospitality from death no less than from birth' (Derrida, 'Hostipitality' 14). The diary entries end with a hopeful pause in the hostile assault on hospitable home(lands) as the 2014 Gaza war ends and Abu Saif can state 'Now I can eat alone with no drone watching over me' (*Drone* 234). Yet, his afterword concludes with 'but for those who were left homeless or bereaved, or with their livelihoods destroyed, the war goes on. The only difference is the world isn't watching anymore' (*Drone* 235), thus reminding us of the persistent implications of the disconnected space-times of witnessing, narration and justice created by continued techno-biopolitical violence, siege and representational negligence with respect to Gaza.

Notes

1. In my current monograph project provisionally titled 'Arab (Im)mobilities,' I engage with the significance of the illustrations by Janice Hickman in *The Drone Eats with Me*.
2. In 'Arab (Im)mobilities', I present a yet more expansive conceptual approach to Gazan war writing linking the medical humanities and techno-biopolitics.
3. For an approach to the banality of media reportage in this context, see, for example, Lee Artz on the *New York Times* coverage of the 2014 Gaza war and Anandi Ramamurthy on the war as a media battleground.

4. My reference to the 'more-than-human' in this chapter develops further my earlier engagement with this concept at the crossroads of biopolitics and environmental concerns in relation to the works of Hassan Blasim (Sakr, 'The More-than-Human') and Behrouz Boochani (Sakr, 'Decolonial Imaginaries') as well as diasporic Arab(ic) literature, while taking into consideration the additional dimension here of what Isla Forsyth calls 'more-than-human warfare'. A very recent monograph, Joseph Pugliese's hugely important *Biopolitics of the More-than-Human: Forensic Ecologies of Violence* devotes two chapters to the Palestinian/Gazan context.
5. Abu Saif's perspective on a multifaceted discourse and practice of banal violence may be situated at the intersection of Hannah Arendt's conceptualisation of 'the banality of evil' and Gil Anidjar's exploration of the 'banality of morals' with respect to Gaza.
6. In this context, Abu Saif's reflections on coffee rituals (*Drone* 214) in relation to hospitality–hostility are deeply evocative of Darwish and what Simone Sibilio calls the poet's 'geopoetics of coffee' (103) – exemplified in this chapter's epigraph.
7. See Iyad Sabbah's 'Worn Out' clay sculpture installations set amidst the destroyed neighbourhood of Shuja'iyya.

2

DAILY ENCOUNTERS: DIARY WRITING AND THE POLITICS OF THE MUNDANE IN OCCUPIED PALESTINE

Hiyem Cheurfa

Palestinian life writing is an expanding field of inquiry in Anglophone postcolonial studies, where postcolonial criticism has increasingly focused on autobiographical literature and its relationship to the ongoing Palestinian colonial predicament. The field is notably acknowledging the significance of autobiographical writing as a compelling cultural form of narration which highlights the intertwined relationship between individual life, national history and political reality. This critical interest in life writing can be particularly attributed to the way the genre is produced and received as a form of Palestinian testimony and its capacity of prescribing the effects of the political conflict on the lives of individuals (Bernard, *Rhetorics* 4). Having achieved a wide critical exposure, Palestinian life writing today is one of the major genres of contemporary Palestinian literature and is, as Karim Mattar notes, 'a uniquely compelling means to transmit the archetypal features of Palestinian reality – exile, diaspora, dispossession, occupation, and war – to international audiences otherwise exposed mainly to foreign, corporate narratives, if to any at all' (54).

This chapter considers the contemporary Palestinian diary as a cultural form of self-expression which reinvigorates the imbrication of personal and national narrations.[1] It argues that the formal and thematic capacities of the diary form enable life writers to present life under occupation as monotonous, daily encounters. The diary form, as I demonstrate, challenges the fundamentally political and conflict-centred discourses that govern the representation of Palestine and Israel which, as Anna Bernard notes, 'continue . . . to determine the conditions of reception for Palestinian and Israeli writing in English and in

English translation' (*Rhetorics* 7). Instead, the diaries under discussion, I argue, are motivated by the desire to record, represent and testify to the mundane dimensions of contemporary local Palestinian life by privileging the quotidian experience of the occupation.[2] While one could argue that examining life writing as politically driven is not a new route of research in Palestinian literature, the study of the diary form, I assert, emerges as an important concern for postcolonial autobiography studies not only as an under-examined subject of inquiry but also as an increasingly emerging form of Palestinian life writing which highlights the discursive relationship between national narration and self-representation as important cultural sites for manifesting Palestinian daily resistance.[3]

While the relationship between non-fictional forms of personal writing and the political status quo has indeed been central to major studies on Palestinian life writing, postcolonial and autobiography critics have been arguably selective. Diary as a form of Palestinian life writing has been at the margin of critical studies with the major scholarly intervention on the genre focusing particularly, or exclusively, on memoir and auto/biography (Hammer; Bugeja; Bernard *Rhetorics*; Nasser *Literary Autobiography*; Moore), partly due to their abundance as compared to diaries. However, this hierarchical interest in terms of critical discussions of life writing forms is not a new phenomenon. Diaries have been both publicly and critically stereotyped as aesthetically unsophisticated as compared to other forms of autobiographical discourses. The founding scholars of autobiographical criticism regarded autobiography as the quintessential self-representational literary model to which they attributed strict formal and thematic rules. These rules, which have dominated the critical field for around three decades,[4] revolve around three major intersecting aspects: the subject's sovereignty, the unitary and developmental aspect of the self, and generic cohesiveness, which have long served as master narratives on and about the genre.[5]

The normative characteristics of autobiography, as a literary form typical to a 'great man' of exceptional accomplishments (Misch; Gusdorf), focusing on the 'development of his personality' (Lejeune, 'The Autobiographical Contract' 193) and presenting in its form and sense of selfhood a homogenous narrative as 'a whole, with unity and direction and significance of its own' (Misch 7–8), have been challenged and revised in many ways – predominantly by feminist, poststructuralist and postcolonial scholars of the 1980s onward.[6] The diary form, however, has retained its reputation as being associated with the feminine, private, secretive and confessional. It was, and arguably still is, stigmatised as 'scandalous, sordid, unmediated, [and] associated with "unprofessional" writers, or with adolescent girls' (Cardell, *Dear World* 5). Unlike the conventional (Western) understanding of autobiography, the diary constitutes often unpublished, frequent records of unexceptional daily experiences in the life of its subject who is usually an ordinary person. It consists of (dated) entries which record life in process rather than retrospective narratives of past, well-grasped experiences. Although it has been recognised as a literary mode of life writing in the 1980s and 1990s, the diary form was, until the early twenty-first century, 'derided as too personal or ephemeral to be taken seriously' (Cardell, 'Life Narrative Methods' 90–1). Contrary to the generic unity and subject's singular sense of self in a conventional autobiography, the diary, as Sidonie Smith and Julia Watson elaborate, 'is fragmented, revisionary, in process. The immediacy of the genre derives from the diarist's lack of foreknowledge about outcomes of the plot of his life' (193). It is thus a serial mode of life writing that lacks generic cohesion and narrative closure. As such, the diary form of life writing constitutes a site of contestation between 'the ideologies of the unitary self [and form] and the more discontinuous subject' conventionally associated with autobiographical writing (Nussbaum 7).

Philippe Lejeune, who is best known for his concept of the 'autobiographical pact', which remains influential in the field of auto/biographical literary criticism,[7] gave much critical – yet less acknowledged – attention to the aesthetics and rhetorics of the diary form. He asserts that the diary is often popularly judged as a simplistic, narcissistic and unprofessional 'self-portrait' and critically derided as being '"discontinuous", "full of gaps", "allusive", "redundant and repetitive"'; as such, it is often considered as 'secondarily a text or a literary genre' (*On Diary* 153, 170). Certainly, diaries are often a critically neglected form of writing because they usually arise from peripheral subjects writing about intimate and personal matters that have been regarded as marginal to historical and national concerns. Having said that, there has been a modest critical interest in the political dimensions of postcolonial modes of diary writing, including fictionalised and digitised diaries (Whitlock; Moore-Gilbert; Anishchenkova; Cardell; Blanchard; Nasser *Literary Autobiography*; Cheurfa; el-Ariss). The central concern of these studies is to call for renewed considerations of the form as allowing new dissident voices, silenced testimonial accounts and marginal experiences to emerge. This chapter responds to the enduring stereotypes associated with the diary form and to the growing critical interest in the political aspects of the sub-genre.

This chapter assesses the Palestinian diary as a cultural form that redefines both the stereotypical reputation of the genre and the geopolitical frameworks of the (literary) representation of the Israeli occupation of Palestine. It examines three diaries whose authors are all insiders living and writing from contemporary Palestinian/Israeli territories: Suad Amiry's *Sharon and My*

Mother-in-Law: Ramallah Diaries (2006), Sayed Kashua's *Native: Dispatches from a Palestinian-Israeli Life* (2016) and Atef Abu Saif's *The Drone Eats with Me: Diaries from a City Under Fire* (2015). In this chapter, I argue that the diarists under scrutiny draw attention to the political capacity of the form by highlighting the relationship between personal discourses and the prevailing colonial predicament. I examine the ways in which the authors' articulation of quotidian experiences of life under occupation revises the tragic–heroic divide that has been characteristically associated with the Palestinian struggle against Israeli occupation in prevailing media and cultural productions. Instead, as I will demonstrate below, the formal and thematic distinctions of the diary form allow the authors to represent the political from the perspective of everyday life that is predominantly domestic, mundane and ordinary. In so doing, these diaries map out intersecting personal and political trajectories that draw attention to the occupation as a daily encounter: a recurrent confrontation with the subjugating machination of Israeli forces which becomes part of ordinary life in its repetitiveness. Thus, they not only present a fresh perspective on life in the Occupied Palestinian Territories but also provide commentaries on the ways in which the political reality is anchored in the daily, personal spheres of experience. This also gestures towards the everydayness of Palestinian resistance (*sumud*), as I will explain. Equally, my choice of these dairies, which reflect different nuances in approach, highlights the aesthetic range of Palestinian diary writing and foregrounds the need for renewed postcolonial critical consideration of the form as an instrumental literary medium of Palestinian national self-(re)definition.

Diary Writing under Curfew: Between the Political and the Domestic

Palestinian architect and author Suad Amiry's *Sharon and My Mother-in-Law: Ramallah Diaries* (2006) illustrates the generic and stylistic capacities of the diary form in drawing important subjective insights into what it means to live under Israeli occupation, as a wife, an academic, a daughter-in-law and a Ramallah resident. In an intimate style that is imbued with ironic humour, Amiry's diary, written originally in English, foregrounds the mundane sphere of experience that is imposed by the repetitiveness of life under curfews, which have become part of life in Ramallah since the occupation of the West Bank in 1967.

Divided into two parts, Amiry's diary covers snapshots of the years 1981–2004. A large part of the narrative is centred around its subject's experience of the 2002 Ramallah siege, which was in response to the Second Intifada, and the curfews imposed by the late Israeli Prime Minister Ariel Sharon. The latter is a figure who has been associated in the Palestinian and Arab imagination with the cruelty of occupation and whose name appears on the title of Amiry's account. In an amusing, and perhaps confusing, combination of figures – a political leader and an elderly mother-in-law – the title of Amiry's narrative, *Sharon and My Mother-in-Law*, signals the juxtaposition that the diary intertwines between the political and the domestic. It announces the narrative's preoccupation with an imbrication of asymmetrical power discourses and their effects on the subject who defines herself as a middle-aged, 'early menopausal woman' (Amiry 67). Amiry is obliged to spend the long curfew hours, which at one point last for thirty-six consecutive days, with her nagging ninety-two-year-old mother-in-law, Um Salim. The latter attempts to impose her strict daily routine on Amiry, who finds herself besieged in her own house. Between the tyranny of Um Salim at home and Sharon's imposed curfew on the street, Amiry composes this diary as a way to recount and reflect on the enduring contradictions and 'absurdity of my life and the lives of others' in occupied Ramallah (xi).

Although Amiry's diary was later compiled and reorganised for publication and mainly aimed at an English-speaking international audience, her daily record was initially cathartic. Part Two of Amiry's account, for instance,[8] is based on electronic correspondences with intimate friends through which she recounts her days under curfew 'as a form of therapy' (ix). Her use of the form meets Lejeune's description of the function of diaries as literary vehicles 'to express oneself', '*to communicate*' and '*to release*, to unload the weight of emotions and thoughts in putting them down on paper' (*On Diary* 195). For Amiry, exchanging serial emails becomes a 'valuable self-defense mechanism', her daily escape towards sanity in order 'to release the tension caused and compounded by Ariel Sharon and my mother-in-law' (Amiry ix, x). Most importantly, the diary form provides Amiry with a site for self-expression through which she can bear witness to everyday life in Ramallah under curfew. Her resort to diary writing is meaningful, as she becomes an insider source of daily news reporting in English to friends who live, for instance, in Italy, Jordan and Scotland. Amiry's narrative, in this sense, also acknowledges the ways in which new communication technologies have revitalised the rhetorics of diary writing.[9] The temporal immediacy characterising the diaristic form, facilitated by the instantaneity of transmission enabled by the Internet, enhances Amiry's testifying capacity. Her account thus becomes an example of what Kylie Cardell defines as 'an embodied act of witness and testimony' ('Life Narrative Methods' 93).

The immediacy, and often urgency, of first-hand eye witnessing that Amiry presents in her account interface the personal and the political. Amiry's stories oscillate between first-hand reportages of 'breaking news' (*Sharon Mother* 145) and her domestic days when she is 'utterly bored' during 'the deadly long curfew day' on which she repeatedly exercises her uninteresting daily routine (180, 178). This juxtaposition, that the narrative foregrounds, highlights the contestatory aspect of the diaristic form, and more generally life narratives, in relation to mainstream representations of Palestine under occupation, which is often, as Noam Chomsky notes in his forward to Atef Abu Saif's diary, 'descriptive and analytical prose [that] is too cold, too remote' from daily human life and individuals' stories (vi). The diary, in this case, emerges in corrective response to the representation of the Palestinian as a subject who embodies a 'predicament of being a "non-person"' (Moore-Gilbert, *Postcolonial* 115); it aims to humanise the Palestinian narrative and to disrupt the political crudeness of official discourses by shifting the focus to the effect of occupation on ordinary life. As Felicity Nussbaum rightly argues in her conceptualisation of the form, 'the marginalized and unauthorized discourse in a diary holds the power to disrupt authorized versions of experience, even, perhaps to reveal what might be called randomness and arbitrariness of the authoritative and public constructs of reality' (10). Choosing to make her account public, by positioning it online and later through traditional publication (thus reorganised and edited), Amiry's account deliberately 'step[s] out of the [dominant] frame' (Amiry xi) of representing Israeli occupation, which tends to focus exclusively on political resistance and violent confrontations.

Amiry exposes the 'randomness' and 'arbitrariness' of mainstream discourses on Palestine as a context from which only heroic/tragic stories emerge. She deliberately attempts to contest the image of the Palestinian victim/hero by presenting herself as a laughing and unheroic subject who exercises daily 'passive resistance to occupation' (*Sharon Mother* 71). For example, driven by self-interest and fearful of deportation, Jordan-born Amiry signs the anti-PLO (the Palestine Liberation Organization) statement in order to obtain a residency card which allows her to stay with her husband in Ramallah; an act which symbolically betrays the Palestinian liberation cause. Moreover, Amiry locates herself in a comedic mode and resorts to humour and ridicule as a dissident strategy which seems, as she writes, 'an effective way of dealing with the unbearable encounters of life under occupation' (189). She presents herself as a subject who is capable of daily laughter despite the horrors of the context in which she lives; this strategy, in turn, challenges both the image of Palestine as a site of mourning and tragedy and the status of women as silent weeping victims (Cheurfa 185–90).

Representing Palestinian ordinary life in its unheroic and mundane dimensions is most notably reminiscent of prominent lawyer and author Raja Shehadeh who prolifically uses the diary form to enact 'the way we were leading our lives ordinarily, not only in times of war' (*When the Bulbul* vi). Like Shehadeh,

Amiry's diary shifts the lyrical frames of representing Palestine and Palestinians through investing in the characteristics of the diary form as emphasising ordinary discourses and everyday life representation. Self-consciously, the narrator claims a subjective position as a witness, a storyteller and a person who strives to lead an ordinary life amidst exceptional circumstances. Amiry deliberately portrays the Israeli occupation as a daily encounter and focuses on the representation of its effects on Palestinian quotidian life; she describes her diaries as 'accounts of my everyday life under occupation and my frequent encounters with the Israeli "Civil Administration" and soldier' (Amiry xi).

Instead of writing exclusively on armed confrontations, political parties, suicide bombers, bloodshed and murder, which dominate mainstream media representation of the so-called Israeli–Palestinian conflict, Amiry chooses to present personal and domestic experiences that are impossible to access otherwise. She writes about her mother-in-law's marmalade and purple dress, her love story with her husband Salim, neighbourhood gossip, married women's affairs, domestic skirmishes, cappuccino machines, Israeli friends, amused soldiers, blacksmiths and misogynist vets. In Amiry's account, the repeated life pattern, especially during curfews, imposes enduring sameness to which West Bankers consciously adapt. Amiry refers to curfew days as '"normal" days' (177) on which she embraces the disruption of life and executes her 'curfew routine' (179–80). She also recounts how, during the few hours when the curfew lifts, she visits her friends whose hospitality is impeccable 'as if there isn't a war' (65). Palestinians, as depicted by Amiry, enjoy the simple blessings of life where Turkish coffee makes 'life under occupation and curfew more tolerable' (81) and in which 'how much weight [they gained] during this curfew' (65) is a more important subject of discussion than the armed siege. This attests to Ramallah residents' resilience to pursue and maintain the normalcy of life despite the chaotic and tragic circumstances of the war. In this sense, Amiry's diary becomes a site through which an insider and humane context is given to the reality of life under occupation. This strategic representational choice highlights the power of life narratives as fundamental 'to the constant creation of what it means to be human and the rights that fall from that' (Whitlock 10). Equally, Amiry's account highlights the role of the diary as 'a key methodology through which subjects . . . have been able to recount and record experiences otherwise left out of the public record' (Cardell, 'Life Narrative Methods' 91).

Indeed, in many ways, Amiry's narrative meets the stereotypical characteristics of the diary as being an intimate form of writing in its negotiation of the domestic and preoccupation with the quotidian experiences of its subject. However, the historical and political are hardly marginal in her account. The narrative simultaneously reinvigorates the readers' expectations from the form by enacting political implications in which the mundane is presented and highlighted. Amiry's diaries are, in her own words, 'personal war diaries' (ix) which recount the socio-political effects of the Israeli occupation from an individual's perspective. Particularly, the effects of the Second Intifada on the mobility of Palestinians are acknowledged in Amiry's narrative. The author details the way Palestinians are subjected to restricted mobility complicated by borders, checkpoints and arbitrary legal statuses. She also speaks to the absurdity of travel permits in which her dog, for instance, who is granted a Jerusalem passport by an Israeli veterinarian, has easier access to the capital than herself. Amiry does not shy away from recounting, often in a sarcastic way, the humiliation that Palestinians must endure as a consequence of the illegal occupation where the simplest chores like food shopping become a frantic task motivated by '[t]he fear of hunger and the fear of endless curfew' (60). In this sense, the daliness that the author depicts does not diminish the machinations and horror of the Israeli illegal occupation of Palestine. It rather renders its effect on daily individual experiences and personal stories that emerge hitherto. Hence, the focus on occupation as a daily encounter in Amiry's narrative becomes a site for negotiating the political reality of the war and its impact on the daily life of a Ramallah resident.

While Amiry's diary presents ordinary life amidst the atrocities of war and curfew, the form of writing constitutes an 'eternal yearning for normality' (*Sharon Mother* 67). Amiry's diary selectively covers twenty-three years in the life of its subject as affected by the occupation. Her narrative reflects spatial and temporal shifts, very often abruptly. The discontinuity which particularly characterises the diary form symbolically renders the temporal and spatial fragmentations and disruptiveness that Israel has brutally inflicted on Palestine since *al-nakba* of 1948. However, the stylistic and generic aspects of the diary enable Amiry to bridge fragmented entries into a single narrative fabric and, as Lejeune argues in relation to diary writing, 'to give life the consistency and continuity it lacks' (*On Diary* 195). Amiry's diaries become a recurrent and consistent confirmation of her entitlement to lead a life ordinarily in a brutal context that strives to deny Palestinians their fundamental rights and freedoms, points which I will explore in detail in the following sections.

'When the War Stopped Being Sexy': The Mundane Face of a Palestinian-Israeli Life

Like Amiry, Palestinian journalist, screenwriter and novelist Sayed Kashua explores the quotidian contours of Palestinian life through the diaristic form. His narrative *Native: Dispatches from a Palestinian-Israeli Life* (2016), translated from Hebrew – the language in which Kashua exclusively writes, mainly as a consequence of being educated in Israeli schools – is a compilation of weekly columns that he wrote for the Israeli newspaper *Haaretz*. Covering the years between 2006 and 2014 of his residency in Jerusalem and ending when the narrator decides to move with his family to Illinois in the United States in the summer of 2014, *Native* recounts the complications and paradoxes of Kashua's days as a Palestinian citizen of Israel.

The weekly entries in *Native* are versatile in form, consisting of dated emails, letters, personal reflections, accounts of everyday events and a few fictionalised sketches and short stories. Although the primary material for Kashua's book is his newspaper columns, his narrative, I argue, falls into the diaristic form. It consists of dated entries organised chronologically – or what the subtitle labels 'dispatches' (alluding to the fragmented nature of the genre) – which revolve around the author's personal and professional life. *Native* meets the characteristics of the diary as a 'form for recording and documenting experience . . . associated rhetorically with both the everyday and the private sphere and the personal voice' (Cardell, 'Life Narrative Methods' 92). It also constitutes 'recording[s] of the thoughts, feelings, and activities of the writer, entered frequently and regularly' (Nussbaum 5). While *Native* falls into the category of diary writing, as defined by Cardell and Nussbaum, it challenges some of its conventional aspects. It does not fully adhere to Lejeune's autobiographical pact which binds the autobiographical subject to absolute truthfulness and non-fictionality. Kashua admits that some of the stories he publishes for *Haaretz*, and includes in his book, are partly fictional. This choice, as he states, is either influenced by his journalistic leaning to what makes a good story or sometimes because the real 'story was very sad' (*Native* 42). However, *Native* does not completely undermine reliability and truthfulness. Kashua asserts that in most of the entries, 'I tried to be honest and tell the truth as I perceived it' (*Native* xii) which he conveyed 'by means of personal stories' (xii). Like Amiry, Kashua acknowledges that diaristic practice is a therapeutic site for self-expression which gradually 'became a way of life for me' (*Native* xii). Although professional in his case, diary writing helped him, like Amiry, 'to create order out of the swirling chaos and find an inner logic in what I saw and experienced' (*Native* xii); it 'gave [him] space to apologize, cry out, be afraid, implore, hate, and love – but above all to look for hope and make my life a little more bearable' (*Native* xii).

Unlike Amiry who composes her diary by choice, the frequent entries written by Kashua are often professionally motivated. His account falls into the category of 'solicited diaries': 'diaries that people have been asked to keep for a particular reason . . . to gain rich insights into certain aspects of life'

(Bartlett and Milligan 3–4). Kashua is authorised as a public voice due to Israel's perception of him as a reputable Arab Israeli intellectual. His journalistic privilege, however, puts pressure on his weekly writing task. Writing primarily for a critical Israeli readership, Kashua describes the stereotypical expectations to provide 'an anthropological experience, a rare look into the mind of an Arab, . . . a journey into the very heart of Arab society' (*Native* 137). On the other hand, Palestinian readers living in Israel expect him to use the platform to 'serve our purpose as a national minority' (*Native* 75) by exploring persisting social and political issues. However, Kashua chooses to explore locations that are seemingly marginal to the political conflict and collective interests. He deliberately uses the column to make visible quotidian personal stories and reveal the person behind the intellectual and the public figure through journalistic media.

The serial form of writing allows Kashua not only to reflect on his individual life and experiences but also to foreground the tension and ethical contours in play when journalistic and diaristic writing are brought together. Often self-critically, Kashua draws attention to the labour involved in the process of diaristic writing, especially writing intended for publication. In her exploration of journalists' life writing from war-torn zones, Gillian Whitlock observes that when journalists use the genre 'as an opportunity to reflect on their craft, an important site in the production and circulation of life narratives comes into view' (133). *Native* is highly self-conscious. In many instances, Kashua invites the reader into the procedure of crafting these weekly entries – and arguably his diaristic practice – by metatextually reflecting on the labour invested in the production of his column, such as his difficulties in writing and the involved editing and publishing procedures. In many of the entries in this collection, Kashua depicts his struggle to find materials for his weekly pitch: 'writing a weekly column can be a real nightmare . . . I found myself wandering the streets of Jerusalem and mulling aloud: "what will I write about this week"' (*Native* xi). Through ethical and moral self-reflection, he challenges the conventional and stereotypical characteristic of the diary as being spontaneous, uncrafted, redundant and non-narrative (Lejeune, *On Diary* 170). Instead, Kashua sheds light on existing forms of diaries that are conscious, filtered, intentionally positioned for publication and consumption and geared toward a particular audience.

Kashua attributes his struggle to produce vignettes that meet the editors' deadlines to the repetitiveness of the collective life in the Palestinian and Israeli territories in which 'the war has looked the same for the past hundred years' and 'the stories are the same stories, very little changes over a year' (*Native* 56, 37). This poses a professional struggle to find material for his weekly column; he comedically comments: 'that's what Zionism is for me: to think that the country is interesting, that Jerusalem is beautiful, and that Tel Aviv is lively' (*Native* 56). In this account, Kashua shifts away from over-politicised journalistic discourses on Palestinian–Israeli relations. Instead, he attests to the mundane nature of the Israeli occupation through his exploration of ordinary daily events in a diaristic form. Kashua writes about his bar conversations with strangers, his daughter's homework and personal stories of his family members whom he exploits 'shamelessly' (*Native* xii).

In his portrayal of occupation as a mundane, and often unheroic, encounter, Kashua's use of humour to deliver political and social commentaries is very reminiscent of Amiry. For example, when he is asked by an Israeli journalist why he does not enjoy Israeli Independence Day – which the Palestinian consider as *al-nakba* (catastrophe) day – he responds that 'on Independence Day I feel bad and depressed' because 'the kids are out of school' and 'I have to be with them the whole day' (*Native* 57). In a predominantly sarcastic tone, Kashua privileges the personal as an important location where the political is often negotiated. What we might perceive as political in Kashua's text is often implied and presented in an amusing disjuncture between the serious and the hilarious and the political and the banal. Even the most poignant incidents, such as death, are presented with a discomforting banality. For example, when the radio announces murders of Palestinians and Israelis in an armed confrontation in October 2010, Kashua and his wife 'launched into our regular game. "Four to one, our advantage," I said; my wife bet 3–2, also in our favour . . . We were both wrong, it was 5–0 for us. I won because I was closer' (*Native* 162). Although this incident might be ethically questionable, because death is generally a comedy taboo, it is important in the way it portrays the absurdity of contexts in which death is normalised and the value of human lives is reduced to numbers of fatalities.

However, when Kashua steps momentarily outside his comic register, Palestinian life is presented with enduring poignancy. In an entry entitled 'The Stories I Do Not Dare Tell', for example, Kashua addresses his deceased grandmother whom he remembers on *al-nakba* day of 2012. In an open-letter entry, Kashua laments his grandmother, her loss of her husband and land in 1948 in the town of Tira, the atrocities she endured to raise his father, and all the Palestinian stories of loss and trauma which remain untold. While he comforts her that 'I've become a storyteller myself', he admits 'how hard it is to tell stories' (*Native* 223). The text gradually becomes more sombre and serious in tone as the narrator realises that 'I lost my little war' (*Native* 286), in reference to his optimistic belief that writing about Palestinians in Hebrew would encourage mutual understanding and coexistence between Jews and

Arabs in a 'place that is worth living in, exactly like the stories with good endings' (*Native* 286). When his car is egged in his new Jewish neighbourhood in West Jerusalem, when he is threatened for one of his columns, when Jewish youth marching in a parade shout 'Death to the Arabs' (*Native* 286), when he is not able to speak Arabic with his daughter in the mall parking, and when Israeli children shout 'yuk' to his son and refuse to play with his daughter because they are Arabs, Kashua confronts himself and his readers with the futility of writing. The persistence of injustice, atrocity and racism leads Kashua to reflect:

> All I have to do is write and the occupation will end . . . tell good stories in Hebrew and I will be safe, another book, and another movie and another column for the newspaper and another script for television and my children will already have a better future . . . Twenty-five years of writing in Hebrew, and nothing has changed. (*Native* 285)

Kashua realises that in the face of the systematic Israeli apartheid, writing about Palestinians for an Israeli audience has not and perhaps will never change the historically persistent politics of discrimination and segregation endured by Palestinians. In the 'Farewell' entry, Kasha leaves Israel for the US and the narrative closes with him reminding his daughter that 'whatever you do in life, for them you will always, but always, be an Arab' (*Native* 287). This realisation raises persistent questions of belonging and citizenship in occupied Palestine, which the title of the diaries – *Native* – both states and interrogates. Unlike Kashua's disenchantment with writing in the face of the recurrent brutality of the occupation, Atef Abu Saif's narrative, which I will now discuss, highlights the importance of diary writing as a strategic medium of resistance and steadfastness.

Daily Survival: The Everydayness of Palestinian Resistance

Gaza-based writer and university professor Atef Abu Saif adopts the diary form to testify to the repetitiveness of life and dailiness of warfare in besieged Gaza. His account *The Drone Eats with Me: Diaries from a City Under Fire* (2015) recounts the brutal Israeli war on the Gaza Strip in July 2014, particularly in Jabalia refugee camp, the largest refugee camp in Gaza city where the author resides. The war was a response to the kidnapping and later murder of three Israeli students by Palestinian militants, which Israel claims was sanctioned by Hamas, Gaza's majority-voted, ruling political party.[10] Abu Saif's self-translated diary is a chronological account of the fifty-one consecutive days of bombing (6 July to 26 August) in the life of its subject under arbitrary curfews and drone surveillance. This bombing campaign resulted in the murder of more than 2,000 Palestinians with over 11,000 injured. Writing in moments of precarity, Abu Saif's account adopts a more serious and poignant tone than Amiry's and Kashua's narratives. Nevertheless, in its diaristic form, it similarly attests to the ordinariness of occupation, the prevalence of violence and trauma, and the everydayness of Palestinian resistance.

Like Amiry's *Sharon*, Abu Saif's *The Drone* was not initially intended for publication but was a cathartic practice. Since the onset of the war, Abu Saif had been keeping a record of his days, first in Arabic (which he later self-translated to include in the published version); 'it never occurred to him that anyone would read them' (Page 246). Later, and as suggested by his friend and Comma Press editor Ra Page, he started writing his diary in English, perhaps with the intention of publishing it. For Abu Saif, writing daily records constitutes 'a simple ritual [that] can help you escape the torment of just sitting and waiting for the unknown to happen. It reassures you' (*Drone* 45). Despite being a potential target of the drone, Abu Saif deliberately maintains the habit of going to the Internet café to transcribe his quotidian experiences which, as described by his editor Page, 'was one of his traditions of war, a survival ritual' (246). Through diary writing, Abu Saif claims and performs the role of both subject and witness. He observes – and symbolically, like the drone – surveys, his life and that of others in a literary form that renders the daily acts of survival under occupation and siege.

Abu Saif's diary writing as a means of 'reassurance' and 'a survival ritual' is arguably attributed to both the chronological order (temporal linearity) and quality of unfinishedness characterising the diary form of life writing. In war-torn Gaza, 'days no longer matter' (*Drone* 91), because its oppressive mechanisms tend to confuse the individuals' consciousness of time. Maintaining a sense of time is not only a difficult task for Gazans, but one which, in its strenuousness, is unimportant because of the cyclical monotony of the days, especially during the long periods of curfews. Abu Saif depicts how 'you don't care if today is a Friday or a Monday, a Saturday or a Tuesday. The name of the day isn't important, nor its whereabouts in the calendar . . . day after day, the days of the week become meaningless' (*Drone* 91).

Although the entry from which the above quote is taken is entitled 'Dateless in Gaza', it is interestingly dated Friday 25 July. While the daily repetitiveness experienced by Gazans due to the war devalues temporal tracking, the daily record that Abu Saif keeps as a witness necessitates accurate marking of date and time. Chronological order is one of the main characteristics of the diary form. The genre is the ideal order-keeping writing mode because, as elaborated by Smith and Watson, 'the pages of a diary are fixed in time and space, available to the diarist for later viewing' (193). Unlike autobiography and memoir which are generally written in retrospect, looking back from a particular point in time, a diary is an immediate account that represents continuity in the present. Being an everyday practice that conventionally requires the transcription of date and time, the diary enables the subject to regain, even relatively, a consciousness of temporality. In this sense, Abu Saif assumes control and order over his own war experience through diaristic narration. His diary keeps him time conscious as compared to his 'dateless' compatriots. It enables him to keep track of the sense of time and days in an attempt to survive the potential distortion of Palestinian temporality.

In addition to time tracking, the unfinished character of the diary form, I suggest, provides Abu Saif with a sense of 'reassurance' because it presupposes continuity, and thus survival in the face of the prevalence of death and mass destruction. In fact, 'the idea of finishing is alien to the idea of a diary' (Lejeune, *On Diary* 172). Diaries 'do not begin in a vantage point that offers strategic finality or closure; nor do they progress teleologically towards such a vantage point' (Moore-Gilbert, 'Time Bandits' 196). Unlike conventional autobiography which 'is turned towards the past', the diary 'is virtually unfinishable from the beginning, because there is always a time lived beyond the writing, making it necessary to write anew' (Lejeune, *On Diary* 191). Abu Saif maintains the practice of diary writing in times of war as a way of assuming survival because its lack of closure presupposes the continuity of life. He thus transcribes his story in an open-ended form as a way to sustain hope under the erasing threats of drone-fired missiles. Abu Saif comments that in Gaza 'it's an uncertain life: you're denied any sense of long-term stability . . . Tomorrow is still the thing you can't depend on. Instead, you make do with the unending, unbroken tunnel of today' (*Drone* 201). He writes today without a defined closure, having the intention that he will be writing another entry the day after. His diary becomes a medium of perseverance, an act of resistance and, as Lejeune points out, the form 'is transformed into battlefield against death . . . the idea of chronicling your struggle day by day . . . seems like a way of holding yourself up' (*On Diary* 197). Wartime diary writing offers Abu Saif a space to unravel his everyday struggle as a non-combatant civilian against potential erasure by Israeli missiles and drones. It simultaneously enables the subject to maintain a sense of understanding of his daily emotions in order 'to survive the [war's] madness' (*Drone* 240).

In these diary entries, Abu Saif portrays the politics of resistance in its everydayness through the collective quest to maintain the normalcy of life despite the complexities and hardships of war. Lasting for fifty-one days, the 2014 war in Gaza 'has almost become normality as people get back into the familiar habits of survival' as days 'don't really feel like different days' (*Drone* 43, 202). Gaza residents as depicted by Abu Saif maintain or adapt their daily routines and domestic practices to the newly imposed circumstances of the war. For example, Abu Saif's routine consists of roaming around Gaza from Jabalia camp to Khan Younis, watching the 2014 Football World Cup in public gatherings and smoking Shisha with his friends under the surveillance of drones. He asserts that 'an otherwise boring routine in such circumstances can make life bearable' (*Drone* 45). This reflects the notion of *sumud*, Arabic for steadfastness, which has been associated with the Palestinian resistance against Israeli occupation. *Sumud* 'indicates a person's ability to remain in place in the face of indignities, injustices and humiliation at the hands of the colonial power, which seeks to place and deny the right to exist of the colonized' (El Said *et al.* 13). While *sumud* does not involve active and armed resistance, it does not denote submission. As Shehadeh defines the term: '*sumud*: [is] to stay put, to cling to our homes and land by all means available'; it '*was not submission*. It was keeping open all options, enduring without giving up anything and waiting to understand' (*The Sealed Room* 6). In Abu Saif's diaries, *sumud*, as an act of resistance and endurance, is carried out through maintaining the rituals of ordinary life despite the siege, the prevalence of violence, the restriction in transfer of food and human aid, control over residents' mobility and recurrent threats of drones: 'we are surrounded by death but the only thing Gazans can think about, in their neverending, daily calculations, is life' (*Drone* 180). Daily rituals such as watering plants despite the shortage of water in the water tanks, gatherings to watch drama series in the few hours of electricity supply and exchanging love letters become strategic acts of survival and daily rituals of *sumud* which aim at sustaining the normality of life in abnormal circumstances.

For instance, Abu Saif's narrative emphasises the role of food and daily culinary practices as everyday means of *sumud* which aims at maintaining life's 'cycle of permanence within the cycle of war and destruction' (Mehta 54). The bombardment of Gaza in July 2014 coincided with the Muslim holy month of Ramadan. Gazans, as portrayed in this narrative, maintain the two-meal ritual of *iftar* and *suhur*,[11] after fasting from dusk to dawn, despite the heavy Israeli bombardment of the strip around these 'feeding times' (Abu Saif, *Drone* 11):

> The food is ready . . . Darkness eats with us. Fear and anxiety eat with us. The unknown eats with us. The F16 eats with us. The drone, and its operator somewhere out in Israel, eat with us. Our hand shiver, our eyes stare at the plates on the floor. The dawn prayers leak into the room from a mosque

somewhere out in the darkness. Suddenly, we remember our hunger, all at once, diving into the delicious, merciful food. (*Drone* 31, 32)

Abu Saif portrays food consumption as a politicised act of defiance. He links nutrition, the most basic act of human survival, to political resistance/ *sumud* because, as he asserts, 'the only real heroism is survival, to win the prize that is your own life' (*Drone* 55). This idea is announced as early as the title of the diary which juxtaposes drone warfare with culinary practices and daily routines. *The Drone Eats with Me* is an unconventional title for a war narrative as it is not situated in a rhetorical tone of patriotism, heroism and/ or tragedy. Instead, it suggests both the familiarity of war – indicated by the subject's daily encounter with the drone – and the everydayness of resistance. While the title *The Drone Eats with Me* indicates the unwanted omnipresence of drones in the daily life of Abu Saif, it simultaneously emphasises the steadfastness of the subject who refuses to relinquish his day-to-day (feeding) activities despite the fatal capabilities of the personified mechanical threat. This reflects the way survival becomes a daily, almost intuitive, act. In the face of the unequal power balance between the Palestinian and the Israeli adversaries, daily routines – as represented by Abu Saif – become one of the focal strategies of survival; it aims to maintain existence under brutal circumstances in which living itself constitutes a form of defiance, an act of *sumud*.

Conclusion

The narratives examined in this chapter demonstrate the ways in which the diary form of life writing enables the representation of the mundane spheres of personal Palestinian life under Israeli occupation. Suad Amiry's, Sayed Kashua's and Atef Abu Saif's diaries considered here reinvigorate a historically and critically marginalised literary form of self-expression in order to articulate the impact of the so-called Israeli–Palestinian conflict on daily life. In doing so, they re-orient the readers' imagination and understanding of what it means to be a Palestinian living in the Occupied Territories. The authors examined in this chapter portray the Israeli occupation of Palestine from a daily perspective which collapses the representational boundaries between the private and the public, the political and the personal, and the national and the domestic. The formal and aesthetic aspects characterising the diary as deployed by Amiry, Kashua and Abu Saif provide compelling alternatives to the authoritative versions of discourse that promote a crudely political narrative on Palestine and Israel, which is generally positioned within two extremes: the heroic or the tragic. Instead, they attempt to humanise the Palestinian narrative through recounting quotidian activities and daily practices of individual life under occupation. However, while these diaries depoliticise the representational discourse on Palestine and Israel, they should not be dismissed as apolitical. The mundane and personal dimensions of life amidst the Israeli–Palestinian conflict as depicted by Amiry, Kashua and Abu Saif are seamlessly in confrontation with the political. Their diaries articulate daily encounters that gesture towards the repetitiveness of Israeli abuse and oppression and portray Palestinian resistance as a mode of existence, which reflects, to a varying degree, the notion of *sumud* as a daily practice. This simultaneously enacts the significance of personal stories and private discourses as a crucial cultural part in the construction, production and consumption of national and public narratives on contemporary Palestine.

Notes

1. The diary is a form of life writing that describes a periodic, often chronological, account of the daily life and experiences of its narrating subject. It is an intimate document that is often kept private. While not all the diaries selected in this chapter have been intended for a large audience, they have all appeared in print and were reworked for publication, as I explain in detail in my textual analysis.
2. The diaristic practice is an increasingly emerging mode of life writing in different forms and cultural media. Among the most prominent and prolific Palestinian diarists is Ramallah-based lawyer and memoirist Raja Shehadeh who has published several diaries in English including *The Sealed Room* (1992), *When the Bulbul Stopped Singing* (2003) and *Occupation Diaries* (2013). Moreover, the use of new communication technologies has also contributed to the popularisation of the practice. For instance, Gaza-based teenager Farah Baker used digital media (particularly Twitter, @Farah_Gazan) as a medium for diaristic writing during the Israeli military attack on Gaza in 2014 and recently in 2021 and has gained unprecedented public and international attention. *From Gaza, with Love* is another important diary-style blog by human rights activist Mona Elfarra.
3. The relationship between daily life and the political reality in Palestine is discussed in Nancy Stohlman and Laurieann Aladin (eds), *Live from Palestine: International and Palestinian Direct Action Against the Israeli Occupation* (2003), an important collection of entries bearing witness to the everyday life under Israeli occupation which includes contributions from prominent figures such as Edward Said and Hanan Ashrawi.
4. It was in the mid-twentieth century that the genre was conceptualised and recognised in Anglo-American scholarship due to critics like James Olney who re-introduced and translated, mainly in his *Autobiography: Essays Theoretical and Critical* (1980), studies by the pioneers of the genre such as Georges Gusdorf's 'Conditions and Limits of Autobiography' ([1956] 1980). However, it was not until the 1980s that rules of the genre set by the founding fathers of

autobiography criticisms started to be questioned, revised and contested, initially by feminist studies of the genre like Estelle C Jelinek's *Women's Autobiography: Essays in Criticism* (1980), Bella Brodzki and Celeste Schenck's *Life/Lines: Theorizing Women's Autobiography* (1988) and Shari Benstock's *The Private Self: Theory and Practice of Women's Autobiographical Writings* (1988).
5. These rules also apply to the memoir form (Gilmore 2) because the terms autobiography and memoir are very often used synonymously (see Smith and Watson 198).
6. For more details, see Linda Anderson's *Autobiography* (2011).
7. Lejeune's autobiographical pact refers to a contractual relationship between the autobiographical subject and the reader which implies that 'the author, the narrator, and the main subject of the narrative are identical' ('The Autobiographical Contract' 193). It declares the non-fictionality of the text and binds the author to truthfulness and sincerity in recounting his/her experiences in an autobiographical form.
8. The English edition of Amiry's diary combines two parts which appeared in other languages as two different books. Part One of *Sharon* was written after Part Two. The latter was published first in Italian translation in 2003.
9. For more details on the impact of the new communication technologies on the conventions of the diary form, see Kylie Cardell's *Dear World: Contemporary Uses of the Diary* (2014).
10. For more details on the background of the war, see Nathan Thrall, 'Hamas's Chances' in *London Review of Books* (21 Aug 14) <https://www.lrb.co.uk/v36/n16/nathan-thrall/hamass-chances>.
11. The two main meals during Ramadan, at sunset and before sunrise, respectively.

3

AMERICAN PALESTINIAN WOMEN AS PUBLIC INTELLECTUALS: NEW NARRATIVES OF RESISTANCE

Sahar al-Shoubaki

So in the end it is the intellectual as a representative figure that matters — someone who visibly represents a standpoint of some kind, and someone who makes articulate representations to his or her public despite all sorts of barriers.

(Said, *Representations of the Intellectual* 12)

As I finished writing this chapter in June 2021, the world was facing a Coronavirus pandemic that has swept the globe and caused millions of deaths worldwide. I was constantly checking on the numbers of COVID-19 cases around the world, and at some point, I stumbled upon the website of Johns Hopkins University's Center for Systems Science and Engineering to get updates on the numbers. I clearly remember that I could not locate Palestine on the map they had up on their website, even though news had it that there were cases in Gaza and Ramallah. It was later revealed by Ali Abunimah on a blog post published on the website of the *Electronic Intifada*, of which he is a co-founder, that the Johns Hopkins University's Center for Systems Science and Engineering initially had an entry called 'Palestine' that was changed to 'oPt,' that is the occupied Palestinian territories, but was later merged with the entry 'Israel'. It was under pressure and objection letters sent to the Center that they later had an entirely different entry listed as 'West Bank and Gaza' (Abunimah, 'Johns Hopkins'). This incident of silencing and erasing Palestine is not the first of its kind, bearing in mind that the permission to narrate Palestine has long been denied, suppressed, manipulated and resisted throughout history as Edward Said argued almost forty years ago.[1] In 'Permission to Narrate,' the late Said remarks that 'The [Palestinians] are there all right, but the narrative of their present actuality – which stems directly from the story of their existence in and displacement from Palestine, later Israel – that narrative is not' (30). What Palestine, as a nation, and Palestinians, as a group of people, suffered and are still suffering from is the result of a combination of settler colonialism, neoliberal capitalism, imperialism, Zionism, and racism – powers that American Palestinian women writers recognise and feel the urgency to contest, resist and universalise in their narratives.

It has been seventy-four years now since the Israeli colonial project started in Palestine and the Palestinian people are still dispossessed, misplaced and denied the right to return to their homelands.[2] As former President Trump and former Prime Minister Netanyahu announced the 'deal of the century'[3] on 28 January 2020, which is basically an apartheid plan that continues to deny Palestinians their basic human rights and legalises the occupation and approves the crimes of the continuous settler-colonial project in Palestine, and the annexation of the West Bank is reinforced by current Prime Minister, Naftali Bennett, Palestinians continue to face another setback in their struggles for freedom, return and rights of self-determination as the world turns a blind eye to such violations.[4] Given the growing calls for justice and solidarity with Palestine by prominent intellectuals and activists, it comes as little to no surprise that the literary production of American Palestinian women writers has begun to take a stand and to ask uncomfortable questions, that is, to challenge the dominant powers and to call for justice in their writings. The American Palestinian women writers whose works I discuss in this chapter – Susan Abulhawa and Ibtisam Barakat – take it upon themselves to assume the role of the public intellectual who does not shy away from deconstructing the narratives that do not acknowledge their existence, identity, or experience. This chapter will show how Abulhawa and Barakat, in their novels and life narratives, fulfil the role of the writer-intellectual in that they, to use Said's words, speak truth to power and 'represent all those people and issues that are routinely forgotten or swept under the rug' (*Representations* 11), in so doing extending our understanding of the public intellectual as a typically male figure to include a specific postcolonial feminist perspective on what it means to speak truth to power.

In her article, 'On Writing and Return,' Lisa Suheir Majaj suggests that Palestinian women

> write not only from an understanding of the personal as political (that tried-and-true dictum of feminism) but also from an understanding of the political as personal. It is to write out of a recognition of the ways in which the multiple layers of history and politics, exile and displacement situate and shape individual lives. (115)

Abulhawa and Barakat certainly write from an understanding of 'the political as personal'. They offer feminist interventions that resist the dominant Western narratives that deny their history and existence; they struggle against deportations, statelessness, uprootedness, exile and violence; they fight for freedom from occupation, for basic human rights and for self-determination; and they express their struggles in the diaspora as they lead lives as migrants who are trying to belong and find a sense of 'home' in places far away from their homeland. But they also recognise that Palestinian women, just like any other women in the world, demand equality with men, call for the end of sexism and discrimination and fight for their rights as women the way any feminist would do. However, it is critical to look at their struggles within a larger political context since the freedom Palestinian women demand cannot be achieved without first obtaining freedom from the settler-colonial regime, the Israeli occupation. Suki Ali, in 'Feminism and Postcolonial: Knowledge/Politics', reminds us that the 'need to think through issues of "race", ethnicity and class as situated within globalized networks of economic, cultural and technological expansion is central to feminist discussions of power and resistance, as it is of course to feminist politics and practice' (197). This is why I take a postcolonial feminist approach whenever the discussion and representation of Palestinian women is involved. Postcolonial feminism allows for an examination of the diverse experiences of (post)colonial subjects and helps analyse the conditions under which they live. It necessitates the acknowledgement of the differences in privilege and position of Palestinian women – differences that are impacted by cascading factors such as the Israeli occupation, patriarchy, daily oppressions, harassments, and harsh economic conditions. Abulhawa and Barakat recognise and write about these differences, and my approach means that any analysis of the issues and concerns of Palestinian women in their works cannot be looked at without first including a critique of the political reality of their situation, which is the existence of a settler-colonial regime and an ongoing occupation of their land.

Both Abulhawa and Barakat were born and have lived in Palestine before they were displaced and became American citizens. When they write about the experiences of Palestinian women in Palestine, they write from first-hand experience since their families have lived through the *nakba* and they both experienced the aftermath of the *naksa*, the 1967 occupation of the Palestinian Territories, and lived under the occupation of the West Bank. It is in this sense that American Palestinian women's new narratives act as a creative form of resistance through the way that they offer a counternarrative that gives voice to the Palestinian people. But they also write as Arab American women writers, who, as Carol Fadda-Conrey argues, 'straddle cultures, fight double battles, and recognize that any location comes closely intertwined with gender, racial, and political context' (17). For Abulhawa and Barakat, diaspora creates a space and a medium of expression for their voices as women and becomes a potential site where they reconfigure, reassemble, 'revisit their past/history, deconstruct it, and reconstruct their own her/stories' (Fadda-Conrey 10). Their writings, thus, push Arab American women as postcolonial feminist public intellectuals to the foreground and help contest and resist the stereotypical Western mainstream view that Arab American women are voiceless and invisible.

The American Palestinian Intellectual and the Right to Write

Before moving on to my discussion of the themes of freedom from the occupation; justice and human rights in Palestine; displacements during the *nakba* and *naksa*; and return to the homeland that Abulhawa and Barakat address in their works, I want to examine why these themes were absent from most fiction books produced by American Palestinian writers until the Second Palestinian Intifada.[5] As Said's famous article, discussed above, explains, the Palestinian narrative has been absent in the West and the United States but in recent years this absence has been further corroborated by an increased fear of criticism of Israel being conflated with anti-Semitism (Bayoumi and Rubin 246).[6] This partly explains why American Palestinian writers have been discouraged from writing about Palestine in their prose fiction until the early 2000s and instead of speaking up and narrating the stories of their displacement from their homeland, they have focused on alternative themes like assimilation with barely any mention of Palestine or the history that led to their displacement and dispossession.[7] Assimilating into American society and narrating stories about the lives of Palestinians in the diaspora are still important themes that American Palestinian women writers write about, but the focus has shifted to allow for more important pressing issues to emerge in their writings – such as the aftermath of the *nakba* and *naksa*, justice, freedom, and return to the homeland.[8] More Arab American intellectuals have started to write counternarratives that register the history of Palestine and reflect the Palestinian experience, whether it is the experience of Palestinians under occupation or in the diaspora.

This shift cannot be examined without looking at the historical background that allowed for its emergence. It is very important to mention the foundation of the BDS (Boycott, Divestment, Sanction) movement in 2005, which is a non-violent grassroots movement that works towards ending all international support for Israel's occupation of Palestine and calls for Palestinians' rights of self-determination, equality, and return. Co-founder of

BDS, Omar Barghouti, in his book, *BDS: Boycott, Divestment, Sanctions: The Global Struggle for Palestinian Rights*, argues that:

> This context of relative change in the US establishment, accompanied by more radical change at the grassroots level in the United States and Europe in reaction to Israel's war crimes and other grave violations of international law in its bloody suppression of the second Palestinian intifada, provided fertile ground for a well-conceived, nonviolent citizens' movement for Palestinian rights to flourish. (4)

Thus, the BDS campaign has played a very important role in shifting the narrative of Palestine, allowing for more room to discuss and address the critical injustices inflicted on Palestinians. Hence, the BDS movement played a major role in bringing agency to American Palestinian intellectuals who have started to reclaim their roles in writing their own narrative. Accompanying this opening up of a space for talking about Palestine in the United States is another important rhetorical shift, as Ali Abunimah has pointed out:

> As one consequence of these [BDS] efforts, the question of Palestine is being redefined not as the 'Palestinian problem,' but as the settler-colonial problem and the problem of Zionism's attempt to deny the rights, the history, and even the existence of the Palestinian people. (*The Battle* xii)

BDS, thus, plays a vital role in legitimising and generating more action and dialogue about Palestine, whether on a political or literary level, which American Palestinian writers create through their works to advocate for justice and freedom within a Palestinian context.

Bearing all of the above in mind, contemporary American Palestinian women writers, two of whose works I refer to in this chapter, speak truth to power by shedding light on the oppressive practices of powerful imperialist regimes and patriarchal systems and by calling out the war crimes and injustices happening in Palestine during the *nakba*, the *naksa*, and under the current occupation. Their works serve as a space for investigating the experiences of the Palestinian refugees who were dispossessed and forced to leave their homeland. They trace war memories, register the untold stories of the (mostly female) victims who survived the wars, struggle to heal from its horrors and try to restore their lost identity while also giving special attention to the urgent calls for freedom, justice, equality, and self-determination – calls that are considered the basic tenets of the BDS which they endorse and advocate for in their public life. Hence, they do not only play an important role as

Palestinian writers and intellectuals but as postcolonial feminist intellectuals whose intersectional approaches to depicting the lives of Palestinian women in Palestine and the diaspora offers a new gendered perspective on the Palestinian story that has long been silenced.

Palestinian Women and Displacements

Susan Abulhawa is one of the most famous women writers in contemporary American Palestinian literature. She is the author of three novels, *Mornings in Jenin* (2010), *The Blue Between Sky and Water* (2015) and *Against the Loveless World* (2020). She is also a human rights activist, a strong advocate of Palestinian rights and a signatory to the BDS campaign. When Abulhawa was asked in an interview about the role her works and literature in general play in talking about the Israeli occupation of Palestine, she answered that:

> Literature is a facet of society and when you belong to a people whose very existence is denied, to whom the world says 'you're not real, you do not exist,' writing your story and creating your art becomes an act of decolonisation. What Palestinian art and Palestinian literature does in this sort of political context is to assert our presence, our existence, our humanity and our ancient history, all of which belong to us. (Abulhawa, 'Interview')

For Abulhawa, writing narratives about Palestine and the experiences of Palestinian women who are going through multiple displacements at times when the world tries to silence such narratives becomes an act of resistance, and by doing so, Abulhawa assumes the role of the female public intellectual whose role it is to challenge the dominant powers. The inseparability of the conditions of Palestinian women and the displacements and occupation that pervade their lives is something Abulhawa recognises and makes an integral part of her narratives in all her novels. While *Against the Loveless World* explores the life of a Palestinian woman estranged in exile and later imprisoned in Israeli jails, *Mornings in Jenin* and *The Blue Between Sky and Water*, which are the focus of my discussion in this chapter, act as oral history accounts that offer a gendered perspective on the Israeli regime and track four generations of women's life narratives during several key historical periods. Abulhawa's novels give the reader the chance to witness the atrocities committed by Israel since its creation in 1948 while paying special attention to the extra price that women pay for colonialism because of their gender. Palestinian women in Abulhawa's narratives are taking on agency by telling their stories and writing history rather than being the silenced other. Not only that, Abulhawa also shows in her narratives that there is a great deal of female solidarity among Palestinian women as they struggle against both the occupation and patriarchy while they try to return to their home cities and homeland. In 'Cartographies of Struggle: Third World Women and the Politics of Feminism', Chandra Talpade Mohanty reminds us that:

> Resistance clearly accompanies all forms of domination . . . [it] inheres in the very gaps, fissures, and silences of hegemonic narratives. Resistance is encoded in the practices of remembering, and of writing. Agency is thus figured in the minute, day-to-day practices and struggles of third world women. (38)

Thus, Abulhawa's act of writing and remembering functions as a way of deconstructing the different forms of oppression from which Palestinian women suffer, as we will see below.

In *Mornings in Jenin*, the main character of the novel is Amal whose family goes through several traumas and tribulations during the *nakba* and the *naksa* and who later becomes an orphan at age fourteen. She lives in an orphanage, later immigrates to the US for her education, then eventually settles there and becomes an American citizen. Because Amal's experience in the US is shaped by her initial displacement from Palestine, her assimilation into American culture is shaped by the political factors that led to her immigration. Once she arrives in the US, she is unable to identify with American life which appears so unusual to her, bearing in mind that she lived in a war zone her entire life. She says, 'I found no commonality with the men and women who walked with purpose and self-possession . . . I felt diminished, out of place, and eager to belong' (172).[9] Since Amal escaped war and violence, she wants to find a place in America where she is not reminded of her sufferings and displacement. She adapts an American name, turning Amal, the Arabic word for hope, into '"Amy" – Amal without the hope . . . a word drained of its meaning' (178). She wants to forget the horrors of wars in Palestine, but her Palestinian national identity always comes back to remind her of her roots in Palestine. Thus, in the middle of her attempts to assimilate into American culture, she is still connected to her homeland and unable to erase her Palestinian identity. She observes that 'The divide could not have been greater, nor could it be bridged. That's how it was. Palestine would just rise up from my bones into the center of my new life, unannounced' (175).

Confirming her national identity as Palestinian after struggling to belong in America, she says, 'I forever belonged to that Palestinian nation of the banished to no place, no man, no honor. My Arabness and Palestine's primal cries were my anchors to the world' (Abulhawa, *Mornings* 179). It is being in her homeland, Palestine, which makes Amal feel rooted and grounded; she 'was Amal there, not Amy' (289). It is in that land and her hometown, Jenin, that Amal also starts to open up and reconnect with her daughter, Sara, with whom she has a cold mother–daughter relationship because the death of her husband, Majid – who was killed by Israelis in Beirut – left her traumatised and unable to care for her daughter. Sara insists on visiting Palestine with Amal to learn about her roots and her mother's past, and Amal agrees to go back after three decades of exile. Being surrounded by familiar faces and places in Jenin, Amal, for the first time, talks about Majid with Sara and builds a closer bond with her by sharing family stories and past experiences; but this is all short-lived because Amal's life comes to an end when she is shot in the head by an Israeli soldier during an Israeli raid on a refugee camp in Jenin. Amal's journey of belonging and un-belonging and her hopes and aspirations for a family, for love, for a home, and for a return to her homeland is crushed by continuous displacements and by the ongoing Israeli occupation of her homeland, Palestine. The tragic life she leads, the separation from her family, the deaths and short-lived moments of happiness are representations and political commentary on the lives of Palestinians as their land is fractured and they are physically and culturally dislocated and separated from their homeland.

The Blue Between Sky and Water is another work where Abulhawa's narrative gives readers the minutest detail of the many atrocities committed by the Israeli regime in Palestine, starting with the *nakba* and ending with the blockade of Gaza (from 2007 to 2011, according to the novel's timeline) while, at the same time, showing how displacements affect the life of Palestinian women at different levels. The novel is about several generations of Palestinian women who are trying to navigate life in the middle of violence and the ongoing Israeli occupation. The story starts during the time of the *nakba* in the Palestinian village of Beit Daras, where a battle occurs in 1948. During this battle, Nazmiyeh, a strong and resilient Palestinian woman, flees with her family to Gaza, but before she is able to reach safety, she gets raped by several Israeli soldiers who kill her little sister in front of her. '"Scream!" the soldier demanded in his language as he shoved himself into her. "Scream!" He pulled her body up by the hair, but Nazmiyeh understood neither his words nor his desire to hear her suffering' (Abulhawa, *The Blue* 37). The horrendous rape scene is described in full detail as a testimonial to the brutality and violence Palestinian women went through during the *nakba* and *naksa* which often goes untold or is not written about. This aligns with Valentine Moghadam's argument that

> Armed conflict has dire effects on all citizens, but women face specific risks ... Wars, and especially occupations by foreign powers, often are accompanied by crises of masculinity that lead to restrictions on women's mobility and increases in violence against women. (83)

Sexualised violence against women (rape in particular) is often seen as a weapon and by-product of war, and whether it is committed as a manifestation of gendered or colonial power, hegemonic and toxic masculinity or as a warring tactic to instil fear and humiliation, women are always at the receiving end and they are the ones who have to bear its horrible consequences. After her thirteenth and last pregnancy brings her the daughter she always wanted, Nazmiyeh tells her husband, Atiyeh, that 'now that we have Alwan, we're not having sex anymore.' He answers her with, 'your abstinence could affect population growth of Palestinians and we'd no longer threaten Israel demographically,' to which she replies laughingly, 'Okay. I'll give you some of this good stuff for the greater good of Palestine' (*The Blue* 60). Palestinian women, because of their gender, do not only get expelled from their homeland, but their bodies, in the realm of war and occupation, also get exploited in different ways, whether it is rape, sexual violence or even the constant childbirth in order to increase the Palestinian population that will fight for freedom from the Israeli occupation. Nazmiyeh acts as the old, wise and funny matriarch who is always resilient in the face of perils and who will crack jokes at times of distress as if to make the plights inflicted upon her lighter and more bearable. From the start to the end of the novel, she is the one who pulls the family together even after the death of her husband; the killing of her daughter's husband during the war on Gaza; the imprisonment of her oldest son, Mazen, by Israelis; the destruction of their houses' and even when her lost granddaughter, Nur, is reunited with them in Gaza and is pregnant out of wedlock. We see Nazmiyeh showing resilience and female solidarity by supporting all the widowed women in the family who are left to provide for themselves; she stands by her daughter Alwan through her breast cancer diagnosis and treatment; and she stands up for her granddaughter – in spite of the conservative society in Gaza – by asking her not to abort her child and finding ways to cover up the fact that she got pregnant without being married so they can raise the child within the family. Nazmiyeh's insistence on living with grace, humour and hope despite the occupation, destruction, loss and death is a symbol of Palestinian resilience. At the end of the novel, when Nazimiyeh is having a family gathering at the beach in celebration of Nur's return and the announcement of Mazen's release from prison, she says, in a hopeful tone, 'My mother once said this land will rise again' (*The Blue* 286).

As an activist, a member of the BDS campaign, and an intellectual, Abulhawa finds it critical to respond to the political and historical events that shape the lives of Palestinians. Her works become a means to defy the silencing of Palestinians, and to show the world how Palestinians' lives (especially women's) are informed and shaped by the occupation that leads to their dispossession, oppression, uprootedness and exile. In the epilogue to *The Blue Between Water and Sky*, Abulhawa writes,

> Shortly after I completed and submitted this novel for publication, Israel attacked Gaza with particular savagery in the summer of 2014 . . . Despite the horrors and terror they suffered, Palestinians in Gaza supported the resistance because, in the words of one man, 'We'd rather die fighting than continue living on our knees as nothing more than worthless lives Israel can use to test their weapons. (288)

The blockade of Gaza has created a humanitarian crisis that negatively impacts all aspects of Gaza's society, whether it is the education system, the economy, the health system or the infrastructure. It has created a shortage of food, medical supplies, energy and fuel as well as leading to restricted movement in and out of Gaza, which makes it impossible for refugees to go back to their villages in the surrounding areas.[10] Writing about such unjust realities and historicising/documenting the specific political events that led to them in literary fiction is the intellectual's approach to demanding justice and freedom as well as a means to bring back the writer's agency and right to narrate, which Palestinians have been denied for decades. There is no denying then that Abulhawa is assuming the role of the public intellectual who is committed to social justice and freedom, especially for women.

Coming of Age under Israeli Occupation: Speaking Truth to Power

Another American Palestinian woman writer who chooses an intersectional approach to write about Palestinians' lives (especially children's and young adults' lives) in the West Bank under the Israeli occupation is Ibtisam Barakat. In her memoirs, *Tasting the Sky: A Palestinian Childhood* (2007) and *Balcony on the Moon: Coming of Age in Palestine* (2016), Barakat pays less attention to the 1948 *nakba* and instead focuses on the Israeli occupation of the West Bank after the 1967 war, that is the *naksa*. Being among the younger generation who were born in Ramallah, having witnessed the 1967 war and having spent her childhood and adolescence in the West Bank under occupation, Barakat's life narratives focus on the effects of the *naksa* and the consequent Israeli occupation of the West Bank on the lives of children and teenagers. In an interview with the news magazine, *The Nation*, Barakat was asked about what prompted her to write her memoir to which she answered,

> I grew up in a world that ached for freedom but could not touch it. So I wrote *Tasting the Sky* as an exercise in freedom and as an expression of it. When I lived in Ramallah, there was the sense that anything I loved or owned could be taken away from me in an instant. In writing this book, I finally could own a piece of my childhood, which itself felt like a piece of Ramallah, in the form of story. (Barakat, 'Interview')

Barakat wants to historicise her story as a child fighting for freedom from the ongoing Israeli occupation and at the same time offer her own personal perspective on how the displacement she and her family suffer from inside their homeland is shaping their future. In *Reading Autobiography: A Guide for Interpreting Life Narratives*, Sidonie Smith and Julia Watson argue that for the writers in the field of postcolonial writing, 'autobiographical writing has often served as a tactic of intervention in colonial repression' (45). Barakat narrates memories of her life as a child growing up under Israeli occupation to offer a feminist intervention against the occupation, providing a criticism of how Palestinians (especially children) are fighting for liberation not only from colonial oppression, but also from patriarchal, economic and cultural oppression. To distinguish between the author, Ibtisam Barakat, and a younger version of the author who is the protagonist in her works, I will use Barakat's last name in my analysis to refer to the author and 'Ibtisam' to refer to the protagonist.

Childhood in Barakat's works is unique in that it is shaped by constant dislocations, wars, harsh social and economic realities, the occupation as well as patriarchal society. In *Tasting the Sky*, when Ibtisam's pen pals – who live in different parts of the world like Great Britain, Spain, Greece, and the US – ask about her childhood, she writes,

> I have nothing to say. It's like a curtain comes down and hides my memories. I do not dare part it and look. So I skip all childhood questions and reply only about the day . . . what would my pen pals say if I told them that I am standing at a detention center because I went to open my postbox for their letters? (11)

Under Israeli occupation, Palestinian children are detained, interrogated, harassed, intimidated and denied basic rights that any child should have. She speaks of how Israeli soldiers point their guns at her head and at other children's heads and how they train and rehearse military manoeuvres on the hill next to their house. She says, 'I realized then that the Israeli soldiers had become part of our daily life. We watched them, imitated them, puzzled over their actions, and talked about them all the time. They were the source of our anxiety and our entertainment' (98–9).

Moreover, Barakat writes about her trauma as an almost four-year-old child getting separated from her family while fleeing to Jordan during the 1967 war, where 'many families were opening their homes to receive West Bank refugees' (*Tasting* 35). Her younger self reveals, 'Fear dug a hole in my heart. I could not grasp what had happened. I wanted to cry aloud . . . but dread stifled my voice' (25). The experience of innocent young Palestinian children getting separated from their family during war is something rarely talked about in literature. In a report published by UNICEF titled, 'Children in the State of Palestine,' it is mentioned that:

> Conflict-related violence leaves a significant impact on the physical and mental well-being of children. In 2017, 15 Palestinian children were killed and 1,160 injured; 4 Israeli children were reported injured – all in incidents related to the armed conflict. Children continue to endure violations of due process when held in Israeli military detention in the West Bank, and when detained pursuant to Israeli domestic law, which Israel applies in East Jerusalem. (UNICEF 10)

By writing about and registering the experiences of Palestinian children during war, Barakat is assuming the role of the intellectual whose job is to educate the public about what usually goes unnoticed and to highlight and bring attention to the injustices that happen to children and Palestinians in general because of the Israeli occupation.

After being reunited with her family, Barakat also documents her life as a refugee in Jordan waiting for the war to end so she and her family can go back home. She writes about homelessness, despair, poverty and the sense of loss as well as the hope to 'return to Ramallah no matter how long the wait' (*Tasting* 55). While many Palestinians were not able to return to Palestine after the war ended, Barakat's family were among the few lucky ones to get their names randomly announced on the radio with a permission to return. But the fact that they return to their old house in Ramallah and are treated as refugees in their own homeland, Palestine, becomes the focus of Barakat's memoir. She highlights the harsh living conditions they experience under occupation where annexing and demolishing of Palestinian homes, cities, towns and villages by the Israeli government increases and where 'many camp families did not have enough food. The flour and sugar *mu'an* ration donated by the UN for refugees came irregularly' (155). Her family struggles with homelessness as they keep moving from one place to the other depending on her father's job, who is struggling to support his family. Moreover, because the 'United Nations schools don't require fees for children of refugees' (107) Barakat and her siblings are enrolled in the UNRWA schools where they have to drink milk and take cod liver oil pills every morning and where 'girls whose hair ha[ve] lice or fleas' (148) because they 'have little water in the camp' (149) stay outside schools to get their hair sprayed with 'a DDT pesticide' (148). Barakat is obviously exposing the crises of the health conditions and health system Palestinians experience under occupation. In 'Palestinian Women Under Israeli Occupation: Implications for Development,' Souad Dajani states that:

> As the Special Committee of the World Health Organization (WHO) has repeatedly emphasized, the health status of Palestinians has been adversely affected by numerous environmental problems. These include the salinity of water supply and nutritional deficiencies due to the lack of essential food-stuffs ... these problems are compounded by specific Israeli policies, such as the refusal to allow the digging of wells, which 'adversely affect' the health conditions of Arabs in the occupied territories. (112)

Barakat's testimony to the existence of a health crisis under occupation in her memoir is a tactic of contesting and speaking truth to the colonial power, the Israeli occupation.

In *Balcony on the Moon*, as the protagonist becomes a teenager, Barakat continues her criticism of the occupation, but at the same time extends it to a criticism of sexism and patriarchy. Hence, she exemplifies that 'the Third World indigenous, migrant and immigrant intellectuals of color make their collective presence known as *decolonizing*, rather than colonized and minor, *subjects*' (Yang 146). Barakat assumes the role of the intellectual whose job it is to ask uncomfortable questions and to decolonise the different dominant powers controlling her life rather than be silent. Her calls for freedom from the occupation become intertwined with her calls for freedom from patriarchal oppression. That is why in her memoir, we see her as a young Palestinian woman who keeps asking questions, demanding answers and calling for her rights. While as a teenager, she is 'filled with bigger questions: Is being Palestinian bad? Would the worlds be happier if there were no Palestinians at all?' (*Balcony* 89) and she also asks why boys are treated better than girls, for example when she objects to the fact that 'girls cook, mop the floors, wash dishes, do laundry, fold the clothes, clean windows, and organize the house while the boys either run errands or have jobs outside, or play sports and spend a lot of time with their friends' (34). Ibtisam, the teenager, makes it her responsibility to point out and contest the fact that she is being discriminated against by the Israeli occupation because of her identity as a Palestinian and by her society because of her gender as a woman. She connects her freedom from the occupation to her freedom from patriarchal roles: 'when I grow up and am free, I promise myself I will not wash even one dish' (34). Moreover, she sees a summary of the declaration at the UNRWA office, copies it in her notebook, and says,

> Having this paper encouraged me, so instead of saying I have the right to do something, I began saying I have thirty rights to do it. I read from the declaration to my mother and father and siblings, always personalizing it. (92)

Ibtisam narrates how she first encounters the declaration of human rights, which she learns by heart and keeps referring to whenever she demands and calls for her rights. The occupation under which she lives contributes to the fact that she is acting older than her age, so we see her character as a young child who is inquisitive and asks big, fundamental questions as to why she and her people are not allowed basic human rights as is the rest of the world. Because the fight and resistance against the occupation is anchored in universal human rights and international law, it becomes urgent and important that Palestinian intellectuals frame their struggles within that context.

In *Human Rights, Inc.: The World Novel, Narrative Form, and International Law*, Joseph Slaughter believes that 'everyone should know why human rights are important, that we do need a little human rights just now, and that literature does have a capacity to minister to that need' (6). Literature that demands the universal human rights declaration and calls out its violations is an obvious confrontation to abusive powers, and it is within this context that Barakat, in her memoirs, acts as a public intellectual who is speaking up and calling out the unjust practices of the Israeli occupation. Insisting once again on situating her struggles as a young Palestinian woman living under occupation within a universal struggle for human rights, Barakat makes her protagonist, Ibtisam, say,

> People in Ramallah are born free, that is article 1. All Palestinians refugees have the right to a nationality, that is article 15. My father has the right to rest, article 24. Everyone has the right to work, article 23. That is what I quote to Mother as we argue about my getting a job. I emphasize the word everyone. (*Balcony* 92–3)

When Ibtisam tells her father that she wants to find a summer job to help support her family because it is a right recognised in many nations, he tells her that 'nothing that applies to other nations applies to us here under the occupation' and he also asks her, 'you want men to laugh at me for not being able to support my family and protect my *sharaf*, my honor?' (93). Barakat thus makes it clear that her younger self's inability to work is due both to the occupation that turns a blind eye on universal human rights and to her patriarchal culture and its 'traditional Arab view of the role of women as housewives and mothers and the restrictions placed on their participation in public life and productive work outside the home' (Dajani 105–6).

It is also worth pointing out here that the protagonist's father's sarcastic tone, when he tells her that human rights do not apply to Palestinians, reflects an overall cynicism that Palestinians feel towards human rights and its industry. This cynicism, as Lori Allen argues, is 'linked to the ongoing, and seemingly unstoppable, Israeli colonization of Palestinian land and the indefatigably brutal occupation. This attitude has been the result of decades of what could be described as "noneventful" history' (*The Rise and Fall* 27). However, Allen sees this cynicism as a tool that Palestinians use 'to critique and search, or at least hope, for something better' (*The Rise and Fall* 27). Young Ibtisam, being the feminist and resilient girl that she is, defies her family and finds a job at an industrial factory while only twelve and a half years old. She starts earning and buying 'some of the family necessities' (*Balcony* 100) and when one of the factory workers gets humiliated while getting paid, Ibtisam speaks up and demands an apology to the worker calling out, 'we are here to work, not be humiliated. We get enough humiliation from living under harsh military rule' (102). Barakat, at a very young age, is constantly battling injustices and oppressions, be it colonial, economic, or patriarchal oppression. She defies any power that tries to deny her her rights, and through the power of her writing, she emerges as a public intellectual who tries to resist and dismantle the dominant structures that shape the realities around her.

The erasure of Palestine from the map and the systematic Zionist attempts to deny its existence is another topic that Barakat talks about at length in her work. Her younger self, Ibtisam, recalls the time she and her classmates had to perform a play at a theatre where,

> On the wall is a big map of the world colored to identify countries we are representing. They are all on the map – except for Palestine. Although no one speaks of this, when we happily touch the countries we are representing, we also press our fingers on the place where Palestine once was on the map, with sadness. (*Balcony* 59)

Young Ibtisam is aware that Palestine exists in spite of the occupation's education system that erases Palestine from the world map. She writes about how her school censors teachers who 'do not choose the books or topics [they] teach and have strict regulations about what [they] can and cannot discuss in the classroom. If [they] teach about Palestine, [they] will be punished' (86). When Ibtisam participates in a writing contest at her school where the assignment asks her to write about what she can see on an empty white screen, she thinks that 'if nothing is on the screen, then the assignment is about what is not visible' (117) and so she defiantly writes in emphatic italics:

> *Here on this white screen, there used to be a country made of many cities that you can count as you ride the bus. Many families lived there, but something happened and all of them lost their ability to count. They began to feel blank. They kept losing, and it was like an eraser was following them wherever they walked, erasing their steps until all that remains is this blank board.* (*Balcony* 118)

The fact that Ibtisam insists on writing about Palestine despite the school's censorship is an expression of the Palestinians' resilience and unwillingness to let the occupation erase Palestine from history, making her writing an act of resistance and speaking truth to power. By depicting Palestine from the perspective of a female Palestinian woman living in the diaspora, Barakat is taking on the role of the public intellectual that Said talks about by challenging, subverting and resisting the Israeli occupation and patriarchal practices imposed on Palestinian women. Bearing in mind the systematic erasure of Palestine mentioned earlier in this chapter, Barakat also realises the importance of defying and challenging the dominant powers that police and manipulate the narratives of her own history. Therefore, she turns her writings into a platform where she fights against various forms of oppression, makes Palestine visible, and calls for freedom, justice, equality, return, and rights of self-determination, especially for Palestinian women.

Conclusion

While in the past the Palestinian public intellectual was mainly considered to be male, following the examples of Ghassan Kanafani, Edward Said, Mahmoud Darwish and Naji Al-Ali, the American Palestinian women writers discussed in this chapter reconfigure the gendered nature of the public intellectual by offering multi-layered feminist interventions that change the dialectics of resistance. Their writings act as a creative form of speaking truth to power, not only against the Israeli occupation, but also against patriarchy in Palestinian society. Most importantly, American Palestinian women writers realise that after long years of failed peace negotiations and systematic attempts to erase and marginalise Palestine, the only fruitful way to resist the Israeli occupation is to build a global movement of solidarity to fight for justice and human rights in Palestine. By making Palestine visible in their writings and by shedding light on themes of justice, freedom, human rights, displacements and return, American Palestinian women intellectuals solicit international solidarity and call for coalition building to support Palestinians in their fight and struggles for freedom and in their resistance to the Israeli occupation. Prominent intellectuals and activists like Angela Davis, Naomi Klein, Marc Lamont Hill, to name a few, have understood this urgency and joined Palestinian solidarity movements.[11] I end this chapter with the words of Angela Davis who is among the first intellectuals and activists to join Palestinians in their struggle for freedom. She states, 'The tendency has been to consider Palestine a separate – and unfortunately too often marginal – issue. This is precisely the moment to encourage everyone who believes in equality and justice to join the call for a free Palestine' (11).

Notes

1. See Edward Said's *The Question of Palestine*.
2. While the colonial project in Palestine dates back to the British mandate, I specifically refer here to the establishment of the state of Israel in Palestine in 1948. For more on the history of the colonial project in Palestine, see Rashid Khalidi's *The Hundred Years War on Palestine: A History of Settler Colonialism and Resistance, 1917–2017*.
3. For a breakdown of this deal, see Yumna Patel, 'Understanding the Trump "Deal of the Century": What It Does, and Doesn't Say.'
4. See Kuttab, 'How will annexation change the legal landscape in the West Bank?'
5. One exception to this rule, but using a non-fictional genre, is Edward Said's memoir, *Out of Place*.
6. This fear is not unfounded as Marc Lamont Hill was fired from CNN and Steven Salaita, a former professor of English, lost his job, because they advocated for Palestine and criticised the Israeli occupation practices. See Steven Salaita's *Inter/Nationalism: Decolonizing Native America and Palestine* and Hannan Adely, 'Free Speech, Politics, and Anti-Semitism: Marc Lamont Hill Tells His Story'.
7. Laila Halaby's *West of the Jordan* (2003) is one example of this trend.
8. See, for example, the works of contemporary American Palestinian women writers, such as Susan Muaddi Darraj's short story collections, *The Inheritance of Exile: Stories from South Philly* (2007) and *A Curious Land: Stories from Home* (2015); Hala Alyan's novel, *Salt Houses* (2017), and collections of poetry, *Four Cities* (2015), *Hijra* (2016) and *The Twenty-Ninth Year* (2019); and Leila Abdelrazaq's graphic novel *Baddawi* (2015).

9. Susan Abulhawa echoes the sentiments of Edward Said's memoir, *Out of Place: A Memoir*, in which Said expressed how estranged and isolated he felt as an American Palestinian intellectual.
10. For an overview of the siege of Gaza, see Ilan Pappé's *The Biggest Prison on Earth: A History of the Occupied Territories* and *Gaza in Crisis: Reflections on Israel's War Against the Palestinians Territories* by Naom Chomsky and Ilan Pappé.
11. See for example, Angela Davis's *Freedom is a Constant Struggle*, Marc Lamont Hill and Noura Erakat's 'Black-Palestinian Transnational Solidarity' and Naomi Klein's 'Israel: Boycott, Divest, Sanction'.

4

THE PALESTINIAN REBEL: LIBERTY AND STATEHOOD IN LITERATURE

Jumana Bayeh

The Palestinian struggle has long produced troubling and tragic but no less arresting images of a people resisting the seemingly insurmountable power of an occupying force. Images of young Palestinians, usually men, hurling rocks at the Israeli military are readily associated with Palestinian rebellion. The picture of Faris Odeh (Figure 4.1), for instance, captured in October 2000, facing an Israeli tank with a rock in hand, quickly became the iconic image of resistance during the Second Intifada (2000–5). Odeh himself, killed shortly after the picture was taken, has become a symbol of a defiant Palestinian rebel.

Odeh's image has been more recently joined by other iconic photographs of Palestinian rebels, notably taken during Gaza's Great March of Return, which began on 30 March 2018. Two in particular were widely circulated on social media: the first was of Saber al-Ashqar (Figure 4.2) who is captured in his wheelchair twirling a slingshot toward Israeli forces; the second was of A'ed Abu Amro (Figure 4.3), shirtless, emerging from heavy smoke with a Palestinian flag in one hand and a slingshot in the other.

Odeh, al-Asqar and Abu Amro can easily be assimilated into the plethora of engaging and powerful images of Palestinians demonstrating against Israeli brutality and occupation. These rebels and many others are rightly assumed to be fighting for statehood, but the recent image of Abu Amro points to a further goal that is tied closely to the quest for statehood. Abu Amro's image has been associated with liberation and thus presents an opportunity for us to probe further how the assumption that the prime goal of Palestinian rebellion is statehood is related to or bound up with liberty. Abu Amro's picture was quickly compared to Eugène Delacroix's *Liberty Leading the People* (Figure 4.4), an 1830 painting of the French people's

Figure 4.1 This iconic image of Faris Odeh throwing a stone at an Israeli tank was taken on 29 October 2000 by photojournalist Laurent Rebours for the Associated Press.

Figure 4.2 Saber al-Ashqar, photographed by Mahmud Hams on 11 May 2018. © Agence France Presse (AFP).

Figure 4.3 A'ed Abu Amro, photographed by Mustafa Hassouna on 22 October 2018. © Anadolu Ajansı TAŞ.

Figure 4.4 Eugène Delacroix, *Liberty Leading the People*, 1830. The Louvre, Paris.

fight for freedom during their revolution. Liberty, personified as a woman by Delacroix, is, like Abu Amro, surrounded by smoke, bare chested and clutching her nation's tricolour flag.

The positioning of Abu Amro's body, the smokiness of the scene and his similar triple-striped flag made the comparison all the more poignant. Abu Amro himself welcomed the resemblance because *Liberty Leading the People* is widely seen, especially in the West, as symbolic of the right to freedom. As he states, through the comparison his image came to be considered as a similar 'symbol of resistance. This has made me determined to remain steadfast and stay among those rejecting the Israeli blockade' (quoted in Yaghi). What preoccupies this rebel, and drives his rebellion, is not unlike what Delacroix captured in his painting – a quest for liberty from oppressive forces. In other words, Abu Amro is motivated by the liberation of Gaza from a blockade which has the effect of restricting, almost to the point of totality, the autonomy of Gazans and the control they can exercise over their daily lives.

Taking this emphasis on liberty as a point of departure, this essay will examine novels published since the Second Intifada that contain rebel characters who, in their acts of resistance, seek liberation from the tyranny of occupation and regimes of control. The Second Intifada, which ended in 2005 – the same year in which Israel withdrew from Gaza – provides the key moment for this exploration. As has been argued by Caroline Mall Dibiasi and outlined in the activist work of B'Tselem, since the end of the Second Intifada Palestinians have incrementally lost more control over their lives. This is not just true for Gazans, who once isolated were more easily besieged and violently intimidated, but has also impacted West Bank Palestinians whose freedom of movement or access to employment became more severely monitored and restricted. This amplified level of containment and brutality occasions a renewed consideration of the figure of the literary rebel, especially the rebel's quest for liberation and autonomy. My focus on the literary rebel draws from a long history of the use and appreciation of the rebel figure in fiction. For the Romantics, John Milton's depiction of Satan in *Paradise Lost* (1667) was not simply seen as a representation of evil, but was interpreted as a rebel fighting against the dictates of ordained power. Milton's God is cast as authoritarian and righteous, especially in the poem's opening books where it is Satan's perspective that is privileged. His resistance to God paints this literary Satan, in the Romantics' appreciation of him, as the original antihero or rebel. In the Victorian era, Charlotte Brontë's *Jane Eyre* (1847) was one of many feminist texts that presented women as rebels working against repressive, patriarchal norms for the sake of personal autonomy.[1]

The texts that form the focus of this chapter, *The Parisian* (2019) by Isabella Hammad, *A Rebel in Gaza* (2018) by Asma al-Ghoul and Selim Nassib and *Mornings in Jenin* (2010) by Susan Abulhawa, can be incorporated into this existing literary history, though they also extend it to fiction concerned with the Middle East. While Hammad, al-Ghoul and Abulhawa's texts contain rebel characters who fight for liberation, they vary both in terms of who is targeted by the rebels and in the different narrative strategies they use to highlight how liberation might be achieved or at least pursued. But before turning to the rebels in these texts, it is important to explore the shifting meaning of this term in media discourse and how the Palestinian literary rebel's pursuit of liberty, as part of the goal for statehood, addresses this volume's broader concern with emergent forms brought to light by the Second Intifada.

The Literary Rebel, Liberation and Palestine

The Arab Spring – which began in Tunisia in 2010 and continued in 2011 in Egypt before spreading to other Arab countries – seems to have transformed the term 'rebel' in the Western media into an acceptable way to describe the people who took to the streets to overthrow several corrupt regimes (see Lang and Théoleyre). This is not to suggest that the appellation of rebels was not used prior to the recent uprisings, but is more a reflection of the positive connotations that imbue the term, particularly as opposed to the negatively perceived and more widely used descriptors of 'terrorist' and 'infidel'.[2] To be sure, as Felix Lang and Malcolm Théoleyre explain, rebels were not always viewed positively in the West but were rehabilitated with a 'positive rebel discourse . . . in the US from the 1950s' (8). Leerom Medovoi links this transformation to mid-century world politics, arguing that entertainers such as Elvis Presley and James Dean as well as writers from the Beat Generation 'emerged at the dawn of the Cold War era because the ideological production of the US as leader of the "free world" required figures who could represent America's emancipatory character' (1). Those rebel figures were 'pitted against a status quo cast as parental, repressive and authoritarian' (Medovoi 1). Repressive and authoritarian is precisely how the youth of the Arab uprisings described the Ben Ali and Mubarak regimes, and rebelling against them, with the aid of digital technology, was largely applauded in Western media outlets. Digitally connected Arab youth could be awarded the title of 'good rebels' (Lang and Théoleyre 8) and were even described as part of an effort to 'Westernise' their countries (Zhuo et al.).

Yet Palestinians have rarely, if ever, been described as 'good rebels' and their intifadas, both first and second, have seldom been seen as legitimate rebellions in the eyes of the Western media. Rather, they have faced international criticism for their continued resistance to Israel's various modes of oppression and endured numerous economic and political penalties – principally from Israel and its most loyal ally, the US – for their continued rebellion against a stultifying occupation. This criticism has only persisted since the Second Intifada despite, as noted above, the increased levels of control and oppression exercised against them. Even the 'metropolitan left', as described by Anna Bernard, who have been sympathetic to the plight of the Palestinians since the 1980s, have largely tied their support to support for international law and human rights, rejecting armed liberation or violent rebellion ('They Are in the Right'). In other words, this sympathetic group tolerates resistance only if it comes through non-violent and legal channels.

The Palestinians, therefore, have not just been denied the label of the 'good rebel', they have also been depicted as more than simply 'bad rebels.' Rather, they are more often seen as violent insurgents and their various acts of resistance, from suicide bombings to rock throwing, are consequently rendered illegitimate. Part of the reason for this denial of legitimacy, I argue, lies in a pivotal aspect of the term rebel that designates, to borrow from Lang and Théoleyre, some rebels 'bad' (terrorists) and others 'good' (pro-Western agitators) (8). As suggested above, Beat Generation writers were hailed as good and necessary rebels because they consolidated America's 'emancipatory' image. Emancipation or liberation is a fundamental aspect of the multiple categories of rebel identified in Hyeran Jo, Rotem Dvir and Yvette Isidor's typology of rebel groups in the contemporary Middle East. What is significant about this observation is that it is the quest for liberation from what is deemed unlawful or unjust oppression that separates a good rebel from a bad one, and what lends legitimacy to a rebellion (Collier and Hoeffler). For instance, it appears that 'greed-based' rebels, like Sierra Leone's Revolutionary United Front, who sell diamonds to accumulate wealth, are heavily criticised and are not supported in the international arena, while 'grievance-based' rebels, such as pro-democracy protestors in Hong Kong resisting extradition to mainland China are viewed in a much more compassionate light (Jo *et al.* 78). What complicates matters for the Palestinians is that the denial of their right to rebel is tied up with their lack of sovereignty. As a non-sovereign or stateless people, their quest for liberation does not easily correspond to an international regime that tends to recognise claims for autonomy and liberty through the modern nation-state system.

This can be explored in further detail via Govand Azeez's notion of 'counter-revolutionary discourse'. In his research on the Western reception of revolution and crowd rebellion in the Middle East from the eighteenth century through to the present, Azeez argues that Palestinians have faced a long and accumulative history that delegitimises their right to resist through a number of discursive strategies. He refers to this as counter-revolutionary discourse, an approach which involves a number of inter-related strategies or 'tools', two of which are apposite here. The first is 'recrudescence of fanaticism' where any 'Oriental resistance was reduced to Islam, and Islam was nothing but terror, destruction, and fanaticism' (Azeez 225). This tool, Azeez argues, was applied by various political officials in Europe, the US and Israel, to explain the political motivations of, for instance, the Palestinian Liberation Organization, a secular group which was nevertheless repeatedly 'exposed' as a 'fanatic movement driven by Islam . . . moved only by religious passion' (225). The second is 'progress fetishism', whereby political, economic, technological and social advancement are fetishised as the dominion of Europe and the West, with no contribution made by the Oriental other (Azeez 257). Palestinian resistance was reduced to terrorism by Western officials, and terrorism was tied to the inability to modernise. In a 1985 US Department of State report cited by Azeez, terrorism was described as 'inherently born out of the "frustrations of traditional societies confronting rapid modernization"' (257). Thus the 'primitive Palestinian' Azeez explains, 'is left behind in the caravan of progress' (257).

Both recrudescence of fanaticism, with its essentialist identity marker of Islam, and progress fetishism, which insists that the Palestinian is always trailing behind, underscore the ways in which the international world system is complicit in the containment of Palestinians. Because they are never perceived as a people with a national (secular) subjectivity, they are not considered worthy of statehood and therefore exist outside the realm of modernity; their claims to liberation, and their acts of rebellion in pursuit of it, are not legible in the modern (Western-dominated) international system. Recrudescence of fanaticism and progress fetishism are not just elements or tools of counter-revolutionary discourse but its ultimate bind – they repudiate all the conditions of modernity (national identity, secularism, progress) that would allow the Palestinians' rebellion for liberation to be deemed legitimate and their grievances to be viewed as justified.

This is where the prominence of the rebel figure in post-Second Intifada literature is significant. As stated, the acts of violence undertaken by the rebel characters in the three texts under examination here can be interpreted as having a specific aim of liberation. In these literary texts, then, the discourse is one that elevates liberty, reminding us that while statism is important and not a lesser goal, liberation is also vital and should not be forgotten in the quest for statehood. As Rana Baker has argued, one of the complications with the perception that the default aim of Palestinians is simply to establish a nation state is that such a view does not engage with questions about the conditions under which this future state will be conceived, and under which Palestinians will be forced to live. The assumption, Baker tells us, of 'present pro-Palestinian discourse is its fixation on statehood' because it posits an autonomous state as the solution to the plight of the Palestinians. But what this assumption fails to acknowledge has become painfully apparent to Palestinians in the wake of the Second Intifada and Israel's withdrawal from Gaza: namely, that liberation from both the oppressive conditions of Zionism (which in turn buttressed the siege of Gaza and the proliferation of illegal settlements in the West Bank) and from corrupt and oppressive Palestinian leadership must be vigorously pursued in order for state-building to proceed. This follows what Franz Fanon recognised in his seminal *The Wretched of the Earth* (1961) and Pierre Bourdieu argued in relation to Algerian independence in his *Algerian Sketches* (2013), which is that achieving statehood should not be seen as a guarantee of liberation.

By recognising that liberty is part of the struggle for statehood, *The Parisian* and *Mornings in Jenin* deploy their rebel characters to address the need for liberation from Zionism, utilising the different narrative techniques of character comparisons and the return of an occulted 'twin' to do so. Likewise, *A Rebel in Gaza* highlights the role of a woman journalist, al-Ghoul, in exposing not just the brutality of Israel but also, and more harshly, Hamas's attempts to control women by enforcing Islamic codes of morality. As will be seen in the discussion below, the response of literary texts to the bind outlined in the previous paragraph is to imagine the kind of state Palestinians deserve by focusing on the rebel's quest for liberation.

The Parisian

Hammad's debut novel follows the life of a young Palestinian, Midhat Kamal, from 1915 to 1936. This was a pivotal period in the history of Palestine, and Midhat's life unfolds alongside significant events including World War I, the Nebi Musa riots of 1920, and the Arab general strike of 1936. Our hero's story begins in Montpellier, France where he has arrived to study medicine, and ends in Mandate Palestine, specifically in his hometown of Nablus. In between he changes majors to study history at Paris's Sorbonne, returns to Nablus to run the local branch of his father's textile business, and suffers a period of mental illness during which he is institutionalised, all while Palestinian resistance to the British Mandate forces and tensions with Jewish settlers are building. Due to the years he spent in France and the particular style he adopted while there – a cane, flamboyant ties and colourful pocket handkerchiefs – Midhat's moniker in Nablus is '*al Barisi*' (the Parisian), sometimes used affectionately and at other times to mock his out-of-place sensibilities.

Midhat, as the above suggests, is no rebel, but he provides an interesting foil to his cousin Jamil Kamal, a founding member of the Nablus Strike Committee and the novel's most closely explored rebel fighter. Both Jamil and the novel's omniscient narrator label him and his fellow committee members as '*thuwwar*' (*Parisian* 502). *Thuwwar* is generally translated as revolutionaries, and *thawra* as revolution. However, according to Mohammad Harbi, Gilbert Meynier and Tahar Khaloufe, more accurate translations of these words would be rebels and rebellion. The authors base their assessment on the claim that a *thawra* – rebellion – lacks the concerted political programme of a revolution. In other words, for Harbi *et al.*, rebellions are devoid of political programmes, planning efforts or goals (5). While Harbi *et al.* do not make it entirely clear what such a programme would entail, it seems it should involve a plan to overthrow a leadership or take over the state (12–13). There are many who would refute this semantic delineation, but that is of less importance here than the fact that these writers – in their efforts to neatly separate one term from its close synonym – have overlooked the importance of recognising liberation as a political goal. It is this stress on liberation that underpins Jamil's actions as a rebel, which are revealed in a chapter that focuses entirely on his rebellious efforts.

That chapter unfolds in the year 1936 in Nablus during the general strike, later recorded by historians as The Great Revolt. It details an evening in which Jamil and a fellow member of the strike committee, Basil Murad, undertake a sniping operation on the roof of a sports club. The chapter oscillates between detailing the characters' strategy and Jamil's inner thoughts as relayed by an omniscient narrator, allowing readers privileged insights into this rebel's primary concerns. A striking example of this oscillation is the swift shift from a crucial moment during a sniping operation to Jamil refuting the possibility of further political discussions: 'the time for witnessing . . . of debating in assemblies and composing memoranda, was over' (*Parisian* 503). But rather than inform the reader what is needed in the current moment, Jamil's thoughts immediately turn to recalling a litany of British acts of violence against the Palestinians in the Mandate period:

> News of British violence gusted through him and flowered out as anger . . . he saw the policemen flogging student protesters on their bare buttocks . . . Peasant women being searched for arms on the roadside and lewdly gestured at. A house demolished, the family holding their belongings beside the soldiers on the hillock, forced to watch as their home exploded. (*Parisian* 503)

These are the reasons behind Jamil's need to act, or as he states, his 'long[ing] to be *doing*' rather than planning, debating and speaking (502). The sniping operation, then, like the several others Jamil had led in Nablus, must be seen as being driven by a need to actively liberate Arab Palestine from the oppressive British Mandate forces, who from Jamil's perspective at least are operating entirely on the side of the Zionist cause by allowing Jewish immigration to Palestine to proceed with little regulation.

This preoccupation with achieving liberation is also expressed as a personal responsibility and an embodied act for Jamil. He notes that he has 'dissolved into his mission' so deeply 'that the strains of his body became idiomatic of the struggle: the energy in his feet was Arab energy, his mind's determination was Nablusi determination, the weakness of his ankles Palestinian weakness, the ache in his bones a Palestinian ache' (*Parisian* 503). The collective weaknesses that strain Jamil's body are the dangerous divisions infecting the Palestinian movement during the strike. As Jamil explains, the revolt produced tensions between 'town and country, Nablusi and fellah [peasant], strike and rebellion' (501). And although Jamil believes such cleavages are being misreported in newspaper editorials, and that both the rural-focused armed uprising and the urban-based general strike were united acts of civil disobedience, he also notes

> reluctance sprouting among the wealthy . . . at being ordered around by the peasants, who were starting to threaten landowners and merchants with defamation and damage to property unless they handed over funds that only one month ago they had been donating with pride. (*Parisian* 501)

Jamil raises this tension again, suggesting that 'condemnation of strike-breakers' had reached fever-pitch, leading him to conclude that the most 'dangerous rage of all was the rage against impurity' (*Parisian* 508). Not only is Jamil a self-labelled *tha'ir* (singular of *thuwwar*) or rebel, he also refers to himself as a 'crossover figure' uniting city and country (501). More poignantly, Jamil does not see himself as a 'public figure' or intellectual like another of the novel's characters, Hani Murad, who speaks of national identity and proposes models of statehood in open fora. Rather, Jamil is 'a quiver of darkness; an actor and also a ligament; a fibre between fighter and fighter' (*Parisian* 502). The strategic role he occupies is to unite the Palestinians to combat the immediacy of the oppressive British forces, and to liberate the Palestinian people from the Mandate power by acting as a bridge between the emerging divisions among the Palestinians. While the concerns in this chapter do not raise the issue of statehood explicitly, Jamil's fixation with freedom from British and Zionist oppressive forces suggests that the struggle for statehood includes and is implicitly bound up with liberation.

The quest for liberation reflected in *The Parisian* extends beyond the figure of Jamil and forms part of Midhat's recovery from an episode of mental breakdown. Midhat is, as stated earlier, no rebel and he concerns himself very little with questions of statehood or liberation. As Jamil states to his mother 'Midhat will never be a fighter' because, as Jamil sarcastically reveals to the reader, 'al-Barisi [could never] cope with wearing patched trousers' (*Parisian* 506, 508). But Midhat's encounter with France and the French family he billeted with when he arrived in Montpellier form the basis for the connection between Midhat and liberation in the novel. While in Montpellier, Midhat eventually learns that the generosity of his host, Doctor Molineu, a professor of a social sciences college, is based on Molineu's desire to study and observe his 'Oriental' mannerisms, language and cultural traits, as if Midhat were an anthropological specimen. Midhat discovers this after reading some of Molineu's notes – in which conversations between himself and the doctor are recorded along with Molineu's pejorative commentary and analysis – and abruptly departs for Paris, leaving behind Molineu's daughter, Jeannette, the object of his deep affection. Years later, when he finds a hidden letter from Jeannette in which she declares her love for him, Midhat experiences a mental breakdown and is transferred to a psychiatric hospital. His inner dialogue reveals that despite being widely associated with France by everyone in Nablus, and being a devoted Francophile who is nostalgically attached to France, he has nonetheless been oppressed and racialised as an inferior Arab Other not only by the French professor but by an entire French and Western system of colonial expansion.

The final scene in the novel stages an encounter between Midhat and Father Antoine, another French professor of sorts who, as earlier sequences in the novel make clear, is compiling a study of Nablus. That Midhat perceives Antoine as a version of Molineu is revealed when he asks, twice: 'are you going to write it [our conversation] down?' and states 'I know you have been writing about Nablus' (*Parisian* 546). The two men briefly engage in some discussion about their lives and Midhat's time in France; however, it is Midhat's final words to Antoine that are most poignant: 'With one long deep inhalation, as if surfacing from underwater, Midhat said "I forgive you"' (*Parisian* 550). As Midhat's forgiveness is offered without an apology from Antoine, the reader can only conclude that this forgiveness is for the France that rejected him by turning him into a racialised subject of anthropological research, and which was partially responsible for keeping him and Jeannette apart. In that sense, Midhat's act in the novel's final scene liberates him from his repressive experience in France. On one level, this liberation is deeply personal and closely tied to Midhat's life experience. However, in relation to the novel's broader commentary on liberation – as facilitated through the rebel character of Jamil – this scene showcases Palestine's pursuit of freedom alongside a political programme that emphasises the state; more specifically, a pursuit of freedom which recognises that liberation and statehood are related and interdependent.

A Rebel in Gaza

Unlike the novels *The Parisian* and *Mornings in Jenin*, *A Rebel in Gaza* is a memoir co-written by Asma al-Ghoul and Selim Nassib. Al-Ghoul, as one of the text's authors but also its main subject, makes the content of her life the focus of the memoir, giving readers insights into her acts of rebellion and her particular opinions of politics and society in Gaza. What is unique about this text, and has not yet been replicated in novelistic form, is its strong representation of a Palestinian woman as a rebel. Unlike the fictional Jamil, al-Ghoul does not engage in military operations. Her chosen form of rebellion is journalism, both in print and online media outlets, through which she reports on the suffering of Gazans. Importantly, the target of her criticism is not predominately Israel but Hamas, the ruling authority in Gaza.

Al-Ghoul credits Gaza and in particular Gaza under Hamas's rule for her rebelliousness. There are two key scenes that suggest this. The first is revealed when al-Ghoul reflects on her childhood in the Emirates, specifically in Abu Dhabi where her father is employed at the time. Al-Ghoul informs the reader that the 'religious power', or Hamas, wants 'Gaza [to] become a society in the image of the Gulf' where people are segregated according to gender, women are veiled, and wives are considered the subjects of their husbands (*Rebel* 57). Under these oppressive conditions, al-Ghoul claims that the Emirates 'can't educate you' as it fails to give one the ability to think independently and critically or, in al-Ghoul's words, 'the capacity to say "This is what I reject, that is what I want"' (*Rebel* 58). This is why, al-Ghoul believes, when her father gave her a headscarf, she 'half went along with it', having no real opinion of her own. 'It's Gaza' she concludes, 'that turned me into [an independently minded] rebel' (*Rebel* 58). The full import of this pronouncement is not made clear to the reader until a later scene in the memoir, the second that explains her rebellious character. That scene takes place in 2006, when Hamas is elected to power in Gaza. Al-Ghoul reacts by yelling, at no one in particular, a 'curse on you all' and 'dash[ing] out into the street like a madwoman. Unveiled!' (*Rebel* 87). Her response to onlookers shocked at the sight of her bare head is 'Hamas is winning – do you think I'm going to stay veiled? I prefer to take off my veil before they force me to keep it on' (*Rebel* 87). Her removal of the veil can be seen as an act of rebellion against the impending religious morality, comprised of 'conservativism and rules of behaviour' fabricated under the guise of the principles of Islamic piety that Hamas will implement (*Rebel* 87). Hamas's victory in 2006 is a turning point for al-Ghoul as it heightens her rebellion against the religious authority, motivating her to pen more strident criticism of the group and speak publicly against their use of Islam to justify the oppression of women.

While the focus of al-Ghoul's criticism is Hamas, she does not exonerate or pardon Israel and even sees the latter's brutal blockade and routine bombing of Gaza as a boost for Hamas. In an article al-Ghoul describes in her memoir as her most famous piece of political writing – an essay called 'Never Ask Me About Peace Again' written during the August 2014 siege in which the author lost multiple family members – she makes a poignant appeal to Israel:

If it is Hamas that you hate, let me tell you that the [women, children, families] . . . you are killing have nothing to do with Hamas . . . let me assure you that you have now created thousands – no, millions – of Hamas loyalists, for we all become Hamas if Hamas, to you, is women, children and innocent families. If Hamas, in your eyes, is ordinary civilians and families, then *I am Hamas*, they are Hamas and we are all Hamas. (Al-Ghoul, 'Never Ask Me')

At this crucial moment, al-Ghoul recognises and lucidly articulates the conditions under which even she becomes, or is made to become, Hamas. This recognition, however, does not lead al-Ghoul to conform to the overriding view that statehood is the solution for the violence that Palestinians, and in particular Gazans, face on a routinised basis from Israel.[3]

It is especially revelatory that at no point in her memoir does al-Ghoul argue the case for statehood or call for Palestinians to return to their homeland. Rather, she openly refutes the notion of return, stating: 'I'm supposed to love the Palestine we have lost, but I refuse to lie and say that I dream of going back to my home country. I regret the loss of that land for my grandmother's sake, but I cannot share her . . . compelling desire for a "return"' (*Rebel* 28). Al-Ghoul acknowledges that this is a highly unconventional position to hold as 'refugees [are] supposed to preserve the dream of return', but she criticises the attachment to return to or to the restoration of a homeland as 'the basis of all our mythology' (*Rebel* 28). Al-Ghoul's position could be read as 'treason', she claims, because it ridicules an important 'national tradition' (*Rebel* 28) for Palestinians and, I add, undermines what many scholars and legal experts have argued as being central to redressing the colonial violence of Zionism. Joseph Massad could not be more precise on this issue: 'The Palestinian struggle today . . . must not waver on the implementation of the Palestinian right of return, as this right is the legal key to undoing the Zionist conquest of Palestine in its entirety.'

While al-Ghoul's position is sceptical of the Palestinian quest for statehood, what appears to direct her disavowal of return is the inertia the mythology cements. She states that the time between refugee life and return is seen as a 'transitory reality', an interim period of waiting for a particular wrong to be corrected (*Rebel* 88). However, for al-Ghoul, there are other 'wrongs' or misfortunes that have befallen the Palestinians which include the corruption of Fatah and, more importantly for al-Ghoul as a resident of Gaza, the 'rigidity of Hamas' (*Rebel* 88). Combatting that rigidity, that distortion of Islam for the sake of patriarchal tyranny, is what focuses al-Ghoul's rebellion in both her journalistic work and her refusal to wear the veil or commit to Hamas's definitions of 'honour' and 'piety' (*Rebel* 112). In a sense, to return to Lang and Théoleyre, what al-Ghoul advocates is a 'notion of *thawra* . . . [that promotes] social and political changes', or cultural shifts in thinking (7); one which would pave the way for and underpin the widely desired Palestinian statehood and return. Al-Ghoul makes clear to her readership that without confronting the issues she raises and without facing up to the oppressive codes of Islam under Hamas, a free Palestine would run the risk of simply replacing Israeli domination with an equally domineering and tyrannical force.

Her commitment to a kind of rebellion that promotes a shift in thinking about Palestinian liberation is explicitly emphasised toward the end of her memoir. After readers have waded through an overbearing number of crippling incidents (wars, deaths, the loss of homes, exile, restrictions on movement) that detail every hardship al-Ghoul and her fellow Gazans have endured, she posits the arts, and literature specifically, as a solution. From her childhood, al-Ghoul has been an avid reader with access to her father's and uncle's libraries. The impact of these books on her mind and understanding of the world leads al-Ghoul to realise the extent to which literature, music and cinema carry a transformative potential, and to lament the fact that these art forms are 'alien to the children of Gaza' (*Rebel* 186). Absent the arts and cultural production, 'there's only a hair's-breadth distance between ending up as a professor/writer/poet or being a [reactionary or fanatical] warrior' (*Rebel* 186). The options in Gaza are limited – residents can either get 'stoned on Tramadol' or join 'the Al Qassam brigades', Hamas's militant wing (*Rebel* 186). The only thing people need to escape this sort of fate, al-Ghoul argues, 'is a good book', which operates as a device that will open Gaza 'up to the world' (*Rebel* 186). Nothing else, she insists, is needed. While this may seem highly hyperbolic, if not naïve, al-Ghoul's push for the arts speaks to the cultural, social and political shifts in attitude, understanding and vision that are needed in the confined space of Gaza – a *thawra* of the mind, or the psyche, must, in al-Ghoul's assessment, precede and is more significant than return and statehood.

Mornings in Jenin

Abulhawa's novel, much like *The Parisian*, narrates the dreadful fate of one Palestinian family, the Abulheja clan, focusing most closely on the youngest family member, Amal. But unlike *The Parisian*, the novel spans the years 1948 to 2002, tracking four generations of the Abulhejas: from the lives of Amal's grandparents in Palestine, through to that of Amal's college student daughter, Sara, in Philadelphia. While the central character here is female, she is not, unlike Asma al-Ghoul, the text's main rebel character. In *Mornings in Jenin* it is Yousef, Amal's older brother, who assumes the role of rebel in similar ways to Jamil in *The Parisian*. Yousef is a *fedayee* or guerrilla fighter (*Mornings* 122) who is labelled a hero in the Battle of Karameh in 1968,[4] and swiftly becomes a high-ranking member of the PLO due to his military skill and prowess. He is even the prime suspect of the 1983 terrorist attack against the US embassy in Beirut, where a truck load of explosives was driven into the highly fortified area (*Mornings* 234).[5] Amal learns this news about her brother when she is questioned regarding his whereabouts by the CIA while she is living in the US, soon after losing her husband in the 1982 Shatila attack,[6] which also saw Yousef lose his wife and newborn child.

In contrast to *A Rebel in Gaza*, this text does not unequivocally disavow the idea of statehood or resist linking national identity to land. This is emphasised through Amal's character, who leaves her hometown of Jenin to study in the US. Her nostalgia for Palestine is never exactly consistent, as at times she longs to be American, even changing her name to Amy when she receives her green card. But, she confesses, no matter the façade she 'forever belonged to that Palestinian nation . . . [and her] Arabness and Palestinian primal cries were [her] anchors to the world' (*Mornings* 179). Amal reaffirms this on a return visit to occupied Palestine with her daughter Sara, where in Jerusalem the sight of a '"Judais[ed] Jerusalem", [made] the Old City seem[] cold. Cruel, even' (*Mornings* 290). Sara, not appreciating the transformation of the city that preoccupies her mother, exclaims that it is 'beautiful', to which Amal replies: 'I'll show you an olive tree in Jenin – Old Lady, she's called – that has more history than the Old City walls. It is more beautiful and authentic than the chiseled stone here' (*Mornings* 290–1). Amal's preference for a tree raises the association of trees with roots and their representation of origins, a strong signifier of lost homelands for many displaced peoples.[7] Yousef also appears to subscribe to such views, telling his sister that he will always fight not only for justice and freedom but also the restoration of the Palestinian homeland (*Mornings* 120).

Such nation-driven or state-focused sentiments are, according to Jo *et al.*, amplified particularly among rebel groups who interact with or fight against 'foreign interventionists'. (80). The extended occupation and control of what is perceived to be an external aggressor – in this case, Israel – leads to 'Palestinian groups such as Fatah [or Hamas] . . . promot[ing] a struggle for Israel's withdrawal and Palestinian independence' (Jo *et al.* 80). This struggle is often oriented by the need to 'create the nation of Palestine' (Jo *et al.* 80) without delving into questions about liberation that entail challenging oppressive organisations like Hamas or the corruption of the PLO; precisely the sort of questions which *A Rebel in Gaza* forces its readers to consider.

Despite this, *Mornings in Jenin* complicates the idea of statehood through an interesting narrative twist by re-introducing to the story the character of David Avaram – the long-lost brother of Yousef and Amal – whom readers have known only as an infant who was kidnapped by a Jewish-Israeli settler and soldier. When we encounter David again, he is a soldier in the Israeli Defense Forces. His return takes place at a checkpoint he is manning, a checkpoint that Yousef must cross. The chance encounter quickly turns violent even though Yousef has a permit to cross, as David is so shocked by the resemblance between them that he flies into a rage, beating Yousef 'again and again until *that* Arab – *that* face – was unconscious' (*Mornings* 106). Everything about Yousef's face troubles David, and he does 'not want to see the Palestinian again. The one who had his [David's] face without a scar' (*Mornings* 105). Although the origins of his scar are not known to David, Yousef is aware he has an older brother who, as a baby, fell from his crib and was permanently disfigured. That brother – then named Ismael – was taken by the Israeli soldier, Moshe Avaram, in 1948 when the Abulheja family and the other residents of their village were forced to flee during the *nakba*. In the chaos of the crowd, Ismael is dropped by his mother and quickly picked up by Moshe – a married man with a wife unable to bear children – even though he sees Ismael's mother frantically searching for her son.

What David represents in the novel, then, is an inability to cleanly separate the Jew from the Arab, the Israeli from the Palestinian. Although he is raised an Israeli Jew, a citizen of that state and a soldier who protects its borders, his Palestinian-Arab heritage and past return to haunt him in the face of Yousef. And even though Yousef fights to reclaim a lost Palestine, the return of David is a reminder that their lives – the lives of the Arab and the Jew – are deeply entangled. Such entanglement was arrestingly described by Edward Said in one of his earliest articles, published in 1974, concerning Arab and Jewish interaction. In the article, aptly titled 'Arabs and Jews', Said argues that neither Israelis nor Palestinians 'can develop without the other there' because

> no Arab today has an identity that can be unconscious of the Jew, that can rule out the Jew as a psychic factor in the Arab identity; conversely . . . no Jew can ignore the Arab in general, nor can he immerse himself in his ancient tradition and so lose the Palestinian Arab in particular and what Zionism has done to him. The more intense these modern struggles for identity become, the more attention is paid by the Arab or the Jew to his chosen opponent, or partner. *Each is the other*. (3; emphasis added)

While Said here writes about imagined identities, and while Abulhawa's novel explores commitments to national identity via Amal, Yousef and

David, identity is not detached from statehood. What underpins the drive for statehood for the Palestinian and the Jew is the belief in their singular and separate subjectivities. National identity in this instance becomes an expression or dimension of territory and statehood. In this mode, the statehood that is envisaged is one that attempts to neatly and cleanly segregate Palestinians and Jews, a prospect that Said suggests is impossible.

The impossibility of separation is realised in *Mornings in Jenin* through Yousef and David, notably in the way their relationships to their respective national identities transform. This transformation begins for David in 2001, when he manages to locate Amal in Philadelphia. David expresses regret at not knowing his Palestinian origins, which he discovers when his dying father confesses the truth. Amal and David's initial awkward encounter is followed by another less angst-riddled meeting in Israel a year later. David takes Amal to meet Dr Ari Perlstein, an old friend of Amal's father, Hasan, who owes his life to Hasan's help and intervention. As Ari states: 'After having lost his home, his land, his son, his identity to the Jewish state, your father risked his life to save mine and my family's' (*Mornings* 289). This historical embrace of the Palestinian and Jew seems to have a profound and revelatory effect not just on Amal, but also on David. Several days later, when David accompanies Ari and Amal to visit the grave of Amal's grandmother, he asks: 'Will you teach it to me? The Fatiha [Muslim prayer]?' (*Mornings* 319). Although not yet a major shift, this gesture highlights David's openness to recognising and becoming his Other. His final appearance in the novel is through an online post on a website set up by Amal's daughter, Sara. Addressing his sister, he writes: 'I'll never be wholly Jew or Muslim. Never wholly Palestinian nor Israeli. Your acceptance made me content to be merely human' (*Mornings* 219–320).

This recognition of a common humanity is replicated in Yousef's appearance in the book's final chapter, set in 2002. Back in 1983, Yousef had promised to avenge the death of his wife and children, who were killed in the Shatila camp massacre. At this time, he lists in detail his origins – 'I am an Arab son. Born of Dalia and Hasan. My grandfather is Yehya Abulheja and my grandmother is Basima. I am the husband of Fatima, father two' – an act that reaffirms his Palestinian-Arab identity. As a man 'haunted . . . by [all] their corpses' he states he will 'seek vengeance' vowing: 'I shall have it. And you shall see no mercy' (*Mornings* 241). By the time of her own death at the hands of an Israeli sniper, Amal still believes that her brother died as a result of the terrorist attack he is accused of leading on the US embassy in Beirut. However, the reader learns that this was not the case. Though he was committed to exacting vengeance, in the end Yousef – the fighter, the rebel – told his commanders he could not go through with it: 'Much as I want them to bleed,

I'll not besmirch my father's name' (*Mornings* 322). He instead opts for the life of a fugitive, working in Basra, Kuwait, Jordan and finally as a school janitor, in an undisclosed location. Reading Sara's website and learning of his sister's death he apologises for being unable to keep his promise of vengeance but explains, in a post on the site: 'I'll keep my humanity . . . and Love shall not be wrested from my veins' (*Mornings* 322). Again, as with David, it is resorting to a shared humanity that dissuades Yousef from continuing with his mission and fulfilling his promise. In light of this, the novel's message is to rebel not against the Other but against the compulsion to subscribe to confining versions of national identity that can underpin the drive to statehood.

Conclusion

Just as al-Ghoul prescribes literature and the arts as a significant remedy against the lure of religious fundamentalism for Gazans and Palestinians, Abulhawa's novel does much the same. Yousef, long assumed dead by his sister Amal, posts his humanist message from his room which is situated under the school library where he is employed. Surrounded by, indeed buried under, the books and literary culture al-Ghoul prescribes for Palestinians, is the place where Yousef not only reneges on his promise of revenge but also reveals his inability to enact a form of Islamic terrorism. In doing so, Yousef reclaims his status as a rebel, rejecting nationally driven forms of segregation and recognising the common humanity between himself and the Other. In these texts, and perhaps more subtly though no less significantly in *The Parisian*, literature becomes a site to consider the relationship between statehood and liberty, and to reimagine and narrate liberty – or more precisely, Palestinian liberation from oppressive forces such as Hamas and Israeli Zionism – as something which must precede and accompany statehood. Palestinian literature published in the wake of the Second Intifada centralises a quest for liberty in its narratives through the rebel figure, showcasing these figures not just as fighters for statehood but also as agitators for liberty, autonomy and freedom.

Notes

1. For further insights on rebels in English literature in the Romantic period see Marilyn Butler's *Romantics, Rebels and Reactionaries: English Literature and Its Background, 1760–1830* (Oxford University Press, 1985).
2. This chapter focuses on how the West has understood the term 'rebel' in relation to the Arab Middle East. This is not to suggest that similar Arabic terms used to describe people like Odeh or Abu Amro are irrelevant or devoid of political bias. Rather I have chosen to focus on the figure of rebel in English or Western language texts (al-Ghoul's memoir was originally composed in French and later translated to English) to explore how Palestinians have been denied the right to rebel in Western discourse.

3. Since the Israeli withdrawal from Gaza in 2005, there have been almost yearly attacks by Israeli forces on Gaza, including: Operation Summer Rains (2006); the Gaza Beach Explosion (2006); the Shelling of Beit Hanoun (2006); Operation Autumn Clouds (2006); the Beit Hanoun Incident (2008); Operation Hot Winter and Operation Cast Lead (2008); twelve separate attacks over the course of February and March of 2009; the Gaza Flotilla Raid (2010); Gaza Strip Air Raids (2011); Operation Returning Echo (2012); Operation Pillar of Defense (2012); Operation Protective Edge (2014); the Khan Yunis Clashes (2018); and the May 2019 Air Strike.
4. The Battle of Karameh was a conflict fought briefly between the Israel Defense Forces and the Jordanian Armed Forces on 21 March 1968, in which the Palestine Liberation Organization participated. The battle occurred when the Israeli forces invaded the town of Karameh, Jordan, and were met with resistance from the Jordanians and their Palestinian allies.
5. This car-bombing, which took place on 18 April 1983, killed sixty-three people, most of them Lebanese. The culprits have never been formally identified, although a pro-Iranian group which called itself the Islamic Jihad Organization initially claimed responsibility, and it has also been widely speculated that Hezbollah was behind the attack.
6. This attack at Shatila was part of the massacre which occurred in 1982 in the Sabra residential district and Shatila refugee camp in Beirut, which were then home to thousands of Palestinians. Lebanon's right-wing Christian Phalange militia – aided by Israeli troops – stormed the camps and indiscriminately murdered refugees, with estimates of the death toll ranging from the hundreds to the thousands.
7. The link between trees, roots and home in a diaspora context is best explored by Ghassan Hage's essay in 'With the Fig, the Olive and the Pomegranate Trees: Thoughts on Australian Belonging'.

5

THE ISRAELI/PALESTINIAN CONFLICT IN *TO THE END OF THE LAND*: SOME THOUGHTS ON DAVID GROSSMAN'S HEBREW IN TRANSLATION

Niva Kaspi

> From experience I can say that the language used by the citizens of a conflict to describe their situation becomes flatter and flatter as the conflict goes on, gradually evolving into a series of clichés and slogans . . . The process eventually seeps into the private, intimate language of the citizens (even if they vehemently deny it).
>
> (Grossman, *Writing in the Dark* 61)

Despite David Grossman's widely publicised views on the Israeli–Palestinian conflict and his ongoing critique of Israeli occupation, his 2008 novel *Isha Borahat Mib'sorah* (published in English as *To the End of the Land*, 2010) is his first significant fictional representation of the subject. Upon its publication, the novel received almost instant – though not undisputed – canonical status, attracting both praise and criticism for its ambitious familial-political scope. Arriving in the wake of the failure of the Oslo Accords, and engaging somewhat with the political escapist leanings of its time (Keren 247), the novel is Grossman's urgent call if not for action, then for a thorough national self-examination.

The novel tells the story of Ora, a soldier's mother who flees her home in order to escape a visit from the Military Casualty Notification Unit whom she is convinced are about to deliver the news of her son Ofer's death in a military operation on Israel's northern border. As she hikes through the Galilee with her companion, Avram, who is Ofer's estranged biological father, Ora composes for Avram a portrait of the son he never knew, and this private biography intertwines with Israel's history of conflict from 1967 until the year 2000. Through Ora's hike-narrative, Grossman creates an intimate portrait of one family whose fate is shattered by the *Matsav*,[1] and he does so while deploying his hallmark linguistic virtuosity which, as Avidov Lipsker-Albeck notes, is formed by and deeply grounded within Israeli and Hebrew specificities (212). In this chapter, I analyse a number of linguistically and culturally dependant features of the text in order to demonstrate how Grossman's writing poses some challenges to the translation of his literary rendition of the conflict. The issues described here are not concerned with aspects of a particular translation or target language but rather with attempts to relocate to a disinterested space those linguistic events that mimic or analogise the conflict. In doing so, the chapter more broadly strives to acknowledge that any analysis of literary representations in translation must be mindful that the process of translation is 'more dark space than connective constellation' (Bertacco and Apter 10), and to make visible some of those spaces which resist retelling. The areas I will focus on here include the depiction of the land's national and imagined borders, the utilisation of particular vocabularies and accents to signify relationships between Jews and Arabs, and the assimilation of military speech into the domestic sphere. The chapter concludes by returning to the land as a site of transformative-regenerative language and narrative.

The Land

'Drive,' she said when she sat down next to Sami.
'Where to?'
She thought for a moment. Without looking at him, she said,
      'To where the country ends.'
'For me it ended a long time ago,' he hissed.

(Grossman, *To the End* 148–9)

With its overarching narrative's exposition of a hiking protagonist, and through foregrounding actual and psychic checkpoints and border-crossings, the novel constructs a land/nation that is territorially indeterminate, reflecting the tendency in early-millennium Israeli literature to present borders as 'geographically and morally' problematic sites (Mendelson-Maoz xiv). As evident in Ruvik Rosenthal's glossary of Second Intifada terms, it is perhaps the same morally problematic motives of that time that have produced a proliferation of euphemistic border metaphors such as 'security belt', 'barrier zone', 'separation fence', 'security strip' and even 'seam sphere' (Rosenthal 'Conducting War').[2] The novel responds by questioning such demarcations between Israel and the once-was/yet-to-be established Palestine, reflecting the paradox expressed by Emily Apter, that 'if there is no Palestinian state, there can be no border, and yet . . ., there *is* a checkpoint' (103, original emphasis). There are persistent reminders in the novel of Israel's history of annexations, occupations, re-zoning, and other such territorial reconfigurations, and of its complex set of regulations, imposed by several governing authorities, around movement between the different segments and applied variously to citizens and non-citizens. Even the division between the spiritual capital, Jerusalem, and its hedonistic counterpart, Tel Aviv, between Left and Right, and between Ashkenazi and Sephardi Jews are coded into the story, at times with clues as subtle as the spelling of a character's name, an accent, a carefully selected object, or a turn of phrase.

The instances in the novel where boundaries are transgressed are often concealed within linguistic–cultural clues that draw on an insider's familiarity with the country and its idiosyncratic design. In the following episode, borders are crossed, and enemy/ally roles are reversed to depict a number of tragi-comic interactions with, and manifestations of, the iconic gate-keeping mechanism that is the checkpoint. It begins when Ora, forgetting the fact of Sami – her taxi-driver's – 'Arabness' (Grossman, *To the End* 54), engages Sami to drive her son to the military meeting point, bound for an operation on Israel's northern border. Placing an Arab – albeit one who holds an Israeli identity card – amidst thousands of battle-primed Jewish-Israeli soldiers is a taboo-breaking aberration. More importantly, this careless act forces Sami to inadvertently 'add his modest contribution to the Israeli war effort' (63). Ora, deeply remorseful, pledges to make it up to Sami, so when he asks her for a favour in return for driving her to Tel Aviv later that night, she agrees. Sami detours via South Tel Aviv 'where he has to take care of something' (103).[3] It turns out the 'something', sitting beside Ora in the taxi, is a young and very ill boy named Rami. 'Raami or Rami?' (106) asks Ora.[4] 'Rami' is Sami's answer, but when Ora presses him, Sami admits that 'his name is called Yazdi' (110).[5] The boy is wearing an old *Shimon Peres, My Hope for Peace* t-shirt and a pair of jeans, and this costume, along with Sami's nervous reaction to the roadblock, reveal to Ora the reason for her being there.[6] It turns out the boy is a Palestinian smuggled from the Territories for urgent medical treatment at a clandestine makeshift hospital in Jaffa.[7] Ora must act the part of the boy's Jewish mother to help him pass undetected through Israeli security checks. Ironically, Sami's Jewish impersonation for the checkpoint guard, garnished with a '*baruch hashem*'[8] (*To the End* 114, transliterated and italicised in the original), is so compelling that it is Ora, and not her two Arab companions, who raises the suspicions of Israeli security. 'Don't worry', Sami reassures the guard conspiratorially, 'she's one of ours', later explaining to Ora that by 'one of ours', he meant a right-wing Jew, 'even though you look like a lefty' (116).

In his debunking of territorial and national signifiers such as the ubiquitous checkpoint, Grossman demonstrates a desire to expose the 'philosophical poverty and even incoherence' of nationalism (B. Anderson 49). He further questions territorial claims by turning to the map of Israel for the purpose of de-naturalising the link between naming the land and possessing it. The institutional Hebraisation of Arabic place names that has taken place since Israel's formation has been viewed as a form of 'colonizing' (Zerner 38) and 'cultural-engineering' (Azaryahu and Golan 328), designed to erase the memory of a historical injustice (Mosih 173).[9] The novel is dotted with reminders of the place's previous inhabitants: monuments, ruins, and also placenames that are rich with some kind of allusion, historical or cultural reference, or some semantic quirk. One such example is when Ora, recalling one of her evening walks on the outskirts of Jerusalem with her now-estranged husband, Ilan, notes the traces of the Arab village that used to be in what is now known as Mevo Beitar (*To the End* 455). Mevo Beitar – a *moshav*[10] – was founded in 1950 by the Beitar movement, the Revisionist Zionist youth movement which is affiliated with the nationalist Likud Party. It was built on the site of the 'depopulated' Arab village of Al Qabu (al-Khalidi, cited in Zochrot).[11] The name Beitar shares the same three-letter root as the Hebrew word *biter*, a verb describing the action of dissecting or tearing meat. In Rosenthal's glossary of Second Intifada terms, the term *bitur*, also derived from the same root, is defined as 'a disconnection of the link between Palestinian land and population'. Rosenthal adds that this term 'is problematic due to its cannibalistic associations' ('Conducting War'), an association which has likely occurred to Grossman and his readers. Ora is unable to remember the name of Al Qabu, but she senses traces of the vanished lives around and underneath the lovers' path, as she notes 'the remnants of quince, walnut, lemon, almond, and olive groves in the Arab villages that had ceased to exist' (*To the End* 455). Both histories – the former lovers' and Al Qabu's – now united in pain and loss in a way that evokes Bashir Bashir and Amos Goldberg's notion of a joint Jewish–Arab sharing of traumatic memories (77), a notion which evidently resonates with Grossman. Grossman, who lost his son, Uri, in the Second Lebanon War, is a regular speaker at the annual joint Israeli–Palestinian Memorial Day ceremony, and despite being labelled 'terrorist' and 'traitor' by right-wing Israeli protesters, he insists, in his 2018 ceremony speech, that 'even old enemies can connect with each other through their grief; precisely because of it' (Roth and Bar).

Naming and commemorating are inseparable acts in Grossman as they are for the displaced Palestinians, and in Jewish thought. The name of the Israeli museum dedicated to the commemoration of the Holocaust references the Book of Isaiah: 'And to them will I give in my house and within my walls a memorial and a name (a "*yad vashem*") that shall not be cut off' (Yad Vashem), highlighting the bond between the memory and its signifier. In translation, however, the identity markers attached to names of people and places can be shed in a way that is similar to the loss incurred through Hebraisation. While translation theory often metaphorically applies the terms 'domestication' and 'foreignisation' to the degree and nature of the source text's assimilation into the target language and culture, these terms are rarely used in relation to the translation of proper nouns such as toponyms. When conveying place names in other languages, options range from offering the common name (e.g. 'Jerusalem'), to transliterating ('*Yerushalayim*'), or – less commonly – translating the meaning of the place name into English ('City of Peace'). These choices impoverish the translated texts by either over-emphasising some biblical or other bond, exoticising the mundane, conspicuously foregrounding the literal meaning, or removing traces of the name's previous incarnation. A translation can thus further contribute to what Rona Sela describes as the 'erasure and concealment' (215) of history and to the perpetuation of the historical narrative endorsed by the dominant sovereign power. A further example of the 'genealogy' (Sela 218) of such erasure took place in recent years when Jerusalem's most common Arab name, *Al Quds*, was removed from road signs, leaving only its Hebrew-kin *Urshalim* on display (al-Ghubari).

Significantly, a name that is exported more or less intact into the target language can also lose its meaning in the course of its reception by the dominant-language readership. In the next section, I examine the character of Sami, Ora's Palestinian Israeli taxi driver. By a fortunate coincidence, Edward Said meditates on the asymmetry in the reception of this name in Arabic – Sami – and its English equivalent, Sammy. In its English version, Said argues, Sammy is an 'inelegant nickname', whilst in Arabic, the name, meaning 'high' or 'heavenly' ('Living in Arabic' 231), is much more dignified and elevated. The two, Said concludes 'coexist in the bilingual ear, unresolved, never at peace' ('Living in Arabic' 231); they are 'false friends', bonded only by a superficial likeness. As with Jerusalem, *Yerushalayim* and *Urshalim* – the very fact of the names' similarity or apparent kinship deceptively conceals the eradication of a layer of meaning that occurs in the process of their conversion.

The Bilingual Arab

Sami's character problematises the translation of national demarcations in ways that also carry thematic and interpretive implications. A master in the art of blending in, Sami dexterously travels between the various actual and symbolic points on the 'Israeli' and 'Arab' identity spectrum and his bi-cultural, bilingual figure clearly reflects the 'hybrid' (Atalia 221), 'hyphenated' (Rabinowitz and Abu-Baker 12; Hammack 368) and 'oxymoronic' (Kashua quoted in Hochberg, 'To Be or Not to Be' 71) experiences of the Palestinian citizens of Israel. Grossman's earlier nonfiction texts, *The Yellow Wind* (1987) and *Sleeping on a Wire: Conversations with Palestinians in Israel* (1992), have undoubtedly informed the construction of Sami's character, and it will be shown later how Sami's speech echoes that of Grossman's interview subjects. Importantly, Sami's particular use of the Hebrew language, his accents, vocabulary, and his code-switching, reveals a transformation of his character which reflects actual changing attitudes documented amongst the Palestinian citizens of Israel towards the governing state during the same period.

Like Sami, most Palestinian citizens of Israel speak Arabic as their first language and learn Hebrew for reasons such as employment, study, dealings with authorities, and accessing services (Mar'i). The daily interaction between the two language groups, be it in the workplace or elsewhere, as well as the shared etymological and historical bond between the sister-languages, has meant that words and expressions have migrated over the years and have been naturalised into their respective lexicons. This process of naturalisation is, however, asymmetrical, with linguistic interferences, or borrowings, between the two languages reflecting the social, cultural and economic relationships between the two sectors. Some examples of this are the adoption into Arabic, through work interaction, of Hebrew specialised and technical terms (Mar'i; Hawker, 'Mirage' 223), the Arabic words that have migrated into early Hebrew military slang (Rosenthal 'The Soldiers'), and the low social status of many Arabic slang words adopted into Hebrew (Henkin-Roitfarm 71). Attitudes towards second-language acquisition by the two groups is also uneven, with only around 10 per cent of Israeli Jews identifying as being proficient in the Arabic language (Shenhav *et al.* 7). Interestingly, while the majority of Jewish Israelis believe a command of the Arabic language is important for 'security-related reasons' (Shenhav *et al.* 8), Palestinians largely regard Hebrew fluency as a means for raising their social status (Henkin-Roitfarm 96).

Over the course of the novel, Sami's language use reflects the changes in attitude detected in the Palestinian Israeli cohort towards the state of Israel, from the post-1967 desire to assimilate and participate as equals in Israeli society, to the disillusioned and politicised 'Stand-Tall Generation' that emerged around the Second Intifada (Rabinowitz and Abu-Baker 2). The power dynamics between Sami and Ora reflect two levels of hierarchy that exist between the two groups in Israel: first, between the Jewish employer and the Arab employee, and second – more symbolically within the microcosm of the taxi – between the Arab owner and the Jewish occupier. Sami and Ora's relationship begins with a period Ora refers to nostalgically as the 'twenty good years' (*To the End* 298), during which the Jewish woman enjoys a friendly coexistence with her Arab driver who largely conforms to an earlier tendency among Palestinian Israelis to 'operate legally and non-violently within the Zionist establishment' (Atalia 191). Within Ora and Ilan's 'little underground cell in the heart of the "situation"' (*To the End* 299), the Arab driver has become – it is narrated with some poignant irony – '*almost* one of the family' (53, my italics).

Grossman captures the complexities of this quasi-honeymoon phase in Jewish–Arab relations in a *mise en abyme* that is overflowing with ideological, linguistic and cultural 'speed-bumps of untranslatability' (Apter 3). In this scene, Ora recruits Sami to join her in scouting 1950's memorabilia for a US-funded project to construct a mini-replica of the state of Israel in the Nevada Desert. The two spend considerable time together traversing the country in search of iconic cultural emblems of that era which they must beg or prise out of their current owners. Once again, it is Sami's charm and his chameleon-like inconspicuousness (perfected over a lifetime of blending in), along with the shared 'epidermic identity' between many Arabs and Jews (Oppenheimer 215, citing Fanon), that wins him the trust of their prospective vendors who variously recognise in him a former *kibbutznik*, an old Hapoel soccer fan from the Nachlaot neighbourhood in Jerusalem, or a Yemenite from the Kerem neighbourhood in Tel Aviv (*To the End* 58–9).

This satirical micro-replication of the conflict, where an Arab is employed on a US-sponsored project to commemorate Jewish settlement on his own land, is an obvious critique of the demands placed on Palestinian Israelis to capitulate to Jewish dominance in Israel, and of the US's and the global Christian community's endorsement of the Jews as chosen custodians of the Holy Land. It also exemplifies the assumption that the Palestinian Israelis should collaborate with the Zionist project, and the extent to which not only the Hebrew language, but also the dominant Jewish-Israeli folklore and collective memory have permeated the cultural vocabulary of Palestinian Israelis. This kind of vocabulary is tremendously difficult to fully convey in translation, since memories, stories and ideas are welded into the word-objects that Ora and Sami collect on their trips and into the places they visit and the people they meet along the way.

One example of such an untranslatable object is the *kolboinik*, a compound word made of *kol* (everything) and *bo* (inside it) with the Russian *nik* suffix commonly attached to early Hebrew slang. In the English version, the word is translated simply to a 'stainless-steel basin' (*To the End* 58). This is a reasonable translational choice, since the word has such wide cultural connotations that it would require a lengthy footnote, if not an entire essay, to explain not only what it means (a stainless-steel container positioned at the centre of a kibbutz's dining-room table for depositing food-scraps), but also the principles on which the kibbutzim were founded, and the significance of the *kolboinik's* disappearance along with the cessation of communal dining in the now largely privatised kibbutzim, which reflect the demise of collectivist values within Israel's political and social landscape. In addition to the nostalgic lament that this humble trash-container conjures, the fact that Sami has internalised this Jewish cultural icon comments on the nature of the power relations between the dominant and the minority cultures and hinges on the reader's ability to decode these dynamics. It must be added that crossing over the linguistic Hebrew–Arabic border, as noted by Hawker, must not be read simply as a sign of the Palestinian's acquiescence, since learning the language of the Other can also constitute a strategic and 'proud act of national resistance' ('Mirage' 232), and one that, in this instance, hints at Sami's shifting sense of belonging, which will be discussed shortly.

In being neither/both Israeli and Palestinian, Sami personifies the 'oxymoronic' or indeterminate status of Palestinian Israelis outlined above. His 'Arabesque' (*To the End* 59) Hebrew is part of the performance of the orientalised persona which initially prevails in his relationship with Ora, who delights in his humorous wit and admires the dignified stoicism he displays through a routine of degradation that he endures as a minority citizen. 'You may shit all over me', he once said to an airport checkpoint guard who called him 'a shitty Arab', 'but that doesn't make me shitty' (*To the End* 61). Indeed, despite the Jewish fluency which gets him through interactions with authorities, Sami remains acutely connected to his fellow Palestinians in his village and, later, beyond. Sami's early signs of subversion emerge in the form of the 'ironic power speech' (Hawker, 'Complexities of Speech' 4) typical of non-Israeli Palestinians at the start of the millennium, which utilises 'Hebrew's connotation of Israel's dominance in paradoxical situations' (Hawker, 'Complexities of Speech' 4). Sami, who is said to have been 'an explicit clause' in Ora and her estranged husband's separation agreement, jokes that as an Arab he is used to being divided up by the Jews (*To the End* 54). He also attributes the reason he is mistaken for a *kibbutznik* to the fact that 'half of Kiryat Anavim's'[12] lands belong to [his] family' (58), and refers to his children as his 'five demographic problems' (62).[13]

Significantly, it is Ora's failure to remember Sami's Palestinian-ness that leads to the eventual crisis in the relationship between the two, which happens in the year 2000. In ordering her Arab driver to deliver a Jewish soldier to battle, Ora forces Sami to pick a side. This crucial moment awakens in Sami the same 'unprecedented support' (Rabinowitz and Abu-Baker 9) documented in Palestinian Israelis towards their fellow non-citizen Palestinians at that time, as expressed in his smuggling of the sick boy, Yazdi. At the same time, Sami also begins to assume the 'Palestinian identity accentuation' that has been observed in Palestinian Israelis during the same period (Hammack 368) which once again aligned them more closely with the Palestinians in the Occupied Territories. Sami's speech takes on a deliberately broad Palestinian accent and syntax, a trait observed years earlier by Grossman in *The Yellow Wind*, during his conversations with Palestinians in the Occupied Territories, where, Grossman notes, 'even those who can pronounce the "p" in "politics," say "bolitics," as a sign of defiance, in which there is a sort of self-mocking' (*Yellow Wind* 8). At the peak of the crisis between Sami and Ora, Sami, who has, incidentally, just reupholstered his taxi in 'Arab taste' (*To the End* 66) fake leopard-skin, takes on a heavily accented, flawed Hebrew as a way of performing to Ora the extent of his withdrawal from her and – by implication – from the Jews more broadly.[14] In the following example, Sami's exaggerated mispronunciations, his tone, and his deliberate grammatical errors, along with – importantly – the use of the Hebrew second-person plural 'you', culminate in a linguistically constructed declaration of the end of his compliant neutrality:

> 'You[15] people,' he hisses through the rearview mirror, 'you're always looking for a story in everything. So you'll have it for your *telefision* show or a movie for your *bestivals*, not so? Ha? Not so?'
>
> Ora pulls back as though she's been slapped. 'You people,' he called her. 'Bestival,' he said, brandishing the accent of Palestinians from the Territories, whom he's always derided. He was defying her with a put-on 'dirty Arab' persona. (*To the End* 111–12, original italics)

Such instances of speech modification by a bilingual character are tremendously complex to replicate in another language. The 'movement' metaphors (Cheetham 245; Jacobs, 'Anna Herman' 297) frequently attached to the act of translation do not apply here, since these metaphors imply a transference from a single language-location to another, whereas in texts such as *To the End*, the markers of social or ethnic marginality – or dominance – are made up of multiple and hybrid modes of speech. Like the Hebrew poetry of the late nineteenth-century European Jews who settled in Israel, which 'acknowledges positions and articulations of in-betweenness *within* linguistic, geographic, and cultural text and contexts' (Jacobs, *Strange Cocktail* 16), Grossman's language similarly considers this 'in-between' space. As Sami's character illustrates, Israel's ambiguous geopolitical demarcations, with its de facto partner, Palestine, sitting both within and without it, spawn languages which are enmeshed together, mingle, infiltrate one another, and struggle for domination in a way that at times mimics the contest between the two peoples. Translating the in-between idiolect of non-standard or accented speakers such as Sami necessitates a renegotiation of the convenient binaries of source/target languages that more neatly apply to a single language or dialect (Grutman 18).

As discussed, there is a certain inherent and unavoidable estrangement between the kinds of Hebrews spoken by the Arab and by the Jew, and their dislocated other-language rendering. In addition, mainstream translations, driven by economic and stylistic conventions, judge the quality of a translated text by its 'fluency' and by the 'invisibility' of the fact of its translation (Venuti 179) in order to 'foster a certain illusion in the reader: that he or she is reading the original language, which is also his or her own language' (Kamuf 3). Since this illusion inevitably affects the translation of non-standard varieties, dialects and code-switching, these smoothed-over aesthetics, says Apter, tend to 'neutralize the politics of translation' (Bertacco and Apter 12). For Sami, who is a bilingual, accented and non-standard variation speaker, there are also delicate issues of 'prestige' (Rosa 213) to maintain in translation, since it is known that readers will tend to attribute a higher status to characters who use the standard language variety than to those who speak in dialect or accents (Ramos Pinto 291). Thus, while this text is not multilingual proper, Grossman's strategic performance of his characters' use of the language of the Other holds some potential ethical implication as seen in the translation of Sami's subversive performance of the Hebrew language.

False Friends

In addition to the character who speaks the language of the dominant culture as a second language, there are also instances in the novel where Jewish characters speak Arabic, with an effect that has potential implications for the reception and interpretation, in translation, of such linguistic events. One example in the novel of what, in linguistics, is aptly termed 'language interference' is when Arabic words invade the holiest of domestic sanctuaries – the family kitchen – in a much-cited monologue sometimes referred to as *Salat Aravi* (Arabic Salad). In this scene, Ora is chopping vegetables for Ofer's favourite Arabic salad when she is suddenly overcome by a rage that manifests as a new kind of 'salad': a verbal one made up of the Arabic incorporated into Hebrew conflict-lexicon.[16] As though lifted from a stream-of-consciousness poetry-slam performance, Ora's monologue is composed of the names of battlegrounds, towns, refugee camps, generals, 'fighters' of various kinds, and weapons, vocalising her aversion not only toward the words' connotative charge, but also to their tone and texture. The English translation leaves the Arabic more or less intact through transliterations, but as the words manifest in a foreign typeface, only echoes of their palpable throaty grittiness are heard through the more agreeable 'gurgles, grants and yammers' (*To the End* 599) of their new attire:

> Ora attacks the vegetables. She grabs a sharp knife, swings it, and lands it down furiously to dice Abd al-Qader al-Husseini with Haj Amin al-Husseini and Shukeiri and Nimeiri and Ayatollah Khomeini and Nashashibi and Arafat and Hamas and Mahmoud Abbas and all their kasbahs and Qaddafis and SCUDs and Izz ad-Din al-Qassam and Qassam rockets and Kafr Qasim and Gamal Abdel Nasser. (*To the End* 600)

It is interesting to reflect here once again on the idea of 'false friends' mentioned earlier in relation to words with an apparent, deceptive, identity in two languages. Such instances of interaction between Arabic and Hebrew as the ones seen in the Arabic Salad monologue present the Arabic spoken by the Jew as a language which is itself a mistranslation. The words and terms imported from Arabic into Hebrew maintain their original façade, but even seemingly innocuous nouns such as *Kasbah* and *Jenin* (*To the End* 600), in this context, are charged – radicalised even – with new, sinister potency when they penetrate the vocabulary of the panic-stricken mother. Later in the same monologue, Ora uses the word *Shaheed* (*To the End* 600), a word commonly translated to the English 'martyr'. In a 2018 court case involving a poem by Palestinian Dareen Tatour, the translation of the word *shaheed* became central to the charges of 'inciting terrorism' made against Tatour. Translator Yoni Mendel argued in court that since in Hebrew, *shaheed* has become synonymous with 'terrorist', it would be more true to the Arabic poem to translate the word as 'victim' (Mendel 6–7). The word *Intifada*, which appears in another text by Tatour, was also brought in as evidence against the poet, with the judge eventually choosing to apply its adopted Hebrew connotation (a violent disobedience) rather than the less incriminating one (a people's struggle against oppression) of the original Arabic (Haifawi 3–4). Tatour was convicted and sent to prison, with one critic condemning the court for acting like 'a heart-kidney scholar who knows what we all think and feel when we hear the word "Intifada"' (Haifawi 3–4). The battles staged in *Salat Aravi*, and in Tatour's case, where the Arabic expression becomes loaded with terror and trauma in the hands of the adopted, dominant language, is one that the translated texts can only observe from the periphery rather than actively participate in.

Military Secrets

A similar linguistic interference is evident in the novel's use of Israeli Defense Force (IDF) 'language' to reflect the ubiquity of the military within Israeli society as well as to heighten the sense of alienation felt by those who have no access to this terminology. The language of the IDF, with its particular vocabulary syntax, and phonology, has trickled into civilian speech (Rosenthal, *Israeli Army Talk* 13) and, once again, Grossman uses this quintessentially Israeli trait symbolically to reflect his characters' attitudes and emotional states, or as a means of eliciting particular responses in his readers. A proliferation of military slang and jargon is used during the scenes from the Yom Kippur War in particular, including acronyms (APC, NCO, SKS), military-specific slang such as *Helmut* (a soldier in shock) and *jobnik* (non-combative soldier), macabre euphemistic idioms such as 'returned his kit' (died), Hebraicised foreign words such as 'jerry cans' and 'signals', and two-way communication codes such as 'matches' for low-rank soldiers, and 'blues' for air force personnel (Rosenthal 'Militarese Dictionary'). There is also military vocabulary taken from the processes of occupation, such as the standard IDF Arabic phrases used for arresting a suspect (*To the End* 499). Some of the terms are commonly known, whilst others are unfamiliar to those outside the milieu or user group.

Indeed, despite the prevalence of the military within the domestic sphere, and the trickling of military speech into civilian life, Rosenthal finds that military slang is often unique to a particular military corps, or even subsections within a corps (*Israeli Army Talk* 30), and is therefore not widely accessible to those outside the particular group of speakers. Further, since the 'front/rear' binary of Western military hegemony, in which the front is predominantly male and the peripheral rear is female, is also true for the Israeli army (Lomsky-Feder and Ben-Ari 229–30), and considering the exclusion of some ethnic minorities from the frontline, access to military speech is in effect also restricted on the basis of gender, religion and ethnicity (Rosenthal, *Israeli Army Talk* 181). In the novel, the military-combative (and predominantly Jewish male) language variation is made up of slang emerging from the Yom Kippur War and the two Intifadas, of a strategic, euphemistic 'language laundry' (Rosenthal 'Conducting War') and – significantly for Ora – of a particular belief system and code of behaviour. Hence, the linguistic difference between Ora and her family represents a fundamental moral incompatibility that places Ora – the mother – in opposition to her husband and sons (all combat soldiers). In the same way that Ora rejects the domestic interference that comes from the Arabic conflict-vocabulary, she refuses the ideologically saturated military speech that has similarly contaminated her family home.

The dialogue below between Ora and Ofer illustrates how Ofer's language, with its euphemistic acronyms, insinuations, pseudo-moralistic rhetoric, and detached, macabre humour, both signifies and deepens the psychic chasm that has opened up between mother and son. The exchange takes place one day when Ora finds Ofer carving a wooden stick:

> She asked what it was, and he looked up at her with his ironic, arched eyebrows and said, 'What does it look like?'
> 'Like a rounded stick.'
> He smiled. 'It's a club. Club, meet Mom. Mom, meet club.'
> 'What do you need a club for?'
> Ofer laughed and said, 'To beat up little foxes'. . . He said, 'But what's wrong with a club, Mom? It's minimal use of force.'
> Ora, with uncharacteristic cynicism, asked if they had an acronym for that, 'MUF, or something.'
> 'But clubs prevent violence, Mom! They don't create it.'
> 'Even so, allow me to feel bad when I see my son sitting here making himself a club.'
> (*To the End* 502–3)

If Ofer adopts IDF language and rhetoric and Ora refuses it, Avram disarms this language by appropriating its vocabulary and syntax into his own inventive idiolect in a way that subverts its original utilitarian–ideological function. Avram is Ora's long-time friend and Ofer's biological father, who was, in his pre-war life, an aspiring writer and a linguistic virtuoso. Avram is the indisputable wordsmith in the novel who incidentally shares a number of biographical similarities with Grossman, as well as the desire to expose and disarm the workings of unimaginative 'language defrauders' (Grossman, *Writing in the Dark* 65). For Avram, the language of the military and the secrets he collects through his role as a translator for military intelligence are a haul to add to his cache; to be tinkered with and moulded and incorporated into his already abundant collection of characters and dialogues. He may have 'adopted military lingo, making it sound like his mother tongue' (*To the End* 552), but he does so as a thespian might, rather than as someone who is taken by its underpinnings. As he does so, this prototypal artist comes to represent the 'centrality of the human voice' (Ben-Dov 287) and it is indeed a singular voice that is expressed in both his tragi-comic battlefield broadcasts, and in his lengthy post-traumatic silences.

Avram's – and perhaps Grossman's – magnum opus in the novel is the two-way radio, one-way monologue he delivers into the ether as he is stranded injured in a deserted post, ahead of his capture and torture by the Egyptian army. This monologue showcases Grossman's characteristic exploitation of the 'strange cocktail' (Jacobs, *Strange Cocktail*) that is the modern Hebrew language, with its multiple historical, cultural and other-worldly influences. The following excerpt from Avram's radio transmission is intertextually and linguistically loaded, deploying military, biblical and popular registers, puns and wordplays, code-switching and neologisms in a comedic performance that – not unlike Dovaleh, the stand-up comic protagonist from Grossman's International Booker prize-winning book *A Horse Walks into a Bar* – fails to conceal the enormous tragedy that simmers beneath it. I bring an excerpt from Avram's monologue that I have annotated in order to demonstrate Grossman's mode of constructing such a 'carnival of Israeli-ness' (Kaspi):

> Ilan . . . you'll probably marry Ora in the end. Way to go,[17] you stud.[18] Just promise me you'll name your son Avram, d'you[19] hear me? But with the 'h'[20] – Avraham! Father of many nations! And tell him about me. I'm warning you,[21] Ilan, if you don't, my ghost will haunt[22] you at night in your bed and bruise your reed.[23] (*To the End* 567)

As noted by Mercel-Padon, it is often Avram who is charged with showcasing Grossman's ways of reformulating language (342) and this quintessential 'Avramese' is as much a part of the character's composition as is his small stature and his gait, but unlike Avram's anatomical features, which can be described to similar effect in any language, his form of speech resists replication, explication or mimicry for its very reliance on the Hebrew language as its base substance.

Defamiliarised Conflict

Like Ora and Sami, Avram is caught up in what Mei-Tal Nadler understands as the tension 'between the desire to dismantle the national space from within . . . and the immersion, willingly or otherwise, within the mechanisms of power' (81). These characters' mode of dismantling the national space comes through imagining a language that subverts common articulations of 'State', 'enemy', 'motherhood', 'the fallen soldier' and other signifiers of the conflict. Shklovsky suggests that 'this thing we call art exists in order to restore the sensation of life, in order to make us feel things, in order to make a stone stony' (162). It comes to counter our 'automized' response to things that have been 'packaged' or presented to us in familiar, nominal signs (161). In Grossman, the de-automatisation of language has metalinguistic and paratextual implications that extend beyond translation proper. His literary idiolect functions in concert with his public push towards rejuvenating a stagnant political dialogue in the nonfictional world, which is made all the more poignant when read alongside the loss of his son, Uri, in the Second Lebanon War. The various dimensions of the author's life and work, as Michael Gluzman observes, 'are not mere paratextual matter useful as background for discussion, but form part of the novel's composition and of the story of its reception' (350).

A few months before Uri's death, in a piece he wrote about life in a conflict zone, Grossman quoted Bertolt Brecht: 'He who laughs has not yet heard the terrible tidings' (Grossman, *Writing in the Dark* 44). Grossman proposed then that when living under the persistent threat of bad tidings, surrounded by fear-inducing stereotypes and generalisations, literature preserves our 'right to individuality and uniqueness' (51), and it does so not so much by exerting thematic victories, such as in allowing good to overcome evil, but through creative means, amongst which is its commitment to 'the precision of words and descriptions' (51). Ora's movement towards the land and away from the notification moment marks her refusal to participate in the nationally sanctioned conflict mythology that produces and glorifies the fallen soldier. Grossman brings an end to the mother's linguistic paralysis (Benziman) by giving Ora agency over her own story. In devising a private language for Ora, Grossman returns to the site of the conflict – the land – and offers its primal, autonomous and natural exuberance as a version of the 'actual' world which is not overcome by the conflict. He draws on the mechanics of the Hebrew language to create and 'legitimize' (Stein 455) organic neologisms, foregrounds the language's sensory features such as sounds and textures, and composes a flourish of unexpected metaphors and hybrid collocations, creating a meticulous natural cosmos of irrepressible vitality. Once more I offer an annotated example to exemplify the methods discussed here:

> Ants bustle along a dry stem of fennel plant, gnawing at the wood[24] and the crumbs of congealed[25] honey left by last year's bees. A tiny scepter of orchid stands tall, purple and light as a butterfly,[26] its pair of tuberous roots[27] in the earth – one slowly emptying out, the other filling up. A little farther away, in the shade of Avram's right upper back, a small white deadnettle, engaged in its complicated affairs, sends out olfactory signals to insects that constantly flit between it and other plants.[28] (*To the End* 215–16)

Grossman stipulates that authors are driven by 'the need to name things by [their] own private names'. He adds that 'by using a personal language – achieved by certain tempo combinations, particular uses of specific words – readers can feel the fingerprint of your inner world' (Grossman, cited in Shainin). As he utilises the inherent features of the Hebrew language, the physicality of an utterance colludes with its 'spiritual' or connotative thrust to promote a particular effect that is understood, intuited and sensed in Hebrew. Just like Ora's outcry over the task of translating the flesh, blood and soul of her beloved son 'with only words' (*To the End* 204), the fleshy qualities of Grossman's private language which are very much rooted in Hebrew and Israeli-ness, at times refuse to be squeezed into foreign 'bodies'. Grossman's Hebrew original constructs a linguistic contribution to the conflict which requires careful decipherment of the source language. The collateral – and unavoidable – loss of meaning in the process of translation must be worked into our consciousness during our reading and interpretation of the conflict as it appears in Grossman's – and perhaps other authors' – translated literature.

Notes

1. A Hebrew euphemism that literally translates to 'the Situation', commonly used to refer to the conflict and its effect.
2. All translations from Hebrew are my own unless otherwise indicated.
3. South Tel Aviv is an area known for its population of foreign workers, asylum seekers, illegal overstayers, and sex workers.
4. Ora is trying to distinguish between the Arab and Jewish pronunciations of the name.
5. A more unambiguously Arab name. Also note Cohen's mimicry of Sami's grammatical error in the original ('הוא קוראים אותו יזדי', p. 134)
6. This is presumably a 1984 campaign t-shirt for the dovish Israeli Labour leader who, along with Itzhak Rabin, received the Nobel Peace Prize in 1994. At the time the story takes place, the right-wing Likud party has been in power for some two decades, Itzhak Rabin had been assassinated, and the peace process championed by Rabin and Peres is as tattered at the old t-shirt.
7. As a resident of the Territories, Yazdi has restrictions on travelling to Israel. Access to Israel for medical treatment can be difficult for non-Israelis who live in the Occupied Territories. Special permits are required and delays at checkpoints often impact on non-Israeli Palestinians travelling to Israel for this purpose (B'tselem, 'Restrictions on Movement').
8. Hebrew for 'praise god'.
9. In *The Yellow Wind*, Grossman quotes author and researcher Nissim Krispil who notes that some place names which were changed to Hebrew are now referred to with the prefix *Ma Rah* ('gone') (29) by Palestinian speakers.
10. A *moshav* is a cooperative agricultural community.
11. On the region's webpage, no mention is made of the place's pre 1950 history, instead Mevo Beitar is described as village 'whose residents live peacefully with each other and . . . lead a rich social life with a strong sense of belonging' (Mateh Yehuda Regional Council).
12. A kibbutz near Abu Ghosh, the village where Sami grew up.

13. This conjures a similar comment made by Aymen Odeh, the Arab-Israeli leader of the Hadash Party, in response to Netanyahu's referring to the Arabs as an existential threat. Odeh tweeted a photograph of his children in pyjamas with the caption 'At the end of a long day, it's time to put these three existential threats to bed!' (Odeh).
14. 'Arab taste' is a derogatory Hebrew slang term for cheap, tacky taste.
15. Grossman uses a single word, אתם, the second-person plural in the original Hebrew but does not include the word 'people'.
16. The Hebrew word for salad, '*salat*', is also slang for 'mess', 'mixture', 'disorder'. Incidentally, what in Jewish-Israeli cooking is known as 'Arabic Salad' (hand-diced tomato, cucumber, onion, parsley), is commonly translated to 'Israeli salad' in English.
17. The original Hebrew word is סחתיין, a common Hebrew slang word borrowed from the Arabic, meaning 'good on you'.
18. Grossman uses the word נקניק (sausage), 1970s Israeli slang for 'you bastard'.
19. The Hebrew version uses the past tense here, שמעת אותי? which is commonly applied in the military for delivering a command.
20. In the Old Testament, as the covenant between man and God is established in the act of the circumcision, God declares: 'Neither shall thy name any more be called Abram, but thy name shall be Abraham; for a father of many nations have I made thee' (Genesis 17:5). The letter 'ה' ('h') is commonly used to denote the sacred name of the Jewish God. The spelling of Avram's name, without the 'ה' ('h'), is uncommon, and some critics have interpreted this as Grossman hinting at Avram's Sephardic origins.
21. דיר באלק is common Hebrew slang based on the Arabic, meaning 'Be warned'.
22. Original: בעתה. The Hebrew language does not have an equivalent verb to 'haunt' for collocation with 'ghost'.
23. The original Hebrew would literally translate to 'flip the end of your sawn-off rifle', which is a word play on a Hebrew idiom 'משענת קנה רצוץ derived from the Book of Kings (The Academy of the Hebrew Language). It is also a pun on Abraham's circumcision during the renaming ceremony mentioned above.
24. The Hebrew text uses a botanical term, 'כלך' ('lignin'). This was possibly left untranslated due to the obscurity of the English term.
25. This replaces a typical Grossman inflection, 'הדבישו'. It takes the root letters of the word 'honey' (ש,ב,ד) and turns into a verb 'honeyed'.
26. Another unusual inflection, 'פרפרני' which is akin to 'butterflied'.
27. A Grossman metaphor using the unusual possessive pair: 'שני אשכי פקעותיו' ('its two testicled-bulbs').
28. Since the deadnettle is female and the insects are male, the erotic tone of this description is diminished in translation to a non-gendered language.

PART 2

REPURPOSING FORM: REIMAGINING THE CONFLICT OUTSIDE OF PALESTINE/ISRAEL

6

'PUBLIC CONFESSION' IN PALESTINIAN LITERARY SELF-NARRATIVES AFTER THE SECOND INTIFADA

Aarushi Punia

The Palestinian struggle against the Israeli occupation and settler colonialism is often characterised as a struggle for 'self-determination' (Said, *The Question of Palestine* 6) where Palestine is imagined as an embodiment of a community of selves that has been erased from official narratives. Since 1948, Israel has enabled settler geopolitics that renders Palestinian existence invisible and forgotten through rhetorical and material instrumentalities. The function of Golda Meir's statement in 1969 to the *Sunday Times* that 'there is no such thing as Palestinians' (Soussi) was not just to deny the national character of Palestinian existence, but to delegitimise the Palestinian nation-in-waiting through rhetorical acts of erasure. This 'logic of elimination' (Wolfe 387) has created an 'architecture of erasure' (Makdisi 519), which consistently tries to hide the presence of Palestinian lives from Israeli citizens and the world. While Golda Meir's statement can be considered as a rhetorical offence, it is pertinent to note that rhetorical offences have material consequences of their own. This chapter argues that Palestinian writers contend with Israel's rhetorical practices of erasure and colonial amnesia through self-narratives that inscribe and memorialise Palestinian existence in a literary life-world.

The Palestinian struggle has always been to determine the self: to make it visible, including to an international public, and this struggle has been reflected in Palestinian literature as well. The struggle for self-determination is not limited to political emancipation but also the creation of a new understanding of Palestinian selfhood altogether, which is undertaken by Palestinian literature through the development of a new narrative form that I would like to characterise as public confession. The development of this form can be traced through the literary works of Ghassan Kanafani's *Men in the*

Sun (1963), Emile Habiby's *The Secret Life of Saeed: The Pessoptimist* (1974) and Mourid Barghouti's *I Saw Ramallah* (1997). It can be found in its most developed form in narratives published during and after the Second Intifada (2000–5), when the representation of Palestinian selfhood to a concerned international public sphere became most crucial. This chapter focuses on the mode of public confession embedded in self-narratives (autobiographical and fictional narratives narrated in first-person) by examining Sayed Kashua's *Dancing Arabs* (2004), Suad Amiry's *Sharon and My Mother-in-Law* (2006) and Samir El-Youssef's 'The Day the Beast Got Thirsty' (2004). Furthermore, this chapter discusses the role of the unheroic Palestinian protagonist in questioning the tradition of Palestinian nationalist propaganda. The unheroic Palestinian paves the way for the creation of what can be described as unheroic literature, which marks a departure from the traditional literary tropes and practices that foreground the heroic aspects of resistance within Palestinian literature, such as the reliance on commemoration, valorisation of martyrdom, emphasis on nationalist pride, and expression of nostalgia for a lost community and land. Unheroic literature continues the project of Palestinian self-determination but it articulates the alienation ordinary Palestinians feel from the nationalist project by critiquing Palestinian politicians, communal commemorative practices, and the representation of Palestinians by humanitarian and media organisations. Particularly after the Second Intifada, unheroic literature adopts humorous, ironic, and self-assertive strategies to narrate a public confession that resists the romanticisation of the Palestinian condition and to articulate modes of survival within a state that is oppressive because of Israeli settlers and military control, and repressive because of orthodox Palestinian politics and societal conventions.

Testifying after the Second Intifada

Ilana Feldman (2009) observes that the Second Intifada (2000–5) forced Palestinians to confront fractures within their own community and acknowledge that their condition was further exploited by their own political leaders. Additionally, Tobias Kelly (2008) explains that most Palestinians turned to activities other than political mobilisation due to a disenchantment with political leadership. Death was no longer glorified in lives held together by a fragile sense of the ordinary. What distinguishes the Second Intifada (2000–5) from the course of the Israel–Palestine conflict is the marked increase in violence (in terms of the military aggression from Israel to suppress the Palestinian revolt and Palestinian resistance to the same), its coverage by the international media after decades of neglect and apathy towards Palestinians, and the international humanitarian response to Palestinian suffering. Lori Allen notes that the Second Intifada carved a 'new martyr geography' ('Getting by' 456) as the Palestinian became internationally visible as the victim of Israeli armed forces or as the suicide bomber who was commemorated as a martyr.

Self-narratives published after the Second Intifada articulate new modes of self-determination that defy the normative imaginations of nationalism, patriarchy and martyrdom to constitute a unique self, distinguished from the imagined Palestinian collective. The unique self constituted in unheroic literature is different from previous articulations of selfhood in two ways: through form and content. In terms of form, instead of swinging between morbid and morose language (for the figure of the martyr) or eternally hopeful expressivity (for the figure of the hero), unheroic literature's unheroic protagonist deploys narrative techniques of tongue-in-cheek humour (Amiry), dark humour (El-Youssef), or irony (Kashua) to blatantly reject the Palestinian literary traditions of expressing nostalgia for the lost land and community, and the desire to return to pre-1948 Palestine. In terms of content, the unheroic protagonist chooses to abandon (or at the very least interrogate) Palestinian community and its commemorative practices to escape the expectations of identification that are imposed on Palestinians. While the unique unheroic protagonist may identify as Palestinian, they also challenge the popular definition of what it means to accommodate oneself within the Palestinian community or what it means to be perceived as Palestinian. Through public confession, the unheroic protagonist narrates experiences that can be read 'against the grain', since they oppose being incorporated within the dominant nationalist or patriarchal rhetoric. Hence, the uniqueness of the unheroic protagonist refers to a Palestinian subjectivity that defies the impositions of assimilating in a collective imagination and articulates a new mode of critical belonging, and in so doing inaugurates the literary figure of the anti-hero. The modern Palestinian anti-hero is shaped by their encounters with traumatic violent experiences within the settler state. Lori Allen (2013) and Rema Hammami (2015) assert that Palestinians often normalise the violence they experience, since their narratives often exhibit an attitude of 'getting by'. They argue that this is not passivity or subordination to the occupation but a different articulation of agency. Allen and Hammami observe that by adopting a stoic attitude in interviews with ethnographers and routinising experiences at the checkpoint, Palestinians subvert Israeli violence and military aggression meant to serve as a 'collective punishment' (Allen, 'Getting by' 457; Hammami, 'On (Not) Suffering' 1).

Yet Palestinian literary works do employ distinct narrative techniques, such as the public confession, to reveal how difficult the process of 'getting by' really is. While on the one hand 'getting by' remains an important survival strategy, on the other hand, it carries the risk of a loss of the agency that it is attempting to articulate, since it can easily be read as submission to the settler-colonial order. 'Getting by' is seen as a continuation of the strategy of *sumud* or steadfastness, where simply existing within the colonial order and continuing with daily life defines resistance. Hammami notes that '[i]n the 1970s, *sumud* meant refusing to leave the land despite the hardships of occupation; now, it connotes something more proactive. Its new meaning, found in the common refrain, "*al-hayat lazim tistamirr*" ("life must go on") is about resisting immobility' (Hammami 'On the Importance of Thugs'). However, the public confession in unheroic literature diverges from the conventional nationalist standpoint of *sumud* and even its new variation theorised by Hammami. The Israeli occupation has incorporated the strategies of 'getting by' to legitimise and extend its authority over Palestinians and their movement. Furthermore, Palestinian nationalism has ensured that resilience is the only strategy available in the face of inefficient political leadership. Hence, unheroic literature distances itself from these strategies and does not allow the reader to forget that the protagonists are forced to choose the path of unheroic acts and pragmatism to escape the impositions of the occupation and nationalist rhetoric.

Furthermore, there are multiple contesting narratives about the life of Palestinians. On the one hand, there is a narrative built and espoused by the Palestinian community, and etched onto the landscape to create a visibly political memory. Lori Allen observes that the image of martyrs dominates the visual geography of Palestine, creating what I would like to call a spatial testimony of the *shahid* (*shahid* in Arabic means 'martyr' as well as 'witness'), where streets are named after martyrs and covered with their posters. This 'hyperrepresentation' (Allen, 'Getting by' 462) has been the result of specific types of commemorative practices where Palestinians produced 'particular forms of social space through memorialising practices' ('Getting by' 475). However, the spatial testimony created through a visual iconography of martyrs is posthumous, since it is not narrated by the *shahid* but by those who stand to gain something through the representation of (usually) his death. The spatial testimony of the *shahid* makes the *shahid* visible, but also unwittingly silences him by narrating on his behalf.

On the other hand, there are self-narratives that resist the hegemonic spatiality of communal memory because it erases the individuality of the self by allowing Palestinians to be seen only as heroes or martyrs. In Palestinian self-narratives, the public confession of an unheroic protagonist constructs an imaginative geography onto which the conflict and Palestinian existence is mapped. This imaginative geography is at odds, and often, in conflict with actual spaces that hyper-represent Palestinians as an undifferentiated community. Each site that is remembered becomes a site to narrate personal experiences that are considered unacceptable within the Palestinian nationalist and commemorative project, thereby creating a literary testimony. Hence, the public confession reveals that the individuality of Palestinians and their everyday struggles have been erased by the commemorative project, which only focuses on the spatial testimony of the *shahid*. By creating a literary testimony, the public confession counters the hegemonic spatiality that glorifies militant resistance, nationalist ideals and commemorative practices.

Laleh Khalili argues that practices of national commemoration 'anthropomorphize the nation, telling its history as if it were a collective biography for all members of the nation' (Khalili 224). When practices of national commemoration are broadcast to an international audience by political organisations and NGOs, they glorify the dead to arouse sympathy in the viewers. The dead are projected to bind the entire community and represent its collective history. The public confession in Palestinian self-narratives articulates the problem inherent in forming a collective biography, which creates the pressure of assimilating within a nationalist narrative irrespective of location and gender. There is no space for dissent or dissociation since 'commemoration' is 'a performance of self-assertion and streamlines a cacophonous and eventful history into a unified nationalist narrative' (Khalili 93). In practices of national commemoration, the assertion of the self becomes a mere means to the end of creating a unified nationalist narrative, burying the distinctions that make the self unique. Even though 'commemoration provides a medium through which those who are often silenced can at least express that they exist' (Khalili 226), practices of national commemoration are institutionally funded and are subsumed within a nationalist commemorative project, such as the projection of the image of the Palestinian in international media as a resilient warrior practicing *sumud*. In commemorative practices, the singular existence of the silenced that is attempting to vocalise itself, is silenced once again. Hence, Palestinian self-narratives are structured as literary testimonies to break the silence imposed by nationalist political parties and international media organisations on Palestinians in their singularity. They narrate experiences of Israeli violence and the pressures of assimilation to the discourse of martyrdom and heroism within Palestinian society and, hence, resist being co-opted within a unified nationalist narrative.

The Narrative Form of Public Confession

A public confession is a specific narrative form that creates the public to whom the confession is made whilst simultaneously articulating the self through confession. The creation of the public allows for the creation of a new political space where the self can become visible in its uniqueness. The self is constructed through the narrative recount of memories of experiences that can be seen as threatening to the larger national unity or an imagined community. Within Palestinian literature, certain self-narratives have to be structured as unique confessions because they deviate from the popular representation of Palestinians and the mainstream discourse of national belonging.

Narratives of public confession reveal their speaker's unique identity in the public and create the public through address. In analysing St Augustine's *Confessions* (400 AD), Matthew Condon suggests of the form of confession that:

> Since the subject narrating is also the subject narrated, confession . . . is a literary device that is profoundly constitutive of self-identity. Its power is found . . . in its ability to reappropriate, to reconfigure and reinscribe one's self-identity and the 'absoluteness' of one's (completed) acts. Confession in and of itself is foremost a verbal act. (44)

Therefore, a literary 'confession' is a rhetorical device that enables self-determination and self-assertion. Each confession is made to an audience, and in literary self-narratives it is made to a rhetorical audience constituted and affected through narrative strategies. The rhetorical audience is constituted by and remains open to persuasion through the confession.

The confession is also dialogical, for it constantly relies on the imagined response of an authorial audience or flesh-and-blood readers. Mikhail Bakhtin asserts that the 'utterance is filled with dialogic overtones' (86), since it always carries the sense of a past address and a future response. In *Confessions*, Augustine draws attention to the rhetorical nature of the confession as it is made to an absent narratee, that is, God. Additionally, he demonstrates awareness of the implied reader in Book X on 'Memory' when he says,

> So what profit is there, I ask, when, to human readers, by this book I confess to you who I now am, not what I once was? . . . So as I make my confession, they wish to learn about my inner self . . . I will reveal not who I was, but what I have now come to be and what I continue to be. (Augustine 180)

Augustine gestures towards the narrative constitution of the self in his attempt to distinguish the 'I' in 'who I now am' from the 'I' in 'what I once was'. He exhibits a consciousness of God as his absent narratee by referring to him as 'you', and displays an awareness of his authorial audience by wondering about the reaction of his 'human readers' to whom he refers as 'they'. The confession works as a confession if it is acknowledged as such, and this acknowledgement is sought here from the authorial audience or the implied reader, and not from the narratee or God. Augustine imagines, in a Bakhtinian dialogical sense, that his readers wish to learn about his 'inner self', which cannot be penetrated through any other means except through narrative. Therefore, narrative is a means of not just revealing but of constituting the changing 'I' through the narration of memory.

Narration produces the self as a unique object of reflection that is distinguished from a collective, since 'narrating enables speakers/writers to disassociate the speaking/writing self from the act of speaking, to take a reflective position vis-à-vis self as character' (Bamberg 132). Self-narratives assert the development of the 'I' and shape the context of its differentiation from a collective 'we' or 'them' by making the individual distinct in plurality. Palestinian self-narratives structured as confessions construct a distinct, unheroic self and reveal it to the public by making it visible in an Arendtian sense. The revelation of the self in public requires an immense amount of courage, which Hannah Arendt characterises in *The Human Condition* (1958) as 'one of the most elemental political attitudes' (35). Therefore, Palestinian self-narratives redefine unheroic acts, for they assert that it is not heroic to prescribe to a community's national ideal, but heroic to critique the community from within. The confession creates a literary public realm or a literary *polis* in times of conflict when acts of courage are extremely crucial. Arendt asserts that 'everything that appears in the public can be seen and heard by everybody' (*The Human Condition* 50), signifying that the public is an apparitional space. It allows the self to move from the realm of invisibility into visibility, and this appearance becomes constitutive of reality. The presence of others (which is the narratee and the authorial audience in the literary confession) creates a sense of plurality from whom the narrating self is distinct and to whom the confession is made. Hence, literary confessions constitute what I would like to call apparitional politics, since they enable the self that has been put through erasure to articulate its existence and make itself visible.

A continuously changing self must create for itself an audience or a discerning public that can track and appreciate its evolution. Michael Warner suggests that a public is 'self-creating and self-organised' (52) and that a public is brought into existence through the means of discourse. In the autobiographical confessions of St Augustine and Jean-Jacques Rousseau, the confession reveals the changing self and causes shifts in the cognition of the public as well. Therefore, the public created through a literary confession is not static and changes along with the evolution of the narrating self. A constant play between what are imagined to be readerly expectations from a text and how the text outmanoeuvres those expectations through narrative devices such as irony and humour, creates a shift in the orientation of the public as well. In the case of unheroic literature, the public confession forces the reader to reconsider whether it is unheroic to critique normative practices within the Palestinian community.

Michael Warner asserts that a public address attempts to 'realize that world through address' (81), implying that the address is constitutive of the public. The public is the space where the self is revealed through articulation and where the public itself is shaped through address. A literary testimony or a public confession is a public discourse, which constitutes the narrating self and moulds the public it addresses. Sara Helman observes that 'testimony and confession . . . are framed as a means to build a new national identity and national solidarity' (380). The unique unheroic Palestinian identity that emerges upon reading the confession will be made evident through the analysis of self-narratives in the following sections. What unites Kashua's *Dancing Arabs*, Amiry's *Sharon and My Mother-in-Law* and El-Youssef's 'The Day the Beast Got Thirsty' is the employment of the form of public confession to question the rigidity of Palestinian nationalism and its emphasis on maintaining antagonism against Jewish-Israelis at the cost of the mental wellbeing and happiness of Palestinian-Israelis, its imposition of limits on the lives and choices of Palestinian women, and its unrelenting construction of posthumous heroes. The unique unheroic Palestinian identity is a critical position that can only be expressed in the form of a confession laced with irony and humour since it resists Palestinian nationalism, which is the dominant discourse that orders Palestinian lives. The following public confessions present Palestinians in a new light since they are published during and after the Second Intifada (2000–5), when refashioning the image of the Palestinian became crucial, and hence, describe the necessity of adopting unheroic pragmatism to survive as a Palestinian.

Confession of the Nameless Narrator: Sayed Kashua's *Dancing Arabs*

Sayed Kashua's *Dancing Arabs* (2004) is the self-narrative of a nameless narrator who is born in Israel to a Palestinian family. The narrative is autodiegetic (narrated in the first person) and, hence, invokes the genre of autobiography upon reading since the narrator and protagonist share the personal pronoun 'I'. Philip Lejeune defines the genre of autobiography as a 'retrospective prose narrative written by a real person concerning his own existence, where the focus is his individual life, in particular the story of his own personality' (*On Autobiography* 4). Lejeune asserts that for a narrative to be an autobiography, there must be an 'autobiographical pact' (*On Autobiography* 13) between the author and the reader, that is, the name of the author must refer to a real person, and the narrator-protagonist must have the same name. He says that 'the reader might be able to quibble over resemblance, but never over identity' (*On Autobiography* 14), implying that self-representation can be dubious, but the existence and identity of the narrated self cannot be in doubt. Lejeune argues that the autobiographical pact 'determines the attitude of the reader' (*On Autobiography* 14) as what defines the autobiography for the reader is above all a contract of identity that is sealed. The namelessness of the narrator in *Dancing Arabs* is a technique intended to violate the autobiographical pact in a text with distinct autobiographical overtones. The text plays with the reader's desire to establish a quick identity between the author and the narrator since the narrative is trying to prove that it is difficult to establish an identity as a Palestinian-Israeli.[1] Gil Hochberg observes that Sayed Kashua's writings

> reject the pre-given status of this identity, emphasizing instead the manner by which it comes into being by bringing together two seemingly incompatible identities – Israeli and Arab – only to re-enforce, validate, and naturalize the current dominant national ideologies of inclusion and exclusion that inevitably render this identity incomplete: Israeli but Arab, Palestinian but Israeli. A split identity, an oxymoron – in sum, an impossibility. ('To Be or Not to Be' 70)

As a self-narrative, *Dancing Arabs* articulates the narrator's misnomeric identity – the identity of Palestinians in Israel, which always seems out of place, whether you place them amongst Palestinians or Israelis. The misnomeric identity reflects the complex politics of naming Palestinians in Israel, since they are called 'Arab Israelis', 'Arabs of Israel' or 'Israeli Arabs'. Such naming of Palestinians has been a part of the official Israeli discourse, dictating how this segment of the Palestinian collective should be referred to in the public. Shourideh Moulavi notes that

> it is not that the Israeli and Palestinian identities are necessarily contradictory, or that one has to be premised on the rejection of the other. But the dilemma here is that they are both incomplete and deficient in different ways, thereby preventing either from fully solidifying as a meaningful and accessible identity. (152)

A misnomeric identity challenges the mainstream Israeli discourse, which erases the Palestinian-ness of Palestinian-Israelis, severs the connection with other segments of the Palestinian population in the Occupied Territories and the diaspora, and imposes Israeli terminology on them. By rejecting being codified as only Palestinian or only Israeli, the misnomeric identity reveals the complexity of the naming terrain, reflecting in the namelessness of the narrator who can be neither fully Palestinian nor fully Israeli.

Palestinian-Israelis have established a literary tradition of being insider-outsiders since they feel out of place within the Palestinian community and the Israeli state. They are considered as traitors by Palestinians living in the Occupied Territories and the diaspora for choosing to live with the oppressor, and are viewed with suspicion by Jewish-Israelis who believe their loyalties will never lie with the Israeli state. Whether it is Emile Habiby's *The Secret Life of Saeed: The Pessoptimist* (1974), where Saeed is a Palestinian who inadvertently becomes an informer for the Israeli state, or Anton Shammas's *Arabesques* (1988), which was originally published in Hebrew and caused an upheaval in the world of Hebrew literature by carving a space for Palestinians writing in Hebrew, the literature of Palestinian-Israelis has always had to speak out from the 'fraught borderline between Hebrew and Arabic' (Levy 1) literature, and between Palestinian and Israeli literature. The misnomeric identity finds itself at home on 'the no-man's-land (which) is at once a space *between* Hebrew and Arabic and a space *outside* the ethnocentric domain that equates Hebrew with "Jewish," Arabic with "Arab"' (Levy 3, original emphasis). *Dancing Arabs* straddles the boundary between an autobiography and a fictionalised autobiographical novel by playing with readerly expectations from both genres. This play engenders a public confession bordering on the unacceptable and incendiary: a literary testimony of a misnomeric identity of a seemingly unheroic Palestinian-Israeli who cannot identify with Palestinians or the Palestinian national cause.

The nameless narrator says that he belongs to a Palestinian family living in a village named Tira in Israel. He suspects that his father was involved in the bombing of a cafe in Israel around 1968 when he was younger and studying at the university. The narrator-protagonist, however, unlike his father has no radical tendencies. He writes

> My father doesn't understand how my brothers and I came out the way we did. We can't even draw a flag. He says kids much smaller than us walk through the streets singing 'P-L-O – Israel, no!' and he shouts at us for not even knowing what PLO stands for. (Kashua, *Dancing* 12)

The narrator begins to establish his distance from the Palestinian national cause of liberation by showing his lack of knowledge about the PLO, the Palestine Liberation Organization. He says that his grandfather was a '*shahid*' (*Dancing* 15) possibly in the 1948 war against the Jews. The narrator distances himself from the idea of the martyr or the stereotypical Palestinian agrarian labourer by saying 'I was the best student in class, and I did what I could to keep from becoming a fruit picker. But I was convinced nothing would help. My grandma had worked as a fruit picker, my father was a fruit picker, and I figured I'd become one too' (*Dancing* 15). He actively resists the idea of family tradition and works hard to unfollow it and distance himself from it. Since *shahid* means both witness and martyr in Arabic, the narrator's refusal to be a *shahid* for the Palestinian cause initiates his public confession about his unheroic distinction from Palestinians and his desire to assimilate within Israeli society. This unheroic protagonist refuses to be sacrificed for the Palestinian national cause but also fails to successfully assimilate within the Israeli state, finding that only a literary testimony can articulate his misnomeric identity.

In another formative incident of the narrator's misnomeric identity, the narrator describes an exchange programme between Palestinian and Jewish schools in Israel, where the narrator is supposed to meet a Jewish child and take him home. The child allotted to the narrator is Nadav Epstein, but a few weeks later, when Nadav is accidentally assigned to another boy, he cries and demands that he be reunited with the narrator, who says 'I was so happy. Nadav felt the same way I did. That Jew really did love me' (*Dancing* 44). As opposed to the stereotypical representation of the Israeli Jew as an object of hatred, the Jew becomes an object of desire, self-fulfilment, and establishing distance from the Palestinian community. The appreciation of the Israeli Jew's love articulates a misnomeric identity that does not seek love or appreciation amongst Palestinians and, in fact, appears as an outlier in the Palestinian collective.

Similarly, in Section Three titled 'I Wanted to Be a Jew', the narrator confesses his delight at having, at least superficially, assimilated in Israeli society when he is transferred to a Jewish-Israeli school on account of his good grades:

> I look more Israeli than the average Israeli. I'm always pleased when Jews tell me this. 'You don't look like an Arab at all,' they say. Some people claim it's a racist thing to say, but I've always taken it as a compliment, a sign of success. That's what I've always wanted to be, after all: a Jew. I've worked hard at it, and I've finally pulled it off.
>
> There was one time when they picked up on the fact that I was an Arab and recognized me. So right after that I became an expert at assuming false identities. It was at the end of my first week of school in Jerusalem. I was on the bus going home to Tira. A soldier got on and told me to get off. I cried like crazy. I'd never felt so humiliated. (*Dancing* 58)

The narrator describes the benchmark of appearances in Israel and implies that he resembles an Ashkenazi or European Jew. He has fashioned his appearance in such a way that he seems unrecognisable and unidentifiable as a Palestinian or an Arab. Contrary to popular imagination, as a Palestinian living in Israel, he takes pride in not looking like a Palestinian. This allows him to escape the routine humiliation of surveillance to which Palestinians are subjected by Israel's aggressive military system and checkpoints. This is by no means a form of simply 'getting by' and routinising the violence experience, but a technique of intelligently evading it and revealing its inanity. Rather than attempting to form a community of or solidarity between Palestinians, the narrator takes pride in blending seamlessly into Israeli society by circumventing its constant surveillance of Palestinians. By 'passing' as Israeli,[2] the narrator challenges the political construction of binaries and animosities between Jewish-Israelis and Palestinian-Israelis, thereby demonstrating the fluidity of a misnomeric identity that resists compartmentalisation.

The process of carving out this misnomeric identity is subject to constant self-editing. Assimilating into a Jewish school is not without its difficulties. The narrator reveals that 'They laughed when I said *bob* music instead of *pop* music. They laughed when I threatened to complain to Principal Binhas – instead of Pinhas' (*Dancing* 59). *Dancing Arabs* is written in Hebrew, and hence one can presume that Kashua's authorial audience is comprised of Hebrew-speaking Jewish- and Palestinian-Israelis. This joke about 'P' and 'B' is, however, a joke about Arabic as the sound 'P' does not exist in Arabic. This joke about the difficulty of assimilating would have been lost on a reader who does not have any knowledge of Arabic, and hence the authorial audience can be extended to Palestinian readers as well. Hence, this is a confessional articulation of misnomeric identity, which constitutes a transcultural audience – a joke is made presuming knowledge of Arabic while bemoaning gauche failures at assimilating into a Hebrew-speaking society. The misnomeric identity forms the core of the nameless narrator's unheroic character as it helps him carve out a survival strategy in a state which discriminates against the Palestinian minority. His confession comes not out of humility, but out of pride at having crafted a fluid identity, even if it is considered unheroic and frowned upon by Palestinians.

However, the misnomeric identity is constantly policed by surveillance structures and practices that seek to undo the fluidity of 'passing'. The narrator describes an encounter when as a teenager he is asked by a Jewish-Israeli soldier to step down from a bus full of Jewish-Israelis at Ben Gurion airport. While he does not specify this as the reason, the reader can gauge that his Palestinian descent is why he was asked to get down. He feels humiliated and cries and rings his father to come and collect him. He says,

> I took that bus line hundreds of times after that. Each time, I'd feel the fear again. It didn't let up until we'd passed the airport. The only time they ever made me get off was on that first trip. After that, they didn't notice me anymore. I felt sorry for the Arabs who were taken off, and I thanked God they hadn't picked on me. (*Dancing* 63)

While the Jewish-Israeli military forces are referred to as 'they', the Palestinians residing or working in Israel are also referred to as 'the Arabs'. The adoption of dominant Israeli terminology for Palestinians reinforces a distance between the narrator and other Palestinians. The narrator does not see himself as a part of an imagined Palestinian collective despite feeling pity for them, because of his misnomeric identity.

Similarly, he describes feeling alienated from the pedagogical project of memorialising Palestine that is executed by schools, syllabi and teachers. In a passage full of comic overtones, he says,

> Once, our history teacher in Tira asked if anyone in the class knew what Palestine was, and nobody did, including me. Then he asked contemptuously if any of us had ever seen a Palestinian, and Mohammed the Fatso, who was afraid of having his knuckles rapped, said he'd once been driving with his father in the dark and they'd seen two Palestinians. (*Dancing* 64)

Following this nadir of historical amnesia, the history teacher whacks all the students with a ruler and exclaims that they are all Palestinians. This creates an effect of bathos, instead of the pathos the reader might have expected given how the Palestinian cause has been historically treated as traumatic and heart-wrenching. Through comedy, the narrator reveals how Palestine may have been constructed as a land that exists in the past and is a source of nostalgia for his father's generation, but for him and his classmates, who do not recognise themselves as Palestinians, it remains an abstract entity. This is perhaps the most unwitting success of Israel's settler-colonial project since it has made Palestine into an abstraction even for Palestinian-Israelis, and yet these people will also never be considered true Israelis as the narrator's father says:

> Once an Arab, always an Arab . . . the Jews can give you the feeling that you're one of them, and you can really like them and think they're the nicest people you've ever known, but sooner or later you realize you don't stand a chance. For them you'll always be an Arab. (*Dancing* 66)

The narrator's misnomeric identity is born out of the difficulties and the systemic racism encountered by Palestinian-Israelis. Not only are they severed from the feeling of a national community, it is also difficult for them to articulate their alienation from the Palestinian community and their lack of desire to bridge existing gaps between geographically dispersed Palestinians. While the narrator consistently attempts to fashion himself as a Jewish-Israeli and applauds himself for developing a survival mechanism that enables him to escape the routine surveillance experienced by most Palestinians at checkpoints, he acknowledges that this farce is only temporary as true assimilation is impossible. The facade of the possibility of assimilation slips when he confesses his love for Naomi, a student at his Jewish school. Naomi's mother says she did not mind her daughter having an Arab boyfriend in school since it is an enclosed world, but would like their relationship to end after school. Naomi tells him that 'her mother had said she'd rather have a lesbian for a daughter than one who hangs out with Arabs' (Kashua, *Dancing* 80). While her mother says she has no hard feelings towards Arabs, her actions and prejudice prove otherwise – leading the narrator to a suicidal attempt. When he grows up, he enters into a loveless marriage with a Palestinian-Israeli girl named Samia and thinks about leaving Tira, although he is unable to because he feels trapped by his father's memories and hopes. The narrator realises that an Arab will always be an Arab, even if he is nameless and trying to confess an elusive and forward-looking misnomeric identity as a Palestinian-Israeli.

It might appear as though the narrator is trapped in an impasse, but it is not so. The misnomeric identity is generated through apparitional politics, which turn the no person's land inhabited by Palestinian-Israelis into a productive space of critical discourses. Remaining nameless and unidentifiable as either Palestinian or Israeli, the misnomeric identity enables him to reflect on what is considered unheroic through a public confession. Since he jokes that he did not know where Palestine was or who Palestinians were or even what PLO was, he says he only loves Jewish people and feels disgusted by dancing Arabs in bars, and is generally indifferent to the fate of other Palestinians, the narrator is anything but a stereotypical or heroic Palestinian. He creates a space for articulation that exists outside and differentiated from the popular imaginations of heroic martyrdom, nationalism and resistance. By refashioning what is considered unheroic, he provides constructive criticism of the Palestinian project of self-determination, which has been blinded by a unilateral perspective, such as the right of return or the unification of Palestinian Territories, ignoring the daily struggles and alienation encountered by most Palestinians. The nameless narrator's public confession about his misnomeric identity associates him with everything that is considered antithetical or detrimental to the communal project of idolising Palestine, thereby refashioning him as an unheroic Palestinian.

Mocking Israeli and Palestinian Patriarchy: Suad Amiry's *Sharon and My Mother-in-Law*

Suad Amiry compiled her 'personal war diaries' (viii) and emails sent to friends and relatives into a book entitled *Sharon and My Mother-in-Law* (2006). While she was writing 'as a form of therapy . . . to release the tension caused and compounded by Ariel Sharon and my mother-in-law' (Amiry viii), what she has consciously attempted to do through her self-narrative is to learn 'how to step out of the frame and observe the senselessness of the moment . . . observe and recount the absurdity of my life and the lives of others' (xii). Self-narratives produce the lifeworld as an object of critical reflection, and in her memoir, Amiry reflects on her encounters with Israeli but also Palestinian patriarchy.

Amiry describes the discrimination experienced by Palestinians when she is detained at the Tel Aviv airport. A pink slip is inserted into her passport at the security check, which implies that she will be held for further questioning. Amiry is interrogated about the purpose of her stay in London, first by a female and then by a male Israeli security officer. She is told that if she fails to cooperate with the security she could be arrested. Amiry continues to joke in an attempt to antagonise her questioners and shocks them by saying she was dancing in London. Her authorial audience is aware of what she would not tell her questioner: 'I was not in the mood to tell the Israeli security woman that I had been on vacation in Scotland with friends, friends I had not seen since 1983, when I had been working on my thesis at the University of Edinburgh' (*Sharon Mother* 9). When Amiry informs her male Palestinian taxi driver that she is being arrested for saying she was dancing in London, he is aghast. Amiry says, 'It seemed that Ibrahim was even more troubled by my dancing in London than the Israeli security officers' (12), implying that he was perhaps more offended by her dancing than her arrest. His reaction is that of a typical patriarch: for whom arrest is a sign of heroic defiance of settler politics, but dancing, as an act of freedom, is to be frowned upon. Amiry mocks the Israeli security officers and Ibrahim in conversation as 'three anti-dancing men' (12), establishing an intermittent community between Palestinian and Israeli men based on their patriarchal beliefs. Julie Peteet notes that the military occupation on the West Bank has had an impact on the construction of Palestinian femininity. She explains that:

> With the enactment of masculinity challenged daily by an occupation that deprives men of the sources of their gender identity – land and the ability to support and defend their families – women's status as markers of family honor and respectability has been enhanced. A culture of shame and control . . . serves to keep women isolated and vitally aware of the consequences of the minutest aspect of their behavior. ('Subordination of Women' 114)

A Palestinian woman's life in this sense becomes doubly controlled: through the Israeli occupation and through Palestinian patriarchy, and Amiry employs tongue-in-cheek humour to shake the hold these structures attempt to exert over her life. Ironic narration becomes a method of confessing unheroic acts, such as antagonising Palestinian and Jewish-Israeli men, which reveals feelings that would have been impossible to express: that the occupation for Palestinian women is doubly compounded because of the similarity that exists between the Israeli occupation and Palestinian patriarchy and their desire to control the lives of Palestinian women. Amiry's confession to her readers reveals that patriarchy in Palestinian society has been conducive to the Israeli military occupation. Patriarchy and military occupation are two seemingly distinct forms of violence, which work in tandem to subordinate Palestinian women's lives.

The Palestinian nationalist imagination has also exerted pressure over Palestinian women's lives and the decisions they make. Amiry recalls attempting to move to Ramallah in 1984 after her marriage and gain a residency card. As a visitor, she is asked to sign an anti-PLO statement at the bridge to the West Bank. She confesses, 'Oh, how unheroic Palestine and Palestinian lovers can be. Until I wrote down these words, I thought this would remain one of my many undisclosed secrets' (*Sharon Mother* 34). She implies that she signed the anti-PLO statement in order to gain a visitor's permit and live with her husband in the West Bank. Amiry's confession creates the new image of the unheroic Palestinian, like the nameless narrator of *Dancing Arabs*, who has to resort to pragmatism to survive under the occupation. This unheroic pragmatism is irreconcilable with the nationalist idealism, which demands multiple sacrifices from Palestinians. Like Kashua, Amiry refashions unheroic acts as practical, since they create a critical standpoint within the Palestinian project of self-determination that is unreflective of the daily struggles and difficulties encountered by Palestinian women in the Occupied Territories.

Amiry's critical discourse extends to the hierarchisation of lives within Palestine, ordered by a masculine practicality that she seeks to subvert. Amiry comments on the patriarchy of Palestinian men when she takes her female dog Antar to a male Palestinian vet for vaccination against rabies:

> 'Antar is a bitch,' said Dr. Hisham with great disappointment.
> 'You mean she is female,' I tried to correct him.
> 'That's what I meant,' said Dr. Hisham.
> 'So . . . ?' I said in an irritated, high-pitched voice.
> 'Do you really want to waste a thirty-dollar vaccine on a *baladi* bitch?'
> 'I can't believe this, Dr. Hisham,' I said, my anger mounting.
> I kept quiet, amazed at how defending a female dog had aroused in me national, feminist and pro-animal rights emotions. (111)

In Arabic, *baladi* means indigenous as well as vulgar. While the incident is narrated humorously, Amiry expresses her outrage at this dismissive evaluation of female Palestinian lives, irrespective of species, by Palestinian men who do not deem them as worthy. Amiry restrains herself in front of the vet, but vocalises her dissent in the confession to her readers. Her mocking dissent articulates the selfhood of a Palestinian woman living under patriarchy reinforced by military occupation and makes feminist irritation visible to her readers through a literary testimony.

Amiry's 'unheroic' confession privileges the lifeworld and choices of Palestinian women. It creates a space where her existence can be thought of in its quotidian resistance to a Palestinian nationalist or patriarchal imagination as well as the Israeli occupation. Amiry's unheroic acts defy conventional nationalist Palestinian heroism and provide a new space of habitation for women through apparitional politics, so that they can appear outside the conventional rhetoric of Palestinian mothers who need to be worshipped, and Palestinian wives or sisters who need to be saved. Her literary testimony produces a position from which Palestinian women can articulate their independence from Palestinian patriarchy and critique the Israeli military occupation.

Rejecting Palestinian Nationalism: Samir El-Youssef's 'The Day the Beast Got Thirsty'

The predicament of Palestinian refugees in camps in Lebanon is unique because they are refused the right to return by Israel and the right to naturalise by Lebanon. In her ethnographic work carried out in Palestinian refugee camps in Lebanon, Diana Allan states that 'refugees' accounts of everyday survival not only reveal tactical resistance to nationalist orthodoxy but also foreground the economic and existential – as opposed to purely political and cultural – dimensions of their struggle' (2). Palestinian refugees are caught in an endless limbo of time and space. They are trapped between memories of the past and imaginations of the future, the dreams of returning to erstwhile Palestine and the hopes of seeking refuge and starting over in other countries. However, they are denied movement and trapped in the eternally timeless camps, which were meant to be temporary homes but have become permanent settlements for them. To create a new space out of the confines of the refugee camp, Palestinian writers create a literary *polis* to express disillusionment with the nationalist commemorative project as camps were not simply 'mnemonic communities' (Allan 4). This is expressed by the seemingly unheroic narrator Bassem in the 'The Day the Beast Got Thirsty' (2004), which is a part of a collection of fictional stories called *Gaza Blues* that contains the collaboration of the Palestinian writer Samir El-Youssef and the Jewish-Israeli writer Etgar Keret.

'The Day the Beast Got Thirsty' is a self-narrative that breaks the autobiographical pact Lejeune theorises since the name of the author, Samir El-Youssef, is distinct from that of the narrator-protagonist, Bassem. Bassem defies nostalgic and national tradition by saying 'unless I leave the country I shall go mad' (111). The narration occurs in a drug-induced haze, wrought with dark humour and satire. Bassem stands out from conventional Palestinian protagonists because of his disinterest and disaffection from the talks of 'our people . . . our just cause' (117). He mocks the political activism of his friend Ahmed who 'knew from experience that political newsletters and leaflets were rarely read and at best they were used for no better purpose than to wrap falafel sandwiches' (122). His dismissive attitude is reflective of a dissociative gap between political propaganda, media reportage, and the everyday struggles of Palestinians.

In order to escape the drudgery of the camp, Bassem visits a travel agent or a 'fixer' who promises to help him escape to Germany. He thinks to himself, 'I felt he was a crook, nevertheless I handed him my travel document and gave him the money. I wanted to question his promise, but did not have the courage to do so' (112). Bassem tries to ask the agent how he can get a visa to Germany when his passport was not valid there, only to see that the agent has put on a performance of being offended and returning his money. Bassem cajoles the agent because he is amused with his performance, and the agent readily accepts the money again and assures him that he will reach Germany. Bassem is almost masochistic when he says 'I knew he was lying. But I liked listening to liars' (116). One might argue that Bassem could have escaped the agent's deception, but that might provoke the reader to view him as a hero. The narrative paints him as unheroic not because he is incapable of being a hero, but because he rejects the path of heroism since even that leads to a dead end.

Upon realising that his attempt to escape the refugee camp in Lebanon and abandon the Palestinian cause and politics has been thwarted by the travel agent who turned out to be a con, Bassem laughs hysterically as it dawns on him that he will forever be stranded in the camp. Rather than be stereotyped as a hero or a martyr, he confesses 'deep down I knew that the moment I would leave the country I would forget everyone and everything' (157). Defying the conventional image of the Palestinian clutching to memorial landscapes and a sense of a community, Bassem is eager to forget his traumatic life in the camp and has no qualms in admitting that he feels trapped within the community. He cannot escape physically, so he relies on cannabis and medication to enter into a stupor and forget his surroundings.

With no means of escape, Bassem envisions his future in the camp with Dalal, a woman he does not love because 'she looked like a monkey' (132) and only visits for sexual gratification:

> Yes, I thought, we must get married, Dalal and I. We will get married and have ten children, but then they will die, and have their photos as huge posters glued to the walls of the Camp, declaring them as heroic martyrs who have died fighting the Zionist enemy. And Dalal and I would be the proud parents of ten martyrs. After that Israel could invade Lebanon again, destroy the camp and fuck us all up, so we die and get the hell out of this fucking life. (170)

While he feels his future is consigned to the inevitability of the martyr geography as discussed earlier, his confession of unheroic thoughts, feelings and actions creates an apparitional space where a dissenting voice that does not follow the Palestinian national rhetoric can be heard. His literary testimony resists the fact that his or his children's lives would be used to construct the spatial testimony of the *shahid*. For Bassem, living in the camp with other Palestinians is nothing less than his worst nightmare and a death sentence, for he says 'that was exactly what I needed for my life to be a total disaster: to remain in Lebanon and get married to a monkey' (132). Lori Allen asserts that such cynicism expressed after the Second Intifada functions as a 'form of awareness and a motor of action by which subjection and subjectification are consciously resisted' (*Rise and Fall* 16). This seemingly unheroic cynicism can only be expressed as a confession for it is still considered unacceptable in a society where Palestinians can only be fashioned and remembered as either heroes or martyrs. Rather than committing himself to the future of the Palestinian cause, Bassem chooses to abandon it in a manner that would traditionally be considered traitorous and unheroic. However, the reader cannot help but sympathise with Bassem. One must pause at too quickly calling his acts traitorous, for his predicament is reminiscent of the soldiers in Wilfred Owen's 'Dulce et Decorum Est', who realise that there is nothing glorious and heroic about dying in a dehumanised manner. Bassem may be physically alive, but he is almost emotionally dead and incapable of any feeling because of so many traumatic years spent in the camp. His emotional growth has been stunted in the camp, where he wanders in a drug-induced haze from cafes to Dalal's house and back.

The only remote inkling of emotion Bassem displays towards anyone is toward his Iraqi friend and drug peddler, Samir. When he goes missing, Bassem is concerned for him and decides to save him from the men who are after him. However, he checks himself and thinks, 'all of a sudden I noticed I kept saying I must save Salim. Who the hell was I? I asked myself, the Scarlet Pimpernel? The brave knight who saved members of the French nobility from the guillotine of the French Revolution?' (143). He deliberately undercuts any heroic attempt or self-imaging because he is painfully aware that he is trapped in a system that has rendered him powerless. When Bassem learns that Samir has been murdered, he says 'I was not shocked. I didn't feel angry or sad. I just nodded as if Ahmed was merely telling me something trivial, in which I had no interest . . . I simply no longer cared about what had happened to Salim' (149). Bassem's apathy is not just a resignation to fate in the camp, but resistance to grieving and mourning the loss of a life that has become so commonplace in the camp.

Peteet notes that since the First Intifada, the experience of physical violence had become central to the social construction of Palestinian masculinity ('Male Gender' 31). Bassem's public confession of unheroic non-participation in nationalist commemorative practices rejects this construction of Arab masculinity and creates an apparitional space for the visibility of unheroic people. His literary testimony reveals the selfhood of the disillusioned, unheroic Palestinian whose existence is constantly put under erasure not just through the occupation but also Palestinian nationalism.

Conclusion

In public confessions after the Second Intifada, the articulation of an unheroic identity through literary testimony helped further the project of Palestinian self-determination by creating a new kind of unheroic literature that is truly representative of the Palestinian condition. It reveals a distinct self that has been put under erasure through the Israeli occupation on the one hand and resists absorption by a homogenous Palestinian nationalist narrative on the other. Resisting two oppositional yet strangely mirrored regimes has led to the creation of the unheroic protagonist in self-narratives, where the protagonist feels alienated from Palestinian nationalist ideals and does not confront the Israeli occupation with the traditional practice of *sumud*. Each of the texts discussed confesses a difference and distance from the collective imagination of Palestinian unity. In *Dancing Arabs* (2004), the nameless narrator confesses a misnomeric identity, which creates a space for narration between Arabic and Hebrew literature and articulates his refusal to be categorised as purely Israeli or Palestinian. Amiry's unheroic confession in *Sharon and My Mother-in-Law* (2006) creates a space for women testifying under the occupation, which reveals the similarities between Palestinian patriarchy and the Israeli occupation. In 'The Day the Beast Got Thirsty' (2004), Bassem's unheroic confession configures an apparitional space for articulating a refugee's disillusionment with Palestinian nationalism and resistance to being remembered as a nationalist martyr. The clearing of this political space by means of narratives creates the possibility of articulating a unique selfhood and identity that defies heroic stereotypes and is distinct from the Arabic-speaking Palestinian, the patriarchal Palestinian, or the nationalist Palestinian respectively.

The triangulation of patriarchy, nationalism and the occupation are countered through what has been called apparitional politics in this chapter. Apparitional politics executed through literary testimonies in the form of public confessions create a space of visibility, dissent and unheroic humour. This space functions as a literary *polis* where the courage expressed in the narratives helps the articulation and appearance of a new unheroic selfhood that does not fit into existing stereotypes of heroes and martyrs. The literary testimony resists being coded in the spatial testimony of the *shahid* and instead it reveals a new identity by refashioning what is considered 'unheroic' – those who were made invisible or silenced are given a chance to narrate and make their selfhood visible. The narrative form of public confession creates an alternate order of knowledge and a scope for a singular articulation of identity in a plurality, which is distinct from a cohesive imagined collective. The self that is determined is one that confesses its distinctness from and among the rest, and creates the apparitional space for its distinction through the confession.

Notes

1. There are problems inherent in most nomenclature related to Palestinian-Israelis or Palestinians who continue to live in erstwhile Palestine and within contemporary Israeli borders. The phrase 'Palestinian citizens of Israel' seems to acknowledge the legitimacy of the state of Israel and erases the fact that Palestinians are mostly treated as second-class citizens whose rights can be easily revoked. While the hyphenation of 'Palestinian-Israeli' may not be ideal, it relays the complexity of living within a settler state, while grappling with a communal Palestinian identity and the desire of assimilation in a predominantly Israeli society.
2. The theme of 'passing', or questioning the rigidity of identities by adopting an oppositional one, is recurrent in Kashua's literary works. It also features in his work *Second Person Singular*, where Amir Lahab assumes a Jewish identity, speaks in Hebrew, and hides his Arab heritage to climb the social ladder in Israel.

7

DETECTIVES IN BETHLEHEM: CRIME FICTION IN THE OCCUPIED TERRITORIES

Anastasia Valassopoulos

In Stephen Knight's essay 'The Postcolonial Crime Novel', his broad investigation into the contours of the transnational detective novel, he writes that in the context of some national crime fiction, the genre is able to 'combine procedural detection with social issues' (172). Moreover, he argues that 'many recent writers around the world have used the modes of crime fiction to juxtapose crime and investigation and explore abuses, corruption, and imbalances of power both past and present in their own countries' (178). Indeed, he points to the ways in which certain authors who follow this trajectory 'adapt and expand the single inquiry form of disciplinary crime fiction to tell a fuller and more complex story about threats and values' (178).[1] Pearson and Singer argue that recent critical work on crime fiction has 'refocused around fundamentally different arguments about how the genre engages structures of knowledge, especially those "external" to the text' (2). These external worlds can often be very complex and involve navigating multiple and diverse iterations of the law and broad differences in the understanding of justice. As such, it is worth looking closely to see what the genre of crime fiction offers to an evolving geopolitical dynamic such as that found in Israel/Palestine.

Tellingly, recent work in the area seems to acknowledge that crime fiction texts 'dramatize the challenges of formulating a genuinely democratic approach to knowledge-production, justice, and human rights in a transnational and postcolonial world' (Pearson and Singer 3). Knowledge-production, questions of justice and the representation of the question of human rights are all issues engaged with at length in Matt Rees' popular detective novels, the Yussef Mysteries (2007–10), set in the West Bank and Gaza. In many ways, these very issues and concerns structure the development of the novels and provide coordinates that shape the trajectory of the schoolteacher-turned-detective Omar Yussef and his investigations.

It is useful then, at the outset, to read these novels in the context of transnational detective fiction. In practice, this encourages us to consider the genre as one that has 'evolved from seeing transgressions of national and racial boundaries as *preconditions* for crime to seeing them as *keys* to its detection and resolution, especially where such solutions include indictments of broader social and political conditions' (Pearson and Singer 7, my emphasis). To unpack this a little in the context of the Matt Rees novels is crucial. Significantly, the crimes committed and solved in the Yussef Mysteries are not solely the result of the occupation – this is a very important idea that we must entertain. Rather, the crimes committed and the routes to resolving them require a near constant re-evaluation of the role of the occupation and its diverse and divergent consequences. In fact, the crimes themselves reorganise contemporary popular thinking about the dynamics of the occupation and force a consideration of *local* social subtleties. In other words, it is precisely these broader social and political conditions to do with intimate ethnic and confessional affiliation, not to mention economic disparities between the communities of West Bank and Gaza, that are not openly attributable to the occupation, especially in the post-Second Intifada era, which take precedence in the novels.

Working within certain features of the crime novel, namely those that apportion exceptional powers of observation to the detective, Yussef's investigations expose domestic power structures local to Palestinian communities and allow a form of socio-cultural complexity to emerge around what might otherwise appear to be straightforward political contexts. In their work on narrating conflict in the Middle East, Matar and Harb argue for the necessity of recognising various cultural forms as routes to 'rethink[ing] questions of power and knowledge at different levels of societal interaction' (5). Alongside other authors working in the detective genre, Matt Rees has 'broadened the theme or investigation to address issues of community, beliefs and identity constructions across geographic and national boundaries, including gender and race relations' (Matzke and Mühleisen 5). Rather than prioritise dynamics produced at the pressure points of the conflict – military collisions, labour opportunities and land grievances among others (though these *do* form part of the overall landscape) – Rees' detective novels permit an altogether different layer of imaginative detail to emerge. Focusing on rich descriptions of the surroundings and providing opportunities afforded for ad hoc dialogue (all in the interests of fact-finding!) these spaces of Palestine are animated. What we as readers discover along the way is the multifaceted Palestinian experience ranging from the extraordinary reach of the Palestinian diaspora to the lingering effects of the British Mandate on contemporary Palestinian life. Food, drink, weather, architecture, fauna and flora, refugee camps, UN officials and local police are among the abundant features that make up the vibrant backdrop that Yussef must navigate in order to solve local crimes. This chapter engages this landscape in order to understand better the contribution of the detective/crime novel genre to contemporary understandings of the role of popular culture in rendering the Israeli/Palestinian context accessible differently to audiences worldwide.

Matt Rees' *The Bethlehem Murders* (2007; also known as *The Collaborator of Bethlehem*) and *The Saladin Murders* (2008; also known as *A Grave in Gaza*) have been praised for shedding much needed light on conditions in the Palestinian territories and a particularly positive review for *The Observer* by Conal Urquhart of *The Bethlehem Murders* in 2007 praised the novel for providing 'insights into Palestinian society' and allowing readers to experience for themselves the 'real frustrations of Palestinians'. The novels interestingly do not address these frustrations as being *primarily* about the relationship with the Israeli state. Though this is unacceptable to some Middle East analysts, such as Nicholas Blincoe, who have gone as far as accusing Rees of thoroughly 'ignoring the occupation', the books in fact prioritise the *internal* dynamics of the various ethnic and religious groups that work and live in and around Bethlehem and Gaza in particular and the Occupied Territories in general. Although the question of degrees of representation is a contentious issue, it is not wholly accurate to say that the novels ignore the occupation. They do, however, seek to prioritise different local contexts and in certain ways perform a parallel investigation – alongside the main plot – into how power dynamics play out differently across the Occupied Palestinian Territories.

Matt Rees' interest in the region derives from the work he undertook as a Middle East correspondent for large news corporations such as *Newsweek* and *Time* magazine. Both novels discussed here are set in the context of the Second Intifada and are sensitive to the emerging social changes that are being felt and experienced across the communities. These changes include the questioning of the role of the official Palestinian police and judiciary; the emerging presence and power of local interest groups or factions; and the changing role of the UN representatives on the ground. The narratives also, in ways that I shall investigate below, '[transcend], if not [invalidate], national boundaries' (Matzke and Mühleisen 8). This bold move is crucial in the context of Palestine where the very lack of geographical boundaries forms the centre of a national and international political discourse. Matt Rees, however, through his protagonist Omar Yussef, seeks to transcend the debate over unity that threatens to overshadow all others, and in so doing brings other matters, such as local interpretations of the crisis and the effect of these on daily life and social interactions, to the fore.

Omar Yussef: Introducing a Palestinian Sleuth

The Bethlehem Murders opens with a stark reference to unhappy students at the United Nations Relief and Works Agency Girls School (an UNRWA institution). Though seemingly an innocuous enough setting, a UN school in the Occupied Territories, located in the Dehaisha refugee camp just south of Bethlehem, the reference makes visible the proximity of the continuing refugee context to the geographical and historical continuity experienced by Yussef and his family. As a resident of Bethlehem, Yussef retains a sense of belonging and authority that does not map easily to communities that rely on aid conferred by the UN. Yussef himself, we later learn, has been educated at the Collège des Frères, a much more prestigious school in Bethlehem itself. He has a clear sense of his surroundings and walks the streets in relative safety, having learnt how to navigate a variety of both imagined and real dangers, all of which he is very aware of.

Yussef, as an educator who has high hopes for his students, performs a powerful trope of the educated Palestinian – a vision for the UN relief agency in its long and often conflicted attempt to maintain and deliver standards of education across the Occupied Territories (Hanafi *et al.* 2014). The UN itself maintains a central place in the book as an institution that has formal powers to develop and deliver resources and educational programmes. However, Matt Rees' observations go beyond these functional descriptions. The novels reveal the potential of such organisations to influence how we experience the political and social multi-layering of the landscape and inhabit a space that is beholden to a variety of ideological and political discourses. Within the first few pages, Yussef tries to ignore the newly founded faction of the Martyrs Brigade sentries as he walks into the Greek Orthodox Club to meet his Christian friend George Saba for dinner. Recalling the origins of his connection to the Saba family, Yussef notes that,

> At that time, there was nothing strange or blameworthy in a close acquaintance between a Roman Catholic priest from the patriarchate near the Jaffa Gate in Jerusalem and the Muslim mukhtar of a village surrounded by olive groves south of the city. By the time Omar Yussef gave the Bible to George Saba, Muslims and Christians *lived more separately, and a little hatefully*. (*Bethlehem* ch. 1, my emphasis)

Rather than rehearse the now familiar hostility between the Israeli Jewish population and the various Arab Palestinian groups, Rees is keen to extend the remit of animosity to the various religious communities that are still forced to share the same space. Here, it is as though the greater socio-historical changes that have affected the population as a whole has had a particular impact between existing relations. Reflecting on the extent to which the Christians living in Bethlehem no longer feel entirely in unquestioned solidarity with the majority Arab population, Yussef recalls that,

> The Christians of George's village, Beit Jala, had followed an early set of emigrants to Chile and built a large community. The comfort in which their relatives in Santiago lived, worshipping as part of the majority religion, was an ever-increasing draw to those left behind, sensing the growing detestation among Muslims of their faith. (*Bethlehem* ch. 1)

Rees here deftly weaves together a rather less discussed aspect of the voluntary Palestinian exodus to South America, a move that Tahia Abdel Nasser reminds us was a very popular one in the 1920s and 1930s ('Palestine and Latin America' 239). Nasser writes that Chile 'is home to the largest Palestinian diaspora made up of Arab immigrants from Beit Jala and Beit Sahour [and that] Arab-Latin American contact dates back to three waves of migration from the Arab world, largely from the Levant to the Americas in the 19th and early 20th centuries' ('Palestine and Latin America' 240–1). In referencing this detail, George Saba's village, Rees expands our view of this small town, showing it up to be part of a much broader social and political network and also revealing the potentially ever-growing sensitivities along confessional lines. This historical fragment also serves to question the contentious although much idealised concept of an untroubled and unified Palestinian identity – an identity that has been at the core of the struggle for Palestinian self-determination and self-governance.

In this way *The Bethlehem Murders* swiftly expands outwards to enlarge the Occupied Territories, showing them up to be the *starting point* for waves of international migration movements, participating in and helping to shape broader ideological and political discourses around diaspora. This is important as the book progresses and we begin to understand the convoluted relationships that lead to the crimes committed. Yussef can see the value of this enlargement, though he often portrays himself as sometimes being alone in appreciating it. In his frustration with the school children who seem to parrot their parents' narrow political views, we hear that:

> He tried not to be [frustrated], but he couldn't stand to listen to them when they rolled through the political clichés of the poor, victimized Arab nation, subjugated by everyone from the Crusaders and the Mongols to the Turks and the British, all the way to the intifada. It wasn't wrong to see the Arabs as victims of a harsh history, but it was a mistake to assume that they bore no responsibility for their own suffering. (*Bethlehem* ch. 2)

This particular reference to a culture of subjugation frames the long history of the post-*nakba* period as one of suffering and victimhood. This is a view of Palestinian history that has to some degree been naturalised and vehemently opposed in equal measure and one that does not permit much outward-facing engagement. The character of an amateur detective can sense that he can see something that others cannot and what he can see is a society that is closing in on itself. Shocked at the overall promotion of a culture of martyrdom that pervades the children, Yussef ruminates that 'no matter how he tried to liberate the minds of Dehaisha's children, there were always many others working still more diligently to enslave them' (*Bethlehem* ch. 3).

There's No Such Thing as a Good Detective

It is clear then that Omar Yussef is set up as a man who tries to rise above what he sees as the petty politics of the everyday. He seems more aware than others of the cost of infighting that threatens to water down the perception of a more united Palestinian front. And yet, at the same time, he is suspicious of such a thing as a Palestinian common identity that has to act in certain scripted ways. This is structurally important, of course, as it means that no one is above suspicion once Yussef becomes involved in the investigation of a series of murders that take place in Bethlehem and later in Gaza over the course of a few days. Each murder offers the possibility of dissecting another aspect of Arab Palestinian society and this is further nuanced by the attention to both financial and confessional affiliations. The detective, however, is not without his own preconceptions and beliefs and, in the context of the Occupied Territories, these are far from straightforward. As Zi-Ling argues,

> the detective's truth-generating capacity, most often characterized as a process of discovery rather than creation, demands scrutiny given the institutional and class biases he or she is often called upon to serve. Complicity with or resistance to cooptation by authority-bearing agencies is tied to the discursive reduction and eventual transmission of the text. (2)

In our case, Yussef's position as an amateur detective, not affiliated to any formal institution, makes him well placed to survey and critique all he sees. Nevertheless, he is very much bound by his educated, middle-class Muslim but also secular worldview – a particular form of being an Arab Palestinian which seems very much at odds with the communities that surround him. And although Yussef does not seem in thrall or beholden to any particular formal body, such as the police or a political party, he is very much aware of the declining ability of all of these institutions to perform independent and impartial investigations. In fact, it is here that his abilities are most at work – in trying to best understand how formal policing organisations and the Arab

Palestinian judiciary can function in the midst of competing political factions, each with its own security infrastructure, in the context of a higher authority: the Israeli occupation.

These intersecting and often competing policing bodies and their very different operational tactics, strategies and command structures all vary wildly. It is very productive in this context to therefore view the work of the detective as 'gift' rather than 'wage labour' as defined by Zi-Ling in the context of hard-boiled detective fiction (2), in the sense that the detective works to understand these intersections and present them to us and perhaps one or two other deserving characters. Yussef is never in receipt of praise or financial rewards. In this sense, there is no wider audience for his feats and there is no witness to his exertion apart from the reader and an atypical 'Watson' type figure in the form of a friend and former PLO operative turned policeman, Khamis Zeydan. The 'gift' in this sense can be seen as a type of nuance or complexity: a complexity sometimes abandoned in a popular press heavily invested in the possibility of a peace process and often unwilling to examine the conflict as puzzling and intractable. Outside of the immediate requirement to provide explanations or air grievances, the Matt Rees novels can take a step back and delve into lesser-examined social dynamics. These dynamics often momentarily shift the focus from the central motif of the occupation and allow for more sustained, even if fictional, interactions with the diverse affiliations and cross-memberships of seemingly non-aligned groups. Yussef is also not obliged to go along with any party lines and in fact comes across as a small-time troublemaker amongst the more 'radical' parents at the UNRWA school in *The Bethlehem Murders*. When the head of the school and Yussef's boss, Mr Steadman, has a local schools inspector evaluate Yussef's supposed unpopularity with the students, the letters that are read out reveal this tension:

> The government inspector read from a series of letters he claimed parents had written to his department. The letters quoted Omar Yussef criticizing the president and the government, lambasting the Aqsa Martyrs Brigades as gangsters, condemning suicide bombings and talking disrespectfully about the sheikhs in some of the local mosques. (*Bethlehem* ch. 3)

Omar defends himself by telling the inspector that what he wants to do is 'encourage intellectual inquiry' (*Bethlehem* ch. 3) rather than promote unthinking reactivity. Yussef's assessment of the society he lives in as dysfunctional centres around his observations on the dangers of factional loyalty that can lead to lawless gang-like behaviour, the loosening of accountability when power lies with those that have the greatest access to weaponry, and the immeasurable problems that arise out of the seductive qualities of bribery and corruption. The communities, un-tethered to a central political authority and unremittingly aware of the volatile nature of Israeli imposition, reach out for alternative means of cohesion. These means – collaboration with various local factions, coercion and intimidation – all provide different ways of engaging with the consequences of a de-centralised Arab Palestinian jurisdiction split across multiple geographic sites. These elements of distrust and misinformation therefore lend themselves very well to the detective story where the amateur sleuth can raise uncomfortable questions and rely on the reader to recall them. As Cothran and Cannon argue, 'generic structures of detective fiction, especially the potential for widespread deception, place intense demands on memory and metacognition' (3). Moreover, the investigative structure can open up many uncomfortable avenues. The reader then 'does not simply consume a world in which meanings are self-evident and revelatory: he is asked to consider the nature of mystery and crime, language and plot' and the mystery therefore has the capacity to '[assault] and [redefine] the reader's vision of personal and public history, psychology, and ethics' (Cothran and Cannon 4).

The Bethlehem Murders encourages such redefinition in a political context that, however, promotes a public discourse of unity, steadfastness and the dream of a return to a unified and unblemished Palestine. These themes are articulated clearly and Arab Palestinian characters voice controversial viewpoints that may put them at odds with official opinion. Omar Yussef's father, for example, is remembered as a stoic man who, when leaving his village in the year following partition, became a displaced refugee and claimed to be absolutely certain that there would never be a 'return'. This claim of return is one that has doggedly haunted the question of Palestine and remains one of the most sought-after concessions in any future decisions over statehood, and was indeed one of the most important items in the Palestine Charters of 1974 and 1978.[2] Rees here points to the centrality of this belief whilst also imagining its feared impossibility. 'Even as a young boy' Rees writes, 'Omar Yussef knew his father was right' (*Bethlehem* ch. 5).

Omar Yussef is therefore a man able to acknowledge the ambivalence that permeates everyday life in his community: ambivalence over loyalty, authority, history and allegiance in all its forms – to religion, to the relevant faction, to extended family, to village, to political ideology. Omar Yussef alleges that his 'clan', the Sirhan, enjoyed a particular privilege on account of their affiliations to the most powerful factions, Hamas and Fatah. Thus, Yussef is no stranger to the advantages of powerful connections but differentiates this from the temptation to 'see the threat of a Zionist conspiracy everywhere' (*Bethlehem* ch. 5). Cothran and Cannon talk of the detective novel's ability to become involved in 'indicting cultures' and *The Bethlehem Murders* and *The*

Saladin Murders spare no attempt to indict what they see as a fractured Palestinian identity. Writing of the chief of police Khamis Zeydan, an old friend of Yussef's, Rees writes that,

> Khamis Zeydan was an early devotee of Palestinian nationalism. He scorned Omar Yussef's faith that the Arabs would unite and liberate Palestine ... Khamis Zeydan followed the PLO around the Mediterranean from Jordan to Syria, to Lebanon and Tunis. He lost touch with Omar Yussef because of the communication restrictions of the Israelis, and he lost his left hand to a grenade in Beirut. (*Bethlehem* ch. 6)

The differing debates on the best course of action for Palestinian political autonomy play a large part in the tension between the two men as they go about trying to solve the crimes, each in very different ways. Yussef at various turns believes his friend to be a corrupt police officer, perhaps even part of the events that have led to the murders. His divergent political past puts him at odds with Yussef's general moral and ethical framework. Although I would hesitate to call the Yussef mysteries *historical* crime novels, in the sense that Scraggs might call *The Name of the Rose* a historical crime novel, it is, however, possible to understand the mysteries as 'trans-historical' (125) in that the setting of the Occupied Territories can be said to not only have 'certain associations in the popular imagination' (126), but also contains within it multiple divergent and contested histories. The trans-historical nature of the Yussef mysteries, however, mostly require a revisiting of established differences in allegiance to the question of 'Palestine'. In the above example, whatever occurs in the present between Zeydan and Yussef is always already overdetermined by their divergent views and experience over the long history of the struggle for Palestinian self-determination. In *The Saladin Murders* in particular, where we witness a vast array of factions and their leaders embroiled in a complicated historical refashioning of Palestinian heritage, it is sometimes difficult to ascertain what exactly everyone is fighting for.

This fundamental difference in perspective over the past and future of Palestine lead to Yussef's constant questioning of Zeydan's reliability and honesty as a police officer and as a friend. Zeydan's impassioned belief in the potential of radical Palestinian nationalism is at great odds with Yussef's more gentle and hopeful approach. In essence this boils down to Zeydan's willingness in the past to take up arms for the cause of Palestinian self-determination whilst Yussef wishes and has always wished for more diplomatic international, even pan-Arab, interventions. The tragedy of course is that in the present of the novel, neither dream has succeeded. Instead, the Martyrs Brigade in *The Bethlehem Murders* (that we are to read as the Al Aqsa Martyrs Brigade which grew out of the Second Intifada) have full control of Bethlehem and are described as 'thugs', 'running the place as a family racket' (*Bethlehem* ch. 6). Yussef can see the problems with this internal and largely unregulated group dispensing justice as they see fit (to an extent this is reproduced in *The Saladin Murders* with the representation of the so-called Saladin Brigade/s in Gaza). Members of the brigade, in a bid to raise revenue, recruit or convince younger Arab Palestinians[3] to get involved in black market activities – in particular the accruing and selling of arms and ammunition. Internal quarrels are often solved by raising the alarm on so-called 'collaborators', thus ensuring that every and any infraction or disagreement with actions of the brigade is seen as siding with the Israeli state and its army. Yussef sits apart in his insistence on facts, rather than hearsay or simple speculation. He is not, however, actually able to stop anyone from being killed. 'In Palestine,' Zeydan tells him, 'there's no such thing as a good detective' (*Bethlehem* ch. 6). Yussef nevertheless resolutely continues in his attempt to dismantle the confusing and sometimes nonsensical rationales that he is given for certain deaths and pursues a much more patient and thoughtful approach that takes the particular social context into consideration. When meeting with the leaders of the Martyrs Brigade in *The Bethlehem Murders* Yussef describes their ferocious nationalism yet he also takes the time to reflect on the fact that insurgents do not always act in the best interests of their community: a community made up of various constituents, each with its own desires and aspirations.

Our People's Struggle is Run like a Crappy Casino

In the introduction to *The Post-Colonial Detective*, Ed Christian notes that 'post-colonial detectives, approaching crime with a special sensitivity enhanced by their marginalized positions, are especially quick to notice societal contradictions because they have always been exploited by them' (2). Where Christian is drawing attention to the tensions that may be found in cross-cultural relations in more traditional postcolonial contexts, in *The Bethlehem Murders* and *The Saladin Murders* the tensions are intra-cultural but unravel in similar ways. Christian's intriguing understanding of detective novels as often offering up a 'practical anthropology' and a reading of why 'people are as they are and why there are benefits to being that way' (2) frames the layered investigations undertaken by Yussef. Rees' description of the Martyrs Brigades' headquarters as an homage to Palestinian nationalism with 'flags' and 'an official crest' emulating 'the office of a government ministry' allows us to consider the ways in which the different factions articulate their version of struggle and justice (*Bethlehem* ch. 14). George Saba, the accused collaborator in *The Bethlehem Murders*, can sense the power of what he calls 'thugs' (*Bethlehem* ch. 10) and sees the Martyrs Brigade as nothing more than petty criminals: 'The criminals have made themselves the law. They shoot at some soldiers, and it transforms them into the representatives of the national struggle. That makes them unassailable and they can abuse anyone they want' (*Bethlehem* ch. 10). This landscape, of various factions rising to power in the supposed context of the national interest, produces vulnerable subjects open to accusations by powerful, unregulated bodies and institutions that, in the absence of a reliable legal infrastructure, are not beholden to a particular set of binding laws. This disorder evoked by the novel has its roots in the context of the occupation that allows for limited and monitored self-regulation among the Arab Palestinian authorities and its subjects. In this context of limited control, ideology, hearsay, word of mouth, anecdote, paranoia and even ennui might propel and bring about various forms of ruthless injustice, such as the one suffered by Saba and investigated by Yussef.

Zeydan, on the other hand, condemns his society outright for not presenting a consistent and united front with respect to its local and international political position, indulging instead in profit-making and corruption. He notes that 'our people's struggle is run like a crappy casino' (*Bethlehem* ch. 11) and his disgust at how political fragmentation and petty infighting has stymied any potential for a unified vision is an experience that he likens to being 'under sentence of death' (*Bethlehem* ch. 11). Yussef understands where this bitterness comes from and prides himself on keeping 'free of the corroding effect of the historical events through which he had lived' (*Bethlehem* ch. 12). Yet this too is soon revealed as a very difficult personal challenge, one that cannot be upheld at all times. In *The Saladin Murders*, we learn that as a younger man Yussef was '*bullied out of politics by the threat of more time in prison*' and '*chose to live a quiet, easy life for so long, whilst there was death and suffering all around*' (*Saladin* ch. 7, italics in the original). No one, it seems, has not in some way been corroded. Yussef has to contend with a past that included moral compromise yet has to retain some sort of elevated ethical stance in the present. As he surveys and adjudicates on the actions of others who are in turn fighting against more conceptual and material forms of injustice in the form of the occupation, his own questionable choices haunt him.

Helping to investigate the imprisonment of an Arab Palestinian schoolteacher in Gaza by local law enforcers in *The Saladin Murders*, Yussef is confronted by the very crux of local corruption. He wonders whether Gazans, having withstood the worst of the Palestinian struggle have perhaps become vulnerable to a particular kind of organised lawlessness: 'This small strip of land – rather than Bethlehem – seemed to represent the desperate reality of the Palestinians: Gaza bellowed and struggled like an injured donkey, while its rulers played the role of the angry farmer, furiously beating the stricken beast, though they knew it couldn't get up' (*Saladin* ch. 1). Fully aware of the sacrifices that have been made by Gaza over the years, Yussef is still disgusted by what he calls the putrid 'scent of Gaza' (*Saladin* ch.1) as he crosses over the checkpoint. On visiting the house of the arrested man, Yussef notices that the garden wall is 'graffitied with the Palestinian flag and a yellow Dome of the Rock. Spiky barbed-wire curlicues [encircle] the cartoon mosque' (*Saladin* ch. 2). Residents of Gaza do not have easy access to this crucial landmark and so must envision it as art, though their entire struggle is based on maintaining its symbolic powers. This duality makes it difficult for us to imagine Yussef undertaking to investigate *rival* Palestinian security and military intelligence forces in Gaza. Eyad, the imprisoned man, has been arrested after uncovering corrupt activities at the university that he is associated with. The irony that a man is arrested for uncovering corruption linking the university to the police force itself is not lost on Yussef: what Eyad uncovers is that the university is selling degrees to the Preventative Security forces, who have in turn arrested him. Angered at these actions, Eyad involves a human rights organisation that demands answers of the university and the security forces – this action ends in his unfortunate arrest and torture.

The discursive and ideological layering here is crucial for us to unpick as it maps out the relative complexity of seeking out justice in a context where the category of victim and perpetrator is multifaceted. It is difficult, in other words, to expect Yussef to take a stand against all of these various institutions: education, the military, security that seek to instil dignity and continuity in Palestinian society. Although as Evans *et al.* note, 'dissent, marginality and often explicit disagreement are often part and parcel of the make-up of the very best detectives' (3),[4] I was struck by how, in the Israeli/Palestinian context, Yussef's dissent and disagreement make him a very dangerous man as he threatens to undermine rival factions, each with their own differing political objectives. Charles J. Rzepka's basic rules of detective fiction, outlined here below, do not align with Yussef's mode of inquiry as the evidence needs to be politically and socially interpreted before it can be utilised:

> first, that all the evidence necessary to win the game will conform to the requirement of scientific induction; and, second, that all necessary evidence will be presented before the solution is announced. As in any game, it's not just the competitors who must 'play fair', but the official in charge as well. (31)

In the context of the Omar Yussef novels, it is very difficult to distinguish the 'necessary evidence' and thus sometimes impossible to follow logical systems of 'scientific induction'. For example, in *The Bethlehem Murders* we find out that the 'real' criminal and collaborator is none other than the most recent leader of the Martyrs Brigade – Yussef had assumed that it was the previous leader who was the collaborator on the basis of a clue connected to his colloquial name Abu-Walid (father of Walid). To his chagrin, the current leader is *also* known as Abu-Walid as he too has a son named Walid. Matt Rees is here quite cunning to play with the various local details that certainly trip up the reader but also have the capacity to trip up the detective, regardless of his inside knowledge. Yussef's marginal status as the teacher-turned-detective who does not associate with the political endeavours of the Martyrs Brigade and their particular brand of insurrectionist activities (raids, suicide bombings, lynching) blinds him from seeing the members as individuals, themselves reacting to their typologising by Israeli forces as terrorists. Anxious to prove his theory, that the collaborator is a member of the Martyrs Brigade, he pursues the first lead that comes his way and in so doing temporarily gives up on nuance.

In Alina Korn's analysis of criminological literature 'within the context of socio-political changes . . . or the context of conflicts between groups' she argues that what came across most prominently were 'the ways whereby a dominant group [made] political use of legal mechanisms and criminalization in order to control a specific ethnic group or any other national group, thereby enforcing political, social or economic change' (208). The contiguous problem that we see articulated in *The Bethlehem Murders* and *The Saladin Murders* is that there are multiple alternative legal or pseudo-legal mechanisms that are operating below the dominant Israeli one. Within those alternatives, there is an operational structure with subtle hierarchies that needs to be understood in order to be navigated. There is a need for cultural sensitivity in navigating these contentious terrains. In *The Saladin Murders*, Yussef can only travel to Gaza because he is a guest of UNRWA. Top Palestinian officials are given VIP passes by the Israeli government so that they do not need to wait at checkpoints. There are various advantages to being affiliated to the various institutions, be they governmental, or non-governmental that operate in the centre of the conflict. Even Yussef is, on occasion, able to exercise some local currency. When asked to a private meeting with one of the Palestinian Fatah members, Professor Maki, he notes that he

> knew why Maki wanted to split him away from the foreigners. There would be appeals to him in the name of the Palestinian struggle. There might even be a payoff to persuade him to throw the UN men off the scent. Still, Omar Yussef considered that, just as Maki thought he could better persuade his fellow Palestinian alone, he also might be able to manipulate the university president through the subtleties of their native language. 'I would be very happy to come, Abu Nabil.' (*Saladin* ch. 4)

By switching to the colloquial 'Abu Nabil', Yussef shows us that he knows how to play this particular game and he is also keenly aware of the appeal to the broader Palestinian struggle. Though Yussef's oft repeated claims to being immune to these appeals works to make him appear ideologically neutral, he does, however, understand these idealistic aspirations and is often seen to be in sympathy with them. In this sense, it is difficult for Yussef or the reader to be fully cognisant of all of the 'necessary evidence' as the revealing of evidence is, in this case, so intimately tied up with the affective dimension of *loyalty*. Whilst Yussef works to uncover the context of Eyad's imprisonment, the UN officials who escort him on his trip have very different loyalties: to the UN institutions, to general UN policies and to the continuing peace negotiations (*Saladin* ch. 5). In many ways, this position reveals the tactical decisions being made every day in what is seen as a volatile environment. When Yussef asks why the UN cannot unequivocally support Eyad's release, he is told that his captor, the head of Preventive Security is the 'most important contact our diplomats have in the security forces' (*Saladin* ch. 5). When a UN official travelling with Yussef is killed, the non-Arab UN workers decide it is too dangerous to be in Gaza and put Yussef in charge. Yussef, it is clear, acts both from his own marginalised position but also at the volatile interstices of many interested parties. Whilst happy to use his cultural capital to gain access to certain spaces, we are also made aware of the many other socio-political spheres that impact and impinge on his and other Arab Palestinians ability to act as independent agents.

Omar Yussef's relative social and political autonomy allows Rees to do something that is often quite complicated in the context of the fractured and geographically dispersed Occupied Territories: to give a sense of place and community that can act as a foil to the otherwise intensely overdetermined actions of groups affiliated to the various political and ideological factions. In a sense, getting it wrong, or assuming he can outsmart another Palestinian on account of their broad shared understanding of struggle, shows up the shaky ground upon which he often relies. Matt Rees' interest in 'place' makes it possible to imagine alternative points of reference. In their introduction to *Crime Fiction in the City*, Andrew and Phelps ascertain that 'crime narratives ... are not only concerned with the authentic representation of the city and the exposure of its secrets but also with the possibility of reconstructing, remapping and, hence, recreating the city' (3). They go on to argue that:

> One of the most obvious ways in which this re-creation occurs is in the physical remapping of the urban space through the process of cultural tourism ... Privileged in literature, fictional crime is reabsorbed into the mythic identity

of the urban space . . . looking through the detective's eyes, armchair *flânerie* if you will, the reader can safely walk streets that normally they may fear to tread. (3)

This is of particular relevance to the imaginative mapping in the novels of the Al-Aqsa mosque and Temple Mount in the context of the Second Intifada and Israeli declaration of sovereignty over the area. This action, understood in international terms to have been 'inflammatory', was seen as both violent and responsible, in the long term, for more draconian security measures and further infringements on Palestinians' right to mobility and assembly. Cities in particular were seen as targets for these actions. Lori Allen's work on the normalisation of acts of everyday violence on populations and infrastructure in the post-Intifada context 'explores the spatial and social practices by which reorientation and adaptation to violence occurred in the occupied Palestinian territories' ('Getting by' 456). Matt Rees also builds up the cities of Bethlehem and Gaza in order to remap and, by extension, to recreate them as sites of multifaceted social and political struggle. This is a powerful motif in the Omar Yussef novels as the overall effect of a fragmented and territorially disparate nation-in-waiting is often the inability to imagine it in any continuous and functional way. This has the adverse effect of contributing to the vision of the Occupied Territories as chaotic, in crisis, hectic and anarchic (Allen, 'Getting by' 453–60). Although Omar's investigations do often lead him to despair at the disordered and callous behaviour of the political and military groups that claim to represent Palestine, he is, however, sensitive and generous in his observations of the landscape and most of all to its people. He is also very aware of the value of the Holy Land to the international community who valorise its basilicas, churches and holy sites. His walks take him to the holy sites in Bethlehem that he describes in detail and where he maintains good relations with clerics of all faiths, and to the homes of his many friends and acquaintances, all of whom greet him with grace, hospitality and great respect. In Gaza, he is invited to a simple meal by Eyad's wife, who treats him with great kindness and reverence. Homes and streets are described in great detail, as are the ubiquitous checkpoints. We have a sense of distances, and means of transport, of the quality of the apartment blocks, the proximity of neighbours and the complexity of travel. There is also a tactile sense of the weather: rain, dust, heat, and intense cold. These all serve to make more tangible an everyday experience that both responds to but also resists the tendency of the occupation to outmanoeuvre other realities. The cities are alive with their various components and have characteristics that make them memorable and distinct, all articulated by an observant Yussef who walks when he can and recreates the old town of Bethlehem and the intensely surveyed Gaza. In Gaza nobody else seems to walk and the UN personnel use huge Suburbans[5] to drive around between meetings. By comparison, Yussef is sensitive to his environment and this helps him better see facts on the ground. The novels incorporate this version of *flânerie* and celebrate its capacity for inclusion.

Rees is also attentive to what Rodgers and O'Neill have called 'infrastructural violence' and which Hanna Bauman, in her article on the Israel/Palestine context in particular, notes is in evidence when structures on which communities depend break down, or are made dysfunctional. In a moving scene, halfway through *The Bethlehem Murders*, an Israeli digger works to burst a main sewage pipe right outside Yussef's home. Unsure what the purpose of this is, other than to cause deep disruption, the pipe eventually spills its contents into Omar Yussef's basement where his son's family live. Bauman describes these 'metabolic' circulations as 'water, sewage and waste', and notes that the curtailment of these services has the capacity to not only '[compound] the sense of exclusion . . . but carries with it the sense of stigma' (145) The inability to access basic municipal services often reduces individuals' and communities' access to washing and laundry facilities (145). However, what happens in this scene is that the neighbours come in to help Yussef and his family and they 'scoured the tiles until the stink of effluent receded' (Rees, *Bethlehem* ch. 18). Bauman argues for the ways in which 'infrastructural warfare also entails the dehumanisation of its targets' (148). Again, what we witness in the novel is the redoubling of Yussef and his neighbours' efforts to work against this dehumanisation and return to what was there before in the full realisation that 'the reek would remain in his nostrils' (*Bethlehem* ch. 17) and the incursion would inevitably re-occur.

As important as these daily acts of mobilisation and struggle might be and as crucial as they remain for an active and engaging resistance to the Israeli occupation, Matt Rees made clear in an interview for *Publishers Weekly* that he

> wanted the characters [in the novel] to represent the Palestinians [he'd] known who stood up against the corrupt politics of their leaders and the gun law in their town. Their struggle wasn't linked to the Israeli-Palestinian conflict and all the clichés that go along with writing about it. It was about having the integrity to think independently at a time when your society is wrapped up in war fever. (Freisinger 237)

Though it is true that in reading Rees' detective fiction we are aided in the navigation of clichés and led to conclusions that surprise us, it would be inaccurate to say that Rees stays clear of the conflict. Rather, he chooses to view it as part of the broader landscape within which more minor though no less significant incursions are at work. It is here that the detective can be most useful, helping us detect the divergent and often subtle socio-political dimensions of contemporary Palestinian society.

Notes

1. I find Knight's discussion on novels dealing with Mafia corruption and the Italian state most aligned with my observations on the Matt Rees novels. Most notably, the issue of dealing with structures that function as mini states within larger state institutions (such as the Martyrs Brigade in *The Bethlehem Murders* or the two iterations of the Saladin Brigades in *The Saladin Murders*) blur the boundaries of who is actually in charge (the Palestinian Authority, the Revolutionary Council, the UN, the Israeli armed forces?).
2. It is perhaps relevant to note that this has been excluded from the more recent Israel–Palestine peace plan unveiled by the US government on Tuesday, 28 January 2020.
3. In this essay I use the term 'Arab Palestinians' to differentiate Palestinians who live in the West Bank and Gaza from 'Israeli Palestinians'.
4. Although Evans *et al.* are predominantly interested in post-1970s European detective fiction, this comment struck me as highly relevant to the Omar Yussef novels, not least because he has to overcome so many seductive national narratives that make up who he is and where he belongs. Having to go against these in the interests of a vague conceptual understanding of justice requires him to often stand alone in his persistence.
5. The Chevy Suburbans are large SUVs used by UN personnel in the Gaza Strip.

8

REFRAMING OCCUPATION AFTER THE SECOND INTIFADA: DRAWING FROM EXPERIENCE IN FRANCOPHONE GRAPHIC NOVELS

Lowry Martin

This chapter examines Francophone representations of the Israeli–Palestinian conflict as it spills over into the twenty-first century. As the European country with the largest Jewish and Arabic-speaking Muslim populations, France is uniquely situated as an observer of these disparate and often competing cultures not only because of its current demographics but also because of its colonial history in the Maghreb and the Levant. French cultural production about and around this continuing geopolitical crisis is particularly relevant in our global conversation about this conflict, because France remains a primary diplomatic force for both Israelis and Palestinians: it was one of the first nations to recognise the state of Israel and also to advocate for the creation of a Palestinian State.[1] While Belgium does not share France's colonial history in the Middle East and North Africa, it does have one of Europe's largest Jewish communities and the economic and diplomatic ties between Israel and Belgium continue to grow stronger, as evidenced by the billions of dollars in trade between the two countries. Like France, Belgium has been committed to Israel's withdrawal from the Occupied Territories and to the Palestinians' rights of self-determination for decades. Belgium's foreign policy can be best described as one of 'ethical diplomacy' or 'equidistance' during the early 2000s, which aimed at treating all parties equally and allowing the EU to play its mediating role (Herremans 81). It is within this foreign policy context that I analyse a European Francophone cultural response to Israeli–Palestinian relations after the Second Intifada through two graphic novels: *Faire le Mur* (a play on words that can alternately mean *Build the Wall*,

Go Over the Wall, or *Sneak Out*) by Maximilien Le Roy from France and *Les Amandes vertes: Lettres de Palestine* (*Green Almonds: Letters from Palestine*) by Anaële and Délphine Hermans from Belgium.

The graphic narrative seems particularly appropriate for historical representations of the ongoing geopolitical struggles between Israel and Palestine because such a narrative spatially juxtaposes 'past, present, and future moments on the page' (Chute 453). Much in the same way that Art Spiegelman's enunciation of history in his *Maus* series weaves through 'paradoxical spaces and shifting temporalities', namely the reliance on space to illustrate time – these French-language graphic narratives and novels incorporate an array of modalities (Chute 456). They are narratives in which the reader must fill in the gaps in meaning for a 'reconstitution on the part of the spectator' that is driven by the complex play of sequentiality such as in the use of photographs (Groensteen 10). Indeed, graphic novels can reflect the difficulties of historical interpretation in that they are often open texts dependent on a constellation of signs, words, aporias and silences, that must be interpreted to make meaning. In graphic novels '[E]ach panel, with its combination of words and images, is embedded in a network of relationships with other panels and media within and beyond the comic book' (M. Ahmed 4). Because graphic novels are 'syntactic-semantico-pragmatic' devices where the 'foreseen interpretation is part of a generative process', readers interpret and create meaning (Fresnault-Deruelle 49) based, in part, on construing meaning through both the collective imagination and one's personal imagination. Thus, graphic novels can require the reader to consider, evaluate and create meaning not only in each panel but between gutters, temporal disjunctions, the ambiguity of signs and sometimes even different media components.

Graphic novelists such as Maximilien Le Roy include photographs, photo albums and interviews as part of their work and these various forms of storytelling form a narrative mosaic that highlights the complexity of representing this geopolitical conflict. The Israeli–Palestinian conflict is often primarily understood through dominant media discourses and images crystalised in sound bites and video clips. The authors' use of personal anecdotes, experiences, photos, and individualised perspectives foreground the multiple layers of history that challenge a meta-narrative. These elements illustrate the voluminous types of evidence, witnessing, 'facts' and viewpoints that create a dominant but unstable historiography. The juxtaposition of the artist's illustrations with actual photos heightens the documentary dimension of this work and its attempt to portray 'reality'. Two of the graphic novels that I discuss, *Les Amandes vertes: Lettres de Palestine* and *Faire le Mur*, written in the first person, create an intimate documentary style not only to convince the reader of the works' authenticity and truth value but also to evoke a sympathetic reader response.[2] The use of these different types of modalities to retell a history creates a more permeable and multi-faceted text that blurs the lines between aesthetics and documentary, and recasts the on-going conflict as a humanitarian crisis perpetuated by discourses around state security and terrorism.

Contrary to what one might assume, these graphic novels do not focus exclusively on the trauma and victimhood of the Palestinians, but they also engage with the human cost of the occupation to Israelis, although Le Roy's work does so to a lesser extent. Ultimately, I argue that the graphic novel has been and remains, especially effective in recounting the trauma of Israeli occupation for both Israelis and Palestinians as it demands that the spectator synthesise an insistent, emotional and compelling visualisation of history with the written accounts of the protagonists. If history, like memory, is a series of snapshots, then the graphic novel's isolated frames, each with their own story, require the spectator to connect them. I argue that these visual/discursive accounts of Israeli-Palestinian life after the Second Intifada not only contribute to our understanding of decades-old tensions but they may also be one of the most effective and subversive forms of representation of 'life on the ground' after the Palestinian uprising that began in September 2000 precisely because one must see the occupation as one reads about it. These visual representations of the conflict combined with the written word can challenge a reader to rethink her or his viewpoint in ways that a written description cannot.

This chapter examines specifically two books by Francophone authors Maximilien Le Roy and Anaële and Délphine Hermans, whose works are more personal than other French-language graphic novels that have attempted to represent Israeli-Palestinian political life after 2005.[3] Le Roy and Anaële personally know the protagonists about whom they write and have lived the experiences about which they write or have interviewed the Palestinian protagonists.[4] Maximilien Le Roy's work has consistently dealt with social issues, and his works bear witness to the lives of the marginalised, from that of a homeless Franco-Maghrebi man in Lyon to hardships of life in Gaza. A significant percentage of his literary corpus has been dedicated to chronicling Palestinian life. He has devoted a large amount of his creative energies to drawing attention to this conflict. Anaële Hermans is a Belgian writer whose works often examine social issues of immigration, marginalisation and social justice. Le Roy's and the Hermans's reliance on personal narratives function not only to personalise Palestine (Thon 72–3), the 'I' and 'We' narrative positions also draw the reader into the actual lives of the protagonists. These narrative positions function as types of witnessing that allow the reader to learn of horrors, process them, and to see them, which removes a historical blind spot that might allow other atrocities, genocides and inhumanities to occur in the future. Nevertheless, the two graphic novels create their intimate reader identification a bit differently. Le Roy's graphic novel *Faire le Mur* conveys his criticism of Israeli occupation of the West Bank through the first-person narration of Mahmoud, a Palestinian who has suffered various humiliations and traumas under Israeli occupation – reminiscent of Joe Sacco's ground-breaking work *Palestine* published as a book in 2001. *Les Amandes vertes* relies on an epistolary structure to create an intimate realism through the sisters' correspondence with each other. Both graphic novels are more aligned with typical Hebrew-language Israeli graphic novels in that they do not rely on 'alternate realities and parallel dimensions to challenge accepted notions regarding existence and human conditions' (Berenstein 142). Thus, the Francophone graphic novels examined are similar to Palestinian and Israeli graphic novels in their realism, but work strategically to offer counter-Zionist perspectives through narratives focused on Palestinian daily life. This focus is in contrast to the works of the most visible Palestinian graphic novelist, Samir Harb, who examines and critiques the political divisions within Palestine rather than Israeli actions and policies.

Relying on scholars such as Wendy Brown and Eyal Weizman and using literary and visual theory, I argue that these Francophone authors' works differ from many Israeli graphic novels and comics examining Israeli–Palestinian relations after the Second Intifada, particularly those graphic novels with superheroes such as *Profile 107* and *Azure Giants* (Berenstein 142–3). While graphic novels increasingly pose complex narratological problems in determining extradiegetic and intradiegetic narrators, these narratives represent the lived experiences of the authors under Israeli occupation and/or their relationships with Palestinians in these lands. Thus, their status as European 'outsiders' underpins their discursive and graphic storytelling with an intimate experiential authority that lends credence to issues central to their stories, such as land grabs, loss of human capital, terrorism. As Westerners, one of the most interesting aspects of their works is the ways in which they invert dominant Western discourses on terrorism by reorienting the reader's perspective to ask what constitutes terrorism. By focusing on the lived experiences of Palestinians as well as their own experiences, the authors illustrate that terrorism is not a fixed signifier but is often a matter of perspective and context. For instance, an Israeli governmental policy of house demolition without due process or meaningful recourse to a fair and impartial legal system might be considered terrorism in other contexts.

Rebranding Terrorism: Drawing Difference and Division

Early in *Faire le Mur* Mahmoud offers a long meditation on terrorism through a discussion of the wall and how one's socio-political positioning within a specific cultural context gives meaning to the term terrorist. Which side of the wall one resides on literally determines how one is defined within one's social group and from outside that group. Le Roy's frames focus not only on the construction of the wall but also its incessant invasive surveillance. For instance, the reader is confronted with a desolate sepia-coloured rendering of a watchtower and radar with the Israeli flag prominently displayed. The accompanying legend states 'the magic of propaganda: it passes off a large process of annexation as a security barrier' (*Faire le Mur* 25), which gestures to increasing governmental invasion into private lives in the name of state security – yet it also illustrates the ultimate failure of such walls as protection.[5] As Wendy Brown has noted,

> It is too simple, for example, to say that the Israeli wall connotes protection and security to one side and aggression, violation and domination to the other. While the wall may comport with an entitlement to safety in a Jewish homeland felt by some Israeli Jews, it carries for others the shame and violence of occupation. (88)

These two graphic novels vividly portray how very different one's phenomenological experiences are on the two sides of the wall.

Le Roy carefully scaffolds a counter-argument about Israeli security and terrorism through several diegetic components. The first comes in two short pages with fourteen mostly small frames portraying the murder of Mahmoud's cousin as the two are walking through their refugee camp. Drawn in stark black and white images, the first frame shows the entrance to their camp with two horizontal frames placed next to it: in the upper frame is Mahmoud and his cousin waving goodbye in the street and directly beneath it is a frame with two Israeli snipers, one of whom is aiming through a window. The rest of the page consists of four side-by-side panels: a close up of a hand pulling a trigger; the impact of the bullet; Mahmoud's startled look towards the sound; and his fallen cousin who had just told Mahmoud that he wanted to get engaged after the Second Intifada. The layout of these frames reminds one of cinema as they both illustrate the dissociative nature of the violent act through distance as well as the horrifying trauma of a reality too emotionally overwhelming to process. A few pages later Le Roy returns to the sepia tones of faded photographs as he recalls how a meeting with his French girlfriend provided a welcomed distraction from the daily threat of Israeli violence against Palestinians. The temporal and thematic shifts underscore violence and death as commonplace in the Palestinian experience: traumatic events so routine that their consequences are not elaborated.

After the unexplained assassination of Mahmoud's cousin, the protagonist clandestinely crosses into Israel through an opening in the chain-linked fence (which delineated Israel from Palestine while the wall was being built) to meet his French girlfriend, Audrey. Mahmoud makes his way to his sister's house in Beersheba where their rendezvous will occur. While Mahmoud is eating dinner, a television broadcast relates that a Palestinian man who had driven a bulldozer into a crowd near Jerusalem's King David Hotel sowing panic and wounding people was killed by Israeli security forces. The interjection of a terrorist attack as Mahmoud's family gathers around the dining room table underscores the daily violence as part of their lived experience. The narrator's enunciation of the event is through a frame showing the television announcer covering the incident followed by images of Mahmoud's smiling family seated around the dinner table. Le Roy's focus on the family having dinner subtly highlights several things: the banality of terrorism – a certain desensitisation after decades of violence; the family as a primary organising principle of a diasporic Palestinian life outside of the West Bank and Gaza; the consequences of the protracted conflict on Palestinian and Israelis within Israel; and the centrality of the media in perpetuating and circulating acceptable tropes of terrorism.

In confronting the reader with the ambiguity of terrorism as a one-sided relationship that most often posits Israelis as victims and Palestinians as aggressors, the reader learns that from age fourteen Mahmoud worked as an agricultural day labourer for six years in Israel. Although he was part of a systematic use of human capital utilised for the construction of the modern Israeli state, he remembers this time as a period of slow rapprochement characterised by interaction and familiarisation with Israelis, which humanised them in his eyes. Mahmoud could no longer conceive of Israelis as just an abstract polity personified by occupying soldiers. He learned Hebrew, saved money and became more familiar with Israeli culture. He casts his time in Israel as a period that allowed him to 'break the logic of separation established in this land' and to see the commonalities between Israeli Jews and Palestinian Arabs (*Faire le Mur* 60–1). Surprisingly, his time in Israel did not further convince him of the possibility of a peaceful two state coexistence but rather it diminished his national aspirations. Mahmoud believed that the way to peace was a single state where Muslims, Jews, Christians and atheists could live in equality before the law. The fragility of this nascent sense of political possibility, of this new sense of 'us/we' is abruptly shattered when Mahmoud says: 'The years spent fashioning this new "us" crumbled one fine morning' (*Faire le Mur* 61).

Subsequently, in *Faire le Mur* the sepia tones change to stark white frames dominated by bold red, yellows and oranges, Mahmoud relives how, after saving his money for six years, he had bought sheep, poultry and pure-bred dogs to keep on his father's land. His dream was of a rural life with his livestock, which would have increased his financial independence and economic prosperity. One morning Israeli soldiers arrived and demanded that Mahmoud and his father follow them to a post for a 'simple formality' (*Faire le Mur* 63). Despite their protests, they were hauled off to an Israeli military post and kept for over an hour. Upon their return, a bulldozer was pushing their home into a river, the sheep had been shot, his chickens gassed and three of his dogs killed – except for his Doberman that he 'had treated like a son' (*Faire le Mur* 62). The novel provides no pretence of legal justification, but instead it seeks to rehearse the ongoing confiscation of Palestinian lands and material goods through various 'legal' and extra-judicial strategies. The previously mentioned words and images deliver a psychic gut-punch that any reader can understand: what it must be like to leave one's home at the occupying state's insistence only to return to discover that one has literally lost everything. If terrorism is generally defined in the West as the 'unlawful use of violence and intimidation, especially against civilians, in the pursuit of political aims', then Le Roy asks the reader how anyone can interpret these actions as anything other than terrorism (United States Congress 18).

Les Amandes vertes and Epistolary Strategies

Les Amandes vertes follows a similar strategy of humanisation and familiarisation through narration, but its diegetic content does not rely on an overt questioning of the political taxonomies of terrorism. Moreover, the graphic novel's panels work in a linear fashion (the most common of story-telling devices) to engage its audience rather than disruptive flashbacks sequences as in Le Roy's *Faire le Mur*. Contrary to *Faire le Mur*, which is a pseudo-memoir told by Mahmoud, *Les Amandes vertes* is an epistolary graphic novel that relates Anaële's (Nan's) experience in Palestine through her correspondence with her sister, Délphine, during her ten-month stay. In *Les Amandes vertes* Anaële introduces the reader to various Palestinians and their quotidian life from her departure from Liège to Israel, life in the West Bank and its hardships, traumas and human rights abuses. Weaving her impressions, experiences and relationships into a narrative that describes confronting Israeli settlers taking Palestinian land, Palestinians' despair at lack of economic and intellectual opportunities, fearful border crossings, and the precariousness of life, she creates a compelling perspective that also describes Israeli–Palestinian collaboration, dialogues and outreach. Le Roy adopts a broader and diverse strategy to draw the reader into the identificatory process, which requires a very different type of reading practice. For instance, Le Roy discusses for several pages how violence can be legitimised in the name of freedom, whether that violence is the French Resistance in World War II or the United States' illegal bombings of Cambodia. His examples underscore the fluidity of overdetermined terms such as terrorism that are defined by dominant transnational discourses. Much like Joe Sacco's *Palestine*, Le Roy uses gutter-closure, non-sequitur frames that create closure by requiring the reader to interpret and fill in the blanks – 'a largely unconsciously fill-in-the-blank process of making-meaning between reader and the context' (McCloud 67), which move the reader through temporal and spatial shifts that disrupt the linearity of the narrative.

Faire le Mur uses news media such as photo-journalism and personal photos to jolt readers into the consideration of their own complicity in circuits of readership or a spectatorship that underscores the multiple layers of meaning, witnessing and intercontextuality (similar traumas resulting from shared historical events) and to disrupt any sense of safety the reader/spectator may feel while being 'on tour' of Palestine. These visual elements erode the distance between the safety of literary/visual consumption and the dangers, poverty and trauma of living in Palestine. *Les Amandes vertes* avoids these larger theoretical stakes by simply relating Nan's experiences in Palestine and those of the people with whom she comes in contact without drawing on broader historical or political contexts (Brister and Walzer 142). The long shadow of Israeli security barriers becomes not only the book's leitmotif but it also informs the protagonist's entire year in the Middle East. Out of approximately 509 panels almost 10 per cent include representations of the wall or surveillance, but the Hermans's work still remains resolutely simplistic or 'naïve' in its structure – even eschewing page numbers. Beginning with the book's cover that depicts Nan walking in the shadow of the wall or crossing back into Israel for her return trip home to Liège, her phenomenological experience of the Middle East is determined by borders and walls – whether it is crossing through Israeli security checkpoints or visiting the ancient town of Qalqilya now walled on all sides except the east. Unlike many Israeli graphic novels such as *Revolt* by Moshik Gulst that promote 'institutional socialization' within an alternative reality framework where historical developments within the text diverge from actual history, these French works are planted firmly in the reality of lived experience, which is the cornerstone of their narrative strategy (Berenstein 142).[6]

The Hermans write in the introduction that 'this book offers a personal look at a complex reality through the prism of an intimate exchange' (1). Unlike *Faire le Mur*, the simplicity of their book's black-and-white illustrations, its primitive figuration and its familiar language create a narrative that feels innocent, intimate and unvarnished. While Le Roy uses numerous graphic techniques in colour, detail and form, *Les Amandes vertes* never deviates from its black-and-white primitive drawings that also recall the epistolary framework: Délphine's interventions are always framed as postcards, while Anaële's experiences are sequential frames. Délphine's postcards are adorned with images of Western Europe and its natural beauty. They remind Nan of works of art, architectural wonders, forests, mountains and freedom of movement. Each postcard from Délphine serves as the gateway to Anaële's anecdotal analysis of life in Palestine after the Second Intifada, which primarily constructs a cartography of confinement – even the book's cover is dominated by the Israeli wall that demarcates the West Bank. While many of Delphine's postcards depict some form of movement from bicycling to river rides to wide open spaces, they serve to remind the reader of the freedom of movement enjoyed not only within Belgium but within the European Union, which stands in stark contrast to the restraints on Palestinians' movement. Most of Nan's narrative relates her travels in Palestine from Bethlehem to Hebron and refugee camps in between, to Tel Aviv and Jerusalem, and the continued establishment of Jewish settlements. Among the most preponderant themes of the Hermans's book are random violence, dislocation and surveillance; yet, among these oppressive tropes are scenes of joy, hope and different forms of outreach between Israelis and Palestinians that might foster understanding, trust and reconciliation.

The narrative moves quickly from Nan's encounter with Israeli security at Ben Gurion airport to settling into her room and her meeting with a Palestinian youth named Mousa. Nan meets him in Beit Umar where she learns that a few weeks prior to her arrival an Israeli raid ('*descente*') had taken place. Curious to know what was happening, Mousa and his friends climbed to his rooftop at which point an Israeli bullet that hit a stone wall sent pieces of it into his brow. The Palestinian doctors did not have the medical supplies to remove all of the pieces, so Mousa lived with the pain of the shrapnel. Rather than allowing resentment or hatred to fester as his injury does, he tells Nan that he dreams of building a youth centre for peace.[7] Thus, *Les Amandes vertes*, like *Faire le Mur*, also uses the personal story of a Palestinian wounded by Israelis to open up a narrative space of reconciliation and hope in the face of abusive and brutal power, and this strategy resonates with Le Roy's inclusion of the Israeli sniper's apparently gratuitous murder of

Mahmoud's cousin. The authors include other moments of random violence to question the dominant binary of victim (Israeli)/aggressor (Palestinian), with stories of a Palestinian boy shot and killed as he ran for a loose soccer ball or Mahmoud's mistreatment when Israeli Defense Forces catch him re-entering Palestinian territory through a breach.

The randomness of violence underpins the narrative, whether through state-sanctioned security checkpoints that authorise body searches of tourists or military incursions. *Les Amandes vertes* is particularly sympathetic to Palestinians but fails to engage with any Palestinian violence beyond rock throwing. This elision may not be as susceptible to accusations of bias or intellectual dishonesty as one might think, when one considers that Nan works in the world of non-profits committed to education, reconciliation – organisations that may be less radical in their methods of opposition to Israeli occupation and policies. The portrayal of daily possibilities of verbal and physical violence, torture and even death are narrative strategies that the authors deploy to deconstruct Western ideas about terrorism and terrorists, but they expand the discussion of violence as a form of terrorism in their exploration of the Israeli occupation's damage to the Palestinian polity.

Labour and Human Capital

After the 1967 annexation of Palestinian lands, Israeli and Palestinian economies became even further integrated and this has been especially true in the labour market (Bulmer 657). It is important to remember that until the late 1980s Palestinians moved relatively freely between the Occupied Territories and Israel earning their livelihood and it was not until 1991 that Israel introduced permit requirements for Palestinians to work in Israel. The imposition of stringent work permits on Palestinian workers had a marked impact on the Palestinian economy, which at one point, saw about 30 per cent of its workforce employed in Israel (Bulmer 657). *Faire le Mur* interweaves the importance of Palestinian labour in Israel's nation building through Mahmoud's recounting of his time as an agricultural labourer in Israel. His story is both compelling and hopeful as he recounts the importance of cultural confrontation, linguistic acquisition and access and social interaction. His memories of working in Israel remind the reader that these so-called 'terrorists' have played an integral role in the economic success of Israel in construction, agriculture and other areas. *Faire le Mur*'s detailing of Mahmoud's loss of property, that is his livelihood, gestures to several things: abusive Israeli power; systematic and wilful impoverishment of Palestinians; ensuing *désœuvrement* (idleness) and the ways that the continuing socio-economic crisis continues to feed cycles of violence.[8]

On the other hand, *Les Amandes vertes* presents a different view of dealing with loss. When Nan's charity offers its space for women to commemorate and discuss their losses after Land Day, a commemoration of Palestinian resistance to Israel's attempts to expropriate thousands of donums of Palestinian land in 1976 and during which six Palestinian Israelis were killed, Anaële recounts how different women relate not only their personal losses but those of family and friends. In four pages with thirteen frames, Nan describes the testimonies of these women. In one long horizontal frame that runs the length of the page and dominates it, one participant in a group of women tells of her cousin that lived in an Arab village in Israel in which the inhabitants had their farmland taken away, which forced them to find alternative sources of income. Moreover, she adds that Israeli law forbade the renovation of their homes – even driving in a nail.[9] The result was a forced decay and abandonment of property. Another woman speaks of losing her olive orchard when the wall was built. The following frame covers three quarters of the next page with a series of houses completely overshadowed by the wall with the caption 'and I don't see the sun rise anymore' (*Les Amandes vertes* 17). Another powerful example of the continued forced Palestinian diaspora is Nan's visit to Jerusalem with a Palestinian architect, Ibrahim, who knows Jerusalem 'like the back of his hand' (*Les Amandes vertes* 108). In the frame he points out a house to Nan stating that two months earlier it had belonged to a Palestinian family. The first frame on the following page is a small rectangular with nothing but the Israeli flag planted on a rooftop with the words, 'Here, we are no longer in a game of Stratego, but of Risk' (*Les Amandes vertes* 108–9). Directly underneath is another simple frame devoid of details with nothing but Ibrahim and Nan's faces: Nan states 'and once again I have the impression that the game is already lost' (*Les Amandes vertes* 109). Her observation is punctuated by a long horizontal frame that runs alongside the two previous frames with a long view of a street on which all of the houses have Israeli flags and the statement that each new power struggle for a house ends with the same victory.

Le Roy and the Hermans use their voices and images to emphasise the suffocating reduction of Palestinian lands by the Israeli government in the name of security while gesturing to a much larger strategy of economic, cultural and physical subjugation. As Eyal Weizman states in *Hollow Land*, the security wall and its concomitant accessories are 'dressed up as a formula for peaceful settlement', but the fragmentation of these lands has led to 'unilaterally imposed domination, oppression' of the Palestinian people and their property (10–11). As in the architecture of South African apartheid, the separation between Israelis and Palestinians in the Occupied Territories is not only geographic partition, but it is also the systematic lack of access to a cultural heritage, diminished educational opportunities, decimated younger generations and bifurcated, dissected and strangled cities.

In addition to the elasticity of borders and the continued disintegration of Palestinian territorial integrity, the authors of *Les Amandes vertes* address the issue of diminished cultural and human capital. As the reader journeys with Nan through Israel and the Occupied Territories, she reiterates what numerous scholars have asserted: that Palestinians have been displaced and/or cut off from their cultural heritage. Specific images are framed throughout *Les Amandes vertes* that depict Israeli cultural appropriation of a commonly shared historical patrimony. From Rachel's Tomb to access to the Tombs of the Patriarchs in Hebron, Nan's peregrinations evidence Israel's strategy of a forced cultural impoverishment that distances Palestinians from their historical and material inheritance wherever they may be.[10] International celebrations of Arabic culture have been prohibited, such as the UNESCO's selection of East Jerusalem as the Arab Capital of Culture, that was banned in 2009, while 'parallel Palestinian sporting events, a literary festival, and a women's festival were also banned' (Davidson 79). *Les Amandes vertes* depicts small groups of Palestinians gathering to celebrate their cultural and religious events in homes, community centres or on their land, but festivals or large-scale celebrations are not depicted. In the photographic epilogue to *Faire le Mur*, only two photos are included that do not overtly portray violence, resistance and the Israeli occupation: the first is of two young female children celebrating Ramadan as they walk down a street with toy pistols and the other one is of a group of children at a small carnival in East Jerusalem. These authors' books make the point that the wall is more than a physical barrier erected to state security: it is a monument to the double-edged sword of nationalism. The wall represents two very different political realities: one side of the wall dilutes or even dissolves the Palestinian people and polity while ensuring a stable national Israeli identity. The Israeli side of the wall precludes the ethnicising effects of immigration and perceived threats to the state from the easy circulation of people. Whether discussing the Israeli–Palestinian conflict or other polemical borders such as the United States's Southwestern boundary with Mexico, barriers and walls designed to prevent or stem the circulation of peoples and goods are ultimately ineffective. 'Security' walls, barriers, enclosures and other protectionist constructions continue to attract scholarly attention in numerous disciplines, and literature is no exception. Walls have become integral mechanisms for the surveillance of the flow of goods and consequently, they cannot be uncoupled from their security function. 'Walls cannot simply be regarded as tools of capital with indifference to what they perform symbolically and materially', and their inefficacy in preventing or barring the flow of illegal immigrant labour and goods is a universal truth (Brown 174). Walls may reroute people and things but they do not interdict their circulation.

From elaborating the confiscation of agricultural lands and homes to commercial depression, Nan describes the wall's economic consequences not in statistics but in personal terms, as does Mahmoud in *Faire le Mur*. The Palestinians Nan encounters have lost livelihoods, homes, lands and economic stability, whereas Mahmoud's tale is primarily about loss, including loss of liberty. Whether in Hebron or Jerusalem, Nan describes the closed and shuttered shops and former commercial centres that are abandoned. In her description of Hebron, she juxtaposes the new Jewish commercial centre, vibrant, busy and with a state-of-the-art security system (*Les Amandes verte*s 58–9), while the following page, dominated by black, portrays an abandoned Palestinian commercial area totally devoid of human activity. However, Le Roy's depictions of Palestinian economic reality are not based on personal testimonies, but rather they are limited primarily to his background graphics of dilapidated or abandoned businesses. The one exception is the portrayal of Mahmoud's family grocery store where he works. Nevertheless, the spectre of economic precariousness haunts both works, recalling for the reader the drastic poverty inflicted on Palestinians in response to the Second Intifada.[11]

Other aspects of human capital to which the authors gesture are the unquantifiable and lasting trauma and psychological damage of the occupation on men, women and children in Gaza and the West Bank. Mahmoud's melancholia stemming from his loss of lands, freedom of movement, property, familial separation and incarceration, characterises his emotional life and these contributing elements are mirrored in Nan's interactions with numerous Palestinian men in her not-for-profit work in Palestine – and even in her own emotional life. By the end of *Les Amandes vertes* she admits that after almost a year in Palestine she does not have the same energy she had – the experience of daily life has simply worn her out (*Les Amandes vertes* 131). Nan's narrative interweaves the psychological toll of life under Israeli occupation through the stories of her Palestinian friends. From the normalisation of interrogation, violence and imprisonment, as evidenced by her friends' reaction to the unexplained imprisonment of Moussa, to the sporadic melancholia and despair of Madji (the director of a youth centre), Nan's words attest to the heavy emotional toll Israeli occupation exacts on Palestinian society. Her testimony is not a psychological diagnosis, but rather, an assertion that trauma is a 'political expression of the state of the world', or in this case, a 'political expression' imposed by the Israeli government (Fassin 532).

Despite the various ways the aforementioned authors have interwoven the material and intangible damages Palestinians have suffered as a result of Israel's response to the Second Intifada, what is strikingly similar is the depictions of the desensitisation of the Palestinians. When Amjad recounts a boy being shot as he chased a loose soccer ball too close to an Israeli settlement or when Akram tells Nan not to worry about Moussa's incarceration and probable mistreatment, both characters tell her not to worry 'It's normal' (*Les Amandes vertes* 33, 47). The damage is inestimable in terms of human development in areas such as educational opportunities, psychological well-being and food security notwithstanding the relation between the land and the people that anchors these narratives. Not only do these works emphasise the deleterious effects of Israeli occupation on Palestinian human capital, but they also emphasise the centrality of ongoing Israeli land grabs as a human-rights violation against the Palestinian people by underscoring that nothing is more central to aspirational nation-building than territorial integrity.

Land Grabs

Not only do the previously mentioned graphic novels show Palestinians as exploited human capital in a larger Israeli neo-liberal economy but also underscore how Jewish 'settlements' are an orchestrated Israeli land-grab in the name of security and Jewish ancestral right. Indisputably, settlement or city-building, typically thought of as purely civilian, has been conflated and reconfigured as a security function as well (Weizman, *Hollow Land* 62, 201). However, Israel's 'Wall' is a complex web of components that includes more than its eight-metre-high concrete blocks: it can be understood as the totality of security devices associated with it, such as its electronic fences, barbed wire, radar, cameras, deep trenches, observations posts and patrol roads that also crisscross through Palestinian territory.

One could argue that *Les Amandes vertes* is a series of discursive and graphic postcards surveying the further contracting of Palestinian borders originally created pursuant to the United Nation's Resolution 181 after the Second Intifada. Nan visits different villages and cities and explores areas of the West Bank and she emphasises not only the difficulties she faces in moving freely but also the confiscation of land in the name of religion and state security.[12] Recounting her visit to Oush Grab where Jewish Israelis were attempting to build a settlement, she tells and draws the story in just a few pages. On the first page of this vignette the only horizontal frame depicts a series of Palestinian hillsides each with Jewish settlements bearing the legend 'everywhere one looks, one sees settlements on the hilltops. It is really remarkable when one crosses the West Bank: it is worse than gruyere cheese' (*Les Amandes vertes* 277). Nan's narration of the different ways that the West Bank wall dices, separates, contains and cuts off Palestinians from family, friends, homes and ancestral areas is a sober reminder of the ways this particular wall has reorganised space and political borders. *Les Amandes vertes* provides both graphic/narrative examples of the 'dynamic morphology of the frontier that resembles an incessant sea dotted with multiplying archipelagos of externally alienated and internally homogenous ethno-national enclaves' (Weizman, *Hollow Land* 7). *Les Amandes vertes*' layout and the expansiveness of the frames in relating this incident highlight the patchwork aspect of Israeli settlements on Palestinian lands and its pictorial representations gesture to a broader Israeli national policy of creating 'organic walls' that bisect, envelop or incorporate Palestinian lands and communities so that these spaces become defamiliarised and resignified. In Oush Grab, Nan states that the confiscated land is justified as part of a new military zone in an asymmetrical game of Stratego. Nan comes to the same conclusion as Ibrahim when discussing Israeli displacement of Israeli Palestinians in Jerusalem: Israel's long-term strategy is the disintegration of Palestinian territorial integrity, which is like the game of Stratego where one of the goals is to capture so many of the opponent's pieces that her or his territory can be freely occupied by the adversary. Despite Nan's sense of despair and futility, she leaves the protest with her Palestinian friends to meet young Israelis in a bar at the foot of the hills: it is again around a table and the sharing of food that the authors provide hope for a future resolution and reconciliation as young Palestinians and Israelis speak of the *nakba*, stereotypes and religion (*Les Amandes vertes* 85). Throughout this work, there is an emphasis on discussion, understanding and potential reconciliation around a table and the sharing of food – a sign of hospitality and friendship so engrained in Middle Eastern cultures.

Another poignant example of the division of Palestinian lands is the Hermans' description of Rachel's Tomb, the third holiest site in Judaism. In Nan's description there are only two frames on the page. The first frame is a large image of a Palestinian house completely surrounded on three sides by a security wall with the legend

> The Israelis decided to annex the Tomb and to build a military base. The dividing wall surrounds the tomb and the Israelis have forbidden Palestinians to enter. It's like that all around my house, there is a house that is surrounded on three sides by the wall. (*Les Amandes vertes* 71)

The panel directly underneath the house depicts a strangled street with the caption that 'before the wall, my street (Nan's) was the city's principal avenue. It linked Bethlehem to Jerusalem to the North and Hebron to the South'

(*Les Amandes vertes* 71). The persistent threat of territorial reorganisation or even appropriation of Palestinian land is exemplified by the frame's towering walls that render the home claustrophobic and prison-like, completely cut off from any geographic anchoring except for the entrance. This experience is echoed in her visit to the town of Qalqilya. After a forty-day curfew during the Second Intifada, residents came out to find their town totally encircled by the wall except for one entrance guarded by a checkpoint.

At Oush Grab, Nan witnesses a protest against the state-supported Israeli settlers and a ragtag group comprised of international witnesses, Israelis against Jewish settlements and Palestinians that attempt to prevent further taking of Palestinian land. This episode conveys to the reader the sense of loss and powerlessness that her Palestinian friends feel as they lose either familial lands or territory that had formed the contours of their lives. This diverse cohort, particularly the Jewish Israelis against further illegal settlements, reminds the reader that no monolithic support among Israelis exists for the settlement of Palestinian lands; such a diverse group also underscores Palestinian efficiency in the mobilisation of world opinion.[13] As Israeli soldiers threaten the protestors and the confrontation heats up, Nan and her Palestinian friends retreat, but the international protestors refuse to move. They are violently thrown to the ground and arrested – an event that she describes as 'super violent' (*Les Amandes vertes* 84). The banality of this violence is emphasised by its placement next to a square frame of equal size that simply depicts Nan's face, while the subsequent frame shows a boy's face slammed to the ground with an Israeli soldier's knees on his back and hand on his face while the barrel of a gun is pointed at his head (*Les Amandes vertes* 84).

In *Faire le Mur*, protagonist Mahmoud's story of land confiscation goes back to his grandfather who was 'chased' from his lands following the 1947–9 war when Arabs in the region fought against the newly formed state of Israel (*Faire le Mur* 58). As was previously discussed, a defining moment in his life was the confiscation of his family's farm and the wholesale destruction of the fruits of his labour, as well as future means of any type of financial independence and stability. Rather than relate individual stories of land confiscation, Le Roy takes a holistic approach in examining Palestine. For example, the prominent display of maps of Palestine and Israel from 1947–8, 1967 and 2007, tell the meta-story of a land-grab not of individually affected families but of a people – the loss of a nation. The intermixing of personal loss with the increasing loss of political sovereignty is part of Le Roy's narrative strategy and the narrative and graphic mapping of confiscated Palestinian land has become a 'geographical tool for advocacy actions against the Israeli government' (Weizman, *Hollow Land* 262).

Whether through Nan's autobiographical account or Le Roy's biographical sketch of Mahmoud, Israel's border wall figures prominently as the controlling symbol of a psychological as well as a physical uprooting. For Mahmoud and the Palestinians that Nan encounters, the wall simultaneously instantiates a psychological alienation from one's cultural past and one's homeland – literally one's roots – as well as a type of containment or patrolled caging complete with checkpoints, guard towers and turnstiles. Although the wall was denominated as officially 'removeable and reroutable' (Tamir), it appears to have become a permanent monument to frustrated Palestinian national aspirations and interminable oppressive occupation.

Conclusion

Because of the eminence of graphic novels in Francophone culture, an examination of this genre's representations of the Second Intifada is a useful lens into Francophone cultural responses to the ongoing Israeli–Palestinian conflict. While political solutions are most often crafted and implemented by elite levels of governments, one cannot discount the power of the arts to encourage citizens to participate in political processes such as peace negotiations. The two particular works discussed in this chapter are not the only Francophone graphic novels focused on this subject, but rather they were chosen because of their similar narrative strategies.[14] This chapter illustrates how graphic novels scholarship can record the breadth and complexity of human rights violations by examining the interplay between historical time, trauma, ethical witnessing and comics narratology. While debate exists among comics scholars as to whether the story determines the form or the form generates the story, what is clear is that 'a holistic approach to the form is necessary in order to understand the layered histories evoked in any given panel sequence or across the entire comic' (Brister and Walzer 142).

These two works, *Faire le Mur* and *Les Amandes vertes*, are indicative of a dominant current in the field of Francophone graphic novels that urge a broader representational model of Palestinians in the ongoing conflict: one that challenges the rigid binaries of victim/terrorist and state security/threat or at the very least, inverts these binaries. Both Le Roy and the Hermans humanise Palestinians by focusing on their individuality, rather than treating them as geopolitical abstractions (often coded as opponent, aggressor and terrorist). The combined power of personal narrative and image creates bonds of commonality and recognition that foster identitarian impulses rather than emphasising differences. Unlike the narrative method used in Israeli–Palestinian reconciliation forums, these Francophone authors do not have to be as concerned with the 'good story', one that does not escalate tensions, alienates, or offend other participants (Moaz 121). However, as we have seen, these writers are very careful to include moments of integration, cooperation, understanding and even support of one group by the other.

The personalisation of daily life in Palestine through Nan's and Mahmoud's stories inverts dominant Western binaries of Palestinian terrorist/Israeli victim and provides a more human and intimate contact with life in places such as Hebron, Nablus or Bethlehem as well as various refugee camps such as Aïda, villages such as Beit Umar. Moreover, *Les Amandes vertes* is careful to insert several depictions of Nan's experiences of Israeli life with Israeli Jews as well as bicultural interactions to further humanise the geopolitical situation. Although *Faire le Mur* provides fewer examples of Israeli–Palestinian amicable social interaction, both works incorporate a strategy of alternating depictions of Palestinian daily life with excursions to Israel that underscores the double helix of two peoples that are inextricably linked politically, geographically and culturally.

Ultimately, these graphic novelists stake claims for human rights in Palestine and they are particularly efficacious because of the genre's spatiotemporal possibilities that disrupt 'linear notions of time and bounded space involved in the denial of Palestinians' rights to property and land and their right of return' (Brister and Walzer 139). Even though the appeal of these graphic novels lies in their autobiographical and biographical dimensions, they are nevertheless highly self-reflexive in that they are marked by the non-transparency of drawing. The author's hand marks the text and reminds the reader of the subjective and potentially unreliable nature of the narration as 'material' history not only through words but through their illustrations (Chute 457). Drawing from experience, the authors succeed in reframing this decades-long geopolitical conflict to highlight Palestinian human rights violations. Similar to Joe Sacco's *Palestine* and other works in this genre, these graphic novelists force the reader to question the West's own complicity in creating the economic, political and social conditions that permit the continued deterritorialisation of Palestine and the oppression suffered by its inhabitants.

Notes

1. On 22 November 1974 France voted in favour of recognising the PLO (Palestine Liberation Organization) as a United Nations observer and reaffirming the inalienable rights of the Palestinian people. France continues to work with both Israeli and Palestinian governments to create a workable peace and two-state solution.
2. It is worth noting that *Les Amandes vertes* has been translated into English, which has not only created a wider reading audience, but it also has received

the Doctors Without Borders Award for best travel diary for calling attention to the living conditions of Palestinian populations in precarious situations in the Occupied Territories.
3. For instance, Farid Boudjellal's graphic novel *JuifsArabes* (*JewsArabs*), published in 2006, does not use the personalising strategy of Le Roy's and the Hermans's works through first person narration or memoir/documentary style.
4. For Le Roy, the Israeli–Palestinian conflict is much larger than a localised geopolitical conflict. Rather, it is a questioning of Western socio-political discourses that have structured their political systems including 'the free world, democracy, and human rights' (Henry). His critical representations of life under Israeli occupation caused the Israeli government to refuse him entry into Israel in 2014 in addition to imposing a ten-year travel ban from returning to Israel, and thus to Palestine. Since Israel's decision to prevent Le Roy from entering the country, he has not subsequently written other graphic novels about Israeli–Palestinian relations.
5. All translations of *Faire le Mur* and *Les Amandes vertes* are the author's translations.
6. I do not wish to argue that Israeli graphic novels, concerned with the realities of the ongoing conflict with Palestinians over issues such as land and sovereignty, do not portray them in a realistic manner. For instance, one can think of Ofer Zanzuri's *Azure Giants* or Ari Folman's *Waltz with Bashir: A Lebanon War Story*.
7. Nan later learns that Mousa has been imprisoned in a round-up, which apparently happens regularly. She never sees Mousa again.
8. For instance, an armed outpost of Israeli Jewish settlers clashes with local Palestinian farmers, and with the tacit approval of the Israeli state, forcefully removes them from their fields and even steals their produce. See Le Roy 62–6. In retaliation, armed Palestinian militants often attack these outposts. In response, the Israeli military builds more outposts as punitive measures on or near where settlers have been attacked or killed. Mahmoud's loss of familial lands and property exemplifies how this cycle might work. See Weizman 4.
9. The villagers had their farmlands confiscated and had to find another source of income. Moreover, Israeli law forbids them from doing work that would enlarge or maintain (the property), even driving in a nail (Hermans 16).
10. Israelis have systematically destroyed ancient mosques, historic houses, and other Palestinian archaeological and historic sites that not only disconnect Palestinians from their historic past but that literally erase it (Chamberlain 'Stealing Palestinian History').
11. Between 2000 and 2002 the poverty rate increased from 21 per cent to 60 per cent according to the World Bank. See World Bank Press Release 'World Bank Expands Support for Emergency Social Services to Palestinians', Washington, 17 December 2002.
12. Wendy Brown provides an insightful and helpful analysis of the evolving imbrication between theology, sovereignty and land (70–8).

13. Israeli activists, politicians and citizens have demonstrated and voice their opposition to settlements. Former Minister of Education, Knesset member and co-founder of Peace Now, Yuli Tamir has called these settlements illegal and has compared the use of Israeli Defense Forces to protect them to a gang of burglars calling up the police and asking for protection because the area where the crime was taking place was dangerous (9).
14. One might also consider Philippe Squarzoni's *Torture Blanche*, Maximilien Le Roy's and Soulman's *Les Chemins de Traverse* and Roannie-Oko's series *L'Intruse-Les Palestiniens* for a broader comparison of representations and discussions of narrative strategies.

9

COMING OF AGE IN GRAPHIC NOVELS REPRESENTING THE PALESTINE/ISRAEL CONFLICT

Ned Curthoys

This chapter will explore different conceptions of the Israeli–Palestinian conflict elaborated in two *Bildungsromane* or coming-of-age themed twenty-first century graphic novels: Harvey Pekar's *Not the Israel My Parents Promised Me* (2012) and Sarah Glidden's *How to Understand Israel in 60 Days or Less* (2010). Both novels are written by Jewish-American authors for whom the Israeli–Palestinian conflict is an abiding personal preoccupation that shapes their sense of self, thus requiring an immersive exploration of their changing relationship to the Jewish state. As neither novel ends with a protagonist who is confident in their judgments about the conflict or reintegrated into a community after a period of wandering and alienation, some commentary on the evolution of the *Bildungsroman* in recent genre studies might be helpful in elucidating the subtleties of Pekar and Glidden's hybrid deployment of autobiography, quest narrative and historical analysis.

A recent article by Harriet Earle reminds us that genre criticism of the *Bildungsroman* has in many ways moved beyond the assumption that the principal animus of the form is to 'trace the journey of the [foundling] protagonist from adolescence to adulthood' and explore their achievement of 'emotional maturity and social position' (430). Where the classic *Bildungsroman*, itself a contested genre concept, was held to have focused on the hero's naïvety and development from innocence to maturity through mistakes and testing ordeals, Earle registers the formal and narratological interest of current criticism. She cites Julia Round's summation of critical tendencies that no longer prioritise the successful self-determination of the protagonist as a defining feature of the genre:

> [This new shift in critical focus] defines the plot events in terms of self-understanding rather than personal growth; emphasizes the dual position of the protagonist (as both reflective narrator and developing subject); and notes a circular (rather than linear) narrative structure. (Round cited in Earle 431)

Earle and the critics she cites deploy a more dialectical and self-reflexive conception of the genre, in which the narrative is often simultaneously about ingenuous child and wizened adult. As a form that blends literary realism with fairy-tale and Gothic elements, the *Bildungsroman* often imbricates developmental plots of youthful formation with recursive psychological and symbolic preoccupations, and as a genre congenial to motivated self-exploration, the *Bildungsroman* renders the formation of the self an ongoing task cathected to the problem of the subject's relationship to the past. Kenneth Millard, for example, rejects the notion of the contemporary coming-of-age story as a linear progression from innocence to achieved maturity and stresses the genre's capacity to interrogate ideological conditioning:

> the contemporary novel of adolescence is often characterized by a concerted attempt to situate the protagonist in relation to historical contexts of origin by which individuals come to understand themselves as having been conditioned . . . the historical awareness that the adolescent acquires is at odds with the faith in the sovereign individual and the mythology of American self-determination that the genre of coming-of-age might appear to endorse. (10)

What gives the *Bildungsroman* its contemporary relevance according to Earle is the dramatisation of a tension between the 'autonomy of the individual and the shaping pressure of history' (431).

The graphic novel, which has had a marked turn towards autobiography and historical reconstruction since the publication of Spiegelman's *Maus* (1986–91), adroitly uses both mature and younger avatars and the flexible visual language of the comics medium. It can blend self-reflexive narration and meta-fictional experimentation with picaresque narratives of ethical and artistic formation. The supple form of the graphic novel, which can tarry in the interstices between word and image, interweaves the 'external spatial world with the internal thoughts of the protagonist into an "inextricable texture"' (Fantasia 83). As a polysemous genre, the graphic novel is a particularly fitting medium for sophisticated coming-of-age narratives that trace the 'protagonist's negotiations with ... external forces – namely, institutional and societal – that influence his or her internal development' (Fantasia 84).

If auto-graphic novels have become a vehicle for examining the individual's continuing and incomplete negotiation of the crucible of political and historical forces that shape psychic individuation, then, as Kenneth Millard argues, the teleological process towards a degree of maturity and identity formation represented is not necessarily bound to the 'specific age of a fictional character' (5). Rather, as Julia Round argues, drawing on the work of Martin Swales, we can displace the interpretive problem of describing *Bildung*, or personal growth in a work of fiction, from the experiences of the hero, which would prioritise their youthful encounters with the world, to the 'narrator's discursive self-understanding' (Round 191). As a reader we are equally attentive to a wry humour and mature perspective which might need to critically incorporate the 'non-fulfilment of consistently intimated expectation' (Swales 34). In the graphic novel in particular, the *Bildungsroman* is revitalised as a sometimes self-ironic quest narrative that does not reward the reader with a conventional happy ending or seek to transcend the problem of entrenched structural oppression with fairy-tale like wish-fulfilment, a narrative desire of the nineteenth century English *Bildungsroman* famously criticised by Franco Moretti in reference to novels such as *Jane Eyre*. The notion of a *Bildungsroman* written 'for the sake of the journey' (Swales 161), would mean a decentred version of the genre that no longer presumes upon the redemption of the emancipatory desires of childhood for personal metamorphosis, social mobility, simplification of circumstances and family stability. As Sara Lyons summarises in her review of recent theories of the *Bildungsroman* and their application to Victorian literary studies, we should recognise that the *Bildungsroman* is not necessarily an optimistic genre, 'that it might refer to either an affirmative or profoundly negative coming-of-age narrative (or to an ambiguous composite of these alternatives) and that such novels may sustain or subvert dominant ideologies' (Lyons 11).

As we shall see in a moment, Harvey Pekar's graphic novel *Not the Israel My Parents Promised Me* (hereafter *NIPPM*) is subversive of dominant narratives of the Israeli–Palestinian conflict and of the rationales for Israeli policies. This is not because *NIPPM* consistently holds to a doctrinaire anti-Zionism intolerant of Israel's existence, but because it understands incremental colonial domination by Israel as a barrier to peace, stability and normalisation, and because the coexistence of Palestinians, Arabs and Jews is not regarded as a chimerical ideal in view of the ebb and flow of diasporic Jewish history.

While not without its complexities as its increasingly uncertain protagonist, a first-time visitor to Israel in the early 2000s, continues to interrogate colonial and racist dimensions of Israel's policies, by contrast Glidden's graphic novel *How to Understand Israel in 60 Days or Less* (hereafter *UI*) '[moves] *towards* Israel, as opposed to *away* from Israel' as reflected in Pekar's dyspeptic narrative of disenchantment with the idealised Israel of his youth (Reingold 538). *UI*, I will suggest, veers towards the consolidation of a more consoling conception of Israel as still capable of fulfilling its early promise as a culturally rejuvenated nation state forged by youthful idealism, aspiring towards peace, and existentially threatened by the trenchant hostility of Palestinians and other Arab neighbours.

Harvey Pekar's *Not the Israel My Parents Promised Me*: The New Left as Found Family

Sara Lyons' conception of the *Bildungsroman* as rife with ambivalence is helpful in regards to my analysis of Harvey Pekar's *NIPPM*, which details the partly autobiographical, partly critical-historical musings of Pekar's aging avatar[1] Harvey, a nebbish, melancholy, kvetching, angst-ridden, but always productively perplexed protagonist. Harvey introduces himself to us as someone who wants to explain his loss of 'faith' in Israel (*Not the Israel* 4) while exploring ways to move beyond the distressing geopolitical quandary the Israeli–Palestinian conflict represents to him, a diasporic American Jew of immigrant Polish-Jewish parents who were profoundly invested in the Jewish state. *NIPPM* is part of a late historical turn in Harvey Pekar's work, following his collaborative graphic novel *Macedonia* (2007), in which he sought to historicise regions of the world, such as the Balkans, which in the popular Western imagination embodied intractable and inevitable ethnic conflict. Pekar wanted instead to entertain the working hypothesis that there might be practical possibilities for coexistence and peace but that progress would require a refreshed perception of the historical and political dynamics in play in particular conflict zones. The late Harvey Pekar might then be considered a participant in the 'multiethnic graphic novel' as it seeks to map 'alternative political genealogies and critical historiographies' so that our sense of the past can be 'provocatively reconfigured, and strategically remade' (Cutter and Schlund-Vials 2).

In certain respects, its motivated relationship to contested histories makes *NIPPM* a quest narrative, a journey towards understanding how we got to a position of conflict and mutual incomprehension that must also take into account the vicissitudes of millennia of Jewish history. Yet the *wanderlust* one might expect to find in a travel narrative is simultaneously parodied by the avatar Harvey's personal narrative of disillusionment, reversals of fortune, and stasis as he remains symbiotically attached to his unfashionable and economically depressed hometown of Cleveland, Ohio. In *NIPPM*, Harvey's youthful enthusiasm for Israel, a reflection of his parents' jubilation at the rebirth of a Jewish homeland, and his flirtation with the possibility of migrating there in the 1960s, segues to his political awakening and subsequent disenchantment with its colonial annexation of Palestinian territories. Harvey's desire to be in some way serviceable to the new Jewish state culminates in a hapless encounter with Israeli officials in which all prospects of *Aliyah* (migrating to Israel) and becoming a 'new Jew' contributing to the birth of a nation are dashed by his practical incompetence and obsessive personality disorder. Rather than journey to new lands, in the present day Harvey and his artistic collaborator JT Waldman, the book's Jewish American illustrator, wander around familiar precincts of his native Cleveland, spending a considerable amount of time talking and arguing on different levels of Zubal's used bookstore, exploring the abundant produce of Gallucci's Italian food emporium, driving around local landmarks, and then finally visiting his second home, a division of the Cleveland public library.[2]

These local and familiar areas are important to the *mise en scène* of *NIPPM*. Harvey readily admits to the younger Waldman – who has performed the hallowed ritual of staying on an Israeli kibbutz – of never having visited Israel and thus not having performed any kind of diasporic pilgrimage to its culturally significant sites. Yet as Harvey points out, that does not mean he is a self-loathing diasporic Jew carping from the side-lines. There is a prominent emphasis in *NIPPM* on the autodidactic Harvey's attempts to understand history and politics through reading and historical research. He 'read[s] a lot' (*Not the Israel* 100) in bookstores, libraries, and then enacts his fluid thought-processes through a conversation that combines sincere anxiety about its topic, absurdist humour in the face of the impasses generated by unrestrained enquiry, and gentle self-mockery. We might say that *NIPPM* dramatises a movement in the *Bildungsroman* from a valorisation of the rewards of personal and social mobility to a sympathetic examination of the intellectual exhilaration and personal equilibrium provided by mature self-understanding as it attaches itself to particular problematics in human affairs.

The point of Harvey's leisurely reading, subtended by tarrying in the gustatory and learned institutions of Cleveland, is to help him '[take] in the big picture' (*Not the Israel* 100) of what's going on in the Middle East. Harvey affirms that his intellectual journey into the problem of Israel/Palestine can only be achieved by examining pre-state Israel from the early twentieth century, the era of mandate Palestine, a time when Zionism was a minority political cause in the Jewish diaspora and when Palestinians and the Arab world were looking to emerge from the yoke of British and European imperialism in the region. This is an era, Harvey makes clear to JT Waldman, in which one must account for the actions of revisionist Jewish paramilitary organisations like *Irgun* and the Stern Gang ('outlaw Jewish groups'; *Not the Israel* 117) in driving away the British and terrorising Arab civilians, and in which famed generals such as Moshe Dayan openly acknowledged the Zionist project as one of dispossession and military conquest; here too we find Israel's legendary founder and first prime minister David Ben-Gurion flirting with the idea of 'transferring' Palestinians into other Arab states (115). It was an era in which the 1948 war of independence drove Palestinians off their land and which still today is recorded by Palestinians as *nakba* or catastrophe. Harvey's historically aware argument, to some degree sympathetic with Palestinian and Arab nationalist aspirations, is that the reclamation of that land and restoration of Arab dignity in a colonial context is a driver of Palestinian nationalism today.

In addition to musing on the need to understand events in mandate Palestine in order to frame the conflict after Israeli independence in 1948, Harvey intersperses his own narrative of political awakening in which he became disengaged from Israel in the 1950s and 1960s despite the ardent pro-Zionism of his immigrant Polish-Jewish parents who were jubilant at the 'miraculous' formation of a Jewish state. In conversation with JT Waldman, who suspects Harvey of having drunk the Kool-Aid of excessive anti-Zionism amongst his Leftist non-Jewish friends, Harvey stresses that his is not a clichéd story of deracination and self-hatred issuing in an abstracted anti-Zionism that ingratiates him with his gentile peers. Harvey wants to make clear the critical and perspectival resources that sustained encounters with the counter-cultural Left offered to him in the 1960s, which presumably stimulated his extensive historical research into the conflict. Harvey spends some time in the novel connecting the dots between Israeli policies towards Palestinians and the anti-Arab racism – his parents had 'plenty of prejudices' against Arabs – (*Not the Israel* 123) and dogmatic resistance to alternative viewpoints he found in his parents and extended family when it came to Israel. This intransigence (ironic in view of popular portrayals of Palestinians as essentially rejectionist in their attitudes and actions) is a sobering discovery for Harvey now that he reflects back on extended family gatherings, having once shared his family's identification with Israel and having been brought up to believe in the essential virtue of the Jewish people. While Harvey's narrative is couched in casual observation and is not searchingly introspective, we are within the narrative code of the *Bildungsroman* in which 'a loss of faith in the value of the hero's home and family . . . leads inevitably to the assertion of the youth's independence' (Buckley, cited in Lima 441).

We might say that Harvey's insistence on the importance of the countercultural or New Left to his changing and more even-handed position on Israel intersects with the 'found family' genre in which Harvey's elective affinities with a non-biological family of progressive, politically aware young people, and his ability to rethink his own conditioning, help to reconstitute the 'genre that one might term "family"' (Millard 2). Harvey finds himself 'on [his] own' (*Not the Israel* 91) by the 1960s and chooses to associate with the New Left because of their intellectual curiosity and spirit of sceptical critique that contrasts with his own family's lack of empathy towards the motivations of Arab leaders. The reader is witness to the aftermath of Harvey's process of pointed recollection and formative deliberation – the 'thought process rolled out over years' (90) – as he rethinks his relationship to his own family's intense and unquestioning pro-Zionist attitudes, informed by Orientalist depictions of Arabs as brutal and treacherous. He reflects with implicit pathos on his own family's hostile denial of the legitimacy of Arab and Palestinian aspirations for postcolonial autonomy. In one example, Harvey recounts his family's attitude towards Egyptian president Nasser as a 'common criminal' without attempting to understand his pan-Arab motives (90) or awareness that, like Israel, Egypt too was a young country in the 1950s seeking its own identity. Harvey tells us that by the 1960s he achieved a perilous independence, tending to meet Leftists, New Leftists, and Marxists who were opposed to at least some of Israel's policies. His Leftist critique of nationalism and racism and his growing awareness that the history of the Middle East has been bedevilled by European imperialism began to inform a growing unease with Israel's actions towards the Palestinians.

Sensitive to the charge that like other diaspora Jews embarrassed by the Jewish state's behaviour Harvey is holding Israel to unreasonably high standards in a world of *realpolitik*, Harvey takes a larger view of history, musing that 'nationalism and ethnic pride, in the long run, delay human development, and the misery they cause must be recognized' (*Not the Israel* 113). The more conventional JT Waldman, half-jokingly suspicious that Harvey's Leftist goyim friends plied him with dope and alcohol and turned him against Israel, represents the more conventional Left-Zionist perspective that Israel is besieged by violent antagonists who reject its existence and so lamentably has no partner for peace. Harvey counters, with a new Left sensitivity to histories of colonialism, that after 1967 'Jews were settling all over the occupied territories, claiming everything', and is drawn in one frame as a younger man reading the newspaper, remarking with alarm on the stupidity of Jewish Israelis 'sabotaging their best chances for lasting peace' (138).

Figure 9.1 'Harvey's consternation at Israeli settlement building.' Excerpts from *Not the Israel My Parents Promised Me* by Harvey Pekar and J. T. Waldman. Text copyright © 2012 by Harvey Pekar and J. T. Waldman. Illustrations copyright © 2012 J. T. Waldman. Reprinted by permission of Hill and Wang, a division of Farrar, Straus and Giroux. All rights reserved.

Figure 9.2 'More like a maze than a process.' Excerpts from *Not the Israel My Parents Promised Me* by Harvey Pekar and J. T. Waldman. Text copyright © 2012 by Harvey Pekar and J. T. Waldman. Illustrations copyright © 2012 J. T. Waldman. Reprinted by permission of Hill and Wang, a division of Farrar, Straus and Giroux. All rights reserved.

Harvey recognises Palestinian terrorist violence and its atrocities but he is also mindful Israel continues to populate Palestinian territories with 'people they can terrorize' (*Not the Israel* 159), is not making a serious effort at building a sustained peace by enabling a Palestinian state, and will not leave the Palestinians alone as it administers Palestinian lives, and builds a wall to contain and isolate them. A splash double-page (158–9) of an aporetic maze in which JT Waldman and Harvey spar over the question of whether Palestinian violence or Israeli colonialism is the real sticking point enacts the collapse of legitimising narratives and ushers in a vertiginous *Kunstchaos* after which, with comic bathos, the tension of the conversation dissipates and it meanders towards self-parody and farce.

A bemused and consternated Harvey, always drawn with a browbeaten frown, a dissident Jew and eccentric outsider-figure, is shown in the final panel sitting alone with his books in the basement of the library, his interlocutors once more leaving him alone with his morbid preoccupations.

While Harvey's intellectual adventure may have had no tangible effects, as like Socrates in an early Platonic dialogue, his penchant for opposition to a conventional interpretation of the conflict has left everyone around him less certain than ever of where they stand, this is a graphic novel written for the sake of its dialogical journey and the reconfigured historical and social relationships it imagines. In the words of Judith Butler, it does succeed in showing that 'there are Jewish resources' for the criticism of state violence and colonial subjugation and the pursuit of social justice for all which would mean that Zionism can no longer control the 'meaning of Jewishness' (*Parting Ways* 3). In the first half of *NIPPM*, Harvey outlines a pluralistic rather than lachrymose version of Jewish history centred on dispersion and oppression before the reclamation of its biblical lands. He points out that Jews were able for a time to enter the mainstream of Babylonian life after their exile and captivity, and enjoyed periods of coexistence with the Islamic world such as in Andalusian Muslim Spain, where the volatility of daily life was 'nothing compared to the barbaric slaughter wrought by the Christian Crusades' (65). Harvey points to a time where Jewish scholars were a major contributor to the Enlightenment through the *Haskalah* led by the philosopher Moses Mendelssohn, enabling learned 'modern Jews' to acquaint themselves with their culture and heritage, and to re-establish Hebrew, once a liturgical language, as the Jewish national language.

So it is that Harvey, the protagonist of a self-willed critical *Bildungsroman*, is able to see otherwise, offering a panoramic and agentic conception of diasporic Jewish history that intersects with other civilisations and movements of ideas. *NIPPM* refuses an ontology of victimhood and acknowledges that Judaism and its meanings continues to be formed and re-formed in cohabitation with the non-Jewish world. It is of a piece, then, that in the epilogue written by Harvey Pekar's widow Joyce Brabner, the ever-stiff-necked Harvey is drawn as having had a moving Jewish service that 'substituted Cleveland, instead of Israel, as Harvey's place of belonging' (*Not the Israel* 172). *NIPPM* in its affirmation of Cleveland as Harvey's elective home could be interpreted as a contribution to Jewish diasporist thinking that allows for invented homelands and complex forms of attachment. As Daniel Boyarin advocates in *A Travelling Homeland: the Babylonian Talmud as Diaspora* (2015), the history of the Jewish diaspora as a mode of textual practice and cultural self-invention demonstrates that diaspora is not an 'essential thing' (Boyarin 4) predicated on a unitary conception of a traumatic past and the projection of one's real or imagined homeland. Diaspora is rather a 'particular kind of cultural hybridity' and a 'mode of analysis' (Boyarin 3–4), a synchronic condition across different cultural locations that allows, as in Harvey's case, for unofficial, affectively intimate, and transnationally conceived expressions of responsibility for one's co-religionists (Boyarin 4).

Sarah Glidden's *How to Understand Israel in 60 Days or Less*: The Release of Psychic Tension

There are similarities and differences as to how Sarah Glidden's *How to Understand Israel in 60 Days or Less* (*UI*), which details her avatar's visit to Israel in March 2007, participates in the layered and historicised conception of the genre that we have discussed. At twenty-six years old, Sarah Glidden's comic avatar is not an adolescent or foundling, she has learnt to appreciate the 'cultural aspects of Judaism' from her family and enjoys a close family circle that loves 'learning, eating, and arguing' (*Understand Israel* 67). It becomes clear, however, that Sarah does have an undefined personality at the liminal threshold of making life-decisions and consolidating an ethical stance and political worldview. As such, both as a younger and more malleable character she is, at first blush, a more recognisable candidate for the genre of *Bildungsroman* than Pekar's avatar. Sarah is on a ten-day birthright or *Taglit* tour throughout Israel with other Jewish Americans that are around her age, and who, like her, are not necessarily observant or deeply attached to Judaism and the Jewish state. As described by Yehonatan Abramson, *Taglit*-Birthright is an educational trip to Israel offered for free to young Jewish adults between the ages of eighteen and twenty-six, and its official goal is to strengthen Jewish identity amongst young Jewish adults who are not part of existing Jewish religious and institutional frameworks (Abramson 659).[3]

The initial scenario is that an introverted but rather smug Sarah, proud of her political awareness, positions herself as a subversive agent amongst a docile group of tourists; her reasons for travelling to Israel less about experiencing the Jewish homeland and reconnecting with Judaism than uncovering the truth about Israel as a colonial power intent on the erasure of the memory of its indigenous inhabitants and as a geopolitical aggressor, a subject that she has recently been 'fixated on' (*Understand Israel* 6). Hugging her Muslim-American boyfriend goodbye, Sarah assures him that there is little chance of her being converted to Zionism. Somewhat smugly she affirms in a flashback prior to her flight out that she is well prepared for whatever 'propaganda they [Israeli spokespeople] try and throw at me' (*Understand Israel* 6).

In quickly registering Sarah's cynicism about Israel *UI* acknowledges a generational shift in which the Leftist perspective on Israel that Pekar gradually had to acquire is now more commonplace amongst the American Left including Leftist Jewish American intellectuals,[4] with US college campuses an alleged hot bed for anti-Israeli sentiment and, according to Israel's defenders, anti-Semitism.[5] As Reingold, who also analyses Pekar and Glidden's graphic novels, suggests, both *UI* and *NIPPM* emerged during a time, in the 2000s, when American Jews were becoming increasingly distant from a romanticised conception of Israel in part because of the failed peace process and increasing cycles of violence (Reingold 528). Sarah, nondescript and sparely drawn by Glidden, usually has a blank if not slightly wary expression in most panels, reflective of the circumstance that as a young person growing up after the two Intifadas and failed or abortive peace processes, she cannot share Harvey's youthful enthusiasm for the Jewish state and arrives instead with a perhaps prematurely settled understanding of its faults. Israel's perceived ethnocentrism, and a critique of Israeli settler colonialism and racism, is the influential narrative that confronts Sarah as a diasporic Left-leaning Jewish American. The college-educated Sarah, likely trained to worry about the Other, and living in a multicultural US environment with a Muslim-American boyfriend presumably reminding her of various counternarratives to Israel as an outpost of Western civilisation in a sea of barbarism, arrives in Israel with a developed hermeneutic of suspicion towards Israel's treatment of the Palestinians and its policy-makers' aggressive posture towards other Arab nations in the region. In the early pages of *UI*, when Sarah feels unsettled by her disarmingly reasonable *Taglit* guides and a protective entourage that include young soldiers serving in the IDF, her conscience whispers to her that she is in fact here to 'pre-judge' (*Understand Israel* 22), while on the subsequent page her friend Melissa, increasingly enthusiastic about the trip, mocks Sarah's defensive claim that she is here to keep an 'open mind' (23).

The implication that Sarah is as ironically prejudiced and doctrinaire as the Israeli state she decries, is itself an aspect of the political work undertaken by *UI*. In the continual redescription of her anti-Israeli attitude as biased, premature, and open to revision by experience, we can see a marked contrast with *NIPPM*, which understands disenchantment with Israel as ethically productive, opening Pekar and his destabilised reader to a range of different perspectives on the conflict and with a more pluralistic understanding of the varied experiences of the Jewish diaspora. By contrast *UI* is largely restorative in its attitude towards Israel, less in the sense that it offers a polemical defence of Israel's policies that renders it blameless, but in that it embraces romantic and idealistic political emotions in regards to Israel's future possibilities as

Figure 9.3 'Prejudging the situation.' © Sarah Glidden. Used with permission from Drawn & Quarterly.

a democratic Jewish state. These maturing affective dispositions might be understood to meliorate a sense of homelessness experienced by diaspora Jews unsure of their cultural and religious identifications. Glidden's confused yet already jaded young traveller Sarah is to gradually re-acquire a sense of Israel's promise, its essential youthfulness as a young and forward-looking nation, a work in progress with humanly understandable aspirations. *UI* redescribes Israel as founded by the energy and hopes of early youthful Zionist pioneers and their spiritual descendants, younger immigrants performing *Aliyah* so they can make a contribution to the Jewish state.

In the tradition of the more classical conception of the *Bildungsroman* in which a young protagonist is capacitated for civic responsibilities, Sarah, who by contrast with Harvey actually visits Israel, will experience the disorienting but self-refreshing aspects of travel to a new land, including varied cultural experiences, new friendships, confrontation with other worldviews, conversations with pedagogical mentors, and the awakening of an artistic vocation. Visits to sites of historical significance give Sarah a much more tangible sense of Jewish history as a living heritage. She will glimpse the possibility of an enhanced sense of belonging to Judaism, thus relinquishing her anti-Zionism as stultifying psychic baggage that renders her aloof, hypercritical, and perpetually uneasy about her anomalous position as a Jewish American with few Jewish friends. It is not hard to find a repertoire of tropes and images that *UI* can draw upon in order to augment Sarah's emergence from a largely abstracted, implicitly deracinated and reified worldview into a more hopeful perception of Israel. As Lorenzo Veracini has argued, there is a settler colonial archive of representations that awaits reanimation, which encourages the US to intimately identify with the fate of Israel as a pioneering settler society (304–5). This elective affinity includes a perception of the Old World, early modern Europe, as degenerate, decaying, hierarchical, and the newly founded settler society as experimental, perfectible, a polity beyond the entropic course of history.[6] In the case of Israel's codification as a young nation, consider the prominence of Zionist youth groups in driving its settlement objectives and desire for Jewish cultural renaissance, the invigorating sabra ideal of the new, muscular Jew restoring fertility to the land, and more recently the enthusiasm for the youthful Israeli Defense Force (IDF) as, in the parlance of Miriam Libicki, a 'fetish object'.[7]

Before we explore how Glidden's own reinvigorated youth, within the context of a *Bildungsroman* that leans more towards the genre's classical possibilities, begins to mirror a refreshed conception of Israel as an essentially ethical and pluralistic nation state, we need to discuss another point of difference in relation to *NIPPM*. Since Joe Sacco's influential if contested work of graphic reportage, *Palestine* (2001), it is something of a convention that the author-avatar uses works of critique as companions or guides on their travels. In Sacco's case this involved the deployment of the writings of Edward Said which assisted him in stressing the investment of many Palestinians in education, and helped him to critique the legacy of Orientalist travel writing as shaping representations of Palestinians as either picturesque camel drivers or irrational terrorists. While Harvey does not explicitly refer to particular readings in his autodidactic researches, we can infer that he has aligned himself with post-Zionist and new histories of Israel and Palestine that includes *inter alia* the historiographical labours of Tom Segev, Ilan Pappé, Baruch Kimmerling and María Rosa Menocal on the history of Al-Andalus.

Despite the existence of this scholarship that has flourished since the early 2000s, Sarah can only gesture towards lacunae and confusion when it comes to understanding the bigger historical and geopolitical picture. While stressing that after deciding to go on the trip she has spent 'every spare moment' reading about 'Israel, Palestine, and the conflict' (*Understand Israel* 11), the results are inconclusive. With the exception of reading *Haaretz* rather than the *New York Times* as her preferred news source and a single frame indicating histories of the region and explorations of Zionism that she decides to leave behind in the US (*Understand Israel* 6), Sarah finds 'objective sources' hard to find, and leaves for Israel with the lament that she 'knew less than when [she] started' (11). Rather than undertaking careful research enabling a broader historicised perspective as she travels, Glidden's fixation on the conflict and her selective reading of left-wing reportage leave her smug about her own rectitude, unhealthily obsessed with the conflict as symbolic spectacle,[8] while still largely ignorant, to all appearances, of the regional and world histories that intrigued Harvey.

Thus, the changing perception we expect from the questing protagonist of a *Bildungsroman* will not come from historical research and political critique as was the case for Sacco and Pekar, but from the affective force of intimacy, of conversing with and sharing experiences with her tour group, growing closer to other diasporic Jews and Jewish Israelis who include former and serving IDF soldiers, and listening empathetically to inspirational speakers on her itinerary. The political criticism that Glidden has read or shares with like-minded progressives in the United States, such as her boyfriend, is recoded as one-sided, determined from a comfortable distance to portray Israel as a villain in a postcolonial narrative that ignores Palestinian terrorism and anti-Semitism in the Arab world.

The epistemic 'gap' that results from not finding reliable sources on Israel/Palestine ultimately also means that Sarah can be consoled whenever a lingering concern about Israel's treatment of the Palestinians arises. Early on her journey, while on the bus to Kibbutz Nachshon, Sarah and her friend Melissa are pleasantly surprised to find multi-lingual signs in Hebrew and Arabic legally mandated by the state. They then encounter the negatively iconic wall or separation barrier which shocks Sarah into realising on the bus trip that she is not in fact in rural Pennsylvania. Their tour guide Gil is once more surprisingly even-handed as he discusses the wall as an issue of some complexity in that it does separate Palestinians from their lands, but in having supposedly reduced Palestinian attacks, is ultimately a guarantor of Israeli-Jewish safety.

This is about the last we hear of the actual mechanisms of the Israeli occupation since Sarah, later enjoying her time in the cultural environs of Jewish west Jerusalem, never visits the Occupied Territories despite her initial intentions and the promptings of her boyfriend. We can contrast Sarah's increasing beguilement by her guides who insist there is no systemic oppression of the Palestinians, to other graphic travelogues which do want to visualise the occupation, such as Guy Delisle's *Jerusalem: Chronicles from the Holy City* (2012). In Delisle's meandering but inquisitive narrative, a foreign correspondent reminds his equable French-Canadian avatar that less than 10 per cent of the

Occupied Territories is under direct Palestinian control, a moot point given that even in centres of Palestinian life like Ramallah, the Israeli army search, arrest and interrogate residents almost every night. When Sarah realises she likes being in Israel more than she thought but finds it hard to enjoy 'the Palestinian situation' because people's homes are being bulldozed and settlement building continues, her idealistic young Israeli friend Nadan quickly consoles her that it is more 'complicated than you think' and that 'nobody's bulldozing for fun' (*Understand Israel* 76), in other words that Israel's security concerns and desire to protect its citizens is a more laudable and rational priority than Sarah suspected at a distance. Sarah's doubts, which, unsupported by extensive empirical knowledge, are often more performed gestures of unease than detailed criticism, are consistently revealed as naïve or simplistic. Sarah is quickly disarmed when her guides routinely respond that it is complicated, implicitly framing Israel's actions as understandable in the fog of war. In conversation with her Israeli antagonist cum mentor Nadan, her tour guide, Sarah is reminded that the Palestinian right of return is in reality an invitation to let people in who 'want to kill us' and that the notion of a Palestinian population wanting peace is a demonstrable pipedream (119). This ethnocentric position, legitimising the prevention of the Palestinian right of return as sanctioned under international law, is left largely undisputed in a text that does not engage with Palestinian narratives of suffering and oppression under military occupation in any detail. It is difficult to agree with Matt Reingold's benign assertion that Glidden simply did not need to tell the story of the Palestinians as Joe Sacco had already done so and that Glidden wants *UI* to 'tell the story of her people and how she came to identify with a community that she thought was entirely foreign to her' (Reingold 533). I would instead interpret Glidden's repositioning of Israel as security conscious rather than systematically punitive or unceasingly land-hungry as a potent exculpatory trope, largely endorsed by the Western media, which can only be challenged by extensive analysis of Israel's domination of many aspects of Palestinian life.

If Sarah's discomfort with 'the situation', as she euphemistically calls it, is complicated by realities on the ground, it is important to *UI* to reveal that Glidden's semiotic training in college, in which critique means a suspicion of naturalised or essentialist representations of self and other, is also poorly equipped to appraise the richly suggestive cultural and religious signifiers in the holy land in which she finds herself. Likely influenced by her undergraduate training in critical theory, Sarah can only see colonialist red flags when speakers use terms like 'hero' or 'pioneer' (*Understand Israel* 64) in discussing the early Zionist founders of kibbutzim such as Kinneret, an early stop on her itinerary. Sarah needs to be reminded by another benign male mentor, an imagined interlocutor named Yosef, an early Kinneret pioneer who intervenes in Sarah's discomfort over her increasing identification with Israel's youthful struggles to found a Jewish homeland, that Zionism is a movement relying on rhetoric and poetry to install visionary courage.

Soon afterwards, other encounters serve to unfreeze Sarah's nominal paralysis in which Israeli self-representation and statements of pride in Jewish-Israeli identity seem to be mired in exclusionary impulses. Sarah is drawn visibly groaning when over dinner the same evening at Kibbutz Kinneret she is asked to engage in a bonding exercise over the meaning of Jewishness, another naff essentialist exercise entailing conformist group-think that in fact, to her pleasant surprise, reveals the diversity of the tour group with vastly different backgrounds. Sarah, as we have mentioned, can celebrate the fact that her family, while not religious, gave her an interest in the cultural aspects of Judaism that include 'learning, eating, and arguing' (*Understand Israel* 67), legible within the text as a microcosm of her educational experience of Israel as vital and self-questioning. That *UI* too is offering a version of the found family genre is more or less confirmed when Sarah is reminded that many Jews and Israelis themselves experience the state of Israel as a 'crazy uncle' for whom they feel responsible, for 'to publicly reject him would expose our family's shame' (109). It is important for *UI* that the state of Israel, a crazy uncle occasionally intoxicated with power or fierce protectiveness, does not encapsulate the Israel she encounters, which is full of idealistic and sensitive young people, sometimes mature before their time due to wartime conditions and the loss of loved ones, working to solve problems and reach a more promising future. These include her patient, thoughtful tour guide Nadan who works as a political staffer for a Left Israeli politician, and a recent young American immigrant named David who made *Aliyah* to overcome the inertia of his own privilege and in order to 'do his part' in a country in which the younger generation is more respected and connected to the problems the country is facing than in the US (*Understand Israel* 184). This particular encounter upsets Sarah's assumption that ideological fanaticism or religious identification is the usual motivating factor for American-Jewish immigration to Israel.

So it is that Glidden's psycho-social isolation and enervating negativity, which masquerades as detached moral superiority, is overwhelmed by eloquent, rhetorically powerful Israeli narratives of youthful participation in the greater good. She can no longer resist a profound identification and thus celebration of Zionist colonialism, taunted by a portrait of one of the founders of Tel Aviv that she would have come here too if she had to flee the Nazis. Embracing a mytho-poetic conception of proto-Zionist Jewish history the longer the journey goes, Sarah is now receptive to the myth of Masada as replete with inspirational symbolism in which Jewish diasporic visitors can understand the resistant Jewish defenders of Masada as role models, setting an example in which Israel is to be defended at all costs.

The incremental framing of Sarah's critique of Israel as a smug academic posture, the fruit of a corrosive diasporic environment, seems to justify a degree of moderate ethnocentrism and familial loyalty as its antidote. Sarah is brought to admit that she likes Israel, and particularly its people, amongst whom she feels strangely at home; towards the end of the novel Sarah will decide not to visit the Occupied Territories, preferring to enjoy a Calderón play with an audience full of cultured young Jewish Israelis, people like herself. Sarah can even begin to feel a connection with the ultimate Leftist bugbear, the IDF, since the soldiers she witnesses are so young, virtually children, while the situation of Palestinians begins to recede as an immediate catalyst for her visit. Indeed, feeling threatened by Palestinian boys in Arab East Jerusalem, Sarah can only wish she is back in civilisation, enjoying the surrounds of a West Jerusalem café.

By this point in the narrative Sarah's experience of Israel is now largely devoid of political ugliness, with Israel expanding her cultural horizons,

Figure 9.4 'Our children.' © Sarah Glidden. Used with permission from Drawn & Quarterly.

impressing her with its resilience and hopefulness, and inviting Jewish comradery, something of a prosthesis for what may have been lacking in her youth. Glidden's graphic novel is by no means, as Reingold notes, simply a pro-Zionist tract as it does not ignore the colonial mistreatment of Palestinians and Bedouins, an issue which receives significant if passing attention. Yet *UI* is nevertheless invested in renovating Jewish subjectivity, affording its protagonist a psychic release from feelings of alienation and detachment, instilling an anti-historicist drive in which the diasporic Jewish self is released from the burden of history.

In this more classically inclined *Bildungsroman*, which, as Franco Moretti argues, as a genre can work to legitimate a social order 'inside the mind of individuals' (Moretti 230), the seemingly sceptical Sarah can psychically incorporate one of the aims of the *Taglit*-Birthright tours, which is to 'strengthen Jewish identity among young Jewish adults' (Abramson 659). In a powerful set of correspondences that accords with the novel's own attention to the imaginative appeal of Zionism as rhetoric, poetry, imaginative lyricism, Israel is repositioned by *UI* as a young nation, full of aspiring and creative individuals who care for the Jewish community, a state sometimes stumbling, yet always on a pathway towards healthy normalisation. Indeed, Sarah is not too dissimilar from the Frédéric of *Sentimental Education* described by Moretti. Like Frédéric, who opposes and postpones separation and exclusion so that no social class or personality is finally excluded from narrative prolongation, Sarah opposes herself to the 'determination' of Israel as a maleficent colonial power, thus preserving the '*unlimited pliability* of the object of fantasy' (Moretti 175, original emphasis) that Israel has long represented in the wake of the Holocaust. The palpable psychic drive in *UI* to relinquish corrosive historicism also dovetails with American optimism about human perfectibility and civilisational mission, suturing divisions between the American Jewish diaspora and Israel. While Pekar and Glidden's texts eventually disagree, partially on generational grounds, about the 'promise' of Israel, both position their protagonists as struggling against ideological conditioning, whether cultural, familial or institutional, allowing their protagonists' tentative coming of age to reshape our perception of the world, thereby 'perceiving and evaluating it according to human proportions' (Moretti 41).

Notes

1. All references to 'Harvey' and 'JT Waldman' in the analysis of *NIPPM* and to 'Sarah' in *UI* are to their fictional avatars.
2. In *Harvey Pekar's Cleveland* (2012), Pekar's avatar mentions Zubal's 'book empire' as critical to his development as a writer and artist (100) and evokes the

capacious collections of the Cleveland public library as a reminder Cleveland was once a historical centre of munificent civic philanthropy (111).
3. In a recent article, Matt Reingold informs us that since the programme's founding, over 600,000 Jews have attended the trip from 67 countries, with around 80 per cent of these participants travelling from the US and Canada (530).
4. For a recent analysis decrying Israel's abandonment by canonised Jewish intellectuals, see Susie Linfield, *The Lions' Den: Zionism and the Left from Hannah Arendt to Noam Chomsky.*
5. Recent polemical complaints about anti-Zionism and anti-Semitism on US college campuses, a distinct target of the Trump administration, include *Anti-Zionism on Campus: The University, Free Speech, and BDS*, edited by Andrew Pessin and Doron S. Ben-Atar, and Cary Nelson, *Israel Denial: Anti-Zionism, Anti-Semitism, and the Faculty Campaign Against the Jewish State.*
6. See Veracini, 'Interacting imaginaries in Israel and the United States' 293–312.
7. In a recent graphic essay, Libicki argues that the new image of desirable, healthy young Jewish soldiers, both young men and women, encouraged American Jewish parents to send their teenagers on 'Israel trips (two weeks to a year post high school) to cement sympathy with the Jewish state and plant the idea that Jews are kinda hot' (18–23).
8. As described by Anna Bernard, Glidden's Sarah would seem to be amongst a demographic of younger American Jews decoupled from the automatic association between Israeli and American interests. In a post 9/11 world, Sarah somewhat unquestioningly participates in the 'metropolitan left's adoption of the Palestinian struggle as "the emblematic solidarity movement of our time . . . our Spanish civil war, our Cuba, our Nicaragua"' (Bernard, 'Consuming Palestine' 200).

10

THE PALESTINE/ISRAEL CONFLICT IN THE YOUNG ADULT ANGLOPHONE *BILDUNGSROMAN*

Isabelle Hesse

In an interview, Canadian children's book author Deborah Ellis has pointed out that 'it is easy to look at the Middle East and only see a colossal mess with people firmly entrenched in their versions of the story and with powerful forces benefitting from keeping the conflict alive' (*Cat* 50). Ellis's statement draws attention to three key aspects of representing the situation in Palestine/Israel, especially outside of the Middle East: first, the idea that it is a complex conflict (what Ellis calls a 'colossal mess') and second, that this is an issue that polarises people. Third, and already implicit in the previous point, is the fact that this conflict is relevant for audiences beyond the Middle East, which is partly due to the fact that it is shaped by the involvement of key international stakeholders, such as the United States and the European Union. As discussed in the introduction to this edited collection, the Palestine/Israel conflict has long fascinated audiences outside of the region. Since the Second Palestinian Intifada, there has been a rise in young adult books from outside the Middle East that imaginatively engage with this conflict, a sample of which will be the focus of my chapter.[1]

While young adult fiction is usually not linked with politics, at least not directly, using Elizabeth Laird's book *A Little Piece of Ground*, which will be discussed later in this chapter, David Belbin has emphasised that 'We should be proud that YA fiction acts as a home for writers with a serious moral agenda' (140). Indeed, many people have emphasised the capacity of young adult readers to engage with complex topics. For instance, Kate Wilson, who was director of Macmillan Books when they published Laird's *A Little Piece of Ground* (2003), a book that was criticised for being too one-sided in favour of the Palestinians, responded by saying that: 'I do not think it is right to underestimate the intelligence and subtlety of young readers' (Wilson quoted in Leibovich-Dar).[2] This statement emphasises that young adult fiction, even though usually aimed at readers aged 12–15, should not automatically include content that is simplified or shies away from complex political matters. In many ways, young adult fiction lends itself to engaging with and representing the Palestine/Israel conflict to an audience outside of the Middle East. First, a key aspect of this genre is that 'reading imaginative works, ones that allow the reader to see the world from other people's point of view, is invaluable in adolescents' journey into adulthood' (Belbin 134). The idea of seeing the world through someone else's eyes is important for engaging with the Palestine/Israel conflict as it allows readers to re-evaluate their preconceived ideas. Second, this is a genre that is 'aimed at emerging readers' which in turn means that 'the educational impulse is at the heart of YA fiction' (Belbin 138). As a result, young adult fiction allows authors to introduce a naïve, innocent, and to a certain extent even ignorant perspective on the Palestine/Israel conflict, which enables their audiences to be educated alongside the characters and to untangle and understand some of the perceived complexities of the conflict in the Middle East. At the same time, young adult fiction offers an informed perspective of the conflict's geopolitical context that can potentially encourage empathy and solidarity with its victims.

In this chapter, I focus on how a specific sub-genre of young adult fiction, the coming-of-age story or *Bildungsroman*, is used to engage with the Palestine/Israel conflict by writers that choose protagonists from different geopolitical backgrounds: Deborah Ellis's *The Cat at the Wall* (2014) focalises its story through the eyes of Clare, a North American eight-grader who dies and is transformed into a cat living in Bethlehem; Elizabeth Laird's novel *A Little Piece of Ground* (2003) tells the story of Karim, a thirteen-year-old Palestinian living in Ramallah; and William Sutcliffe's *The Wall* (2013) focuses on a twelve-year-old boy named Joshua who lives in a town that is a thinly veiled allusion to a Jewish settlement in the West Bank. The *Bildungsroman* in its emphasis on self-discovery and development lends itself to being used as a didactic tool, and as Carla L. Peterson notes, in the process of 'witness[ing] a growth from naiveté to experience' (22) by the protagonist, the reader experiences the desire to undergo a similar development. Franco Moretti also emphasises that in the *Bildungsroman* 'the reader perceive[s] the text through the eyes of the protagonist: which is logical, since the protagonist is undergoing the experience of formation, and the reading too is intended to be a formative process' (56). Hence, the protagonist's journey to self-development can be used to parallel the audience's development and self-discovery as regards their understanding of, and positioning in relation to, the conflict.

However, critics have drawn attention to the problems inherent in using the *Bildungsroman* as a European genre in relation to non-European contexts. Kaisa Ilmonen, for example, in discussing the use of this genre in postcolonial contexts, has argued that 'it institutionalizes the presentation of an emancipated, individual and coherent *Western* self' (61, my emphasis). In her view, one key distinction between the European and the postcolonial *Bildungsroman* is that for the latter 'becoming is not always directed towards harmonious closure, but instead towards fragmentation and friction between the self's different axes of identity' (72). I am interested in how the novels under discussion use the *Bildungsroman* as a genre familiar to their 'Western' audiences, but equally I interrogate how their mainly 'non-Western' protagonists challenge the narrative conventions of the European *Bildungsroman*.

Although Palestine/Israel is not strictly a postcolonial context, as the Palestinian Territories are still occupied by Israel, the protagonists situated in this geopolitical context exhibit similar struggles to their postcolonial counterparts, including defining a coherent identity in relation to their community: the (Jewish settler) community of his town in the case of Sutcliffe's Joshua, and the Palestinian community in the West Bank in the case of Laird's Karim. Even though Ellis's displaced protagonist Clare does not have a local community in the West Bank, she develops an ethical identity by assuming 'social responsibility'. The latter idea is also pertinent to the development of the two other protagonists and as Marianne Hirsch has noted, in the classical German *Bildungsroman*, it is through 'the assumption of social responsibility' that 'the individual discovers his authentic self and realizes his personal destiny' (302). I argue that this process of self-discovery is closely linked to encountering the 'other', which in the case of Sutcliffe's and Ellis's protagonists is the Palestinian, while for Laird's main character this 'other', or rather that which is unfamiliar or unknown, is the Palestine/Israel conflict. Encountering this 'other', who can be both a character and the conflict itself, plays an important role in defining the identity of the self, following Sara Ahmed who has argued that: 'The journey towards the stranger becomes a form of self-discovery, in which the stranger functions yet again to establish and define the "I"' (6). As I will show below, encountering the 'other' not only defines the identity of the self but can also actively destabilise it. Hence, this chapter shows that identity formation is interactive and dialogic, emphasising how both self and other are transformed through this encounter.

The type of dynamic identity formation depicted in these novels contributes to what Joseph R. Slaughter has identified as one of the key features of the *Bildungsroman*, namely its ability to do 'literary social work ... that articulates certain social relations' (7). This literary social work manifests itself through an engagement with the Palestine/Israel conflict, which helps the narrators of the three novels discussed in this chapter to gain a better understanding of their place within a wider national or global community, specifically in relation to transnational concerns about empathy with and the human rights of the Palestinian people. However, the young adult novel's literary social work also manifests itself in the use of conventions of the *Bildungsroman* to render the conflict in Palestine/Israel accessible to a wider audience, using generic conventions and aesthetic strategies to depict a historical and geopolitical context that is often seen as too complex to understand for both adult and young adult readers from outside the region. Taking up the challenge, the three novels under discussion depict everyday life under occupation, asking readers to consider the effects of the occupation on the lives of young Israeli Jews and Palestinians and to interrogate deeply rooted ideas about conflicting religious or ethnic identities. Overall, they ask readers to revise their perceptions of the conflict, including how walls create segregations of the mind.

Deborah Ellis's *The Cat at the Wall*: Metamorphosis, Empathy and Individual Choice

Canadian author Deborah Ellis is an award-winning children's book author, best known for her *Breadwinner* trilogy, which focuses on the life of eleven-year-old Parvana in war-torn Afghanistan. She has also published non-fictional work on the Middle East, since her publisher Groundwood Books sent her to Israel and the Gaza Strip to research a book about oral history among Palestinian and Israeli children.[3] Her interest in the region and in depicting the conflict from the perspective of a child, or rather a young adult, is continued in her novel *The Cat at the Wall* (2014), which follows the story of thirteen-year-old Clare who lives in Bethlehem, Pennsylvania. After her death, she is transformed into a cat and finds herself in Bethlehem, in the West Bank. Metamorphosis, as Marina Warner reminds us, is often linked to 'spaces (temporal, geographical, and mental) that were crossroads, cross-cultural zones, points of interchange' (17). Ellis sets up a cross-cultural geographical connection by having Clare live in Bethlehem, Pennsylvania and then moving her to Bethlehem in the West Bank. Moreover, her metamorphosis happens at a key juncture in her life, just after she has started to realise that she had been misbehaving in school because she had not processed her beloved grandmother's death yet.

Clare initially thinks that being transformed into a cat is a punishment for the way she behaved as a human. In a series of flashbacks, she reveals to the reader that she was not a very likeable person but arrogant, self-absorbed and cruel and that she often lied to get an advantage. As a cat, she realises that she is unable to lie, exemplifying the fact that her magical 'punishment' fits the crime, which is a common trope in fairy tales and fables, as Bruno Bettelheim has noted (186). In narrative terms, Clare's transformation also has a practical aspect to it, as Ellis has explained in an interview:

> I wanted to be a fly on the wall in one of these situations, but thought that a cat would be just as good as an interloper. But I didn't want to write in the voice of a cat. That's how Clare came into the picture. (*Cat* 149)

While Ellis wants to preserve a human voice, it is important that a cat can witness and participate in situations where a human would be conspicuous. The perspective of a cat can to a certain extent be seen as more detached, especially since cats are often seen as manipulative and less interested in human validation than for example dogs. An anthropomorphic cat allows Ellis to depict the situation in the West Bank, and especially the hardships of children, from a perspective that will not immediately be discarded as too politicised. In addition, the feline perspective results in the adult reader being doubly removed from the conflict as they not only experience the somewhat comic distance of the animal's perspective but equally the innocence and at times bemusement achieved through Clare's young adult perspective.

Typical of the growth trajectory of the *Bildungsroman*, Clare slowly develops as a character as she is increasingly able to feel empathy and starts exhibiting a sense of social responsibility towards other human beings. This change is catalysed through her encounter with Omar, a Palestinian boy into whose house she sneaks when two Israeli soldiers take it over for surveillance purposes. At first, however, Clare uses being a cat as a way to evade responsibility: 'What did I care if a boy wanted to hide? It had nothing to do with me. The best thing about being a cat is that nothing is my fault' (*Cat* 24). This sentiment can be extrapolated to Ellis's readers, especially if we read Clare's refusal to take responsibility in light of a statement that Ellis has made in the preface to her book *Three Wishes: Palestinian and Israeli Children Speak Out*: 'war, like almost everything else humans do, is a choice . . . Sitting on the sidelines and doing nothing to stop something that's wrong is a choice' (x). Clare soon models this change in commitment, when she decides to bring Omar his inhaler because she realises that he has asthma, admitting that this is not something she would have done in her previous life: 'It took me a while to figure out what [I should do], because I'm not used to doing things for other people' (*Cat* 39). In many ways, Clare's encounter with Omar exemplifies Sara Ahmed's argument, mentioned in the introduction to this chapter, that the journey towards the other is a form of self-discovery, helping to shape the identity of the self. In Clare's case it equally serves to re-evaluate her previous behaviour and moral standards. However, and this is a trope of the *Bildungsroman*, this scene confirms that Clare's development was only possible once removed from her old life, both geographically and in terms of species, confirming how transformation plays a key role as a 'figure of thought for negotiating our "selves" and our world' (Gildenhard and Zissos 2). Moreover, this altruistic scene can be read in light of a philosophical tradition in which cats have played a crucial role in encouraging critical thinking. Mario Ortiz-Robles has pointed out that cats 'have always had a special fascination for humans: they are enigmatic creatures that seem to question the right of humans to think' (115–16). Jacques Derrida similarly used the example of the cat's gaze to discuss notions of alterity:

> It [the cat] has its point of view regarding me. The point of view of the absolute other, and nothing will have ever done more to make me think through this absolute alterity of the neighbour, than these moments when I see myself naked under the gaze of a cat. ('The Animal' 380)

If we follow both of these lines of argument, we can argue that the cat's perspective, especially its emphasis on asking humans to interrogate the 'otherness' of those around them, encourages a critical engagement with the Palestine/Israel conflict, asking Anglophone audiences not only to reconsider their preconceptions about this conflict but equally their ideas about 'otherness', particularly in relation to the Palestinians.

This development of the audience's perceptions is paralleled by Clare's development as a character, which becomes even more pronounced towards the end of the novel, when she takes a picture of Omar and his parents to the boy who is feeling distressed, telling the reader that 'I wanted to comfort him' (*Cat* 110). In addition to having moved from passivity to action, a key trope in the *Bildungsroman*, as Susan Rubin Suleiman notes (65), Clare's desire to comfort Omar is motivated by a sense of social responsibility, which originates from her having witnessed Omar's father and pregnant mother being killed at a checkpoint because the Israeli soldiers thought Omar's father was taking a rifle out of his violin case when he was looking for his identity papers. This scene at the checkpoint is a key moment where the presence of a cat would be inconspicuous. Through Clare's disinterested gaze, as she is mainly hoping to get food at the checkpoint, Ellis is able to describe quite a harrowing scene from a distanced perspective. In this flashback, Clare initially uses quite simple and unemotive language, but her descriptions of Omar's father nevertheless reveal how he gets increasingly flustered and worried, for example when she comments 'The man kept looking around wildly, as if he already knew he was trapped' (*Cat* 112). Moreover, Ellis uses the cat as a mediator between both sides, at least for the audience. Since as a cat Clare understands all languages, she is able to follow the exchange, and particularly the misunderstandings between Omar's father, who speaks Arabic, and the Israeli soldiers, who speak Hebrew: 'They were talking in two different languages. I understood everything but the soldier and the guy at the checkpoint did not understand. They were also not listening to each other' (*Cat* 113). Clare's feline perspective allows Ellis to achieve a balanced appraisal of the conflict, something that she similarly asks her audiences to do.

A key aspect of this balanced perspective is the assumption of social responsibility, which in Clare's case becomes most pronounced when she decides to do something that she would have considered undignified in her former life, in order to diffuse a tense situation between the Israeli army and Palestinians:

> I leapt down from the boy's arms and out into the little space between the enemies.
> I started to dance.
> I danced for all of them, up on my hind legs.
> . . .
> And everybody shut up and stopped to watch. (*Cat* 140)

Ellis has said in an interview that the novel 'tries to figure out a place for individual choice in the face of big events' (*Cat* 148). Through her choice to intervene rather than observe, Clare shows that she has developed a sense of social responsibility not only for individuals such as Omar but also at a collective level as she tries to mediate between the two opposing sides, at least temporarily. This emphasis on choice is a common ending for the *Bildungsroman*, as David J. Mickelsen reminds us: 'Bildungsromane typically conclude with the protagonist making some choice, thereby confirming that the protagonist has achieved a coherent self' (418). In Clare's case, her development as a character is further exemplified in her reflection on her choice:

> It's the sort of thing that should make me feel very sorry for myself. And I've tried. I've tried to go back to my old thoughts . . . but it's not working.
> I did something useful, even though it was a very small thing. It wasn't like I brought peace to the world or anything. I just kept some people from killing each other for a little while. I was useful. It felt good. (*Cat* 142)

While this reflection is a clear example of how Clare has moved from ignorance to knowledge of the self, another key element of the *Bildungsroman*, the ending of the novel challenges the emergence of a coherent self as well as the harmonious closure of the European *Bildungsroman* (Suleiman 65). Ellis achieves this not only through the animal protagonist who is unable to develop further or attain significant power but also by leaving Clare in limbo, not telling the reader whether she is able to return to her previous life as a human. Through her choice of turning Clare into a cat and not returning her to her human form, Ellis refuses the socialisation of the self into society, which is reinforced at the end of the novel when Clare wonders whether she can be part of Omar's family, moving away from traditional ideas of family as an entity linked by blood usually presented as the starting point of a *Bildungsroman*. Moreover, unlike traditional protagonists of the *Bildungsroman*, Clare 'establish[es] links of solidarity with other individuals' (Vazquez 34) and shows a clear sense of empathy for Omar's fate, encouraging the readers to experience the same. As such, Ellis's use of the genre works well to allow her readers to achieve a critical distance from the conflict, while at the same time encouraging solidarity with the Palestinians and their plight through her protagonist's perspective. Ellis is careful not to suggest that Clare's small act will change the situation, which serves to illustrate that there is no easy solution to the conflict and that dialogue and empathy alone cannot resolve this conflict if they are not accompanied by political concessions. Nevertheless, her novel reimagines the future of the conflict by stressing the importance of assuming social responsibility on an individual level, which for a young adult reader might mean considering the impact of their actions on their immediate environments, while for an adult reader this more easily translates into reconsidering the importance of individual choices in relation to wider issues, including the situation in Palestine/Israel.

Education under Occupation: Self and Palestinian Society in Elizabeth Laird's *A Little Piece of Ground*

Fostering empathy for and solidarity with the Palestinians is also a key aspect of *A Little Piece of Ground* (2003), which British author Elizabeth Laird wrote together with Palestinian academic and children's book author Sonia Nimr.[4] Laird first visited Israel in 1968 and she became aware of the plight of Palestinian refugees while living in Beirut between 1975 and 1978, during the Lebanese Civil War. In January 2002, she held workshops for Palestinian children's writers in Gaza and Ramallah, which is when she met Sonia Nimr, and in September the same year they decided to write this book together. Nimr explains their collaboration in strategic terms: 'If a Palestinian were to write a book about the situation in the territories by herself, publishers wouldn't take an interest in it, because they would think it's one-sided' (Nimr quoted in Leibovich-Dar). Laird, on the other hand, saw this as an opportunity to make the Palestinian story more widely known as during her time in the Occupied Palestinian Territories, she 'became aware that we in the West know very little of what life is like for Palestinians living under military occupation' ('A Little Piece'). The novel is set against the backdrop of the events of Operation Defensive Shield in 2002, which was a large-scale military operation by the Israeli Defense Force in the West Bank during the Second Palestinian Intifada. In spite of this very specific historic context and the novel's geographical location, the epigraph states that 'The boys in this book stand for all who live their lives in such circumstances and manage, against the odds, to go on growing up' (*Ground* n.p.). This statement raises two key issues: first, it confirms John Collins's claim that Palestine is both 'microcosmic and prophetic' (137), making the experience of the boys in the book, which is in many ways specifically Palestinian, stand in for other experiences of military and/or colonial occupation (obliquely referred to as 'such circumstances'). Second, this book, from the start, positions itself as a *Bildungsroman*, a novel that focuses on the experience of 'growing up'.

A Little Piece of Ground opens with Karim Aboudi, the protagonist of the novel, making a list of 'The ten best things that I want to do (or be) in my life' (*Ground* 1). Apart from showing Karim's ambitions in terms of developing as a character, this list serves to underline that he is an ordinary boy who wants ordinary things, including becoming 'champion footballer of the entire world' (*Ground* 1). At the same time, it indicates that Karim is not just any boy but someone living in a specific context marked by oppressive conflict and military incursion, which most clearly emerges through the second list that he makes: 'The ten things I don't want to do (or be)', where at least four items are clearly linked to living under occupation, including not wanting to be shot in the back and not having their house demolished, and the tenth is particularly poignant in its brevity: 'Not dead.' (*Ground* 2). Even though the content of these two lists might suggest otherwise, at the start of the novel Karim is not very interested in the broader dimensions of the Palestine/Israel conflict, thus in many ways refusing the 'main task of the hero or heroine' of the *Bildungsroman*, which 'is to accommodate self to society' (Peterson 22). Karim's refusal of awareness could, however, be read, as a refusal to be normalised into a life exclusively defined by occupation and conflict. Karim's anger at the occupation, which is mainly directed at the fact that it prevents him from playing football whenever he wants to, increasingly builds up and turns into anger at the occupation as a whole, which is accompanied by his gradual socialisation into Palestinian society.

This development is catalysed through a scene at a flying checkpoint on the way to his grandmother who lives in Deir Aldalab. All the men are asked to step out of their cars and forced to strip down to their underwear. Karim's reaction is described as follows: he 'watched in horrified fascination. Giggles of embarrassment were bubbling up inside him. The men, standing out on the road in their underpants, looked funny and pathetic, helpless and stupid' (*Ground* 39). But when he realises that this is what the Israeli soldiers want them to experience, Karim sees this scene in a new light and '[h]ot, red anger pulsed behind his eyes' (*Ground* 40). This exemplifies how in the *Bildungsroman*, 'the protagonist is portrayed as being at the mercy of overwhelming social forces' (Peterson 22), even though in this case it is not Karim's society that oppresses him but the Israeli soldiers. However, the reader also witnesses a typical 'conflict between the ideal of self-determination and the equally imperious demands of socialization' (Moretti 15), when Karim and his family are harassed by Jewish settlers while picking olives and Karim exclaims: '"Nobody *does* anything!" he burst out. "My father – they *stripped* him! Then they shot at him – us – in our own olive groves! But he doesn't *do* anything"' (*Ground* 56, original emphasis). This scene is a key moment in Karim's identity formation, as it shows his initial opposition to the older generation and to their non-violent resistance to the occupation, until he himself is ready to become part of a community that advocates and practises non-violent resistance. Moreover, this generational conflict, as Muhammad Masud has noted, 'is likely to resonate with adolescents because for most of them it is a natural part of their daily lives' (605–6), which contributes to creating a sense of connection and solidarity between the Palestinian protagonist and the mainly non-Palestinian readers of the novel.

When they return home, Karim feels increasingly depressed by living under occupation and being confined in his house: 'Whatever you tried to do in this country, wherever you wanted to go, the enemy was always there to stop you. Even a simple game of football was impossible' (*Ground* 79). His development is progressed further when he hides from Israeli tanks in an abandoned car on Hopper's ground, which is the eponymous piece of land he and his friends have cleared from rubble to create a space for playing football. Staying put in the car – which recalls the practice of *sumud*, or steadfastness, staying put on the land – makes Karim realise that 'he was resisting too, in a way. Just being here, holding out on his own under their very noses, was an act of resistance' (*Ground* 166). This marks a key turning point in Karim's development as he now becomes part of a community of Palestinians who resist the occupation. In many ways, this challenges the depiction of the relationship between individual and collective in the traditional *Bildungsroman*, which is usually characterised by 'the conflict between the autonomy of the individual and the need to integrate into a society that the hero does not feel identified with' (Vazquez 33). While Karim certainly exemplified an alienated hero at the start of the novel – when he feels indifferent to Palestinian society, especially the older generation – he now experiences a stronger sense of belonging, albeit not one that is exclusively based on the emergence of an individual self, a relational perspective which is often a key aspect of the postcolonial *Bildungsroman*, as discussed earlier.

This trajectory from disengaged youth to someone who is aware of their surroundings mirrors the journey of the audience, who is encouraged, through the character of Karim, to feel empathy for his individual experience and by extension for the Palestinian people as a whole. As such, Laird's novel can be considered as an example of the *Bildungsroman* as a comment on humanity where an individual's development from growth towards maturity 'is undertaken in the service of a further end' (Beddow 5). Unlike Ellis's novel, the ending of Laird's book confirms the emergence of a new, more mature personality – one that is not just focused on his own needs but is now part of a larger community of Palestinians who resist the occupation. The novel ends with a celebration of the release of Palestinian prisoners and the end of the curfew on Al-Manarah square, Ramallah's main square. The novel ends on a hopeful note, which emphasises both persistence and the importance of being part of a community for Karim: 'We'll get through all right, he told himself . . . We'll survive' (*Ground* 214). While this ending constitutes a typical example of the Palestinian political *Bildungsroman*, whose 'natural endpoint' is when 'the protagonist assumes his role in the national struggle' (Bernard, *Rhetorics* 61), Laird's novel can also be examined as a postcolonial *Bildungsroman*, which 'often makes the hero representative of his community' (Vazquez 34). As such, it can be interpreted as a continued call for Palestinians to resist the Israeli occupation, especially through the practice of *sumud*. Laird's ending can be read as an example of a harmonious closure and a happy ending, since even though the reader knows that Karim still lives under occupation, he has now found the tools to define his identity in relation to his community and to become a part of Palestinian non-violent resistance. This is what the novel encourages the reader to do: to use their sense of empathy and solidarity to revise their preconceived ideas about the situation in the Palestinian Territories and the equation between Palestinian resistance and violence that has gained renewed currency since the Second Palestinian Intifada.

Walled Identities and Imaginary Nationhood in William Sutcliffe's *The Wall*

British writer William Sutcliffe's *The Wall* (2013) is similarly aimed at revising perceptions of the conflict in Israel and the Occupied Palestinian Territories, at least for its adult readers. The main character Joshua lives in Amarias,[5] a fictional town next to a wall in the 'Occupied Zone', which as Sutcliffe emphasises 'should not be taken as an accurate representation of any specific place' (*Wall* 289). However, when he had finished a rough draft of the novel, he asked himself 'Was this, or was it not, a novel about the West Bank?' ('The Power of the West Bank Wall'). In order to address this question, he decided to visit the West Bank as part of the Palestinian Literature Festival in 2010 to decide 'how specific [he] wanted [his] novel to be' ('The Power of the Wall'). The result, as Sutcliffe notes, is a novel that – inspired by George Orwell's *Animal Farm*, which offers a morality tale to young adult readers while adult readers are able to read the story in its specific political context – is close to reportage while it also 'feels fantastical' (Allfree). This dual approach contributes to making his tale both specific and universal and, in some ways, this achieves a similar goal to Ellis's choice to have a cat as a witness to the conflict, as it allows for a more universal perspective and one that is easier for the reader to apply to a range of different contexts.

Sutcliffe's use of a young adult narrator allows him to depict many aspects of the wall from a naïve and innocent perspective and to follow the conventions of the *Bildungsroman*, tracing Joshua's personal development, which is shaped by ideas imposed by his family and community, into a more independent and critical engagement with the situation in the 'Occupied Zone'. Here Joshua demonstrates another characteristic of the *Bildungsroman*, namely that 'the personal history can be read as an allegory of a particular trajectory within a national history' (Buchanan n.p.), as Joshua's initial engagement with the wall can be seen as typical for the people living in his community. However, as his 'education' progresses, Joshua's position deviates from the 'trajectory' of his 'national history' and instead can be considered a suggestion for how people should perceive and engage with the wall in the West Bank and the ways in which it influences their identity and their understanding of the other, following Joseph R. Slaughter's concept of the *Bildungsroman* as 'articulat[ing] certain social relations' (7). These social relations are not only the ones between Joshua and the community in Amarias, but can be extrapolated to the Israeli Jewish context, as we will see below.

Joshua's understanding of his position within a national community is initially shaped through his mother's description of their town: 'This isn't an ordinary town . . . Things happen here. We have lots of protection but no amount is enough. There are people living very, very close who want to get us. They want us out' (*Wall* 13). But his perception of the situation in the 'Occupied Zone' slowly starts to change through his engagement with the people living on the other side of the wall. During his first journey across the wall, using a tunnel he finds under a demolished house, Joshua meets Leila, a girl who saves him from a group of boys that are chasing him. Sutcliffe has explained that in his novel he has inverted a common trope in children's literature where characters escape through a portal into a parallel, fantastical universe by writing the story of a character 'raised in a world of fantasy who discovers a portal to reality' (Allfree). Not only does Joshua see the people that the wall usually obscures but he also encounters the other and experiences how this other sees him, reflecting Sara Ahmed's argument regarding how others establish and define the self. However, this encounter with the other, rather than establishing and defining Joshua's identity, actively destabilises it. While his mother and his community made it clear to him that the people on the other side would attack them without the wall, Joshua realises that the boys, who chase him, seem to hate him 'just for being who [he] is, for coming from the other side of The Wall' (*Wall* 22). Joshua was not prepared for them to hate him as an individual without knowing him, which contributes to his rethinking of his own identity, especially as part of a collective.

This first journey across the wall is accompanied by a gradual questioning of the foundations of his own identity as well as the collective identity in Amarias. While the former is typical for the traditional, read European, *Bildungsroman*, the latter challenges the conventions of the genre. Maria Lima has argued that 'The Bildungsroman has been constructed as a fundamentally affirmative, conservative genre, confident in the legitimacy of the society it depicts, and anxious to suggest ways in which both hero and reader can find a productive place within that world' (438). However, in Joshua's case he challenges the society he is supposed to feel part of and, increasingly, he is unable to find a place for himself within his community. This becomes obvious when he returns home and looks at the cardboard town with a wall that he had built as a child. Before destroying it, he comments that 'Now for the first time, it strikes me as strange that I put this wall at the edge, with nothing on the other side of it' (*Wall* 61), which shows that life on the other side had been rendered invisible to Joshua before encountering the people living there. The cardboard wall that Joshua built and the absence of any people beyond its perimeter suggest that the wall has been effective in obscuring and negating the presence of the people living on the other side. Read in the context of Palestine/Israel, this cardboard wall also confirms that not only are Palestinians made invisible through the presence of the wall but also the 'act of erasure itself', as Gil Z. Hochberg has argued, is concealed, as the wall functions as a blinding mechanism (*Visual Occupations* 21). However, in destroying the wall, Joshua draws attention to the wall as 'a symptom of a larger failure of conciliation and justice' (Sorkin xx) and takes a decisive step in wanting to encounter the other and to subvert the control that the wall holds over his identity. As Joshua explains, the identity of people living in Amarias is defined above all through their common enemy on the other side of the wall: 'In Amarias, if you don't know who your enemy is, you don't know anything at all' (*Wall* 99). By taking this other away, selfhood suddenly becomes empty, which confirms Wendy Brown's argument that walls 'contribute to the imaginary of intact nationhood' (104).

Joshua's sense of belonging to an 'intact' nation, whose borders need to be policed, is further questioned when he goes to the checkpoint and witnesses how people from the other side are treated, describing the checkpoint as 'a network of metal cages, like something for funnelling livestock' (*Wall* 89), which emphasises the inhuman treatment of the people at the wall. This inequality and the recurring images of what he saw on the other side of the wall leads Joshua to venture once more into the town on the other side. This second visit again significantly changes Joshua as he learns more about Leila and her family, and especially the hardships they endure on a daily basis, including not being able to access and tend to their olive grove, which is on the other side of the wall. When Joshua puts his Amarias clothes back on, he remarks that 'It is as if these clothes belong to a boy who doesn't exist anymore' (*Wall* 132), which in the style of the *Bildungsroman* not only suggests that Joshua is now becoming an adult but it equally shows that he is in the process of 'discover[ing] his authentic self . . . in the assumption of social responsibility' (Hirsch 302). Joshua feels unable to return to the identity imposed on him in Amarias, which is founded upon a clear distinction between us and them, a distinction he no longer believes in. This becomes clear when his mother asks him to tell her where the tunnel under the wall is to protect 'their' people and Joshua asks who 'their' people are, to which the mother replies 'all of us who live here' (*Wall* 224). His mother's statement exemplifies how walls can create and corroborate a closed and nationalistic collective identity that excludes others. Joshua questions this worldview by interrogating the notion of 'here' when he asks, 'on both sides of the wall?' (*Wall* 224), emphasising that for him 'here' is no longer demarcated by the wall as a boundary, thus challenging the wall's function to 'ossif[y] a social physics that holds that two national bodies cannot share the same space at the same time' (Sorkin vii). He further illustrates this point when he says that 'But I have friends on the other side of The Wall. And there are people on this side of The Wall that I hate' (*Wall* 224), interrogating the assumption that the wall creates an automatic sense of belonging and a sense of national coherence.

But even when Joshua and his mother move away from Amarias to an unnamed seaside town outside of 'The Zone', after he is left a paraplegic because he was shot by an Israeli soldier when trying to cross back into Amarias, he realises that some of these issues are hard to leave behind: 'I hated that place [Amarias] because it felt like a huge lie, but this place doesn't feel so different . . . The lie here is different, but more convincing, easier to fall for' (*Wall* 284). Being further away from the wall allows people to forget what is happening in 'The Zone', including the suffering of the people living on the other side of the wall. As such, Sutcliffe's novel criticises how a delineation between us and them and an emphasis on a walled collective identity can lead to people no longer considering the concerns of human beings outside of their community as worthy, especially if they live behind a wall, whether literal or figurative. This criticism can be extrapolated to the Israeli Jewish collective and their relationship with Palestinians, to the international community and their engagement with Israel and the Occupied Palestinian Territories, as well as any national community that builds a wall or barrier to protect its collective identity from outsiders.

Conclusion

Palestinian writer Susan Abulhawa has argued that 'Writing a novel that depicts an oppressed society when you are not a member of that society is a risky undertaking' (Abulhawa '*The Wall*'). In an ideal world, there would be no need for Anglophone writers to engage with and represent the Palestine/Israel conflict to 'Western' audiences but unfortunately, as Nimr outlined above, there is a strategic need for this kind of literary social work, and for collaborations between Palestinian authors from the region and writers from the UK, the US or Australia. Journalism and commentary engaging with Israel and the Occupied Palestinian Territories is often seen as being one-sided and even more so if published by Palestinian writers. Bearing in mind the ethical implications of writing about the conflict in Palestine/Israel as an outsider, which not only applies to the authors discussed here but also the author of this chapter, I would suggest that Deborah Ellis, Elizabeth Laird and William Sutcliffe are making an important contribution to how the actual situation in Israel and the Occupied Palestinian Territories is represented to younger and some mature audiences outside of the Middle East.

By combining the young adult genre with the ethical formation implicit in the *Bildungsroman*, these writers are able to engage with a politically challenging topic through an aesthetic form that is accessible to a wide range of audiences. As a result, Ellis, Laird and Sutcliffe foreground the dynamics of the occupation of the Palestinian Territories, including everyday encounters between Israeli Jews and Palestinians and the concomitant power dynamics, rather than foregrounding 'ethnic' tension and identities. Although Ellis could be accused of using the West Bank, and the Palestine/Israel conflict, as a moral purgatory for her character, her unusual narrative choice of depicting this conflict from the perspective of a cat not only allows her to represent it to younger readers but equally to encourage her older readers to consider their own involvement in the conflict in Palestine/Israel and, like Clare, to assume social responsibility, even if it is only on a very small scale. While Laird's novel unambiguously focuses on the story of a Palestinian boy living in the West Bank during the Second Intifada, as she wants her readers to get a more informed understanding of what it is like to live under Israeli occupation, readers are similarly encouraged to question their own assumptions about the conflict while developing a sense of empathy with the Palestinians. In Sutcliffe's case, it could be argued that using the wall separating Israeli Jews from the Palestinians living in the Occupied Territories to make a wider point about borders and segregation takes away the specificity of the geopolitical context that this novel is addressing but I would suggest that the use of the fable is an apt genre to approach this context from a critical distance. Through Joshua's perspective, Sutcliffe encourages his readers to question their ideas about Israel and the Occupied Palestinian Territories and to extrapolate these ideas to considering whether they have figurative walls that insidiously encourage them to perceive individuals or communities as being different from, and potentially threatening to, their own identity. What all of these novels, with their courageous protagonists, have in common is that they enable their audiences to develop their own independent ideas about the conflict in Palestine/Israel. Hence, these novels not only function as a comment on the situation in the Middle East and the involvement of global powers in the region, but in their pages the Palestine/Israel conflict becomes a signifier for larger concerns about contemporary society, including the perennial importance of making the independent choice to assume responsibility for others.

Notes

1. There are earlier examples of young adult books from outside of the Middle East that engage with the conflict, such as Lynne Reid Banks's book *One More River* (1973), but these are rare.
2. For a summary of the criticisms levelled at the book, see Sara Leibovich-Dar, 'About a Boy'.
3. The resulting book was entitled *Three Wishes: Palestinian and Israeli Children Speak Out*.
4. Nimr is not acknowledged on the book cover of the edition that I am using in this chapter but she is mentioned as a co-author on the cover page inside the novel and she does appear on the cover of other editions.
5. Amarias is an anagram for 'Samaria'.

11

FEEDING WORDS WITH SUGAR: RESURRECTING PALESTINE IN CHILDREN'S PICTURE BOOKS FROM EGYPT

Magda Hasabelnaby and Radwa R. Mahmoud

The poet Mahmoud Darwish (1964–2008) is regarded widely as 'the voice of Palestine' (N. Bernard 52) and 'one of the finest poets of his entire generation' (R. Khalidi, '*Remembering*' 75). His goal was to prevent those who had colonised the land from 'colonizing memory' (Abu Eid 64). Today, one way of preventing such colonisation of memory is by teaching children about, and reminding adults of, the modern history of Palestine, mainly the 1948 catastrophe known as *al-nakba*, and its subsequent Palestinian struggle and displacement, which continue into the present. In his poem 'al-ward wal Qamus' ('The Rose and the Dictionary'), Mahmoud Darwish writes,

> No matter what happens, I must refuse to die
> Even if my legends do
> I am searching into ruins for light, for new poetry
> . . . how would all these words breathe! How would they sprout? How would they grow? We still are feeding them with memories, tears, metaphors, and sugar! (Darwish, *Akhr al-layl* 10)

This chapter analyses how an Egyptian illustrator, Sahar Abdallah, and an Egyptian publisher, Tanmia, use picture books to give Mahmoud Darwish the 'new poetry' of which he had endlessly dreamt. The chapter investigates an Egyptian artistic reinvention into picture books of three poems originally written for adults by Darwish. The poems are entitled 'ila Ummi' ('To My Mother'; 1966); 'hakadha qalat ash-shajaratu al-muhmalah' ('According to the Neglected Tree'; 1977); and 'Fakkir bi-ghayrika' ('Think of Others'; 2005).[1] It also considers how the emergent genre of children's picture books can help Darwish, and Palestinians, to 'refuse to die' in oblivion, and to stay vivid in a troubled region where voices calling for resistance to the Israeli occupation are getting fewer every day. These books, addressing readers of all ages, are written and published against, and in spite of, deliberate attempts to erase Palestinian history.

Haim Bresheeth notes that 'the narrative of Palestine in the cultural arena carved out by Zionism is, first and foremost, a story of erasure, denial, and active silencing by historians and intellectuals' (179). Such Zionist erasure does not find adequate resistance in Egypt, especially following the 'Arab Spring', which placed the individual and the collective challenges of Egyptians before the Palestinian struggle. In 2013, two years after Egypt's 25 January revolution, Yezid Sayigh expresses his doubt that 'Egypt can significantly realign itself on the Palestine issue. I also doubt this would be a source of strain domestically, again because of all the negative socio-economic indicators' (73). Due to the slowdown of economic activity following the revolution, basic needs of food and shelter are keeping individuals busy with their own and their families' day-to-day safety, while the official leadership appears to be neither capable of, nor eager for, conflict with Israel for the time being. In fact, normalisation with Israel, rather than conflict over the rights of Palestinians, has started to be the rule; the Gulf states 'sought the approval of Washington . . . [through] the groundbreaking normalization agreements signed by the UAE and Bahrain with Israel at the White House on September 15, 2020, marketed collectively as the "Abraham Accords"'(Rahman).

Asma al-Ghoul claims that 'Palestine has receded from the hearts of Arabs since they announced their spring' ('About Palestine') and she enumerates the following reasons: first, Palestinians often played the role of the victim among their neighbours; instead of showing empathy for the peoples of the Arab Spring during their struggles for democracy, they are perceived to have rather selfishly waited to support the winner. Secondly, the Arab interest in Palestine has waned due to the political division and mutual media battles between the Fatah and Hamas movements for nearly thirteen years, which made the question of Palestine appear to Arabs as a power game between two parties. The third factor, according to al-Ghoul, which has affected the passion towards Palestine among the Arab masses, is the exaggerated media rhetoric in dealing with the Palestinian resistance throughout the Arab region, which gives the impression that Palestine is capable of liberating itself and has a military power that can resist Israeli aggression. Finally, al-Ghoul adds, associating Palestine with political Islam in the media has made it appear as if supporting Palestine were the business of specific religious groups. This association sparked an aversion to Palestine on an official rather than a popular level, especially after confronting the Muslim Brotherhood movement in Egypt and Tunisia. Another factor contributing to apathy towards Palestine is specifically relevant to Egypt and can be described as chauvinist Egyptian nationalism. The people who adopt this attitude come from different backgrounds; some claim the pharaonic identity of Egyptians, others advocate the bond to the north bank of the Mediterranean during the two eras of the Greeks and the Romans. A third group simply hates everything related to the Nasser era, or to Arab or/ and Muslim nationalism. However, amidst such apathy and sometimes hostility towards the Palestinian cause, and silence in response to the Israeli erasure of Palestinian history, reviving threatened archive products indicates an undiminished political resistance on the popular and cultural levels. By reviving the poetry of Mahmoud Darwish, Tanmia has joined many emergent voices that shout out against the deliberate erasure of Palestinian history, which is escalating inside Israel and reverberating in the whole region.[2]

There has been a rise in the production and circulation of children's literature after the second Palestinian Intifada, which has affected the ways in which Israel and Palestine have been represented in regional and international popular culture (Stein and Swedenburg 13–14). As Israeli historical revisionism grew, alongside and building on the historiography of Palestinian scholars,[3] 'Zionist Israel [wa]s rapidly losing the discursive war of legitimacy in world opinion compared to rising concern for the rights of the Palestinians' (Rashed *et al.* 9). A negative image of Israel and a growing and increasingly positive image of Palestine reverberated worldwide and has been reflected in children's literature, which began to offer rich portraits of Palestinian children engaging in daily struggles for survival. Such literature has featured Palestinian children with hopes and fears similar to other children all over the world.[4] For the first time, during the 1980s and up until the present, Palestinians were humanised and demystified in picture books and young adult fiction. Having children as its main characters, children's literature about Palestine poignantly revealed the tragic cost of the Palestinian occupation and the urgent need for its resolution, while playing two other important roles: one, keeping Palestine alive in the minds and hearts of Palestinian children and caregivers in the diaspora, and two, educating children worldwide about the Palestinian–Israeli conflict and its history.[5]

The picture books by the Egyptian illustrator Sahar Abdallah perform both roles in a unique fashion by reawakening the poetry of Mahmoud Darwish, and the Palestinian cause for which he stands.[6] Abdallah held an exhibition in the Toronto Public Library in Canada, entitled *Visual Poems*, in November 2018, featuring the original illustrations of the poems. In the same year, she published these illustrations in Cairo, posthumously giving Darwish the 'new poetry' he always desired. This revival of Darwish in Egypt can be seen as a new 'intifada', an uprising, in that it re-members for the Egyptian reader the endangered archive of Palestinian modern history that has almost been lost amid the internal turmoil in Egypt and in the whole region. In addition, such revival not only signals the preservation of Darwish's poems, but rather the growth of his poems into multimodal forms, which utilise a new aesthetic much needed in the twenty first century, wherein what Keefe calls 'the postmodern society of the spectacle' (135) prioritises the image over the word and authentic social life has been substituted with its representation.[7]

This chapter asks whether, and how, Darwish's poems can 'sprout' and 'grow' after all these years in Egyptian soil, and during the post-Arab Spring era. What 'memories', 'tears', 'metaphors' and 'sugar' does the Egyptian illustrator add to the poems through lines and colours? How do the poems travel across time, nations, genders and genres: from 2005 to 2018–19; from Palestine to Egypt; from masculine to feminine creativity; from the verbal to the visual; and from poetry for adults, to picture books for children?

Adaptations and Crossover Picture Books

Transformation of adult poetry into children's picture books has been a common process throughout the history of children's literature. Canonical texts written by Edgar Allan Poe, Emily Dickinson, Franz Kafka, Pablo Neruda, E. E. Cummings, John Irving, Langston Hughes and others have been transformed into picture book versions, which introduce canonical texts by great writers to children and young readers. Adaptations of canonical texts have always played an important role in the history of children's literature; they are considered, to use the words of Linda Hutcheon, 'educationally important for children', because they give them a taste for reading the literary texts on which these adaptations are based and this 'get-them-to-read motivation' is what now drives an entire education industry (118). Anja Müller highlights the aim of such adaptations of adult texts for children: 'to introduce young readers to a literary canon that is deemed essential for sharing a common cultural heritage' (2). By means of such picture books, 'young or inexperienced readers . . . experience "world literature" at an early age and ideally re-read the pre-texts later on' (Zöhrer 488). These picture books can be regarded as 'an active attempt at canonization, whereby literary traditions are kept alive over generations, times, and countries' (Zöhrer 488). In the case of Darwish's poetry, this chapter argues, the picture books under discussion are attempts at both canonisation and decolonisation; they are meant to canonise Darwish, while at the same time they keep the Palestinian cause alive and vivid in the face of deliberate attempts at colonising land and memory simultaneously.[8]

Contemporary picture books presenting illustrated texts of canonical works of world literature are books for all ages, frequently referred to as 'crossover' picture books that support 'intergenerational communication' (Beckett 111). Adult readers may enjoy the creative reinvention of contemporary illustrators who offer new perspectives on canonical texts long familiar to them. This form of adaptation appeals to the 'intellectual and aesthetic pleasure' of understanding the interplay between the verbal and the visual, which is a crossover of media of expression (Hutcheon 117). According to Hutcheon, 'the appeal of adaptations for audiences lies in their mixture of repetition and difference, of familiarity and novelty' (14). Adaptation 'creates the doubled pleasure of the palimpsest: more than one text is experienced – and knowingly so' (Hutcheon 116). Children, on the other hand, will not pay much attention to the author's name, which 'functions as an intertextual clue that addresses the adult reader, who is the intended buyer of the book for children or even himself' (Zöhrer 487).

Mediating the conflict in Israel/Palestine for younger audiences cannot happen without engaging the adult reader and inspiring him or her to tell the story to the young reader. Illustrations can make the original work attractive for both readers. Crossover picture books blur the borderline between two traditionally separate readerships: children and adults. These picture books address two implied readers: 'a pseudo addressee' (the child) and a real one (the adult) (Shavit 71). According to Zohar Shavit, 'the child, the official reader of the text, is not meant to [fully comprehend it] and is much more an excuse for the text rather than its genuine addressee' (71). The picture books under discussion, this chapter argues, speak to children and adults at the same time, introducing Palestine to the former and reviving it for the latter, the adult who has probably witnessed the events described first hand through mass media at the time of their occurrence. A caregiver (especially an adult one) is the 'genuine addressee' of the book, who may have a great deal of Palestinian history to tell to 'the pseudo addressee', the child. We assume that adult caregivers, to whom a disadvantageous 'peace' with Israel is a new and unwarranted phase, and for whom Darwish represents a legal claim for a usurped land, would buy Abdallah's picture books curious about how familiar poems are recreated. Darwish's poetry can bring to readers, particularly older readers, a nostalgia for a pre-1967 pan-Arabism, and can alleviate the psychological burden of neglecting Palestine, through entrusting its narrative to a younger generation and ensuring the continuity of memory and traditions.

Innocence and experience thus intersect: while enjoying the art of Abdallah, adults may recount narratives of the Palestinian calamities for the children, such as stories of a people's expulsion from their land and of their ongoing resistance from 1948 to the present. In his important book *Words about Pictures* (1988), Perry Nodelman argues that

[p]icturebooks are clearly recognizable as children's books simply because they do speak to us of childlike qualities, of youthful simplicity and youthful exuberance; yet paradoxically, they do so in terms that imply a vast sophistication, in regard to both visual and verbal codes. Indeed, it is part of the charm of many of the most interesting picturebooks that they so strangely combine the childlike and the sophisticated – that the viewer they imply is both very learned and very ingenuous. (21)

Dyads of child and adult readers will jointly contemplate the pictures of Abdallah's books while listening to the music of Darwish's poetry, and smelling Palestinian oranges and olives that grow from both lines and words. The binary oppositions of innocence and experience, child and adult, dissolve in the act of the common reading/viewing of such picture books, whereby the child inside the adult will 'grow' with the music in the poetry and the colours in the drawings. It is interesting that Darwish himself is famous for a 'childhood that was growing [in him] and never departing' (al-Saqr 1). In 'ila Ummi' ('To My Mother'), Darwish says:

> I crave my mother's bread,
> My mother's coffee,
> My mother's touch
> Childhood grows in me
> One day on a bosom of a day (*'Ashiq min filastin*)

The brilliant personification/paradox 'childhood grows' which Darwish uses to depict his relationship both to his real mother and to his metaphorical one, Palestine, can serve as metaphor for the two readers/viewers of Abdallah's books: the child and the adult. While the adult-in-the-child can 'grow' in the act of reading/viewing Abdallah's picture books, the experienced adult will also paradoxically 'grow' into a receptive child, who is capable of love and empathy in a world that favours jaded experience to innocence.

It is this child-in-the-adult which led Darwish to fall in love with his Israeli friend Rita. It is also the child whom Darwish addresses in 'Fakkir bi-ghayrika' ('Think of Others') saying:

> As you prepare your breakfast, think of others
> (do not forget the pigeon's food).
> . . .
> As you think of others far away, think of yourself
> (Say: If only I were a candle in the dark). (*Almond Blossoms* 3)

Darwish's poetry thus lends itself to the genre of crossover picture books that simultaneously speak to children and adults. The straightforwardness of the message is comprehensible to the child; yet, the memories and the yearnings will grip the adult in mysteriously poignant ways. In fact, the poems were originally written for adults, but they can be shared with young readers. According to Katharine Davies Samway '[Darwish's] compelling poetry captures life for Palestinians, from their forced dislocation when the state of Israel was formed, through exile and occupation, and many of his poems can be shared with intermediate grade readers.'

Picture Books as an Intifada

Through Abdallah's books, and their poetic intertexts, Egyptian children, with the aid of a knowledgeable adult, thus come to terms with the Israeli colonisation of the land of Palestine, along with the exile of Palestinians, their resistance, and their dream of return.[9] Tanmia's initiative and Abdallah's books can therefore be understood as acts of resistance, an aesthetic intifada, whereby the bitterness of the Palestinian problem is rendered appealing for both children and adults, as the title of the present chapter suggests. Children, in particular, cannot be directly exposed to the details of what Ilan Pappé calls 'the Ethnic Cleansing of Palestine' in his book of the same name. Alternatively, the picture books at hand offer an example of what Freire calls 'problem-posing education', a method of teaching that emphasises critical thinking for the purpose of liberation. Freire used 'problem-posing' as a substitute to the 'banking model of education', in which students are treated as containers into which educators must put knowledge (Freire, *Pedagogy* 71).[10]

The drawings by Sahar Abdallah in the three picture books analysed in this chapter, and the poetry which inspired them, can stimulate critical thinking through instigating dialogue between the child and the adult. This dialogue can develop, in both the child and the adult reader/viewer of the picture books, what Freire has termed 'conscientization', which can be defined as the aptitude to 'intervene in reality in order to change it' (*Critical Consciousness* 3). This process takes place through the identification of 'generative themes', which involve iconic representations that have a strong emotional impact on learners. Through this process, individual awareness can eventually bring to an end a 'culture of silence' in which the politically dispossessed internalise self-destructive images propagated by the oppressor (Freire, *Critical Consciousness* 139, *Pedagogy* 30).

The Intertexts of the Picture Books

The three poems at the heart of Abdallah's picture books make no direct reference to the Palestinian–Israeli conflict and do not include any overt mention of Palestine, of Israel, or of any specific geographical locations or historical events. Even though the three poems belong to different phases of Darwish's poetry, they have much in common.[11] First, they can be read as universal accounts of forced exile and the yearning for return that is not exclusive to Palestinians. Second, they highlight physical attachment to the land through images of nature such as grass, birds, trees, pigeons and clouds. Third, they reveal a state of symbiosis between the human, the natural and the cultural, which shows itself in what Tahar Ben Jelloun termed 'a new rigorous direction [of Arab poetry], a new life that was closer to surrealism or a raw, poignant realism' (22).

The first poem, 'ila Ummi' ('To my Mother'), which is taken from *'Ashiq min filastin* (*A Lover from Palestine*) (1966), the second poetry collection by Darwish, is a melancholic portrayal of detachment from, and nostalgia for the mother, her bread, her coffee, and her 'touch'. The poem goes beyond nostalgia for the mother to a foreshadowing of the death of the persona, presumably a son (a representative of Darwish himself): 'I love my years/for, if I die, my mother's tears would shame me' (*'Ashiq min Filastin* 6–8). This foreshadowing is repeated in the plea from the son to the mother: 'Take me, if I ever return, as a veil for your eyelashes/Cover my bones with grass baptized with the purity of your heel' (*'Ashiq min Filastin* 9–12). The poem merges the physical with the metaphysical; the prosaic with the sacred; and the melancholic with the optimistic. It endows the mother, who is also a metonym for home and the land, with magic power who can give back the joy of pre-*nakba* childhood and make return to Palestine a reality:

> I aged! So give me back the stars of childhood
> So I can share
> With those young birds
> The return route
> To your waiting nest! (*'Ashiq min filastin* 24–8)

The second poem in the Tanmia project is 'hakadha qalat ash-shajaratu al-muhmalah' ('According to the Neglected Tree'), published as part of the collection *A'ras* (*Weddings*) (1977). The poem can be read as a response to the implicit call for return in 'ila Ummi' (1966). Separated by ten years, the earlier poem gives voice to the exiled son, while the latter allows the tree to speak, and to reassure the birds, the deer, the lovers, and the readers that, although the tree was neglected, it is still waiting for everyone's return. The tree in this poem corresponds with the mother in the earlier one; both stand for home and for the land that is awaiting its people.

Though these two poems belong to what critics call 'the militant phase' and 'the dreaming revolutionary phase' of Darwish's poetry respectively, they both show resistance in very subtle ways that make them suitable for a children's picture book. 'Ila Ummi' alludes to the death of the son, and his willingness to die, had it not been for the shame of bringing tears to his mother, but no clue is given to the nature of such death, and no elaboration is made on the causes instigating Palestinian resistance. Likewise, there is a reference in 'hakadha qalat ash-shajaratu al-muhmalah' to the tree being either a dagger or a source of rain. Yet, such passing reference occurs in an overarching context of the tree providing shelter, food and love: (In the drought that breaks the wind/ Do the poor know that/I am /the source of wind? (20–3).[12]

The last poem, 'Fakkir bi-ghayrika' ('Think of Others') was originally published in 2005. It belongs to the last phase of Darwish's poetic career, where 'the local and national theme is raised into a wider human space in which Palestinian groaning is heard together with human pain elsewhere in the world' (Amjad Nasser 32–3). It is a direct poem, which departs from the surrealism of the other two, and adopts a universal call for empathy. The poem is a simple plea for justice, peace and the fair distribution of human resources. Its rhythm maintains a perfect balance between the haves and the have-nots, and an acceptance, at this stage of the poet's career, of the stark contrast that has always existed between the two. As if words were calculated and divided equally between the privileged and the deprived, the poem, and the world it represents, maintains its balance through 'thinking of others', which best represents the universal vision common in Darwish's latest poems.

Adding Sugar: Abdallah's Pleasing Picture Books

The three picture books we will now analyse are *Fakkir bi-ghayrika* (*Think of Others*; 2018); *hakadha qalat ash-shajaratu al-muhmalah* (*According to the Neglected Tree*; 2018); and *Khobz Ummi* (*My Mother's Bread*; 2019). Abdallah reinvents the three poems in aesthetically pleasurable lines and colours; she challenges the widely spread stereotype of the Palestinian as 'a violent, barbaric and inherently anti-Semitic opponent of modernity', often a male figure in a black-and-white chequered *keffiyeh*. Abdallah replaces these rigid stereotypes with diverse images of ordinary men, women and children who constitute the majority of the Palestinian population whether in Palestine or in their new homes in the diaspora.

Abdallah can be said to 'readwithize' the original poems. We coin this term as a reverse-coinage of Cole Swensen's term 'to writewithize', which she uses to describe her ekphrastic poetry (69). In ekphrasis, 'to writewithize': 'as in "to hybridize," "to ritualize," "to ionize," etc.' (Swensen 69) is to 'write "with eyes" in order to enact some kind of transformative change in the form, language, and sound of the poem and, perhaps, in the world in which the poem exists' (Keefe 135). Whereas, in ekphrasis, the painting precedes the writing and inspires it; in the case of the poetry picture book, a reverse process takes place, where the artists 'readwithize' the poem before they reproduce it.

Reading Darwish with her own eyes, Abdallah feminises the characters in the poems; her drawings often represent girls and women as shown in the covers of the three books. Such feminisation of the characters is partly responsible for the portrayal of Palestinians as victims rather than aggressors, and as peace-loving and home-loving exiles, rather than as terrorists targeting Israeli civilians, as often portrayed in the media worldwide, or at best, as militant fighters who risk their lives to protect their people against repeated Israeli demolitions of their homes.

In an interview, Abdallah highlights her intention in adapting Darwish's poems. She says she wishes

> to achieve a visual text parallel to the written one, where the words of the poems are transformed into visual shapes, built together on a background of pleasing colors, to enable the organic lines to connect the elements and narrate the real meaning behind the words where passion of both poetry and illustration is accomplished. ('On Illustrating')

Abdallah thus believes in the narrative capabilities of her lines and colours to 'please' and 'narrate'. In his 2007 Patrick Hardy lecture, Michael Rosen sings the praise of the generic picture book in similar terms:

> it sits like some massive inflorescence, budding and flowering and reproducing in all its delightful, complex and beautiful ways, all freighted with the same impulse – how to please, intrigue, and amuse young children and their carers and teachers. And it does this . . . in many different ways: visually, orally, textually and in any combinations of all three. Eye and ear are constantly challenged to look and listen here, there and everywhere. ('The Bigger Picture')

While the music in the poetry challenges the ears of readers/listeners, Abdallah challenges their visual perception; her drawings merge the human, the cultural and the natural, portraying their inseparable fusion. In all three picture books, human legs surreally turn into plant roots, and human veins into branches. On the other hand, trees acquire eyes and long hair, wear keys symbolic of lost homes, and speak poignantly of the ongoing dream of return. In his poem, 'Trees of Words', Palestinian poet Yusuf Abu Lauz writes: 'Our homeland flows in our blood. We carry it with us in this world, wherever we go, no matter how far' (94). In one of the pictures in Abdallah's *Khubz Ummi*, the tree, as metonymy of the land, surreally turns into veins and arteries of the mother, whose pale colour and sad looks speak of a looming death due to the cutting of trees and land confiscation. Dark brownish and greyish colours are in fact maintained throughout this book to reflect the melancholy, the nostalgia and the death of the son the poem foreshadows, though never portrays. The only green page amid those dark brown and greyish ones is the one in which the persona reconstructs an imaginary home, of past or future Palestine, where the daily cooking and washing takes place.

It is interesting here to note that the persona in the poem, whom Darwish's readers may have long visualised as a young male fighter in a chequered *keffiyeh*, transforms in the picture book into a young daughter in a flowing dress. This transformation, along with the change of the title from *'ila Ummi'* (To my Mother) to *Khubz Ummi* (My Mother's Bread), with the emphasis on the culinary, are decisions that are made by Abdallah so as to give voice to Palestinian girls in diaspora, and underscore women's day-to-day baking as an act of resistance or *sumud*. We can think of Abdallah's book as her endeavour to 'readwithize' Darwish's poems from a woman's perspective.

What Abdallah highlights in these picture books corresponds to various metaphors used by scholars in describing the interaction between words and pictures: Allan Ahlberg talks about 'interweaving' (Moss 21) for the word and image relationship, while Margaret Meek uses 'interanimate' to suggest the dynamic way words and images work together (176). Nikolajeva and Scott use the term 'complementary' for the dynamic cooperation of word and image in picture books where the images reflect and expand on the written text, or where each fills the other's gaps (12). Meek's analogy of pictures and words 'interanimating' each other can best be represented with reference to a scene from Abdallah's *hakadha qalat ash-shajaratu al-muhmalah*. The scene illustrates the following stanza:

> In the evening which hikes
> From eye to eye
> Blue, green or gold
> Is my body.
> Do lovers feel that I am, for them
> A balcony or a moon?
> I am waiting (*Al-diwan vol. 2* 317)

Abdallah fills in the gaps in the stanza to reveal the beauty and the vibrant lives animating the evening which 'hikes from eye to eye' in peace and love. The breathing and moving creatures in the illustration are not exclusive to the tree, the moon, and the lovers in the Darwishian stanza, but Abdallah 'readwithizes' the 'evening that hikes' by creating more living couples in the background. Birds, cats, and even houses, come to life in this much needed make-believe dream of return. The white window spaces, which reveal the absence of life inside the houses, stand as witnesses to the expulsion of people from their homes during the *nakba*. In addition, the worried look in the eyes of the two lovers, reminiscent of the eyes of the daughter in *Khubz Ummi*, casts doubt on an imminent fulfilment of the dream.

The rosette-shaped reliefs on the domes of one of the houses are identical to the tresses/oranges in the 'waiting' tree and the curls in the hair of the male lover. These proliferate with variations on the dress of the female lover and on the fur of the cat in the background. Such harmony among male, female, flora, fauna and cultural artifacts is Abdallah's depiction of the idyllic ambiance of Palestine prior to the *nakba*. This image conforms to a tradition of representing Palestine, whereby as Benay Blend argues, Palestinian poets commonly reveal 'repeated references to all things Palestinian – almond groves, fig trees, oranges, Arabian jasmine, thyme, all items which bring to mind a graphic image of the landscape' (81).

Furthermore, the multiplication indicated by the pairs of cats, birds and humans stand as a sign of resistance to the killing of people, the razing of villages, and the destruction of the ecosystem. Abdallah's decision to feature human and animal pairs renders Palestine into a Noah's ark threatened by an Israeli flood. By doing this, Abdallah is writing back to the religious rhetoric of Israel, and is reclaiming the biblical Hebrew narrative: *Tevat Noah*, in which God saves Noah, his family, and examples of all the world's animals from a world-engulfing flood.[13] The flood as a destructive force stands for the Israeli incursion, which has caused ecological harm to the flora and fauna of Palestine. Several studies have assessed the impact of the Israeli policies on the environment and highlighted the grim results of the segregation wall and the cutting of trees on biodiversity and environmentally sustainable development in Palestine. Land confiscation, destruction of species and soil erosion, together with loss of water resources have all affected the Palestinians and increased their poverty.[14] Such ecological and economic consequences are interpreted by Abdallah in an outstanding illustration of the following stanza:

> In the drought that breaks the wind
> Do the poor know that I am
> the source of wind?
> Do they feel that I am,
> for them
> A dagger, or a rainfall?
> I am waiting (*Al-diwan vol. 2* 317)

The bleak illustration of these lines stands in sharp contrast with the previous one of the joyous lovers' evening in the green, blue and golden colours specified by Darwish, together with the red and orange of the mosaic tiles added by Abdallah. The only exception to the dark colours in this image is the shining orange in the dress/trunk of the tree and its matching Palestinian earring. The colour stands out as a reminder of the power residing in the tree/the land, and the hope in regeneration in spite of everything. This corresponds with Darwish's lines in which the tree reminds the people that she alone can give them the dagger and the rain, symbolic of resistance and regeneration, respectively. Abdallah, however, decides to change the lines by not representing the dagger, a choice that the genre of children's picture book, political constraints, or ideological convictions may have dictated.

Both *Khubz Ummi* and *hakadha qalat ash-shajaratu al-muhmalah* end in the dream of return. In the former, a girl is sharing the route of the birds back home while closing her eyes as befitting a dream. Facing her, in the latter picture book, in a manner of call and response, is the mother/homeland symbol of the 'neglected tree' who stands in pride and in confidence that her 'lost branches', her people, are coming back. It is interesting how the tree is facing outside the frame of the book in the direction opposite to the running/flying girl/birds who face inside in the other picture book, as if the two characters in the separate books are going to meet each other. The look in the eye of the tree, similar to that of the lovers and the nostalgic girl in the pictures from Abdallah's *hakadha qalat ash-shajaratu al-muhmalah*, betrays a mixture of anguish and hope, while the key, the main cultural symbol of Palestinian diaspora, is dangling from a huge orange sun in the background. Abdallah demonstrates Pierre Nora's argument that memory has to rely 'on the materiality of the trace . . . the visibility of the image' (13). For Palestinian refugees, 'the act of holding on to the original house key is not merely an exercise in nostalgia, but also stands for a continual reminder of the loss and the story of that loss that has to be told and retold' (Nashef 4).

The finale of each of these two picture books exemplify early phases of Darwish's poetry, which reveal that restoring the land of Palestine by Arab joint forces, whether armed or diplomatic, was still an option before 1967. However, the third book, *Fakkir bi-ghayrika*, does not share the same optimism; it does not portray the journey back home either through words, or through pictures. Instead, Darwish's lines call for the minimal Palestinian rights of food and shelter on a portion of their land. In this evenly balanced poem in terms of message, lines and rhythms, Darwish aims at 'conscientizing' readers, to use Freire's term discussed above. At this stage of his career, Darwish had already lost hope in both political and armed solutions for the Palestinian problem, and had become content with raising awareness of the socioeconomic factors that determine the lives of his oppressed people and with evoking empathy for them. In *Fakkir bi-ghayrika* (*Think of Others*), both words and pictures depict the displacement of the Palestinians and underscore their connection to the land. Abdallah's illustrations provide a rich visual discourse, an abundance of connotations and symbolism, open to multi-layered interpretations, which the child, 'the pseudo addressee', can make with the help of the 'genuine addressee', the adult (Shavit 71). The illustrations can guide the reading process and stimulate dialogue between child and caregiver/teacher. They underline the Palestinian diaspora as the topic of the poem and reiterate themes of connection to the land, colonial oppression, and ecological problems already raised in the other two books. Illustrations emphasise these themes in a manner that both appeals to the child reader and encourages the adult reader to narrate complimentary stories.

Furthermore, Abdallah's illustrations interpret Darwish's poem by rendering the verbal text as a visual chronotope specific to Palestine. The poem, without the illustrations, could refer to any refugee population and could be read as a call for empathy and the fair distribution of planetary resources in the absolute. Yet, Abdallah's use of symbols, which are particular to the Palestinian experience – the key, the dove, the Arabic letters and the olive tree – is what makes the book a narrative about Palestinian suffering in particular. In addition to illustrating metaphors from Darwish's 'Fakkir bi-ghayrika' ('Think of Others'): the sustenance for the pigeons, the cloud and the tent, Abdallah uses images from other books by Darwish, such as the suitcase and the butterfly.[15] She also draws on symbols from the wider political and cultural context of the Arab–Israeli conflict such as fences, bombs, houses, keys and olive branches.

The three most significant motifs in Abdallah's *Fakkir bi-ghayrika* are the key, the suitcase and the fish. The heavy old key, the concrete reminder of loss of the ancestral home, is one significant trace that Abdallah foregrounds in all three books. Darwish's words read:

> As you return home,
> Your home,
> Think of others
> Do not forget the people of the camps (*Almond Blossoms* 3)

The illustration of the above lines is surrealist; it juxtaposes three unexpected variations of home in exile: one girl literally lives in a suitcase, while also holding the key, which denotes the 'right of return' and the right of entry to her ancestral home. The suitcase is a recurrent metaphor of exile in Darwish's poetry. In 'Yawmiyyat jurh filastin' ('Diary of a Palestinian Wound'; 1970), he writes, 'My homeland is not a suitcase and I am no traveler/I am the lover and the land is the beloved' (*Al-diwan vol. 1* 356). Thirteen years later, in 1983, he realises the painful truth. In a poem entitled 'Madih al-zill al-aly' ('In Praise of the High Shadow'), Darwish declares, 'My homeland is a suitcase/and my suitcase is my homeland/at night, it becomes my bed/I sleep within/I die within' (*Al-diwan vol. 2* 331). Such change from rejection of the suitcase symbol to acceptance of its relevance marks the poet's journey from defiance to experience and corresponds to the difficulty of attaining the right of return for millions of Palestinians.

Abdallah's pictures of suitcases thus complement Darwish's reference to home, filling in the gaps in the verbal narrative both from history and from Darwish's entire oeuvre. The suitcase Abdallah has created is surrealist: it is transparent, revealing a dress that contains doors, a book that is symbolic of history, and a heart that connects with a fine thread to the girl's body. Abdallah's images correspond with Suheir Hammad's expression of memory and endurance in the Palestinian diaspora: 'Home is within me. I carry everyone and everything I am with me wherever I go' (11). The same page shows another girl holding an umbrella without a canopy reminiscent of the flimsy nature of the tents in which the refugees are forced to live. In place of the canopy, the umbrella has three keys, a fish, a pigeon and a rainy cloud. The fish which Abdallah frequently uses is a recurrent symbol in Palestinian art: Palestinian refugees, who lived in the coastal cities until 1948, had a direct connection with the sea before being moved to the hilly region. For the refugee, the sea is the source of livelihood and freedom.[16] In another picture, a girl is walking while carrying a mobile home on her shoulders and holding a key of another home, presumably a distant one, in her hand; her two legs are visible below the house to foreground her constant walking in an endless diaspora. Her face, which appears from a small window, reflects the same melancholic expression recurrent in the three picture books.

Conclusion

In the picture books analysed, the illustrations make Mahmoud Darwish's poems accessible for children in spite of the historical complexity of the Palestinian crisis they represent, which speaks to the adult reader of the books. These books, therefore, fit into the crossover genre of children's books, which speak to both children and adults. This emergent genre resurrects a free Palestine in a manner that is engaging and enticing for both children and adults without being too political; the picture books subtly provoke children and adults to imagine a free Palestine and to view this in context of a historical determinism. Sahar Abdallah's adaptation of Darwish's poetry introduces young readers to canonical texts and gives them the ability to gain easier access to Palestinian literary heritage. Abdallah's picture books demonstrate Perry Nodelman's argument that placing words and pictures 'into relationship with each other inevitably changes the meaning of both', so that they are 'more than just a sum of their parts' (199). Abdallah and Tanmia publishing house offer the Arabic reader a unique cultural product that brings to life the history of Palestine, and the suffering of its people through the synergy between pictures and words. The books help Palestine, through its great poet of resistance, to stay alive across generations of readers, and to remain free and festive in the imagination of children and adult.

Notes

1. All translations of the poetry in this chapter are by the author (Magda Hasabelnaby) unless stated otherwise.
2. Voices against such deliberate erasure can be heard even in Israel itself. See, for example, Hagar Shezaf.
3. See John Docker, 'Instrumentalising the Holocaust' 28. Docker highlights the historiographical achievement of Palestinian scholars, such as Walid Khalidi, Edward W. Said, Nur Masalha and Saree Makdisi who have investigated and analysed the tragedy for the Palestinian people that Zionist settler-colonial genocide has produced and continues to inflict.
4. The following are some examples of post-Second Intifada books for children and young adults: *A Stone in My Hand* (2002) by Cathryn Clinton; 'The Second Day' by Ibtisam Barakat in *Shattered: Stories of Children at War* (2002); *The Enemy Has a Face* by Gloria Miklowitz (2003); *Dreaming of Palestine* (2002) by Randa Ghazy; and *A Little Piece of Ground* (2003) by Elizabeth Laird.
5. For more detailed explorations of the portrayal of Israel and Palestine in children's literature, see Fouad Moughrabi, 'Three Representations' and Elsa Marston, 'More than Just Stories'.
6. Though Sahar Abdallah was a pioneer in using canonical Palestinian poetry in picture books, she was not the first to portray Palestine in children's picture books. In 1994, the Arab American poet Naomi Shihab Nye paved the way for depicting Palestine in children's literature with her picture book *Sitti's Secrets*, beautifully illustrated by Nancy Carpenter. Many other books followed: working with children at Lajee Center in The West Bank, Amahl Bishara has co-produced two bilingual children's books, *The Boy and the Wall* and *The Aida Camp Alphabet* in 2006. Both books presented a child's view of the separation wall. In 2017, Golbarg Bashi published *P is for Palestine*, an ABC storybook about Palestine, told in simple language with prominent illustrations that reveal the beauty and strength of Palestinian culture. In 2019, Bashi published another book, *Counting up the Olive Tree: A Palestine Number Book* illustrated by Nabi H. Ali, highlighting Palestinians' love of the land and their attachment to olive trees.
7. The term 'society of the spectacle' was first coined by Guy Louis Debord in his book *La société du spectacle* (1967), a book which critiques the commodification of the spectacular created by post-industrial technologies, and calls for altering the images produced by the spectacle in order to communicate subversive messages.
8. Following the ethnic cleansing of Palestine in 1948, Israel pursued methods whose main features were memoricide, erasure and culturecide. Palestinian historian Nur Masalha explores how the formation of Israeli identity was premised on the erasure of Palestinian history and identity. Masalha explains that 'culturecide' denotes the 'destruction and elimination of cultural patterns of a

group, including language, local traditions, shrines, monuments, place names, landscape, historical records, archives, libraries, churches – in brief the soul of a nation' (*The Palestine Nakba* 11). For a detailed discussion of deliberate attempts at colonizing memory, see Nur Masalha's book *The Palestine Nakba* and his article 'Settler-Colonialism, Memoricide and Indigenous Toponymic Memory'.
9. The standard Arabic of Darwish's powerful poetry, in spite of its marked simplicity, may be challenging for those children whose educational systems value English and other European languages over Arabic.
10. For further discussion of the concepts of banking education and problem-posing education, see Paulo Freire, *Pedagogy of the Oppressed*, chapter 2, 71–86.
11. For a discussion of the different phases in Darwish's poetry, see Randa Abou-Bakr, *The Conflict of Voices in the Poetry of Dennis Brutus and Mahmud Darwish: A Comparative Study* and Amjad Nasser, 'Mahmoud Darwish between the Political and the Aesthetic.'
12. The word 'dagger' in the poem has changed into 'cloud' when the poem was republished in the complete works of Darwish in 2005. Abdallah, however, used the original version of the poem from the 1977 collection published during the 'resistance' phase of Darwish's poetry. The tree being described as a dagger is a metaphor for resistance. For more details on the different versions of Darwish's poems, see Hussein Hamza, 'al-siyaghat al-niha'ieyya w tahawul al-ma'na.' (Final Formulations and the Transformations of Meaning).
13. The story of Nuh (Noah) is mentioned in the Quran in several places, most notably in Surat Nuh (Chapter 71), which is named after him.
14. See Tanya Abdallah and Km Swaileh, 'Effects of the Israeli Segregation Wall on biodiversity and Environmental Sustainable Development in the West Bank, Palestine'.
15. See Darwish's 'Yawmiyyat jurh filastini' ('Diary of a Palestinian Wound') in his collection *Habibati Tanhado Min Nawmiha* (*My Lover Wakes Up*), 1970; 'Madih al-zill al-aly' ('In Praise of the High Shadow'), 1983; Mahmoud Darwish and Fady Joudah's *The Butterfly's Burden: Poems*, 2007.
16. Palestinian artist Alaa Albaba used the image of the fish in his graffiti project 'Route of the Fish' (2013–18) that depicts the Palestinian *nakba* and the refugee experience. His project reveals the tragedy of the Palestinian people not through the traditional association with the land, but rather via the experience of being cut off from the sea. For further information, see Daniel Monterescu, 'The Palestinian Trail of Fish: Artist's Graffiti Dives into Heart of Refugee Struggle'.

AFTERWORD

Anna Bernard

In 'broken and beirut', the closing poem of her 1996 debut collection *Born Palestinian, Born Black*, the Palestinian-American poet Suheir Hammad describes Palestinian life as an unending state of siege:

> we return to what we know
> it's 1996 and beirut all over again
> this time the murdered are those who survived the last time
> and this time's survivors are preparing for the next time
> when fire will rain down on heads bowed in prayer (83)

The lines evoke two massacres of Palestinian and Lebanese civilians: the 1994 Al-Ibrahimi Mosque massacre in Hebron, when the American settler Baruch Goldstein opened fire on worshippers, killing twenty-nine people; and the 1996 Qana massacre in South Lebanon, when the Israeli military shelled a UN compound sheltering 800 refugees who had fled bombing in Beirut, killing 106 people, half of them children. Hammad sharply reminds her reader that despite the promises of the Oslo Accords, the Palestinian catastrophe continues unabated. The only return that Palestinians can be certain of is the return of more violence and destruction.

This book's focus on international representations of Palestine/Israel since 2000 asks us to take stock of what has changed since Hammad wrote these lines, and what has stayed the same. In many ways, the Palestinians' political and socioeconomic situation is even bleaker, reflecting the consolidation of the US-backed 'imperial restoration' in the region that has taken place from the early 1970s onwards, facilitated not only by Israel but also by counter-revolutionary regimes in Saudi Arabia, Jordan, Egypt, Iraq, and other Arab states (Abu-Manneh 32). Since the Palestinian leadership's 'capitulation' in Oslo, as Edward Said famously put it ('The Morning After'), Palestinians in the Occupied Territories have lived through the eruption of the al-Aqsa intifada and Israel's massive retaliatory invasion of the West Bank; the transformation of Gaza into what is routinely described as the world's largest open-air prison; the vast expansion of Israeli settlements and of the system of checkpoints, barriers and permits restricting Palestinian movement in the West Bank; and the Israeli aerial and ground assaults on Gaza in 2008–9 and 2014. Meanwhile, hundreds of thousands of Palestinian refugees in Syria have been displaced once again, and the already precarious living conditions of Palestinian refugees in Lebanon (whose numbers now include many Palestinian refugees from Syria) have deteriorated even further (UNRWA; McCloskey). This period has also been marked by the loss of Edward Said, still the Palestinians' most influential metropolitan spokesperson nearly two decades after his death; the changed regional picture since the Arab uprisings of 2011 and the authoritarian restorations that followed in their wake (Achcar; see also Hasabelnaby and Mahmoud, this volume); the political ascendancy of the Israeli 'hardliners', emblematised by Benjamin Netanyahu's long tenure as Prime Minister and the passage of the Basic Law defining Israel as the nation state of the Jewish people in 2018; and the Israeli state's coordination of a massive public diplomacy campaign across traditional and social media, known by the Hebrew term *hasbara* (explanation, or propaganda), which dismisses evidence of Israeli violence against Palestinians as 'Pallywood' fiction (Roth-Rowland).

Yet alongside this litany of oppression and defeat, the twenty-first century has also seen an expansion of international support for the Palestinian struggle. This shift in popular opinion extends beyond the global south and the metropolitan radical left to include a significant proportion of the general public even in countries like the United States, Germany and France, where public and institutional support for Israel historically has been high. This is due in no small part to Palestinians' own turn – or return, since the Palestinian struggle has always also been international – to the rest of the world for support, in the face of declining local and regional options for resistance. This change in tactics has resulted in some symbolic victories, like the granting of United Nations non-member observer state status to Palestine in 2012 and its admission as a state to the International Criminal Court (ICC) in 2015, as well as the ICC's opening of an investigation of war crimes in the Palestinian territories in 2021. It has also enabled the rapid expansion of the international Boycott, Divestment and Sanctions (BDS) campaign since 2005. The rise in support for the Palestinian cause additionally reflects the impact of the international outcry against the invasions of Gaza in 2008–9 and 2014, which raised the profile of the struggle in much the same way that the Sabra and Shatila massacre in Beirut had three decades before. These organisational successes have taken place alongside a global renewal of the language of revolution and struggle since the financial crash of 2008 and the uprisings of 2011. It is now much more common to hear Israel described as an apartheid state and as a settler-colonial state in both academic and popular contexts, including among some American and Israeli Jews (Weiss; Waxman; B'Tselem, 'A Regime').

What has not changed is the profound asymmetry of this conflict and the Palestinians' refusal to disappear. In this regard, literature's role in this conflict also has not really changed. Many of the texts that are discussed in this book, by Palestinians and non-Palestinians alike, are examples of international Palestine advocacy (with exceptions such as Sarah Glidden's troubling renunciation of anti-Zionism in *How to Understand Israel in 60 Days or Less*, as Ned Curthoys observes, and the 'internal' critiques of Zionism advanced by the canonical Jewish Israeli novelists Amos Oz, A. B. Yehoshua and David Grossman). Works of Palestine advocacy have different intended audiences, different forms, and different political outlooks, but all are meant to travel, and to persuade their largely non-Palestinian readerships of the justness of this cause. They thus participate in what Timothy Brennan describes as an international 'civic tradition' of literature that exhorts its readers to recognise a bad reality and take a stand against it. Such texts are characterised by their commitment to the provision of information and documentation, their earnest and direct tone, and their understanding of language as 'fundamentally interpretable rather than cryptic' (Brennan, 'Homiletic Realism' 269–70). These texts may entertain, challenge or surprise their readers, but they set out above all to make sure they know what is going on. This does not prevent them from looking critically at various aspects of the Palestinian national movement, nor does it commit them to a particularly radical view of it: a number of them are better described as liberal and/or humanitarian than revolutionary. (Oz, Yehoshua and Grossman's interventions should also be understood as part of the landscape of liberal humanitarianism, though this orientation clashes with the writers' Zionist commitments.) My point is that each effort to raise the reader's awareness of the Palestinian struggle seeks to contribute, in one way or another, to the advancement of international solidarity with this cause.

Refusing to disappear means fighting against the orchestrated silencing and erasure that Palestinians have faced since Arthur Balfour declared Britain's support for the creation of a Jewish national home in Palestine over a century ago. It means claiming again and again the 'permission to narrate' that Said observed was structurally denied to Palestinians even after Sabra and Shatila

('Permission to Narrate'), and then telling again and again the same story, which is no less true for not being new. This political demand poses significant aesthetic challenges that centre on the problem of making Palestinian life visible: not only its present forms, but also its possible future. In a recent essay, Refqa Abu-Remaileh describes the 'enigmas' faced by Palestinian writers as follows: 'writing a national literature without a nation-state, writing silence and non-linearity, and writing fragmentation and wholeness' (21). This summary points to the specific contribution that literature and other art forms make to the representation of the Palestinian struggle, beyond the documentary role that they share with journalism and human rights reports. These works attest to dispossession, fragmentation and disempowerment, but they also assert a sense of national unity – Abu-Remaileh calls it a 're-Palestinization' (24) – that is not based solely on a commemoration of the past but is oriented towards a better future for all Palestinians. This affirmation of a common future draws on a heterogeneous but shared set of experiences and a belief in the Palestinians' collective right to self-determination, whatever political form that might take. As Brennan points out, the civic tradition of letters is not just about resistance to the current dispensation, but also 'about the colonized *in power* – or the promise of their being in power – with a stake in the political system' ('Against Modernism' 35). Works that seek to raise awareness of the Palestinian struggle also 'anticipat[e] the return of democratic possibility' (Abu-Manneh 150) by looking forward to a future in which this particular form of struggle will not be required, because Palestinians will have achieved genuine political representation. Works that focus instead on tensions within Jewish Israeli society or between Israeli and non-Israeli Jews gesture towards such a future too, even if inadvertently, since they implicitly invoke a time when Jewish Israeli identity will not depend upon the exclusion of the Palestinian as 'other' (see Nadler, this volume).

This claim recalls Jumana Bayeh's important reminder, in her contribution to this volume, that Palestinian 'statehood and liberation are not coterminous'. As the outcomes of so many of the anticolonial struggles that have taken place alongside the Palestinian resistance have shown, political independence is not the same thing as decolonisation: a nominally independent state that is unwilling or unable to guarantee the equal status and livelihood of everyone it governs has not achieved the liberation that its champions promised. What Bayeh also suggests, however, is that literature is a site where this broader, truer liberation is repeatedly envisioned, and where the institutions and alliances that stand in its way can be honestly confronted. It is up to the Palestinians to collectively imagine what this future liberation might look like for them, but the task of working towards it falls on all of us. Reading about the Palestinian struggle is a first step; taking part in the forms of resistance that the Palestinian national movement asks of us is the next. As the novelist Kamila Shamsie puts it in a defence of the BDS cultural boycott: 'In a world of too much interventionism here is a chance for internationalism; in a situation that can often seem intractable and in which we feel ourselves powerless, here is a chance to help make change in a non-violent way' (5).

In keeping with what I have been saying, it is worth noting that Suheir Hammad's lament for the dead and their dream of return ends on a more hopeful note than the stanza I began with suggests. As the poem continues, return comes to mean a renewal of the struggle, as the speaker moves from a cry of despair to a call to survive and rebuild:

> come back   and make no mistake
> be precise   get back to work
> shifting through the rubble   mathematically
> building a new day
> with offerings of honey and memory
>
> never forgetting
> where we come from
> where we've been
> and how sweet honey
> on the lips of survivors (84)

With these lines, the poem introduces an expansive idea of return, one that does not exclude the physical return of the refugees, but also extends to the political and personal rejuvenation that can be forged through collective struggle. The 'we' of Hammad's poem is a Palestinian 'we', but the demand to get back to work includes us all.

WORKS CITED

Abdallah, Sahar (illustrator), *Fakkir bi-ghayrika* [*Think of Others*] (Tanmia Publishing, 2018).
— (illustrator), *Hakadha qalat ash-shajaratu al-muhmalah* [*According to the Neglected Tree*] (Tanmia Publishing, 2018).
— (illustrator), *Khubz Ummi* [*My Mother's Bread*] (Tanmia Publishing, 2019).
—, 'Sahar Abdallah: On Illustrating Darwish's "Think of Others" for Kids (interview)', *Arabic Literature and Translation*, 5 November 2018, www.arablit.org/2018/11/05/sahar-abdallah-on-illustrating-darwishs-think-of-others-for-kids/ (accessed 28 October 2021).
Abdallah, Tanya, and Khaled Swaileh, 'Effects of the Israeli Segregation Wall on Biodiversity and Environmental Sustainable Development in the West Bank, Palestine', *International Journal of Environmental Studies*, vol. 68, no. 4, 2011, pp. 543–55, https://doi.org/10.1080/00207233.2011.608504.
Abdelrazaq, Leila, *Baddawi* (Just World Books, 2015).
Abou-Bakr, Randa, *The Conflict of Voices in the Poetry of Dennis Brutus and Mahmud Darwish: A Comparative Study* (Dr Ludwig Reichert Verlag, 2004).
Abramson, Yehonatan, 'Securing the Diasporic "Self" by Travelling Abroad: Taglit-Birthright and Ontological Security', *Journal of Ethnic and Migration*, vol. 45, no. 4, 2019, pp. 656–73, https://doi.org/10.1080/1369183x.2017.1409176.
Abu Eid, Muna, *Mahmoud Darwish: Literature and the Politics of Palestinian Identity* (I. B. Tauris, 2016).
Abu Lauz, Yusuf, 'Trees of Words', in Salma Khadra Jayyusi (ed.), *Anthology of Modern Palestinian Literature* (Columbia University Press, 1992).
Abu-Manneh, Bashir, *The Palestinian Novel: From 1948 to the Present* (Cambridge University Press, 2016).

Abu-Remaileh, Refqa, 'The Three Enigmas of Palestinian Literature', *Journal of Palestine Studies*, vol. 48, no. 3, 2019, pp. 21–5, https://doi.org/10.1525/jps.2019.48.3.21.

Abu Saif, Atef, *The Drone Eats with Me: Diaries from a City Under Fire* (Comma Press, 2015).

—, 'A Journey in the Opposite Direction', in Atef Abu Saif (ed.), *The Book of Gaza* (Comma Press, 2014), pp. 1–18.

Abuelaish, Izzeldin, *I Shall Not Hate: A Gaza Doctor's Journey on the Road to Peace and Human Dignity* (Bloomsbury, 2012).

Abulhawa, Susan, *Against the Loveless World* (Bloomsbury, 2020).

—, *The Blue Between Sky and Water* (Bloomsbury, 2015).

—, 'Interview by Miriam Abdollahi', *Qantara.de*, 24 May 2017, https://en.qantara.de/node/27868 (accessed 20 March 2020).

—, *Mornings in Jenin* (Bloomsbury, 2010).

—, '*The Wall* by William Sutcliffe – Book Review', *The Palestine Chronicle*, 7 June 2013, www.palestinechronicle.com/the-wall-by-william-sutcliffe-book-review/ (accessed 28 October 2021).

Abunimah, Ali, *The Battle for Justice in Palestine* (Haymarket Books, 2014).

—, 'Johns Hopkins COVID-19 Map Faulted for Erasing Palestinians', *Electronic Intifada*, 27 March 2020, https://electronicintifada.net/blogs/ali-abunimah/johns-hopkins-covid-19-map-faulted-erasing-palestinians (accessed 27 October 2021).

Achcar, Gilbert, *Morbid Symptoms: Relapse in the Arab Spring* (Stanford University Press, 2016).

Adely, Hannan, 'Free Speech, Politics, and Anti-Semitism: Marc Lamont Hill Tells His Story', *NorthJersey.com*, 25 March 2019, https://www.northjersey.com/story/news/passaic/clifton/2019/03/25/marc-lamont-hill-fired-cnn-tells-his-free-speech-story-nj/3238443002/ (accessed 28 October 2021).

Agamben, Giorgio, *Means Without End: Notes on Politics*, trans. Vincenzo Canetti and Cesare Casarino (University of Minnesota Press, 2000).

Ahmed, Maaheen, *Openness of Comics: Generating Meaning within Flexible Structures* (University of Mississippi Press, 2016).

Ahmed, Sara, *Strange Encounters: Embodied Others in Postcoloniality* (Routledge, 2000).

Al-Ghoul, Asma, 'About Palestine, which has receded in the hearts of Arabs since they announce their spring!', *Aljazeera Media Network*, 9 April 2020, www.aljazeera.net/knowledgegate/opinions/2019/11/27 (accessed 27 October 2021).

—, 'Never Ask Me About Peace Again', *Al-Monitor*, 4 August 2014, https://www.al-monitor.com/pulse/originals/2014/08/rafah-gaza-war-hospitals-filled-bodies-palestinians.html (accessed 28 October 2021).

Al-Ghoul, Asma, and Selim Nassib, *A Rebel in Gaza: Behind the Lines of the Arab Spring, One Woman's Story*, trans. Mike Mitchell (DoppelHouse Press, 2018).

Al-Ghubari, Umar, 'בעזרת השם מוחקים את "אלקודס" מהמרחב ומהתודעה' ['God Willing "Al Quds" is Erased from Both Space and Consciousness'], *Haokets*, 20 November 2015, https://www.haokets.org/2015/11/20/בעזרת-השם-מוחקים-את-"אלקודס"-מהמרחב-ומ/ (accessed 29 August 2021).

Al-Saqr, Hatim, 'Ahin ila khubz Ummi tawsiat al-hanin al-shi'ria,' *Al-ittihad*, 16 June 2010, www.alittihad.ae/article/35710/2010/أحن-إلى-خبز-أمي-توسيعات-الحنين-الشعرية (accessed 28 October 2021).

Ali, Suki, 'Feminism and Postcolonial: Knowledge/Politics', *Ethnic and Racial Studies*, vol. 30, no. 2, 2007, pp. 191–212, https://doi.org/10.1080/01419870601143877.

Allan, Diana, *Refugees of the Revolution: Experiences of Palestinian Exile* (Stanford University Press, 2014).

Allen, Lori, 'Getting by the Occupation: How Violence Became Normal during the Second Palestinian Intifada', *Cultural Anthropology*, vol. 23, no. 3, 2008, pp. 453–87, www.jstor.org/stable/20484513.

—, *The Rise and Fall of Human Rights: Cynicism and Politics in Occupied Palestine* (Stanford University Press, 2013).

Allfree, Claire, 'William Sutcliffe: It is Immoral to Ignore Injustice, Oppression and Racism', *Metro News*, 16 April 2013, https://metro.co.uk/2013/04/16/five-questions-for-author-william-sutcliffe-3616634/ (accessed 28 October 2021).

Alyan, Hala, *Four Cities* (Houghton Mifflin Harcourt, 2015).

—, *Hijra* (Houghton Mifflin Harcourt, 2016).

—, *Salt Houses* (Houghton Mifflin Harcourt, 2017).

—, *The Twenty-Ninth Year* (Houghton Mifflin Harcourt, 2019).

Amiry, Suad, *Sharon and My Mother-in-Law: Ramallah Diaries* (Granta, 2005).

Anderson, Benedict, 'Imagined Communities', in Philip Spencer (ed.), *Nations and Nationalism: A Reader* (Rutgers University Press, 2005), pp. 48–60.

Anderson, Linda, *Autobiography*, 2nd edn (Routledge, 2011).

Andrew, Lucy, and Catherine Phelps, 'Introduction', in Lucy Andrew and Catherine Phelps (eds), *Crime Fiction in the City: Capital Crimes* (University of Wales Press, 2013), pp. 1–5.

Anidjar, Gil, 'Gaza: Banality of Morals', *Economic and Political Weekly*, vol. 44, no. 6, 2009, pp. 18–20, http://www.jstor.org/stable/40278473.

Anishchenkova, Valerie, *Autobiographical Identities in Contemporary Arab Culture* (Edinburgh University Press, 2014).

Apter, Emily, *Against World Literature: The Politics of Untranslatability* (Verso, 2013).

Arendt, Hannah, *Eichmann in Jerusalem: A Report on the Banality of Evil* (Viking, 1963).

—, *The Human Condition* (University of Chicago Press, 1958).

Artz, Lee, 'Banal Balance, Selective Identification and Factual Omissions: The *New York Times* Coverage of the 2014 War in Gaza', *Journal of Arab & Muslim Media Research*, vol. 7, no. 2–3, 2014, pp. 97–112, https://doi.org/10.1386/jammr.7.2-3.97_1.

Atalia, Omer, 'Subaltern Visions of Peace I: The Case of the Arab Palestinian Citizens of Israel', in Atalier Omer, *When Peace is Not Enough: How the Israeli Peace*

Camp Thinks about Religion, Nationalism, and Justice (University of Chicago Press, 2014), pp. 183–225.
Augustine, *Confessions*, trans. Henry Chadwick (Oxford University Press, 1992).
Azaryahu, Maoz, and Arnon Golan, '(Re)Naming the Landscape: The Formation of the Hebrew Map of Israel 1949–1960', *Journal of Historical Geography*, vol. 27, no.2, 2001, pp. 178–95, https://doi.org/10.1006/jhge.2001.0297.
Azeez, Govand, 'The Oriental Rebel in Western History', *Arab Studies Quarterly*, vol. 37, no. 3 2015, pp. 244–63, https://doi.org/10.13169/arabstudquar.37.3.0244.
Baker, Rana, 'Return to What? Against Misreadings of Gaza's Great March', *Mada Masr*, 14 October 2019, https://madamasr.com/en/2019/10/14/opinion/u/return-to-what-against-misreadings-of-gazas-great-march/ (accessed 27 October 2021).
Bakhtin, M. M., 'Speech Genres', in Pam Morris and Edward Arnold (eds), *The Bakhtin Reader: Selected Essays of Bakhtin, Medvedev, and Voloshinov* (Arnold, 1994), pp. 80–7.
Bamberg, Michael, 'Identity and Narration', in Peter Huhn *et al.* (eds), *Handbook of Narratology* (W. de Gruyter, 2009), pp. 132–43.
Banks, Lynne Reid, *One More River* (Vallentine Mitchell, 1973).
Barakat, Ibtisam, *Balcony on the Moon: Coming of Age in Palestine* (Macmillan Publishing Group, 2016).
—, 'Interview by Molly Bennet', *The Nation*, 4 June 2007, https://www.thenation.com/article/archive/tasting-sky-interview-ibtisam-barakat/ (accessed 1 April 2020).
—, *Tasting the Sky: A Palestinian Childhood* (Macmillan Publishing Group, 2007).
Barghouti, Mourid, *I Saw Ramallah*, trans. Ahdaf Soueif (Anchor, [1997] 2003).
Barghouti, Omar, *BDS: Boycott, Divestment, Sanctions: The Global Struggle for Palestinian Rights* (Haymarket Books, 2001).
Bartlett, Ruth, and Christine Milligan, *What is Diary Method?* (Bloomsbury Academic, 2015).
Bashir, Bashir, and Amos Goldberg, 'Deliberating the Holocaust and the Nakba: Disruptive Empathy and Binationalism in Israel/Palestine', *Journal of Genocide Research*, vol 16.1, 2014, pp. 77–99, https://doi.org/10.1080/14623528.2014.878114.
Bayoumi, Moustafa, and Andrew Rubin, *The Selected Works of Edward Said*, 2nd edn (Vintage Books, 2019).
Beckett, Sandra L., *Crossover Fiction: Global and Historical Perspectives* (Routledge, 2009).
Beddow, Michael, *The Fiction of Humanity: Studies in the Bildungsroman from Wieland to Mann* (Cambridge University Press, 1982).
Belbin, David, 'What is Young Adult Fiction?', *English in Education*, vol. 45, no. 2, 2011, pp. 132–45, https://doi.org/10.1111/j.1754-8845.2011.01094.x.
Ben-Atar, Doron, and Andrew Pessin (eds), *Anti-Zionism on Campus: The University, Free Speech, and BDS* (Indiana University Press, 2018).
Ben-Dov, Nitza, 'Voices of War, Illness, and Dream', *Hebrew Studies*, vol. 54, 2013, pp. 287–98.

Ben Jelloun, Tahar, 'Mahmoud Darwish is dead. Long live his poetry!', *Banipal Magazine of Modern Arabic Literature*, vol. 33, autumn/winter 2008, p. 22.

Benstock, Shari, *The Private Self: Theory and Practice of Women's Autobiographical Writings* (University of North Carolina Press, 1988).

Benziman, Galia, 'Backup Disk for Life', *Haaretz*, 15 May 2008, https://www.haaretz.com/1.4980609 (accessed 27 October 2021).

Berenstein, Ofer, 'The Third Temple: Alternative Realities' Depiction of Israel in Israeli Comic Books and What it Tells Us About Consensus in Israeli Politics', in Derek Parker Royal (ed.), *Visualizing Jewish Narrative: Jewish Comics and Jewish Graphic Novels* (Bloomsbury Academic Press, 2016), pp. 141–53.

Bernard, Anna, 'Consuming Palestine: The Israeli-Palestinian Conflict in Metropolitan Popular Culture', *Journal for Cultural Research*, vol. 16, no. 2–3, 2012, pp. 197–216, https://doi.org/10.1080/14797585.2012.647669.

—, *Rhetorics of Belonging: Nation, Narration, and Israel/Palestine* (Liverpool University Press, 2013).

—, '"They are in the Right because I Love Them": Literature and Palestine Solidarity in the 1980s', in Anna Ball and Karim Mattar (eds), *The Edinburgh Companion to the Postcolonial Middle East* (Edinburgh University Press, 2018), pp. 275–92.

Bernard, Noel, 'A Universal Poet', *Banipal Magazine of Modern Arab Literature*, vol. 33, autumn/winter 2008, p. 52.

Bertacco, Simona, and Emily Apter, 'An Interview with Emily Apter', *The New Centennial Review*, vol. 16, no. 1, 2016, pp. 9–27, https://doi.org/10.14321/crnewcentrevi.16.1.0009.

Bettelheim, Bruno, *The Uses of Enchantment: The Meaning and Importance of Fairy Tales* (Thames and Hudson, 1976).

Blanchard, Rebecca, 'Ferdinand Oyono and Ahmadou Kourouma: Subverting the Personal Diary in the Quest for Identity', in Benaouda Lebdai (ed.), *Autobiography as a Writing Strategy in Postcolonial Literature* (Cambridge Scholars Publishing, 2015), pp. 113–33.

Blend, Benay, '"Neither Homeland nor Exile are Words": "Situated Knowledge" in the Works of Palestinian and Native American Writers', in Isabel Sobral Campos (ed.), *Ecopoetics and the Global Landscape. Ecocritical Theory and Practice* (Lexington Books, 2019), pp. 79–104.

Blincoe, Nicholas, 'Columbo in Palestine', *The Guardian*, 24 January 2009, https://www.theguardian.com/books/2009/jan/24/matt-rees-samaritans-secret (accessed 27 October 2021).

Boochani, Behrouz, *No Friend But the Mountains*, trans. Omid Tofighian (Picador, 2018).

Boudjellal, Farid, *JuifsArabes* (Futuropolis, 2006).

Bourdieu, Pierre, *Algerian Sketches*, trans. David Fernbach (Polity Press, 2013).

Bowman, Glenn, 'Gaza: Encystation', in Helga Tawil-Souri and Dina Matar (eds), *Gaza as Metaphor* (Hurst, 2016), pp. 113–24.

Breaking the Silence, https://www.breakingthesilence.org.il/.
Brennan, Timothy, 'Against Modernism', in Sharae Deckard and Rashmi Varma (eds), *Marxism, Postcolonial Studies, and the Future of Critique* (Routledge, 2018), pp. 21–36.
—, 'Homiletic Realism', in Eddy Kent and Terri Tomsky (eds), *Negative Cosmopolitanisms* (McGill-Queen's University Press, 2017), pp. 263–82.
Bresheeth, Haim, 'The Continuity of Trauma and Struggle: Recent Cinematic Representations of the Nakba', in A. H. Sa'di and L. Abu-Lughod (eds), *Nakba: Palestine, 1948, and the Claims of Memory* (Columbia University Press, 2007), pp. 161–87.
Brister, Rose, and Belinda Walzer, '*Kairos* and Comics: Reading Human Rights Intercontextually in Joe Sacco's Graphic Narratives', *College Literature*, vol. 4, no. 3, 2013, pp. 138–55, https://doi.org/10.1353/lit.2013.0032.
Brodzki, Bella, and Celeste Marguerite Schenck (eds), *Life/Lines: Theorizing Women's Autobiography* (Cornell University Press, 1988).
Brown, Wendy, *Walled States, Waning Sovereignty* (Zone Books, 2010).
B'Tselem, 'A Regime of Jewish Supremacy from the Jordan River to the Mediterranean Sea: This is Apartheid', *B'Tselem*, 12 January 2021, www.btselem.org/publications/fulltext/202101_this_is_apartheid (accessed 27 October 2021).
—, 'Restrictions on Movement', *B'Tselem*, 11 November 2017, https://www.btselem.org/freedom_of_movement (accessed 30 January 2020).
Buchanan, Ian, *A Dictionary of Critical Theory* (Oxford University Press, 2010).
Bugeja, Norbert, *Postcolonial Memoir in the Middle East: Rethinking the Liminal in Mashriqi Writing* (Routledge, 2012).
Bulmer, Ruppert Elizabeth, 'The Impact of Israeli Border Policy on the Palestinian Labor Market', *Economic Development and Cultural Change*, vol. 51, no. 3, April 2003, pp. 657–77, https://doi.org/10.1086/374801.
Butler, Judith, *Frames of War: When is Life Grievable?* (Verso, 2009).
—, *Parting Ways: Jewishness and the Critique of Zionism* (Columbia University Press, 2012).
Butler, Marilyn, *Romantics, Rebels and Reactionaries: English Literature and Its Background, 1760–1830* (Oxford University Press, 1985).
Cardell, Kaylie, *Dear World: Contemporary Uses of the Diary* (University of Wisconsin Press, 2014).
—, 'Life Narrative Methods for Working with Diaries', in Kate Douglas and Ashley Barnwell (eds), *Research Methodology for Auto/Biography Studies* (Routledge, 2019), pp. 90–5.
Chamberlain, K., 'Stealing Palestinian History', *This Week in Palestine*, October 2005, http://www.thisweekinpalestine.com/details.php?id=1451&ed=107&edid=107 (accessed 14 June 2021).
Cheetham, Dominic, 'Literary Translation and Conceptual Metaphors: From Movement to Performance', *Translation Studies*, vol. 9, no. 3, 2016, pp. 241–55, https://doi.org/10.1080/14781700.2016.1180543.

Cheurfa, Hiyem, 'Comedic Resilience: Arab Women's Diaries of National Struggles and Dissident Humour', *Comedy Studies*, vol. 10, no. 2, 2019, pp. 183–98, https://doi.org/10.1080/2040610x.2019.1623501.

Chomsky, Noam. 'Foreword'. *The Drone Eats with Me: Diaries from a City under Fire*, by Atef Abu Saif. Comma Press, 2015, pp, v–vi.

Chomsky, Noam, and Ilan Pappé, *Gaza in Crisis: Reflections on Israel's War Against the Palestinians Territories* (Haymarket Books, 2010).

Christian, Ed, 'Introducing the Post-Colonial Detective: Putting Marginality to Work', in Ed Christian (ed.), *The Post-Colonial Detective* (Palgrave, 2001), pp. 1–16.

Chute, Hillary, 'Comics as Literature? Reading Graphic Narrative', *PMLA*, vol. 123, no. 2, 2008, pp. 452–65, https://doi.org/10.1632/pmla.2008.123.2.452.

Collier, Paul, and Anke Hoeffler, 'Greed and Grievance in Civil War', World Bank Policy Research Working Paper, no. 2355 World Bank, 2000), http://documents.worldbank.org/curated/en/359271468739530199/Greed-and-grievance-in-civil-war.

Collins, John, *Global Palestine* (Hurst, 2011).

Condon, Matthew G., 'The Unnamed and the Defaced: The Limits of Rhetoric in Augustine's *Confessiones*', *Journal of the American Academy of Religion*, vol. 69, no. 1, 2001, pp. 43–63, www.jstor.org/stable/1466069.

Cothran, Casey A., and Mercy Cannon, 'Introduction: Embarking on a New Investigation', in Casey A. Cothran and Mercy Cannon (eds), *New Perspectives on Detective Fiction: Mysteries Magnified* (Routledge, 2016), pp. 1–13.

Craps, Stef, *Postcolonial Witnessing: Trauma out of Bounds* (Palgrave Macmillan, 2015).

Cutter, M. J., and C. J. Schlund-Vials (eds), *Redrawing the Historical Past: History, Memory, and Multiethnic Graphic Novels* (University of Georgia Press, 2018).

Dajani, Souad, 'Palestinian Women Under Israeli Occupation: Implications for Development', in Judith E. Tucker (ed.), *Arab Women: Old Boundaries, New Frontiers* (Indiana University Press, 1993), pp. 102–26.

Darraj, Susan Muaddi, *A Curious Land: Stories from Home* (University of Massachusetts Press, 2015).

—, *The Inheritance of Exile: Stories from South Philly* (University of Notre Dame Press, 2007).

Darwish, Mahmoud, *Akhr al-layl* [*The End of the Night*] (Dar al-Audah, 1993), https://www.dopdfwn.com/cacnretra/scgdfnya/591.pdf.

—, *Al-diwan: al-a'mal al-ula* [*Al-Diwan: The Early Works, volume 1*] (Riad El-Rayyes Books, 2005).

—, *Al-diwan: al-a'mal al-ula* [*Al-Diwan: The Early Works, volume 2*) (Riad El-Rayyes Books, 2005).

—, *Almond Blossoms and Beyond*, trans. Mohamed Shaheen (Interlink Pub. Group, 2009).

—, *A'ras* [*Weddings*] (Dar al-Audah, 1977).

—, *'Ashiq min filastin* [*A Lover from Palestine*] (Dar al-Audah, [1966] 1993).
—, *Habibati Tanhado Min Nawmiha* [*My Lover Wakes Up*] (Dar al-Audah, 1970).
—, *Madih al-zill al-aly* [*In Praise of the High Shadow*] (Dar al-Audah, 1983).
—, *State of Siege*, trans. Munir Akash and Daniel Abdel-Hayy Moore (Jusoor/Syracuse University Press, [2002] 2010).
Darwish, Mahmoud, and Fady Joudah, *The Butterfly's Burden: Poems* (Copper Canyon Press, 2007).
Davidson, Lawrence, *Cultural Genocide* (Rutgers University Press, 2012).
Davis, Angela Y., *Freedom is a Constant Struggle: Ferguson, Palestine, and the Foundations of a Movement* (Haymarket Books, 2016).
Debord, Guy, et al., *The Society of the Spectacle* (Bureau of Public Secrets, 2014).
Delisle, Guy, *Jerusalem: Chronicles from the Holy City* (Drawn and Quarterly, 2012).
Derrida, Jacques, 'The Animal That Therefore I Am (More to Follow)', trans. David Willis, *Critical Inquiry*, vol. 28, no. 2, 2002, pp. 369–418, https://doi.org/10.1086/449046.
—, 'Hostipitality', *Angelaki*, vol. 5, no. 3, 2000, pp. 3–18, https://doi.org/10.1080/09697250020034706.
Dibiasi, Caroline Mall, 'Changing Trends in Palestinian Political Activism: The Second Intifada, the Wall Protests, and the Human Rights Turn', *Geopolitics*, vol. 20, no. 3, 2015, pp. 669–95, https://doi.org/10.1080/14650045.2015.1028028.
Docker, John, 'Instrumentalising the Holocaust: Israel, Settler-Colonialism, Genocide (Creating a Conversation between Raphaël Lemkin and Ilan Pappé)', *Holy Land Studies: A Multidisciplinary Journal*, vol. 11, no. 1, 2012, pp. 1–32, https://doi.org/10.3366/hls.2012.0027.
Earle, Harriet, 'My Friend Dahmer: The Comic as *Bildungsroman*', *Journal of Graphic Novels and Comics*, vol. 5, no. 4, 2014, pp. 429–40, https://doi.org/10.1080/21504857.2014.916329.
El-Ariss, Tarek, *Leaks, Hacks, and Scandals: Arab Culture in the Digital Age* (Princeton University Press, 2019).
El Said, Maha, Lena Meari and Nicola Christine Pratt, 'Introduction', in Maha El Said, Lena Meari and Nicola Christine Pratt (eds), *Rethinking Gender in Revolutions and Resistance: Lessons from the Arab World* (Zed Books, 2015), pp. 1–32.
El-Youssef, Samir, 'The Day the Beast Got Thirsty', in Samir El-Youssef and Etgar Keret, *Gaza Blues: Different Stories* (David Paul, 2004), pp. 111–72.
Elfarra, Mona, *From Gaza, with Love*, http://fromgaza.blogspot.com/.
Ellis, Deborah, *The Cat at the Wall* (Groundwood Books, 2014).
—, *Three Wishes: Palestinian and Israeli Children Speak Out* (Allen and Unwin, 2005).
Evans, Mary, Sarah E. H. Moore, with Hazel Johnstone, 'Introduction', in Mary Evans, Sarah E. H. Moore with Hazel Johnstone (eds), *Detecting the Social Order: Order and Disorder in Post-1970s Detective Fiction* (Palgrave Macmillan, 2019), pp. 1–25.
Fadda-Conrey, Carol, *Contemporary Arab-American Literature: Transnational Reconfigurations of Citizenship and Belonging* (New York University Press, 2014).

Fanon, Franz, *The Wretched of the Earth*, trans. Richard Philcox (Grove Press, 2004).
Fantasia, Annette, 'The Paterian Bildungsroman Reenvisioned: "Brain-Building" in Alison Bechdel's *Fun Home: A Family Tragicomic*', *Criticism*, vol. 53, no. 1, 2011, pp. 83–97.
Fassin, Didier, 'The Humanitarian Politics of Testimony: The Subjectification Through Trauma in the Israeli-Palestinian Conflict', *Cultural Anthropology*, vol. 23, no. 3, 2008, pp. 531–58, https://doi.org/10.1111/j.1548-1360.2008.00017.x.
Feldman, Ilana, 'Gaza's Humanitarianism Problem', *Journal of Palestine Studies*, vol. 38, no. 3, 2009, pp. 22–37, www.jstor.org/stable/10.1525/jps.2009.xxxviii.3.22.
Folman, Ari, *Waltz with Bashir: A Lebanon War Story* (Metropolitan Books, 2009).
Forsyth, Isla, 'More-than-human Warfare', *Social & Cultural Geography*, vol. 17, no. 6, 2016, pp. 798–802, https://doi.org/10.1080/14649365.2016.1147060.
Freire, Paulo, *Education for Critical Consciousness* (Continuum International Publishing Group, 2005).
—, *Pedagogy of the Oppressed* (Bloomsbury Academic, 2014).
Freisinger, Alison, 'A Decent and Honorable Detective', *Publishers Weekly*, vol. 37, 2006.
Fresnault-Deruelle, Pierre, *La Bande Dessinée, Essai d'Analyse Sémiotique* (Hachette, 1972).
Gallien, Claire, 'Minding (About) the Gazan Border in Contemporary Palestinian Literature', *Commonwealth: Essays and Studies*, vol. 39, no. 1, 2016, pp. 57–68, https://doi.org/10.4000/ces.4753.
Gaza, [film], Gary Keane and Andrew McConnell (dirs.). Fine Point Films and Real Films, 2019.
Genesis, *King James Bible Online*, https://www.kingjamesbibleonline.org/Genesis-Chapter-1/.
Gildenhard, Ingo, and Andrew Zissos, 'General Introduction: *Metamorphosis: A Phenomenology*', in Ingo Gildenhard and Andrew Zissos (eds), *Transformative Change in Western Thought: A History of Metamorphosis from Homer to Hollywood* (Routledge, 2013), pp. 1–34.
Gilmore, Leigh, *The Limits of Autobiography: Trauma and Testimony* (Cornell University Press, 2001).
Glidden, Sarah, *How to Understand Israel in 60 Days or Less* (Drawn & Quarterly, 2016).
Gluzman, Michael, 'כתיבת השכול של דויד גרוסמן' [David Grossman's Bereavement Writing], עיונים [*Iyunim*], vol. 31, 2019, pp. 349–80.
Google Arts and Culture, 'Al Baseera #1', https://artsandculture.google.com/asset/al-baseera-1-hazem-harb/4gH6xe8CGh3J1g (accessed 25 October 2021).
Groensteen, Thierry, *The Systems of Comics* (University of Mississippi Press, 2007).
Grossman, David, *A Horse Walks into a Bar*, trans. Jessica Cohen (Alfred A. Knopf, 2016).
—, נוכחים נפקדים, [*Sleeping on a Wire: Conversations with Palestinians in Israel*] (The New Library, 1992).

—, *To the End of the Land* [Kindle Edition], trans. Jessica Cohen (Random House eBooks, 2010).
—, אשה בורחת מבשורה, [*To the End of the Land*] (Hasifria Hahadasha, 2008).
—, הזמן הצהוב, [*The Yellow Wind*] (Hasifria Hahadasha, 1987).
—, *The Yellow Wind*, trans. Haim Watzman (Picador, 1988).
—, *Writing in the Dark: Essays on Literature and Politics*, trans. Jessica Cohen (Farrar, Straus and Giroux, 2008).
Grutman, Rainier, 'Refraction and Recognition: Literary Multilingualism in Translation', *Target*, vol. 18, no. 1, 2006, pp. 17–47, https://doi.org/10.1075/target.18.1.03gru.
Gusdorf, Georges, 'Conditions and Limits of Autobiography', in James Olney (ed.), *Autobiography: Essays Theoretical and Critical* (Princeton University Press, [1956] 1980), pp. 28–48.
Habiby, Emile, *The Secret Life of Saeed: The Pessoptimist*, trans. S. K. Jayyusi and T. LeGassick (Interlink Books, [1974] 2003).
Hage, Ghassan, 'With the Fig, the Olive and the Pomegranate Trees: Thoughts on Australian Belonging', in Paul Tabar and Jennifer Skulte-Ouaiss (eds), *Politics, Culture and the Lebanese Diaspora* (Cambridge Scholars Press, 2011), pp. 151–60.
Haifawi, Yoav, 'מדוע הורשעה המשוררת דארין טאטור' [Why Was the Poet Dareen Tatour Convicted], *Haokets*, 29 July 2018, https://www.haokets.org/2018/07/29/מדוע-הורשעה-המשוררת-דארין-טאטור/ (accessed 4 September 2021).
Halaby, Laila, *West of the Jordan* (Beacon Press, 2003).
Hammack, Phillip L., 'Narrating Hyphenated Selves: Intergroup Contact and Configurations of Identity among Young Palestinian Citizens of Israel', *International Journal of Intercultural Relations*, vol. 34, no. 4, 2010, pp. 368–85, https://doi.org/10.1016/j.ijintrel.2010.03.002.
Hammad, Isabella, *The Parisian* (Jonathan Cape, 2019).
Hammad, Suheir, *Born Palestinian, Born Black*, 2nd edn (UpSet Press, 2010).
Hammami, Rema, 'On (Not) Suffering at the Checkpoint: Palestinian Narrative Strategies of Surviving Israel's Carceral Geography', *Borderlands*, vol. 14, no. 1, 2015, pp. 1–17.
—, 'On the Importance of Thugs', *Middle East Report*, vol. 231, summer 2004 (accessed 30 August 2021).
Hammer, Juliane, 'A Crisis of Memory: Homeland and Exile in Contemporary Palestinian Memoirs', in Ken Seigneurie (ed.), *Crisis and Memory: The Representation of Space in Modern Levantine Narrative* (Reichert Verlag, 2003), pp. 177–98.
Hamza, Hussein, 'Al-siyaghat al-niha'ieyya w tahawul al-ma'na' [Final Formulations and the Transformations of Meaning], *AL-MAJALLA Journal of the Arabic Language Academy*, vol. 3, 2012, pp. 7–56.
Hanafi, Sari, Leila Hilal and Lex Takkenberg, *UNRWA and Palestinian Refugees: From Relief and Works to Human Development* (Routledge, 2014).
Harbi, Mohammed, Gilbert Meynier and Tahar Khaloufe, 'Mouvements du Monde Arabe', *Raison Présente*, vol. 181, 2012, pp. 5–18, https://doi.org/10.3406/raipr.2012.4362.

Harlow, Barbara, 'The Drone Imprint: Literature in the Age of UAVs', *Race & Class*, vol. 60, no. 3, 2018, pp. 59–72, https://doi.org/10.1177/0306396818810988.

Hashim, Norma (ed.), *The Prisoners' Diaries: Palestinian Voices from the Israeli Gulag* (Islamic Human Rights Commission, 2013).

Hawker, Nancy, 'Complexities of Speech in Palestinian Refugee Camps', *Bulletin du Centre de recherche français à Jérusalem*, vol. 21, 2010, pp. 1–5, https://journals.openedition.org/bcrfj/6395.

—, 'The Mirage of "Arabrew": Ideologies for Understanding Arabic-Hebrew Contact', *Language in Society*, vol. 47, 2018, pp. 219–44, https://doi.org/10.1017/S0047404518000015.

Heaney, Seamus, *The Cure at Troy* (Faber, 2018).

Helman, Sara, 'Challenging the Israeli Occupation Through Testimony and Confession: The Case of Anti-Denial SMOs Machsom Watch and Breaking the Silence', *International Journal of Politics, Culture, and Society*, vol. 28, no. 4, 2015, pp. 377–94, www.jstor.org/stable/24713997.

Henkin-Roitfarm, Roni, 'Hebrew and Arabic in Asymmetric Contact in Israel', *Lodz Papers in Pragmatics*, vol. 7, no. 1, 2011, pp. 61–100, https://doi.org/10.2478/v10016-011-0004-7.

Henry, Vincent, 'Les Interviews BD: Interview avec Maximilien Le Roy', *Bdthèque*, 24 May 2010, https://www.bdtheque.com/interviews/141/maximilien-le-roy (accessed 28 October 2021).

Hermans, Anaële, and Délphine Hermans, *Les Amandes Vertes: Lettre de Palestines* (Warum, 2011).

Herremans, Brigitte, 'Belgium and the Israeli-Palestinian Conflict: The Cautious Pursuit of a Just Peace', *Studia Diplomatica*, vol. 66, no. 4, 2013, pp. 77–94, https://www.jstor.org/stable/26531597.

Hesse, Isabelle, 'Sensory Siege: Dromocolonisation, Slow Violence, and Poetic Realism in the Twenty-first Century Short Story from Gaza', *Journal for Cultural Research*, vol. 21, no. 2, 2017, pp. 190–203, https://doi.org/10.1080/14797585.2016.1272786.

Hirsch, Marianne, 'The Novel of Formation as a Genre: Between Great Expectation and Lost Illusion', *Genre*, XII, 1979, pp. 293–311.

Hochberg, Gil Z., *In Spite of Partition: Jews, Arabs, and the Limits of Separatist Imagination* (Princeton University Press, 2007).

—, 'To Be or Not to Be an Israeli Arab: Sayed Kashua and the Prospect of Minority Speech-Acts', *Comparative Literature*, vol 62, no. 1, 2010, pp. 68–88, https://doi.org/10.1215/00104124-2009-033.

—, *Visual Occupations: Violence and Visibility in a Conflict Zone* (Duke University Press, 2015).

Hutcheon, Linda, *A Theory of Adaptation* (Routledge, 2006).

Holy Bible: New International Version, www.biblegateway.com (accessed 12 June 2021).

Ilmonen, Kaisa, 'Talking Back to the Bildungsroman: Caribbean Literature and the Dis/location of the Genre', *Journal of West Indian Literature*, vol. 25, no. 1, 2017, pp. 60–76, https://www.jstor.org/stable/e90005820.

Jacobs, Adriana X., *Strange Cocktail: Translation and the Making of Modern Hebrew Poetry* (University of Michigan Press, 2018).
—, 'Translating Anna Herman's "Mmhmm"', *Michigan Quarterly Review*, vol. 52, no. 2, 2013, pp. 290–8, http://hdl.handle.net/2027/spo.act2080.0052.226.
Jelinek, Estelle C., *Women's Autobiography: Essays in Criticism* (Indiana University Press, 1980).
Jo, Hyeran, Rotem Dvir and Yvette Isidori, 'Who Is a Rebel? Typology and Rebel Groups in the Contemporary Middle East', *Middle East: Topics & Arguments*, vol. 6, 2016, pp. 76–86, https://doi.org/10.17192/meta.2016.6.4571.
Kamuf, Peggy, '*Caracol*: Translator's Notes', *Differences: A Journal of Feminist Cultural Studies*, vol. 25, no. 3, 2015, pp. 1–13, https://doi.org/10.1215/10407391-2847937.
Kanafani, Ghassan, *Men in the Sun*, trans. Hilary Kilpatrick (Lynne Rienner Publishers, 1999).
Karmi, Ghada, *In Search of Fatima: A Palestinian Story*, 2nd edn (Verso, 2009).
—, *Return: A Palestinian Memoir* (Verso, 2015).
Kashua, Sayed, *Dancing Arabs*, trans. Miriam Shlesinger (Grove Press, 2004).
—, *Native: Dispatches from a Palestinian-Israeli Life*, trans. Ralph Mandel (Saqi Books, 2016).
—, *Second Person Singular*, trans. Mitch Ginsburg (Grove Press, 2010).
Kaspi, Niva, 'Standing up for Soul-Searching', *Sydney Review of Books*, 20 March 2018, https://sydneyreviewofbooks.com/review/a-horse-walks-into-a-bar-david-grossman-review/ (accessed 27 October 2021).
Katz, Kimberly (ed. and trans), *A Young Palestinian's Diary, 1941–45: the Life of Sami 'Amr* (University of Texas Press, 2010).
Keefe, Anne, 'The Ecstatic Embrace of Verbal and Visual: Twenty-First Century Lyric Beyond the Ekphrastic Paragone', *Word & Image*, vol. 27, no. 2, 2011, pp. 135–47, https://doi.org/10.1080/02666286.2010.516891.
Kelly, Tobias, 'The Attractions of Accountancy: Living an Ordinary Life during the Second Palestinian Intifada', *Ethnography*, vol. 9, no. 3, 2008, pp. 351–76, https://doi.org/10.1177/1466138108094975.
Keren, Michael, 'Political Escapism in Contemporary Israel: Lessons from David Grossman's to the End of the Land', *Journal of Modern Jewish Studies*, vol. 14, no. 2, 2015, pp. 246–60, https://doi.org/10.1080/14725886.2014.992184.
Khalidi, Rashid, *The Hundred Years War on Palestine: A History of Settler Colonialism and Resistance, 1917–2017* (Metropolitan Books, 2020).
—, 'Remembering Mahmud Darwish (1941–2008)', *Journal of Palestine Studies*, vol. 38, no. 1, 2008, pp. 74–7, https://doi.org/10.1525/jps.2008.38.1.74.
Khalili, Laleh, *Heroes and Martyrs of Palestine: The Politics of National Commemoration* (Cambridge University Press, 2006).
Kimmerling, Baruch, *Politicide: Ariel Sharon's War Against the Palestinians* (Verso, 2003).
Klein, Naomi, 'Israel: Boycott, Divest, Sanction', *The Nation*, vol. 288, no. 3, 2009, p. 10.

Knight, Stephen, 'The Postcolonial Crime Novel', in Ato Quayson (ed.), *The Cambridge Companion to the Postcolonial Novel* (Cambridge University Press, 2014), pp. 166–87.

Korn, Alina, 'Crime and Legal Control: The Israeli Arab population During the Military Government Period (1948–66)', in Ilan Pappé (ed.), *The Israel/Palestine Question: A Reader* (Routledge, 1999), pp. 207–31.

Kuttab, Jonathan, 'How Will Annexation Change the Legal Landscape in the West Bank?', *Electronic Intifada*, 7 August 2020, https://electronicintifada.net/content/how-will-annexation-change-legal-landscape-west-bank/30881 (accessed 1 October 2020).

Laird, Elizabeth, with Sonia Nimr, *A Little Piece of Ground* (Macmillan, 2003).

—, 'A Little Piece of Ground', *Elizabeth Laird* (blog), http://www.elizabethlaird.co.uk/books/a-little-piece-of-ground (accessed 26 November 2019).

Lamont Hill, Marc, and Noura Erakat, 'Black-Palestinian Transnational Solidarity: Renewals, Returns, and Practice', *Journal of Palestine Studies*, vol. 48, no. 4, 2020, pp. 7–16.

Lang, Felix, and Malcolm Théoleyre, 'The Rebel', *Middle East: Topics & Arguments*, vol. 6, 2016, pp. 5–11, https://doi.org/10.17192/meta.2016.6.4571.

Leibovich-Dar, Sara, 'About a Boy', *Haaretz*, 23 October 2003, https://www.haaretz.com/1.4742337. Accessed 26 November 2019.

Lejeune, Philippe, 'The Autobiographical Contract', in Tzvetan Todorov (ed.), *French Literary Theory Today: A Reader*, trans. R. Carter (Cambridge University Press, [1975] 1982), pp. 192–222.

—, *On Autobiography* (University of Minnesota Press, 1989).

—, *On Diary*, ed. Jeremy D. Popkin and Julie Rak, trans. Katherine Durnin (University of Hawai'i Press, 2009).

Le Roy, Maximilien, *Faire le Mur* (Casterman, 2009).

Le Roy, Maximilien, and Soulman, *Les Chemins de Traverse* (Boîtes à bulles, 2010).

Levy, Lital, *Poetic Trespass: Writing Between Hebrew and Arabic in Israel/Palestine* (Princeton University Press, 2014).

Libicki, Miriam, *Towards a Hot Jew: The Israeli Soldier as Fetish Object* (Firenze University Press, 2016).

Lima, Maria Helena, 'Decolonizing Genre: Jamaica Kincaid and the *Bildungsroman*', *Genre*, XXVI, 1993, pp. 431–59.

Linfield, Susie, *The Lions' Den: Zionism and the Left from Hannah Arendt to Noam Chomsky* (Yale University Press, 2019).

Lipsker-Albeck, Avidov, 'הדיבור והכתב או באיזה מובן דויד גרוסמן צמחוני?' [Oral or Textual?: In What Sense is David Grossman a Vegetarian?], *Ot: A Journal for Literature and Theory*, vol. 2, 2012, pp. 205–17.

Litvin, Margaret, and Johanna Sellman, 'Interview with Hassan Blasim', *Tank*, vol. 69, 2019, Tankmagazine.com/issue-69/talk/hassan-blasim (accessed 10 March 2018).

Lomsky-Feder, Edna, and Eyal Ben-Ari, *The Military and Militarism in Israeli Society* (State University of New York Press, 1999).

Luckhurst, Roger, *The Trauma Question* (Routledge, 2013).

Lustig, Kfir Cohen, *Makers of Worlds, Readers of Signs: Israeli and Palestinian Literatures of the Global Contemporary* (Verso, 2019).

Lyons, Sara, 'Recent Work in Victorian Studies and the Bildungsroman', *Literature Compass*, vol. 15, no. 4, 2018, pp. 1–12, https://doi.org/10.1111/lic3.12460.

Majaj, Lisa Suhair, 'On Writing and Return', *Meridians*, vol. 2, no. 1, 2000, pp. 113–26.

Makdisi, Saree, 'The Architecture of Erasure', *Critical Inquiry*, vol. 36, no. 3, 2010, pp. 519–59, https://doi.org/10.1086/653411.

Mar'i, Abdul Rahman, 'ערבים מדברים עברית' [Arabs Speaking Hebrew], *Alaxon*, 30 December 2013, https://alaxon.co.il/article/ערבים-מדברים-עברית/ (accessed 27 September 2021).

Marston, Elsa, 'More than Just Stories: The Portrayal of Palestinians in American Children's Literature', *Electronic Intifada*, 11 March 2004, https://electronicintifada.net/content/more-just-stories-portrayal-palestinians-american-childrens-literature/5012 (accessed 27 October 2021).

Masalha, Nur, *The Palestine Nakba: Decolonising History, Narrating the Subaltern, Reclaiming Memory* (Zed Books, 2012).

—, 'Settler-Colonialism, Memoricide and Indigenous Toponymic Memory: The Appropriation of Palestinian Place Names by the Israeli State', *Journal of Holy Land and Palestine Studies*, vol. 14, no. 1, 2015, pp. 3–57, https://doi.org/10.3366/hlps.2015.0103.

Massad, Joseph, 'Palestinian Right of Return: The Legal Key to Undoing the Zionist Conquest', *Middle East Eye*, 4 December 2019, https://www.middleeasteye.net/opinion/palestinian-right-return-legal-key-undoing-zionist-conquest (accessed 27 October 2021).

Masud, Muhammad, 'Giving Voice at a Price: Imagining the Arab World in the Work of Elizabeth Laird', *Arab Studies Quarterly*, vol. 38, no. 3, 2016, pp. 601–19, https://doi.org/10.13169/arabstudquar.38.3.0601.

Matar, Dina, and Helga Tawil-Souri (eds), *Gaza as Metaphor* (Hurst, 2016).

Matar, Dina, and Zahera Harb (eds), *Narrating Conflict in the Middle East: Discourse, Image and Communications Practices in Lebanon and Palestine* (I. B. Tauris, 2013).

Mateh Yehuda Regional Council, 'מבוא ביתר' [Mevo Beitar], 29 August 2021, https://www.m-yehuda.org.il/מבוא-ביתר/ (accessed 27 October 2021).

Mattar, Karim, 'Review: *Chief Complaint: A Country Doctor's Tales of Life in Galilee*, by Hatim Kanaaneh, and *Return: A Palestinian Memoir*, by Ghada Karmi', *Journal of Palestinian Studies*, vol. 45, no. 3, 2016, pp. 54–7, https://doi.org/10.1525/jps.2016.45.3.54.

Matzke, Christine, and Susanne Mühleisen, 'Postcolonial Postmortems: Issues and Perspectives', *Postcolonial Postmortems: Crime Fiction from a Transcultural Perspective* (Rodopi, 2006), pp. 1–16.

Mbembe, Achille, *Necropolitics* (Duke University Press, 2019).

McCloskey, Stephen, 'COVID-19 Has Deepened the 'Pandemic of Poverty' for Palestinian Refugees in Lebanon', *openDemocracy*, 23 November 2020, www.opendemocracy.net/en/north-africa-west-asia/covid-19-has-deepened-pandemic-poverty-palestinian-refugees-lebanon (accessed 7 April 2021).

McCloud, Scott, *Understanding Comics: The Invisible Art* (Kitchen Sink, 1993).

Medovoi, Leerom, *Rebels: Youth and the Cold War Origins of Identity* (Duke University Press, 2005).

Meek, Margaret, 'Children Reading – Now', in M. Styles, E. Bearne and V. Watson (eds), *After Alice: Exploring Children's Literature* (Cassell, 1992), pp. 172–88.

Mehta, Brinda, *Rituals of Memory in Contemporary Arab Women's Writing* (Syracuse University Press, 2007).

Mendel, Yonatan, 'איך אומרים שהיד בעברית' [How Do You Say Shaheed in Hebrew], שבוע הספר - הערת המתרגמ.ת [*Book Week: Translator's Comments*], 4 September 2019, https://www.haokets.org/2019/06/19/ת-המתרגמ-הערת-הספר-שבוע/ (accessed 27 September 2021).

Mendelson-Maoz, Adia, *Borders, Territories, and Ethics: Hebrew Literature in the Shadow of the Intifada* (Purdue University Press, 2018).

Menocal, María Rosa, *The Ornament of the World: How Muslims, Jews, and Christians Created a Culture of Tolerance in Medieval Spain* (Little, Brown, and Company, 2002).

Mickelsen, David J., 'The Bildungsroman in Africa: The Case of *Mission Terminée*', *The French Review*, vol. 59, no. 3, 1986, pp. 418–27.

Millard, Kenneth, *Coming of Age in Contemporary American Fiction* (Edinburgh University Press, 2007).

Misch, Georg, *A History of Autobiography in Antiquity*, vol 1 (Greenwood Press, [1907] 1973).

Moaz, Ifat, 'Does Contact Work in Protracted Asymmetrical Conflict: Appraising 20 years of Reconciliation-Aimed Encounters between Israeli Jews and Palestinians', *Journal of Peace Research*, vol. 28, no. 1, 2011, pp. 115–25, https://doi.org/10.1177/0022343310389506.

Moghadam, Valentine, 'Afghanistan: Are Human Security and Gender Justice Possible?', *Works and Days* (Special issue: *Invisible Battlegrounds: Feminist Resistance in the Global Age of War and Imperialism*, ed. Susan Comfort), vol. 29, nos. 1 & 2, 2011, pp. 81–97.

Mohanty, Chandra Talpade, 'Cartographies of Struggle: Third World Women and the Politics of Feminism', in Chandra Mohanty *et al.* (eds), *Third World Women and the Politics of Feminism* (Indiana University Press, 1991), pp. 1–47.

Monterescu, Daniel, 'The Palestinian Trail of Fish: Artist's Graffiti Dives into Heart of Refugee Struggle', *Haaretz*, 30 November 2017, www.haaretz.com/life/.premium.MAGAZINE-trail-of-fish-graffiti-dives-into-heart-of-palestinian-struggle-1.5627199 (accessed 27 October 2021).

Moore, Lindsey, *Narrating Postcolonial Arab Nations: Egypt, Algeria, Lebanon, Palestine* (Routledge, 2018).

Moore-Gilbert, Bart, *Postcolonial Life-Writing: Culture, Politics, and Self-Representation* (Routledge, 2009).
—, 'Time Bandits: Temporality and the Politics of Form in Palestinian Women's Life-Writing', *Journal of Postcolonial Writing*, vol. 50, no. 2, 2014, pp. 189–201, https://doi.org/10.1080/17449855.2014.883178.
Moretti, Franco, *The Way of the World: The Bildungsroman in European Culture*, trans. Albert Sbragia (Verso, 2000).
Mosih, Norma, 'להשקיף על הנוף, לראות מקום ולקרוא לו בשם: על הסיורים של עמותת זוכרות' [To Observe the Landscape, See a Place and Call It by Name: On the Zochrot Foundation's Guided Tours], in Amer Dahamshe and Yossef Schwartz (eds), *שמות מקומות וזהות מרחבית בישראל-פלסטין: יחסי רוב-מיעוט, השכחה וזיכרון* [*Spatial Identity in Israel-Palestine: Majority-Minority Relations, Oblivion and Memory*] (Resling, 2018), pp. 167–90.
Moss, Elaine, 'A Certain Particularity: An Interview with Janet and Allan Ahlberg', *Signal*, vol. 61, 1990, pp. 20–6.
Moughrabi, Fouad, 'Three Representations of the Israeli-Palestinian Conflict in Children's Literature', *Electronic Intifada*, 2007, https://electronicintifada.net/content/three-representations-israeli-palestinian-conflict-childrens-literature-part-2/6740 (accessed 27 October 2021).
Müller, Anja, *Adapting Canonical Texts in Children's Literature* (Bloomsbury Academic, 2014).
Nadler, Mei-Tal, '"תקשיב, לשבילים בארץ יש קול": מרחב אלטרנטיבי לאטיקה אלטרנטיבית באשה בורחת מבשורה מאת דויד גרוסמן' ['Listen, the Path Has Sounds: Alternative Space for Alternative Ethics in *To the End of the Land* by David Grossman'], Mikan: Ben Gurion University, 2017, pp. 76–111.
Nashef, Hania A. M., *Palestinian Culture and the Nakba: Bearing Witness* (Routledge Advances in Middle East and Islamic Studies, 2018).
Nasser, Amjad, 'Mahmoud Darwish between the Political and the Aesthetic', *Banipal Magazine of Modern Arabic Literature*, vol. 33, autumn/winter 2008, pp. 32–3.
Nasser, Tahia Abdel, *Literary Autobiography and Arab National Struggles* (Edinburgh University Press, 2017).
—, 'Palestine and Latin America: Lina Meruane's *Volverse Palestina* and Nathalie Handal's *La Estrella Invisible*', *Journal of Postcolonial Writing*, vol. 5, no. 2, 2018, pp. 239–53, https://doi.org/10.1080/17449855.2017.1325771.
Nathanson, Stephen, *Terrorism and the Ethics of War* (Cambridge University Press, 2010).
Nelson, Cary, *Israel Denial: Anti-Zionism, Anti-Semitism, and the Faculty Campaign Against the Jewish State* (Indiana University Press, 2019).
Nikolajeva, Maria, and Carole Scott, *How Picturebooks Work* (Psychology Press, 2001).
Nodelman, Perry, *Words about Pictures: The Narrative Art of Children's Picture Books* (University of Georgia Press, 1988).

Nora, Pierre, 'Between Memory and History: Les Lieux de Memoire', *Memory and Counter-Memory*, vol. 26, 1989, pp. 7–24, https://doi.org/10.2307/2928520.

Nussbaum, Felicity A., 'Towards Conceptualizing Diary', in Trev Lynn Broughton (ed.), *Autobiography* (Routledge, 2007), pp. 1–10.

Nye, Naomi Shihab, *Sitti's Secrets*, illust. Nancy Carpenter (Simon & Schuster, 1994).

Odeh, Ayman, 'בסוף יום ארוך צריך לשים את שלושת האיומים הקיומיים האלה לישון!' [At the End of a Long Day, It's Time to Put These Three Existential Threats to Bed!], *Twitter*, 19 November 2019, https://twitter.com/ayodeh/status/1196157580046942210?lang=en (accessed 27 October 2021).

Olney, James (ed.), *Autobiography: Essays Theoretical and Critical* (Princeton University Press, 1980).

Oppenheimer, Yochai, 'The Arab in the Mirror: The Image of the Arab in Israeli Fiction', *Prooftexts*, vol. 19, no. 3, 1999, pp. 205–34.

Ortiz-Robles, Mario, *Literature and Animal Studies* (Routledge, 2016).

Owen, Wilfred, 'Dulce et Decorum Est', *Poetry Foundation*, https://www.poetryfoundation.org/poems/46560/dulce-et-decorum-est (accessed 24 September 2021).

Page, Ra, 'Editor's Note', in Atef Abu Saif, *The Drone Eats with Me: Diaries from a City Under Fire* (Comma Press, 2015), pp. 243–9.

Pappé, Ilan, *The Biggest Prison on Earth: A History of the Occupied Territories* (Oneworld Publications, 2017).

—, *The Ethnic Cleansing of Palestine* (Oneworld, 2006).

Patel, Yumna, 'Understanding the Trump "Deal of the Century": What It Does, and Doesn't Say', *Mondoweiss*, February 2020, https://mondoweiss.net/2020/02/understanding-the-trump-deal-of-the-century-what-it-does-and-doesnt-say/ (accessed 20 March 2020).

Pearson, Nels, and Marc Singer (eds), *Detective Fiction in a Postcolonial and Transnational World* (Oxford University Press, 2012).

Pekar, Harvey, *Harvey Pekar's Cleveland*, illust. Joseph Remnant, (Z2 Comics, 2012).

Pekar, Harvey, *Not the Israel My Parents Promised Me,* illust. J. T. Waldman (Hill and Wang, 2012).

Peteet, Julie, 'Male Gender and Rituals of Resistance in the Palestinian "Intifada": A Cultural Politics of Violence', *American Ethnologist*, vol. 21, no. 1, 1994, pp. 31–49, www.jstor.org/stable/646520. https://doi.org/10.1525/ae.1994.21.1.02a00020.

—, 'Subordination of Women. Review of *Palestinian Women: Patriarchy and Resistance in the West Bank*', *Journal of Palestine Studies*, vol. 33, no. 3, [University of California Press, Institute for Palestine Studies], 2004, pp. 113–15, https://doi.org/10.1525/jps.2004.33.3.113.

Peterson, Carla L., *The Determined Reader: Gender and Culture in the Novel from Napoleon to Victoria* (Rutgers University Press, 1986).

Pugliese, Joseph, *Biopolitics of the More-than-Human: Forensic Ecologies of Violence* (Duke University Press, 2020).

Rabinowitz, Dan, and Khawla Abu-Baker, *Coffins on Our Shoulders: The Experience of the Palestinian Citizens of Israel* (University of California Press, 2005).

Rahman, Omar, 'The emergence of GCC–Israel Relations in a Changing Middle East', Brookings Report, Brookings Doha Centre, 26 July 2021, https://www.brookings.edu/research/the-emergence-of-gcc-israel-relations-in-a-changing-middle-east/ (accessed 27 October 2021).

Ramamurthy, Anandi, 'Contesting the Visualization of Gaza', *Photographies*, vol. 9, no. 1, 2016, pp. 31–50, https://doi.org/10.1080/17540763.2016.1138994.

Ramos Pinto, Sara, 'How Important Is the Way You Say It?: A Discussion on the Translation of Linguistic Varieties', *Target*, vol. 21, no. 2, 2009, pp. 289–307, https://doi.org/10.1075/target.21.2.04pin.

Rashed, Haifa, *et al.*, 'Nakba Memoricide: Genocide Studies and the Zionist/Israeli Genocide of Palestine', *Holy Land Studies*, vol. 13, 2014, pp. 1–23, https://doi.org/10.3366/hls.2014.0076.

Rees, Matt, *The Bethlehem Murders* [E-book] (Soho Press, 2007).

—, *The Saladin Murders* [E-book] (Soho Press, 2008).

Reingold, Matt, 'American Jews Explore Israel: Jewish and Israel Identity Exploration with Harvey Pekar and Sarah Glidden', *Journal of Graphic Novels and Comics*, vol. 10, no. 5–6, 2019, pp. 525–42, https://doi.org/10.1080/21504857.2018.1532920.

Roannie-Oko, *L'Intruse-Les Palestiniens* (Vertige Graphic, 2013).

Rodgers, Dennis, and Bruce O'Neill, 'Infrastructural Violence: Introduction to the Special Issue', *Ethnography*, vol. 13, no. 4, 2012, pp. 401–12, https://doi.org/10.1177/1466138111435738.

Rosa, Alexandra Assis, 'Translating Orality, Recreating Otherness', *Translation Studies*, vol. 8, no. 2, 2015, pp. 209–25, https://doi.org/10.1080/14781700.2015.1017833.

Rosen, Michael, 'The Patrick Hardy Lecture: The Bigger Picture', *Michael Rosen*, 2007, www.michaelrosen.co.uk/patrick-hardy/.

Rosenthal, Ruvik, 'עושים מלחמה בלשון' [Conducting War with the Tongue], *הזירה הלשונית* [*Hazira Haleshonit*], 19 September 2003, https://www.ruvik.co.il/השבועי-הטור/2003/19092003.aspx (accessed 27 October 2021).

—, 'המילון לצבאית מדוברת' [The Dictionary of Spoken Militarese], *הזירה הלשונית* [*Hazira Haleshonit*], 2021, https://www.ruvik.co.il/כחולים/כ/מדוברת-לצבאית-המילון.aspx (accessed 27 October 2021).

—, 'מדברים צה״לית: דיוקן שפת הצבא הישראלי' [*Israeli Army Talk: Portrait of the Israeli Military Language*] (Mosad Byalik, 2020).

—, 'החיילים' [The Soldiers], *הזירה הלשונית* [*Hazira Haleshonit*], 18 March 2016, https://www.ruvik.co.il/הישראלי-הלקסיקון/2016/החיילים.aspx (accessed 27 October 2021).

Roth, Yami, and Yuval Bar, '"גרוסמן בטקס האלטרנטיבי: "אם לפלסטינים לא יהיה בית - גם לנו לא יהיה' ['Grossman at the Alternative Ceremony: "If the Palestinians Will Not Have a Home – Neither Will We"'], *Maariv*, 17 April 2018 (accessed 27 October 2021).

Roth-Rowland, Natasha, 'Why the "Pallywood" Myth Endures', *972*, 15 October 2020, www.972mag.com/pallywood-trope-second-intifada (accessed 7 April 2021).
Rousseau, Jean-Jacques, *The Confessions and Correspondence, Including the Letters to Malesherbes*, trans. Christopher Kelly (University Press of New England, 1995).
Rzepka, Charles J., *Detective Fiction* (Polity, 2005).
Sabbah, Iyad, 'Gaza Sculptures Depicting Displacement and Suffering', *My Modern Met*, 23 October 2014, mymodernmet.com/iyad-sabbah-worn-out/ (accessed 15 November 2020).
Sacco, Joe, *Palestine* (Jonathan Cape, 2001).
Said, Edward, and Jean Mohr, *After the Last Sky: Palestinian Lives* (Columbia University Press, 1999).
Said, Edward W., 'Arabs and Jews', *Journal of Palestine Studies*, vol. 3, no. 2, 1974, pp. 3–14, https://doi.org/10.2307/2535796.
—, 'Living in Arabic', *Raritan: A Quarterly Review*, vol. 21, no. 4, 2002, pp. 220–36.
—, 'The Morning After', *London Review of Books*, vol. 15, no. 20, 1993, pp. 3–5, www.lrb.co.uk/the-paper/v15/n20/edward-said/the-morning-after (accessed 7 April 2021).
—, *Out of Place* (Vintage Books, 2000).
—, 'Permission to Narrate', *Journal of Palestine Studies*, vol. 13, no. 3, 1984, pp. 27–48, https://doi.org/10.1525/jps.1984.13.3.00p0033m.
—, *The Question of Palestine* (Vintage Books, [1979] 1992).
—, *Representations of the Intellectual* (Vintage Books, 1996).
Sakr, Rita, 'Decolonial Imaginaries of Sanctuary in Behrouz Boochani's Work', *Crossings: Journal of Migration & Culture*, vol. 11, no. 2, 2020, pp. 231–49, https://doi.org/10.1386/cjmc_00027_1.
—, 'The More-than-Human Refugee Journey: Hassan Blasim's Short Stories', *Journal of Postcolonial Writing* (Special Issue: Refugee Literature), vol. 54, no. 6, 2018, pp. 766–80, https://doi.org/10.1080/17449855.2018.1551269.
Salaita, Steven, *Inter/Nationalism: Decolonizing Native America and Palestine* (University of Minnesota Press, 2016).
Salih, Ruba, 'Bodies That Walk, Bodies That Talk, Bodies That Love: Palestinian Women Refugees, Affectivity, and the Politics of the Ordinary', *Antipode*, vol. 49, no. 3, 2017, pp. 742–60, https://doi.org/10.1111/anti.12299.
Samway, Katharine Davies, 'Children's Books About Palestine', *Teach Palestine*, https://teachpalestine.org/articles/childrens-books-palestine/ (accessed 25 October 2021).
Sayigh, Yezid, 'The Palestine Question amid Regional Transformations', *Journal of Palestine Studies*, vol. 42, no. 2, 2013, pp. 71–92, https://doi.org/10.1525/jps.2013.42.2.71.
Schwarz, Elke, 'Prescription Drones: On the Techno-biopolitical Regimes of Contemporary "Ethical Killing"', *Security Dialogue*, vol. 47, no. 1, 2016, pp. 59–75, https://doi.org/10.1177/0967010615601388.

Scraggs, John, *Crime Fiction* (Routledge, 2005).
Segev, Tom, *The Seventh Million: The Israelis and the Holocaust*, trans. Haim Watzman (Hill and Wang, 1993).
Sela, Rona, 'The Genealogy of Colonial Plunder and Erasure – Israel's Control over Palestinian Archives', *Social Semiotics*, vol. 28, no. 2, 2018, pp. 201–29, https://doi.org/10.1080/10350330.2017.1291140.
Shainin, Jonathan, 'David Grossman Interview, the Art of Fiction No. 194', *The Paris Review*, vol. 182, autumn, 2007.
Shammas, Anton, *Arabesques*, trans. Vivian Eden (Harper & Row, 1989).
Shamsie, Kamila, 'Foreword', in Artists for Palestine UK (eds), *The Case for a Cultural Boycott of Israel* (Artists for Palestine UK, 2015), p. 5.
Shavit, Zohar, *Poetics of Children's Literature* (University of Georgia Press, 1987).
Shehadeh, Raja, *Language of War, Language of Peace: Palestine, Israel, and the Search for Justice* (Profile, 2015).
—, *Occupation Diaries* (Profile, 2012).
—, *The Sealed Room: Selections from the Diary of a Palestinian Living Under Israeli Occupation: September 1990–August 1991* (Quartet Books, 1992).
—, *The Third Way: A Journal of Life in the West Bank* (Quartet Books, 1982).
—, *When the Bulbul Stopped Singing: A Diary of Ramallah Under Siege* (Profile Books, 2003).
Shenhav, Yehuda, *et al.*, [Print] *Command of Arabic among Israeli Jews* (The Van Leer Jerusalem Institute, 2015).
Shezaf, Hagar, 'Burying the Nakba: How Israel Systematically Hides Evidence of 1948 Expulsion of Arabs', *Haaretz*, 5 July 2019, www.haaretz.com/israel-news/.premium.MAGAZINE-how-israel-systematically-hides-evidence-of-1948-expulsion-of-arabs-1.7435103 (accessed 27 October 2021).
Shklovsky, Viktor, 'Art, as Device', *Poetics Today*, vol. 36, no. 3, 2015, pp. 151–74, https://doi.org/10.1215/03335372-3160709.
Sibilio, Simone, 'The Aroma of the Land: Mahmud Darwish's Geopoetics of Coffee', *Quaderni di Studi Arabi*, vol. 10, 2015, pp. 103–24.
Slaughter, Joseph R., *Human Rights, Inc.: The World Novel, Narrative Form, and International Law* (Fordham University Press, 2007).
Smith, Sidonie, and Julia Watson, *Reading Autobiography: A Guide for Interpreting Life Narratives* (University of Minnesota Press, 2001).
Sorkin, Michael, 'Introduction: Up Against the Wall', in Michael Sorkin (ed.), *Against the Wall: Israel's Barrier to Peace* (New Press, 2005), pp. vi–xxi.
Soussi, Alasdair, 'The Mixed Legacy of Golda Meir, Israel's First Female PM', *Al Jazeera*, https://www.aljazeera.com/indepth/features/mixed-legacy-golda-meir-israel-female-pm-190316050933152.html (accessed 18 March 2019).
Squarzoni, Philippe, *Torture Blanche* (Éditions Delcourt, 2018).
Stein, Efrat, 'אוי. "The Oyness of Life" – לדרכו של גרוסמן ביצירת תחדישים מטא-לשוניים' ['"The Oyness of Life" – Grossman's Mode of Creating Metalingual Neologisms'], in Rina Ben-Shahar and Gideon Toury (eds), העברית שפה חיה [*Hebrew*

– *a Living Language: Studies on the Language in Its Social and Cultural Contexts*] (The Porter Institute for Poetics & Semiotics, Tel Aviv University/Hakibbutz Hameuchad, 2006), pp. 452–68.

Stein, Rebecca L., and Ted Swedenburg, 'Introduction: Popular Culture, Transnationality, and Radical History', in Rebecca L. Stein and Ted Swedenburg (eds), *Palestine, Israel, and the Politics of Popular Culture* (Duke University Press, 2005), pp. 1–23.

Stohlman, Nancy, and Laurieann Aladin (eds), *Live from Palestine: International and Palestinian Direct Action Against the Israeli Occupation* (South End Press, 2003).

Suleiman, Susan Rubin, *Authoritarian Fictions: The Ideological Novel as a Literary Genre* (Columbia University Press, 1983).

Sutcliffe, William, 'The Power of the West Bank Wall', *The Guardian*, 11 May 2013, https://www.theguardian.com/books/2013/may/10/william-sutcliffe-west-bank-wall_(accessed 26 November 2019).

—, *The Wall* (Bloomsbury, 2014).

Swales, Martin, *The German Bildungsroman from Wieland to Hesse* (Princeton University Press, 1978).

Swensen, Cole, 'To Writewithize', in Cole Swensen, *Noise That Stays Noise: Essays* (University of Michigan Press, 2011), pp. 69–73.

Tamir, Yuli, 'Protection in the Territories', *Haaretz*, 18 March 2003, https://www.haaretz.com/1.4844213 (accessed 28 October 2021).

Thon, Jan Noël, 'Subjectivity Across Media: On Transmedial Strategies of Subjective Representation in Contemporary Feature Films, Graphic Novels, and Computer Games', in Marie-Laure Ryan and Jan Noel Thon (eds), *Storyworld Across Media: Toward a Media Conscious Narratology* (University of Nebraska Press, 2014), pp. 67–102.

Thrall, Nathan, 'Hamas's Chances', *London Review of Books*, 21 August 2014, vol. 36, no. 14, https://www.lrb.co.uk/v36/n16/nathan-thrall/hamas-s-chances (accessed 27 October 2021).

UNICEF, 'Children in the State of Palestine', *UNICEF*, November 2018, https://www.unicef.org/mena/reports/children-state-palestine (accessed 29 September 2021).

United States Congress, *United States Code: Terrorism*, Title 18, section 2331, (Office of the Law Revision Counsel, [1946] Supp. 2, 1988).

UNRWA, 'Syria@10', *UNRWA*, n.d., www.unrwa.org/syria-crisis (accessed 7 April 2021).

Urquhart, Conal, 'Morse, Rebus … and now Yussef', *The Observer*, 15 July 2007, https://www.theguardian.com/books/2007/jul/15/crimebooks.features (accessed 27 October 2021).

Vazquez, Jose Santiago Fernandez, 'Subverting the Bildungsroman in Postcolonial Fiction: Romesh Gunesekera's *Reef*', *World Literature Written in English*, vol. 36, no. 1, 1997, pp. 30–8, https://doi.org/10.1080/17449859708589260.

Venuti, Lawrence, 'The Translator's Invisibility', *Criticism*, vol. 88, no. 2, spring 1986, pp. 179–212, https://www.jstor.org/stable/23110425.

Veracini, Lorenzo, 'Interacting Imaginaries in Israel and the United States', in Ned Curthoys and Debjani Ganguly (eds), *Edward Said: The Legacy of a Public Intellectual* (Melbourne University Press, 2007), pp. 293–312.

Warner, Marina, *Fantastic Metamorphoses, Other Worlds: Ways of Telling the Self* (Oxford University Press, 2002).

Warner, Michael, 'Publics and Counterpublics', *Public Culture*, vol. 14 no. 1, 2002, pp. 49–90, https://doi.org/10.1215/08992363-14-1-49; *Project MUSE* muse.jhu.edu/article/26277.

Waxman, Dov, *Trouble in the Tribe: The American Jewish Conflict over Israel* (Princeton University Press, 2006).

Weiss, Philip, 'Up to 1 in 4 American Jews Sees Zionism as Racist, Colonialist Apartheid Movement! (Says Rightwing Israeli Thinktank)', *Mondoweiss*, 18 September 2020, mondoweiss.net/2020/09/up-to-1-in-4-us-jews-sees-zionism-as-racist-colonialist-apartheid-movement-says-rightwing-israeli-thinktank (accessed 7 April 2021).

Weizman, Eyal, *Hollow Land: Israel's Architecture of Occupation* (Verso, 2017).

Weizman, Eyal, and Zachary Manfredi, '"From Figure to Ground": A Conversation with Eyal Weizman on the Politics of the Humanitarian Present', *Qui Parle: Critical Humanities and Social Humanities*, vol. 22, no. 1, 2013, pp. 167–92, https://doi.org/10.5250/quiparle.22.1.0167.

Whitlock, Gillian, *Soft Weapons: Autobiography in Transit* (University of Chicago Press, 2007).

Williams, Patrick, 'Gaps, Silences and Absences: Palestine and Postcolonial Studies', in Anna Bernard, Ziad Elmarsafy and Stuart Murray (eds), *What Postcolonial Theory Doesn't Say* (Routledge, 2016), pp. 87–104.

Winter, Yves, 'The Siege of Gaza: Spatial Violence, Humanitarian Strategies, and the Biopolitics of Punishment', *Constellations*, vol. 23, no. 2, 2016, pp. 308–19, https://doi.org/10.1111/1467-8675.12185.

Wolfe, Patrick, 'Settler Colonialism and the Elimination of the Native', *Journal of Genocide Research*, vol. 8, no. 4, pp. 387–409, https://doi.org/10.1080/14623520601056240.

Yad Vashem, The World Holocaust Remembrance Centre, 'What is Yad Vashem', *Yad Vashem*, https://www.yadvashem.org/about/yad-vashem.html (accessed 29 August 2021).

Yaghi, Amjad Ayman, 'Liberty Leads the People: Fighting for a Decent Life in Gaza', *Electronic Intifada*, 5 April 2019, https://electronicintifada.net/content/liberty-leads-people-fighting-decent-life-gaza/27051 (accessed 10 January 2020).

Yang, Lingyan, 'Theorizing Asian America: On Asian American and Postcolonial Asian Diasporic Women Intellectuals', *Journal of Asian American Studies*, vol. 5, no. 2, 2002, pp. 139–78, https://doi.org/10.1353/jaas.2003.0010.

Zanzuri, Ofer, *Azure Giants* (Zanzuria Publishing, 2004).

Zerner, Charles, 'Landscapes in Translation: Traveling the Occupied Palestinian Territories and Israel with Raja Shehade and David Grossman', *Ecozone*, vol. 5, no. 1, 2014, pp. 33–53, https://doi.org/10.37536/ECOZONA.2014.5.1.585.

Zhuo, Xiaolin, Barry Wellman and Justine Yu, 'Egypt: The First Internet Revolt?', *Peace Magazine*, vol. 27, no. 3, July/September 2011, pp. 6–10, http://peacemagazine.org/archive/v27n3p06.htm (accessed 30 January 2020).

Zi-Ling, Yan, *Economic Investigations in Twentieth-Century Detective Fiction* (Routledge, 2015).

Zochrot, 'Al-Qabu', *Zochrot*, https://www.zochrot.org/en/village/49455 (accessed 27 October 2021).

Zöhrer, Marlene, 'Picturebooks and Adaptations of World Literature', in Bettina Kümmerling-Meibauer (ed.), *The Routledge Companion to Picturebooks* (Routledge, 2018), pp. 485–95.

INDEX

Note: *f* indicates a figure

Abdallah, Sahar, 200, 202, 205, 206–7, 209, 214
   Fakkir bi-ghayrika (*Think of Others*), 208, 209, 212–14
   hakadha qalat ash-shajaratu al-muhmalah (*According to the Neglected Tree*), 208, 209, 210–12
   Khobz Ummi (*My Mother's Bread*), 208, 209–10, 211, 212
   Visual Poems exhibition, 202
Abraham Accords, 201
Abu Lauz, Yusuf
   'Trees of Words', 209
Abu-Manneh, Bashir 13
Abu Saif, Atef, 15, 45, 46
   'Dateless in Gaza', 45
   Drone Eats with Me: Diaries from a City Under Fire, The see *Drone Eats with Me: Diaries from a City Under Fire, The*
   'Journey in the Opposite Direction, A', 21
Abuelaish, Izzeldin
   I Shall Not Hate: A Gaza Doctor's Journey on the Road to Peace and Human Dignity, 14

Abulhawa, Susan, 52–4, 56–7, 60, 198
   Against the Loveless World, 56
   Blue Sky Between Sky and Water, The, 56, 58–9, 60
   Mornings in Jenin, 56, 57–8, 72, 76, 82–6
Abunimah, Ali, 51, 55
adaptation, 204
Ahmed, Sara, 186, 188, 196
Al-Ibrahimi Mosque massacre, 217
Allen, Lori, 65, 108–9, 110, 125, 142
alterity *see* other, the
America *see* US
American Left, 175
American Palestinian intellectuals, 54–6
American Palestinian Women, 52–3, 55–6, 66–7
   Abulhawa, Susan, 52–4, 56–7, 60
   Barakat, Ibtisam, 52–4, 60–6
   displacements of Palestinian women, 56–60
Amiry, Suad, 36, 109
   Sharon and My Mother-in-Law: Ramallah Diaries, 14, 35–40, 108, 114, 121–3, 126
anti-heroes, 109
anti-Semitism, 54, 175
apparitional politics, 113, 120, 127

Apter, Emily, 90
Al Aqsa Martyrs Brigade, 136–7
Arab identity, 44, 57, 84, 115
Arab Spring, 72–3, 201
Arabic, 93, 116, 118
　Hebraisation of, 91
　language interference, 97–8
Arafat, Yasser 98
Arendt, Hannah
　Human Condition, The, 113
audiences, 112–14, 184, 189, 204
Augustine, Saint
　Confessions, 112–13
autobiographical pact, 35, 41, 114–15, 124
autobiography, 34, 35, 114–15

Balfour Declaration, 219; *see also* British Mandate
Bakhtin, Mikhail, 112
Barakat, Ibtisam, 52–4, 60–6
　Balcony on the Moon: Coming of Age in Palestine, 60, 63–4
　Tasting the Sky: A Palestinian Childhood, 60, 61
Barghouti, Mourid, 22
　I Saw Ramallah, 14, 108
Barghouti, Omar, 55
Bashir, Bashir, 91
BDS (Boycott, Divestment, Sanction) movement, 2, 54–5, 60, 218, 221
Ben-Gurion, David, 170
Bennett, Naftali, 52
Bethlehem, 131–2, 142
Bettelheim, Bruno, 188
Bildungsroman, 165–8, 182, 185–7, 196
　Cat at the Wall, The, 185, 186, 187–91, 198–9
　choice, 190
　How to Understand Israel in 60 Days or Less, 165, 168, 174–82, 219
　Little Piece of Ground, A, 184–5, 186, 191–4, 199
　Not the Israel My Parents Promised Me, 165, 167, 168–74, 175, 177, 182
　postcolonial, 186, 194
　Sentimental Education, 182
　under occupation, 61–6
　Wall, The, 185, 186, 194–8, 199

bilingualism, 92, 93, 95, 96, 97
borders, 89–92, 130, 140, 156–7; *see also* Israeli wall
Bourdieu, Pierre
　Algerian Sketches, 75
Boyarin, Daniel
　Travelling Homeland: the Babylonian Talmud as Diaspora, A, 173–4
Breaking the Silence, 2
Brecht, Bertolt, 102
Brennan, Timothy, 219, 220
British Mandate, 77, 169–70
Brontë, Charlotte
　Jane Eyre, 72
Brown, Wendy, 149, 197
Butler, Judith, 173

canonical texts, 203
children, 61–3
children's literature, 202; *see also* picture books
children's picture books *see* picture books
Chomsky, Noam, 37
Christianity, 131–2
commemoration, 110–11, 155
confession, 112, 113–14; *see also* public confession
confinement, 153
conflict zones, 168
'conscentization', 206, 212
corruption, 138, 139
counter-culture, the, 170, 171
counter-revolutionary discourse, 74–5
Craps, Stef, 21, 25–6, 30
crime fiction, 128, 134, 135, 137, 139, 140, 141–2; *see also* Rees, Matt
cultural vocabulary, 94–5
culture, 82
　prohibition, 156
'culturecide', 215n
curfews, 36, 37–8, 39

Darwish, Mahmoud, 3, 200, 202–3, 204, 205–6, 212, 214
　A'ras (Weddings), 207
　'Ashiq min filastin (A Lover from Palestine), 207
　'Fakkir bi-ghayrika' ('Think of Others'), 200, 205, 206–7, 208, 212

'hakadha qalat ash-shajaratu al-muhmalah' ('According to the Neglected Tree'), 200, 206–7, 208, 210
'ila Ummi' ('To My Mother'), 200, 205, 206–8, 209
'Madih al-zill al-aly' ('In Praise of the High Shadow'), 213
State of Siege, 14
symbolism, 212, 213–14, 216n
'al-ward wal Qamus' ('The Rose and the Dictionary'), 200
'Yawmiyyat jurh filastin' ('Diary of a Palestinian Wound'), 213
see also Abdallah, Sahar
Davis, Angela, 67
Dayan, Moshe, 170
dead, glorification of, 111
Delacroix, Eugène
Liberty Leading the People, 69, 71*f*
Delisle, Guy
Jerusalem: Chronicles from the Holy City, 178–9
Derrida, Jacques, 13–14, 20, 21, 189
detective fiction *see* crime novels
diaries, 14, 33–6, 38, 45
 chronology, 45–6
 labour of, 42
 solicited 41
 unfinishedness, 45, 46
diaspora, 132, 173–4, 176, 181; *see also* refugees
discrimination, 44, 64, 120, 121, 170
Drone Eats with Me: Diaries from a City Under Fire, The (Abu Saif, Atef) 13, 14, 36
 anthropomorphism 26
 embodied relationality, 15–19, 28, 29
 everydayness, 44–8
 hope, 31
 horrific surrealism, 20–1, 29
 hospitality–hostility, 20, 21, 24, 25, 31
 Jabalia refugee camp, 17–18
 metaphor, 19–21, 22
 nutrition, 47–8
 Operation Protective Edge, 16, 17–25, 44–5
 postcolonial witnessing, 21–2
 Ramadan, 47–8

representational aesthetic, 29–30
severed limb, the, 15–16, 17, 20, 22
socio-spatial connectivity, 22
sumud, 47–8
survival, 45, 46–8
techno-biopolitical violence, 13, 16, 20, 22, 23, 24–5, 26, 28, 29–31
techno-biopolitics, 16, 19, 22
women, 28–9
drones, 19, 23–4, 26, 31

East Jerusalem, 156
ecology, 211
education, 131, 203
 banking model, 206
 problem-posing, 206
Egypt, 201–3
ekphrasis, 208
El-Youssef, Samir, 109
 'Day the Beast Got Thirsty, The', 108, 114, 123–7
 Gaza Blues, 123
Ellis, Deborah, 184, 187, 198
 Cat at the Wall, The, 185, 186, 187–91, 198–9
 Three Wishes: Palestinian and Israeli Children Speak Out, 188
embodied relationality, 15–21, 28, 29
environment, the, 211
epistolary novels, 153–4

Fadda-Conrey, Carol, 53–4
Faire le Mur (*Build the Wall; Go Over the Wall; Sneak Out*) (Le Roy, Maximilien), 145–6, 148, 149–51, 152, 153, 161–2
 culture, 156
 economy, 157
 labour market, 154
 trauma, 157–8
fanaticism, recrudescence of, 74–5
Fanon, Franz
 Wretched of the Earth, The, 75
feminism, 63–4; *see also* American Palestinian Women
fiction, 54
 epistolary novels, 153–4
 literary rebels, 75–86
 see also crime fiction; young adult fiction

flânerie, 142, 143
form, 1, 2, 161; *see also* genre
fragmentary compositions, 15
Freire, Paulo, 206

Gaza, 138–9, 142–3, 218
  blockade, 60, 71
  culture, 82
  Hamas, 80–2
  Operation Protective Edge, 16, 17–25, 44–5
  routine in, 47
  uncertain life in, 46
  see also refugees
Gaza (documentary), 21
genre, 2–3
  adaptation, 204
  autobiography, 34, 35, 114–15
  canonical texts, 203
  children's literature, 202
  epistolary novels, 153–4
  journalism 40–3, 80
  life writing, 33, 34
  poetry, 203, 208
  see also *Bildungsroman*; crime fiction; diaries; fiction; graphic novels; narratives; picture books
'getting by' attitude, 109–10
al-Ghoul, Asma, 79–82, 86, 201
al-Ghoul, Asma and Nassib, Selim
  Rebel in Gaza, A, 72, 76, 79–82, 83
Glidden, Sarah
  How to Understand Israel in 60 Days or Less, 165, 168, 174–82, 219
Goldberg, Amos, 91
Goldstein, Baruch, 217
graphic novels, 146–8, 161, 162, 166–8
  Amandes vertes: Lettres de Palestine, Les (*Green Almonds: Letters from Palestine*), 146, 148, 151–4, 156–60, 161–2
  Harvey Pekar's Cleveland, 182n
  How to Understand Israel in 60 Days or Less, 165, 168, 174–82, 219
  Macedonia, 168
  Not the Israel My Parents Promised Me, 165, 167, 168–74, 175, 177, 182
  Palestine, 148, 152, 162, 177

Revolt, 152
  see also *Faire le Mur* (*Build the Wall*; *Go Over the Wall*; *Sneak Out*)
Great Revolt, The, 77–8
Grossman, David, 3–4, 88, 89, 91, 101–3, 219
  Horse Walks into a Bar, A, 101
  Sleeping on a Wire: Conversations with Palestinians in Israel, 93
  To the End of the Land, 88–92, 97–8, 99–103
  Yellow Wind, The, 93, 96

Habiby, Emile
  Secret Life of Saeed: The Pessoptimist, The, 108, 116
Hamas, 44, 80–2
Hammad, Isabella
  Parisian, The, 72, 76–9
Hammad, Suheir, 214
  Born Palestinian, Born Black, 217
  'broken and beirut', 217, 221
Hammami, Rema, 109, 110
Harlow, Barbara, 24
hasbara (explanation; propaganda), 218
Hashim, Norma
  Prisoners' Diaries: Palestinian Voices from the Israeli Gulag, The, 15
Haskalah (Jewish Enlightenment), 173
Heaney, Seamus
  Cure at Troy, The, 31
Hebraisation, 91
Hebrew 41, 43–4, 93, 94–5, 97, 116
  Grossman, David, 102–3
  re-establishment of, 173
Hebron, 153, 156, 157, 159, 217
Hermans, Anaële and Hermans, Délphine, 147, 153
  Amandes vertes: Lettres de Palestine, Les (*Green Almonds: Letters from Palestine*), 146, 148, 151–4, 156–60, 161–2
Hirsch, Marianne, 186
history, 92, 146–7, 169–71, 173
  Bildungsroman, 195
  remembering, 200–1
  revisionism, 202

INDEX | 249

Hochberg, Gil Z., 115, 196
Holocaust, the, 92
homeland, 173–4
horrific surrealism, 20–1, 29
hospitality, 13–14, 20, 21, 24, 25, 31
hostility, 14, 20, 21, 24, 25
human capital, 150, 154–8
human rights, 64–5
humour, 38, 43, 109, 118, 119, 121
Hutcheon, Linda, 203, 204

identity, 93, 126
   Arab, 44, 57, 84, 115
   collective, 196, 197
   formation, 186–7
   Israeli, 115, 215n, 220
   Jewish, 84, 174, 180, 182, 186, 220
   misnomeric, 115–16, 117–20, 126
   names, 91–2
   national 84–5
   Palestinian, 57–8, 96, 109, 114, 115, 136, 186
   unheroic, 126
   see also self-determination
infrastructural violence, 143
intellectuals, 52, 54–6, 60, 63, 64, 66
international attention, 184, 218–21
International Criminal Court (ICC), 218
Intifada (uprising; shaking off), 73, 98, 203, 206
Islam, 74, 131–2, 201–2
Israel/Israelis, 4, 169–70, 218, 219
   anti-Semitism, 54, 175
   Belgium, 145
   critiques, 167–8, 170, 171–2, 174–6, 178–81, 202
   cultural icons, 94–5
   France, 145
   Hamas, 80–1
   Hebrew 41, 43–4, 93, 94–5, 97
   historical revisionism, 202
   Holocaust, the, 92
   identity, 115, 215n, 220
   Independence Day, 43
   language 93, 94–5
   Operation Protective Edge, 16, 17–25
   Palestinians in, 93–4, 95, 96, 115–20

   Palestinians, entanglement with, 84
   perception, 182
   representations of, 184
   Second Palestinian Intifada, 1–2
   social hierarchy, 93–4, 97
   sovereignty declaration, 142
   strategy, 159
   territorial history, 90
   Zionism, 169–71, 173, 177, 179–80, 182, 201, 219
   see also Separation Wall, the
Israeli Defense Force (IDF), 2, 177, 181*f*
   language 99–100
Israeli Independence Day, 43

Jabalia refugee camp, 17–18, 44
Jane Eyre (Brontë, Charlotte), 167
Jerusalem, 92, 142
Jewish Enlightenment, 173
Jewish history, 173
Jewish identity, 84, 174, 180, 182, 186, 220
Jewish paramilitary organisations, 179
journalism 40–3, 80
Judaism, 173
judiciary, 134, 140
justice, 128, 137–8, 139

Kanafani, Ghassan
   Men in the Sun, 107–8
Karameh, Battle of, 87n
Karmi, Ghada
   In Search of Fatima, 14
   Return, 14
Kashua, Sayed, 40–2, 109
   Dancing Arabs, 108, 114–20, 126
   'Farewell', 44
   Native: Dispatches from a Palestinian-Israeli Life, 36, 40–4
   'Stories I Do Not Dare Tell, The', 43
Katz, Kimberly
   A Young Palestinian's Diary, 1941–45: the Life of Sami 'Amr, 14
Keret, Etgar
   Gaza Blues, 123
Khalili, Laleh, 111
kibbutz, 95, 169, 179

labour market, 154–8
Laird, Elizabeth, 191–2, 198
  Little Piece of Ground, A, 184–5, 186, 191–4, 199
Land Day, 155
language, 91, 92, 93, 94–5, 96–102, 116
  false friends, 92, 98
  military, 99–101
  personal, 102–3
  see also Arabic; Hebrew
language interference, 97–8
Le Roy, Maximilien, 147
  Faire le Mur (Build the Wall; Go Over the Wall; Sneak Out) see *Faire le Mur (Build the Wall; Go Over the Wall; Sneak Out)*
Lejeune, Philippe, 35, 37, 40, 41, 46, 114–15, 124
liberal humanitarianism, 219
liberation/liberty, 69, 71f–2, 220
  freedom of movement, 153, 154
  literary rebels, 75–86
  Mornings in Jenin 76, 82–6
  Parisian, The 76–9
  Rebel in Gaza, A, 76, 79–82, 83
  rebels, 74, 75
life writing, 33
  autobiography, 34, 35, 114–15
  hierarchy of, 34
  see also diaries
literary form *see* form
literary rebels, 75–86
literary social work, 186–7, 198
literature, 82, 86, 102, 219, 220–1
  children's, 202
  one-sided, 198
  unheroic, 108, 109, 110, 114, 120, 122–3, 125–7
  see also genre
Luckhurst, Roger, 30

Masada, 180–1
Masalha, Nur, 215n
masculinity, 126
Massad, Joseph, 81
Matar, Dina and Tawil-Souri, Helga
  Gaza as Metaphor 17

Mbembe, Achille, 18, 20
  Necropolitics, 18
media, 146
Meir, Golda, 107
memory, 91–2, 212, 214
  colonising, 200
  see also commemoration
Mendelssohn, Moses, 173
metamorphosis, 187–91
migration, 180; *see also* diaspora; refugees
military language, 99–101
Milton, John
  Paradise Lost, 72
misnomeric identity, 115–16, 117–20
Moghadam, Valentine, 58–9
Mohanty, Chandra Talpade, 57
Mohr, Jean and Said, Edward
  After the Last Sky: Palestinian Lives, 1, 15, 29
Moretti, Franco, 167, 182, 185

Nablus 76–9, 162
nakba (catastrophe), 3, 58, 170, 200
al-nakba (catastrophe) day, 43
naksa (setback), 3, 58, 60
narratives
  Palestinian, 15, 29, 54, 56–7, 201, 219–20
  personal, 147–8
  quest, 168
  trauma, 30
  war, 15, 19–19, 26
  see also public confession narratives; self-narratives
Nasser, Gamal Abdel, 171
Nassib, Selim and al-Ghoul, Asma
  Rebel in Gaza, A, 72, 76, 79–82, 83
nationalism, 3, 108, 110, 111, 114, 123, 126–7, 170
  Bethlehem Murders, The 136, 137
  'Day the Beast Got Thirsty, The', 123, 126
  Egyptian, 202
  literature, 220
  women, 122, 123
nationhood *see* statehood
nature, 207; *see also* trees

necropolitics, 18, 19, 22
Netanyahu, Benjamin, 52, 218
New Left, 170, 171
Nodelman, Perry, 214
  Words About Pictures, 204–5
Nora, Pierre, 212
Nussbaum, Felicity, 35, 38, 41
nutrition, 47–8, 62–3

occupation, 36–40, 43, 178–9
  coming of age under, 61–6
  crime novels, 129, 130
  emotional response to, 157–8
  graphic novels, 147
  health, 63
  human rights 64–5
  patriarchy, 121–3
Operation Cast Lead 3, 87
Operation Defensive Shield, 192
Operation Protective Edge, 16, 17–25, 44–5
Orientalism, 74, 171, 177
Orwell, George
  Animal Farm, 195
Oslo Accords, 217
other, the, 74, 186, 189, 196–7, 220
Owen, Wilfred
  'Dulce et Decorum Est', 125
Oz, Amos, 219

Palestine/Palestinians, 4, 38, 52, 217–18
  appearance 117–19
  Arab interest in, 201–2
  assimilation, 117–18, 120
  Belgium, 145
  British Mandate, 77, 169–70
  children, 61–3
  diaries 33–4, 35–6
  diaspora, 132
  discrimination, 44
  displacements, 56–8, 83
  economy, 157
  erasure, 51–2, 65–6, 92, 107, 110–11, 119, 196, 201–2, 215n, 219–20
  everyday/ordinary life 16, 28, 36, 38–40, 41, 43, 44–8
  France, 145
  Hamas, 44, 80–2
  ICC 218
  identity, 57–8, 109, 114, 115, 136, 186
  'imperial restoration', 217–18
  Israel, living in, 93–4, 95, 96, 115–20
  Israelis, entanglement with, 84
  language, 93
  as martyr, 109, 110
  mobility, 40
  nakba (catastrophe), 3, 58, 170, 200
  naksa (setback), 3, 58, 60
  narrative, 15, 29, 54, 56–7, 201, 219–20
  novels, 4
  othering, 26
  portrayal, 208, 209, 211
  rebels, 73–5
  representations of, 184, 202
  right of return, 81, 135, 179, 212, 221
  Second Palestinian Intifada, 1–2
  self-determination, 107, 109, 112, 120, 126, 136, 193, 220
  society, 129–30, 134–5, 137–8, 140
  sovereignty, 74
  statehood, 69, 75, 81, 83–5, 197, 220
  stoicism, 109–10
  sumud, 3
  support for, 218–21
  survival, 45, 46–8
  symbolism, 212, 213–14, 216n
  UN, 218
  victimhood, 133
  women, 56–60
  see also American Palestinian Women; Gaza; nationalism; occupation; resistance
Palestine Liberation Organization (PLO), 38, 74
Pappé, Ilan, 206
patriarchy, the, 63–5, 121–3
peace, 172*f,* 179
Pekar, Harvey
  Harvey Pekar's Cleveland, 182n
  Macedonia, 168
  Not the Israel My Parents Promised Me, 165, 167, 168–74, 175, 177, 182
Peres, Shimon, 90

picture books, 200, 202–6
　adaptations, 203, 204
　crossover, 203–4, 205–6, 214
　Fakkir bi-ghayrika (*Think of Others*), 208, 209, 212–14
　hakadha qalat ash-shajaratu al-muhmalah (*According to the Neglected Tree*), 208, 209, 210–12
　as an *Intifada*, 206
　Khobz Ummi (*My Mother's Bread*), 208, 209–10, 211, 212
poetry, 203, 208
politics, 108, 133–4, 137, 138, 220
　apparitional, 113, 120, 127
　power, 140
postcolonial feminism, 53
postcolonial witnessing, 21–2
postcolonialism, 30–1, 33, 53, 61, 186, 194
progress fetishism, 74–5
public, the 113–14
public confession narratives, 107–8, 110–14, 126–7
　Dancing Arabs, 108, 114–20, 126
　'Day the Beast Got Thirsty, The', 108, 114, 123–7
　Sharon and My Mother-in-Law: Ramallah Diaries, 108, 114, 121–3, 126
Pugliese, Joseph, 18, 29

Qana massacre, 217
quest narratives, 168

Rabin, Itzhak, 103n
Rachel's Tomb, 159
racism, 170, 171
Ramadan, 47–8
Ramallah, 14, 36–40, 179
　Amiry, Suad, 36–40, 122
　Balcony on the Moon, 64
　Barakat, Ibtisam, 60, 61, 62
　Children's writers' workshops, 191
　Little Piece of Ground, A, 185, 194
'readwithize', 208, 210
rebellions, 76–7
　Arab Spring, 72–3, 201
rebels
　Arab Spring, 72–3, 201
　counter-revolutionary discourse, 74–5
　greed-based, 74
　grievance-based, 74
　legitimacy, 73–5
　literary rebels, 75–86
　view of, 73–4
Rees, Matt, 128–31, 134, 143–4
　Bethlehem Murders, The (*The Collaborator of Bethlehem*), 130, 131–8, 139–40, 143
　infrastructural violence, 143
　place 141–3
　Saladin Murders, The (*A Grave in Gaza*), 130, 136, 137, 138–9, 140–1
refugees 25, 62–3
　Jabalia refugee camp, 17–18, 44
　Lebanon, 123–6, 218
　right of return, 81, 135, 179, 212, 221
　symbolism, 212, 213–14, 216n
　Syria, 218
　see also diaspora
religious tolerance, 131–2
resistance, 2
　Abu Saif, Atef, 20, 27, 28, 31, 44–8
　American Palestinian Women, 53
　Amiry, Suad, 38
　images, 69, 70f, 71
　literary rebel, the, 75–86
　Mohanty, Chandra Talpade, 57
　non-violent, 193
　picture books, 206
　see also sumud
revolutions, 76–7
　Arab Spring, 72–3, 201
　Great Revolt, The, 77–8
　see also rebellions
Rousseau, Jean-Jacques, 113

Sacco, Joe, 177
　Palestine, 148, 152, 162, 177
Said, Edward, 3, 92, 177, 217, 218, 219
　'Arabs and Jews', 84–5
　Palestinian narrative, 15
　'Permission to Narrate', 26, 51–2, 54
Said, Edward and Mohr, Jean
　After the Last Sky: Palestinian Lives, 1, 15, 29

Second Palestinian Intifada, 1–2, 40, 69, 70f, 108–9
   Operation Defensive Shield, 192
   Qalqilya, 160
   terms of, 89, 91
security, 149, 158, 178, 179
self-determination, 107, 109, 112, 120, 126, 136, 193, 220
self-narratives, 110–14
   Dancing Arabs, 108, 114–20, 126
   'Day the Beast Got Thirsty, The', 108, 114, 123–7
   Sharon and My Mother-in-Law: Ramallah Diaries, 108, 114, 121–3, 126
Sentimental Education (Flaubert, Gustave), 182
Separation Wall, the, 2, 149, 152, 155, 156, 158–60, 161, 178
   Wall, The, 185, 186, 194–8, 199
settlements, 75, 158–60, 172, 218
   Amandes vertes: Lettres de Palestine, Les (*Green Almonds: Letters from Palestine*), 153
   refugees, 123
   Wall, The, 185
settler societies, 177
severed limb, the, 15–16, 17, 20, 22
shahid; *shaheed* (martyr; witness), 98, 110, 111, 116–17, 125
Shammas, Anton
   Arabesques, 116
Shamsie, Kamila, 221
Sharon, Ariel, 36–7
Shehadeh, Raja, 3, 17, 38, 47
Slaughter, Joseph R., 186–7, 195
   Human Rights, Inc.: The World Novel, Narrative Form, and International Law, 64
Smith, Sidonie and Watson, Julia, 35, 45–6
   Reading Autobiography: A Guide for Interpreting Life Narratives, 61
social relations, 195
social responsibility, 186, 188, 189, 190, 191
Spiegelman, Art
   Maus, 146, 166
statehood, 69, 75, 81, 83–5, 197, 220
   borders, 90, 130, 197

Stein, Rebecca L. and Swedenburg, Ted, 4
suitcases, 213–14
sumud (steadfastness), 3, 36, 47–8, 110, 193, 194
   women's resilience, 28, 59
Sutcliffe, William, 195, 198
   Wall, The, 185, 186, 194–8, 199

Taglit-Birthright, 174, 175, 182
Tanmia, 200, 202, 206
Tawil-Souri, Helga and Matar, Dina
   Gaza as Metaphor 17
techno-biopolitical violence, 13, 16, 20, 22, 23, 24–5, 26, 28, 29–31
technology, 37, 73
temporality, 45–6, 146
terrorism, 26–7, 74–5, 148–51, 153
   Not the Israel My Parents Promised Me 172
   victim/terrorist binary, 161–2, 209
thawra (rebellion; revolution), 76, 82
thuwwar (rebels; revolutionaries), 76
To the End of the Land (Grossman, David), 88–9
   bilingual Arab, 92–7
   borders, 89–92
   defamiliarised conflict 101–3
   false friends, 92, 98
   language interference, 97–8
   military language, 99–101
   translation, 89, 92, 94–5, 96–7, 103
   false friends, 92, 98
   language interference, 97–8
trauma, 157–8
trauma narratives, 30
traumatic memories, 91
trees, 83, 207, 208, 209, 211–12
Trump, Donald, 52

unheroic literature, 108, 109, 110, 114, 120, 122–3, 125–7
United Nations (UN), 131, 218
urban space, 141–2
US, 177, 217
   American Left, 175
   American Palestinian intellectuals, 54–6
   anti-Semitism, 175

US (*cont.*)
  Beat Generation, 73, 74
  Beirut embassy bombing, 83
  Israel, migration to, 180
  optimism, 182
  see also American Palestinian women

victimhood, 133
  victim/terrorist binary, 161–2, 209
violence, 108, 218
banality of, 160
  children, 62
  everyday, 142, 149–50
  infrastructural, 143
  legitimacy, 152
  masculinity, 126
  massacres, 217
  randomness of, 154
  sexualised war, 58–9
  stoicism, 109–10
  techno-biopolitical, 13, 16, 20, 22, 23, 24–5, 26, 28, 29–31

war narratives, 15, 18–19, 26
Watson, Julia and Smith, Sidonie, 35, 45–6
  Reading Autobiography: A Guide for Interpreting Life Narratives, 61
Weizman, Eyal, 25, 27
  Hollow Land, 155
West Bank, 52, 62, 72, 158
  Abulhawa, Susan, 53
  Amandes vertes: Lettres de Palestine, Les (*Green Almonds: Letters from Palestine*), 151, 153, 157, 158
  Amiry, Suad, 36, 122
  Barakat, Ibtisam, 53, 60, 62
  Cat at the Wall, The, 187, 188, 198
  economy, 129
  Faire le Mur (*Build the Wall; Go Over the Wall; Sneak Out*), 148, 150
  femininity 121
  Little Piece of Ground, A, 186, 192, 199
  occupation, 36
  Operation Defensive Shield 192
  Rees, Matt, 128
  repetitive life in, 36, 39
  Separation Wall, the, 2
  trauma 157
  Wall, The, 185, 195
  see also Bethlehem; Hebron; Nablus; Ramallah
Whitlock, Gillian, 42
Williams, Patrick, 14, 30–1
women, 28–9, 210
commemorating loss, 155
  Hamas, 80
  Palestinian, 56–60
  patriarchy, the, 63–5, 121–3
  resilience of, 28, 59
  sexualised war violence, 58–9
  see also American Palestinian Women
'writewithize', 208

Yehoshua, A. B., 219
young adult fiction, 184–7
  Cat at the Wall, The, 185, 186, 187–91, 198–9
  Little Piece of Ground, A, 184–5, 186, 191–4, 199
  Wall, The, 185, 186, 194–8, 199

Zionism, 169–71, 173, 177, 179–80, 182, 201
  critiques, 219